Arabs and Jews in Israel

Arabs and Jews in Israel

Volume 2
Change and Continuity in Mutual Intolerance

Sammy Smooha

Westview Press
BOULDER • SAN FRANCISCO • OXFORD

Westview Special Studies on the Middle East

This Westview softcover edition is printed on acid-free paper and bound in library-quality, coated covers that carry the highest rating of the National Association of State Textbook Administrators, in consultation with the Association of American Publishers and the Book Manufacturers' Institute.

Published in 1992 in the United States of America by Westview Press, Inc., 5500 Central Avenue, Boulder, Colorado 80301-2847, and in the United Kingdom by Westview Press, 36 Lonsdale Road, Summertown, Oxford OX2 7EW

Library of Congress Cataloging-in-Publication Data
Smooha, Sammy.
Arabs and Jews in Israel / by Sammy Smooha
p. cm—(Westview Special Studies on the Middle East)
Contents: v. 1. Conflicting and shared attitudes in a divided society—v. 2. Change and continuity in mutual intolerance.
ISBN 0-8133-0755-4 (v. 1). ISBN 0-8133-0756-2 (v. 2).
1. Jewish-Arab relations—1973- —Public opinion. 2. Israel—Ethnic relations—Public opinion. 3. Public opinion—Israel. 4. Palestinian Arabs—Israel—Attitudes. 5. Jews—Israel—Attitudes. I. Title II. Series.
DS119.7.S622 1992
956.94'004924—dc19 88-14266
CIP

Printed and bound in the United States of America

The paper used in this publication meets the requirements of the American National Standard for Permanence of Paper for Printed Library Materials Z39.48-1984.

10 9 8 7 6 5 4 3 2 1

To Gil, Adi, Shahar, and Tsofiya

Contents

Part Two
TYPOLOGIES

Part Three
TRENDS

Part Four
CONCLUSIONS

Part Five
APPENDIXES

Tables

Acknowledgments

This volume is part of a continuing research project on the relations between the Arab minority and Jewish majority in Israel within its pre-1967 borders. The first book, based on surveys conducted in 1976, appeared initially in 1980 and then was published in a revised book edition in 1984 (Smooha, 1984). The second book reports the findings of the 1980 surveys (Smooha, 1989). The present book focuses on the 1985 and 1988 surveys.

The book and the research it is based on would not have been possible without the support and help of numerous persons and institutions. It is a pleasure to record my deep gratitude to all of them. There is, of course, nothing in the following acknowledgments to absolve me from the responsibility for any fault in the information, analysis, interpretation, and views contained in the book.

The fieldwork for the Arab surveys was organized and managed by Mr. Taha Ashkar with the help of Mr. Mostafa Hasouna, who supervised the interviewing in the Triangle and Negev in 1985, and of Mr. Riyad Kabha, who coordinated the work in the Triangle in 1988. The fieldwork for both the 1985 and 1988 Jewish surveys was contracted to the Dahaf Research Institute, headed by Dr. Mina Zemah. Thanks are also due to the interviewers and respondents who all cooperated in producing standard interviews with 4,816 rank and file (2,407 in 1985 and 2,409 in 1988) respondents and 281 public figures (in 1985) and in completing scores of non-structured interviews.

Mr. Taha Ashkar, Ms. Edna Zaretzki, Mr. Asa'd Ghanem, and Ms. Amalia Sa'ar served as dedicated and able research assistants throughout the project, and their assistance and contribution are highly appreciated.

The Jewish-Arab Center at the University of Haifa supplied services. I wish to thank Professors Arnon Soffer and George Kanazi, who served as chairmen of the Center, as well as Mrs. Sara Tamir, the executive director. David Boka'i, Aliza Brown, and Haya Markovitz, of the University's Research Authority and Accounting Office, were very helpful in the efficient administration of the research funds.

The data-analysis and the writing of several drafts were conducted at Brown University and the Annenberg Research Institute, in addition to my home base at the University of Haifa. During my 1987-89 stay at the Program in Judaic Studies at Brown University, I received generous facilities from the Program, the Social Science Data Center, and the computer center. I also enjoyed the company and encouragement of many persons, and especially Professors Calvin Goldscheider, Ernest Frerichs, Alan Zuckerman, and Sidney Goldstein. Equally rewarding was my 1989-90 fellowship year at the Annenberg Research Institute, a Center for Advanced Research in Judaic and Near Eastern Studies, in Philadelphia. I am indebted for the facilities, time release, and congenial atmosphere. Thanks are extended to the former Director, Professor Bernard Lewis, and the Associate Director, Dr. David Goldenberg, to the secretarial assistants, Mrs. Etty Lassman and Mrs. Gail Group, and to the computer experts, Dr. John Bloom and Mr. Hal Dell, as well as to the other members of the staff. I am heartily grateful to them for letting me come back for a three-week period in September 1991 to finalize the typing.

Thanks are also due Mr. Asher Goldstein for copy-editing and Mrs. Renee Ben-David for typing the first draft. Discovering the wonders of desk-top publishing, Mrs. Etty Lassman worked enthusiastically, tirelessly, and efficiently on formatting most of the typescript. Mr. Joshua Bell, of Verbatim Word Processing Services in Providence, RI, finished the formatting and produced the master, camera-ready copy. Ms. Barbara Ellington, Ms. Rebecca Ritke, and Mr. Amos Zubrow, of Westview Press, oversaw publication.

Several institutions lent valuable support for the study. The funding for the 1985 surveys was provided by a grant from The Ford Foundation received through the Israel Foundations Trustees, a direct grant from The Ford Foundation in the United States, and a supplementary grant from the National Council for Research and Development of the Israel Ministry of Science and Development. The 1988 surveys were funded by a grant from the DFG (Deutsche Forschungsgemeinschaft) received through the Arnold Bergstraesser Institut, Freiburg, Germany. I wish to thank these foundations and their executive directors, Mrs. Ruth Sharshevski-Atir in Tel Aviv, Mr. Steven Riskin in New York City, Dr. David Hinitz in Jerusalem, and Prof. Theodor Hanf and Dr. Heribert Weiland in Freiburg, respectively, for their support. I am also grateful for a grant for publication from the Jaffe Foundation.

This book is dedicated, with love, to my three children and my wife, just a small gesture for the time taken away from them for the necessary research work and writing chores.

Sammy Smooha
University of Haifa
September 1991

1

Introduction

In early 1991, 730,000 Arab and 4 million Jewish citizens lived in Israel in its pre-1967 borders (excluding the Gaza Strip, the West Bank, East Jerusalem, and the Golan Heights). Both groups constitute only a part of scattered peoples who claim exclusive rights to the area West of the Jordan river. The Arabs are only one seventh of the 4.7 million Palestinian Arabs, whereas the Jews make up about 30% of the 13.5 million Jews around the world. The Arabs are also part of the Arab nation of over 200 million, most of whom are still hostile to the State of Israel. Their brethren in the West Bank and Gaza Strip, the core of their dispersed people, are placed under Israeli military occupation and engaged in the intifada, the Palestinian uprising which began on December 9, 1987. Furthermore, over three quarters of the Palestinians in Israel are Sunni Moslems, who lack a tradition of life as a minority under a non-Moslem population. The anomalous position of the Arabs as a subordinate minority in a Jewish state is even more striking: living as subordinates in a Waqf land (which was liberated by Islam and destined to be ruled by Moslems) under the Jews, a people traditionally subject to a Moslem rule. The picture of the other side is not brighter: the Jews themselves are an inexperienced, new majority, internally divided by ethnicity and religious observance and profoundly suspicious of the Arabs. Seen together, the two communities differ in ethnic origin, religion, language, nationality, and culture – prescriptions for estrangement and animosity. They are also sharply split by key issues and strong, intolerant nationalism. Substantial class gaps, power disparities, separation, prejudice, discrimination, and exclusion further strain their relations.

This snapshot of the division between the Arab minority and Jewish majority brings into sharp focus Israel's structure as a deeply divided society. It is discouraging just to think of the dangers of political instability and violence, including genocidal attempts, to which this special type of society is exposed (Kuper, 1990). It would be sufficient to recall Cyprus, Sudan, Iraq, Northern Ireland, and Sri Lanka in order to appreciate the dislocations of civil war and bloodshed lurking at Israel's doorstep. After all, Israel shares many structural similarities with these strife-ridden countries. For many Jews, these threats, posed by its restive minority, seem more real than apparent. Similarly, many Arabs are afraid that the Jews will resort to repression and forced transfer against them. Both communities tend to view the trend of change in the other side to be hardening and intensifying hostility.

This volume takes this common view to task, tries to show that neither the "Arab radicalization thesis" nor the "Jewish intransigence thesis" is factually valid, and sets forth alternative explanations. Since these and the alternative theses are presented in detail in a previous volume (Smooha, 1989: chapter 1), it suffices us to take up the main line of analysis and to update the sources.

Arab Radicalization and Jewish Intransigence

Researchers and commentators tend to conceive of Arab-Jewish relations in terms of Jewish intransigence, Arab radicalization, or both. They fall into two distinct categories. One category emphasizes Jewish intransigence and underplays Arab radicalization. It consists of those who concentrate on Israel's policies of discrimination against the Arabs, implying that the real problem is Jewish intransigence, which breeds a firm Arab response. Although they do not characterize the Arab response as radical or radicalizing, Arab radicalization is strongly suggested by their conceptualization. The other category underscores Arab radicalization and attaches only small importance to Jewish intransigence. It includes those who stress Arab radicalization, seen mostly as a result of Arab-related forces inside and outside the Arab community, and only partly stemming from state policies or other adverse effects of Jewish intransigence.

The most radical view advanced by researchers belonging to the first category conceptualizes Jewish intransigence as inherent in the very nature of the state. The best-known idea within this stream of thought is the notion of Israel as a colonial state and the Arabs as an internal colony (Zureik, 1979). After its proclamation, Israel expelled most of the Arabs, expropriated half of the lands of the remaining Arabs, imposed a military government in Arab areas, induced the transformation of the Arab peasants into a working class dependent for wages on the Jewish economy, left Arab localities underdeveloped, and pursued various policies of exclusion, discrimination, cultural dominance, and Zionist hegemony against the native Palestinians. According to Zureik, the colonial perspective continues to determine Jewish orientation; it lies at the root of the delegitimation and policing campaign against the Arabs in Israel during the intifada, but it is no longer relevant to understanding Arab attitudes and behavior (Zureik, 1991). This statement notwithstanding, Arab radicalization is the most likely outcome according to the rationale of the internal colonial model.

According to a related account, Israel, being one of the few settler states still in existence, is a caste society (Weitzer, 1990). The Arabs are treated as a lower caste, excluded, dominated economically and politically, and considered innately inferior and politically subversive. As in most settler societies, concessions made to the indigenous population are too little and too late. This failure of reformism "is rooted in the settlers' continuing refusal to relinquish state power and in the subordinate community's resulting radicalization. Faced with the futility of reform, the subordinate population typically abandons peaceful opposition in favor of armed struggle" (ibid.: 34). The Arabs, like the Catholic minority in Northern Ireland before 1968, are too powerless to affect the settler regime (ibid.: 35).

Like the settler model, the control model also traces the Arab problem to the nature of the state (Lustick, 1980). Since Israel is constituted as a Jewish state, it serves only Jews, alienates Arabs, extracts their resources (lands, labor), generates considerable disaffection among them, and subjects them to "a system of control" in order to keep them compliant and to preserve political stability. Lustick portrays this system as consisting of Arabs' segmentation (internal fragmentation and isolation from the Jews), economic dependence, and cooption of elites. He elaborates on the entrenched, undemocratic character of the state in treating its national minority. According to the logic of the control model, Arab actions, under effective control, remain accommodating, whereas their attitudes become antagonistic, but both are bound to radicalize once control erodes or crumbles. Yet, after the outbreak of the intifada, Lustick revised his position, conceded that the system of control was mostly dismantled, and redrew a new picture of Israel as transforming from officially intransigent and Jewish to a practically flexible, binational state. He also portrays Israeli Arabs as playing a new political role: integration into Israeli politics through "strategic voting" (capitalization on the nearly even split between Labor and Likud by voting to install a government of their liking instead of registering a protest but wasteful vote) and a move (the formation of the coalition-oriented Democratic Arab Party in 1988) toward participation in coalition governments (Lustick, 1990).

Rouhana (1991) presents Israel's Jewish character as the overwhelming factor in the fashioning of the Palestinian identity of the Arabs in Israel. The Jewish state does not let Arabs be Israelis, because it reserves Israeli identity to Jews who fully accept the goals of Zionism. This is why the Arabs' Israeli identity is superficial and inconsequential, compared with their potent, central Palestinian identity. It is the pervasive policy of exclusion, springing directly from the nature of the state, that determines the fate of the Arabs as "accentuated" Palestinians rather than as Israelis.

Falah studied Arabs and Jews in the Galilee. His point of departure was that rather than being a liberal, neutral democracy, Israel is a Zionist, only nominally democratic state, geared to institutionalize Jewish dominance and anti-Arab discrimination. "The unequal distribution of land, water, and local budget as regional resources between Jewish and Arab settlements in the Galilee reflects a geography of power along lines of ethnic cleavage. Rather than being 'a neutral' agent in resource distribution and allocation, the central government plays a key role in allocational policies distinctly skewed in favor of the Jewish population in the Galilee, resulting in highly uneven development patterns and other disparities" (Falah, 1990: 335-336). The Arab reaction to this "institutionalized discrimination," which "has touched every single Arab village in Galilee," is "to develop their own institutions and initiatives, independent of any government financing," and "to struggle for equality of allocation and economic rights in a context of growing national awareness as a discriminated Arab-Palestinian national minority in the Jewish state." Both responses are expected to intensify by the massive settlement of Soviet Jews and the possible resettlement in the Galilee of Jews from the Golan Heights as well as the redeployment of military forces there in the event of a peace agreement with Syria.

A similar but less radical analysis of Jewish intransigence that engenders Arab radicalization takes Israel's continued discriminatory policies against the Arabs as given or as a result of policymakers' neglect, myopia, wrongdoing, or distorted set of priorities, rather than attributing it to an intractable Jewish-Zionist nature. Yiftachel, in his study of land-use planning in the Galilee for the 1985-88 period (1990: abstract), concludes that Israel has been applying a policy of control that "has been expressed by the territorial containment and lengthy planning delays experienced by most Arab villages, as well as the location of new Jewish settlements in areas densely populated by Arabs." He finds that "while Israel's land use planning policies have created economic benefits for the Arabs, they have also intensified Arab-Jewish competition over land control, slightly widened interethnic socioeconomic gaps, and mostly maintained a status quo in Arab-Jewish power disparities." Although Israel has managed to maintain a reasonable level of stability for the time being, the clear, direct Arab response to these policies is radicalization: "most indicators of political instability, such as anti-governmental protest, ethnic political polarization, and expressions of regime illegitimacy, appear to be intensifying." Yiftachel considers Arab radicalization to Jewish intransigence in the Galilee as a confirmation of the general thesis that "the use of consociational mechanisms by governments of plural democracies is likely to enhance long-term stability, while the use of control policies is likely to make conditions susceptible to long-term instability."

A public policy of discrimination against Arabs looms prominently in a large-scale research project on the condition and status of the Arabs in Israel that was conducted under the direction of Rosenfeld in the late 1980s. The project consists of eight studies on the Arab minority: local government by Al-Haj and Rosenfeld (1990), legal status by Kretzmer (1990), social welfare services by Haidar (1991), the economy by Haidar (1990), health care by Reiss (1991), planning and housing by Hamaissi (1990), crime and justice by S. Cohen (1990), and education by Al-Haj (1991). These studies well document the gravity and pervasiveness of the discriminatory policies against the Arabs and their dire consequences in all these fields. Yet none of them explicitly attributes discrimination to the Jewish nature of the state.

Al-Haj (forthcoming) sees the intifada as a watershed that has reinforced the double-periphery status of the Arabs in Israel. When forced by both Israel and the Palestinian resistance movement to take sides, the Arabs have shown a clear choice in favor of Israel by opting not to take an active part in the intifada. As a result, they have lost the trust of other Palestinians and were written off in any solution to the Palestinian question. Instead of seizing upon this historical opportunity to accommodate the Arabs, Jewish suspicions have been exacerbated by the Arabs' strong solidarity with the intifada. The state has continued to dismiss Arab demands for equality of opportunities and funding; furthermore, the sympathetic Zionist left has abandoned its traditional posture of protecting Arab rights. It is Israel's hardline policy that looms largest in the Arab predicament.

On the other hand, the state's discriminatory policies are underplayed by the researchers and commentators in the other category, who dwell on Arab radicalism and radicalization. They see Israeli public policies as contributing to the Arab drift, but attribute it mostly to diverse unfoldings within the Arab community and the Arab world, far beyond Israel's control. Figuring highly among these radicalizing developments is the rise of the Arabs to the point of a critical mass consisting of a large population, a network of community institutions, an independent national leadership that instills a sense of power in them, and a drive for autonomy. The Arabs suffer from various deprivations as a developing minority in a developed society and from a policy of neglect. Growing modernization further exacerbates the Arabs' disillusionment with Israel by widening the gaps between their personal and community needs and aspirations, on the one hand, and their accomplishments, on the other. Another alienating factor is the spread in the 1980s of Islamic fundamentalism among Israeli Arabs. The Israeli-Arab conflict is another central factor in shaping the Israeli Arab mind and behavior. As they become increasingly Palestinized, the Arabs find themselves asserting their identity as Palestinian, supporting the PLO, and fusing with their brethren on the West Bank and Gaza Strip.

The proponents of the Arab radicalization thesis notice progressive deterioration in Arab accommodation to Israel. R. Cohen (1989, 1990), for instance, sees the steady decline in the Arab vote for Zionist parties as a vote of no-confidence in the Israeli system and a harbinger of a shift to confrontation politics. Regev analyzes various developments that may lead to a fundamental change in the goals of the Arab struggle. Rather than fighting for equal rights and for a two-state solution, the Arabs will be demanding "a change of status of the State of Israel from the state of the Jewish people to a status of binational state. This demand might alter radically the orientation of the Jewish majority toward the Arab minority" (1989: 25). Arab radicalization is conceived of as the main determinant of Jewish attitudes and policies.

Within academia, Rekhess is the best representative of this trend of thought. He detects a historical process of convergence between the Palestinians on both sides of the Green Line. He emphasizes the political affinity and national solidarity among them, to the extent that the internal political cleavages among Israeli Arabs have diminished considerably. To quote: "The many facets of permitted and existing cooperation attest to two major conclusions: (1) when it comes to Palestinian affairs, the old dividing lines between the various trends within the Israeli Arab community are becoming increasingly blurred; (2) Palestinian solidarity is no longer a matter of politics alone but has branched out into social concerns, art, literature, poetry, religion, folklore, common heritage, and more recently into economics as well" (1989: 147). Rekhess also stresses the intensification of these growing ties by the intifada: "Israeli Arabs came to identify even more fully with them {the Palestinians} and a new sense of sharing a common fate sprang up" (ibid.: 148). Furthermore, he interprets the spread of the Islamic Movement and the 1988 Declaration of

Independence of the State of Palestine (which was based on the 1947 United Nations partition resolution 181) as strong alienating forces in the Arab sector.

Arab radicalization is the working assumption underlying all the confidential policy statements submitted to the government since the early 1970s by the Prime Minister's Advisors on Arab Affairs (Benziman and Mansur, forthcoming: chapter 3). The recurrent themes include Israeli Arabs' rising numbers and power, deepening Palestinization, increasing support for the PLO, gradual crossing of the intifada into the Green Line, mushrooming of autonomous institutions, a demand of autonomy, massive squatting on state land, migration to Jewish towns, and growth in rejectionist Islamic fundamentalism. The Advisors have recommended a policy of non-discrimination in the allocation of resources as a means to slow down the Arab radicalization processes on which the state has limited influence.

The differences between the two above approaches to Arab-Jewish relations in Israel are obvious. One puts the emphasis on Jewish intransigence, locates the problem in the state's discriminatory policies, blames the Jews for the Arab predicament, and calls for a radical change in the system. In contrast, the perspective stressing Arab radicalization focuses on the Israeli-Arab conflict and Israeli Arab objective privations, and suggests only amelioration of state policies. Taken together, however, the two approaches can be seen as complementary, presenting a picture of Jewish intransigence, Arab radicalization, and strained relations heading toward collision.

Arab Politicization and Jewish Accessibility

It is the central thesis of this study that Arab-Jewish relations since 1948 can better be understood by Arab politicization and Jewish accessibility, rather than by Arab radicalization and Jewish intransigence. That is to say, the Arabs are not drifting away, but rather are fighting to improve their status in Israeli society; the Jews are not hardening their treatment of the Arabs, but rather are gradually opening up to them: Arab-Jewish relations are increasingly marked, not by growing intolerance and violence, but by piecemeal mutual accommodation.

Arab-Jewish relations follow the pattern of dominance, neither consociationalism nor liberal pluralism. The Arabs are subordinate or disadvantaged to Jews in virtually all areas: membership in the society, power, class, opportunity structure, privilege, culture, and ideology. The Arabs do not enjoy the advantages of consociationalism; i.e., autonomy, recognized leadership, proportional share of resources, veto power on matters vital to their interests, or participation in national decision-making. Similarly, the fact that Israel is not an open democracy, in which the individual is the cornerstone of society, national origin is privatized, merit is the criterion for allocation of roles and jobs, and people are free to assimilate or keep apart, attests to the inapplicability of liberal pluralism.

While domination has persisted, the contrast between the Arab status at the beginning and end of the 1948-91 period clearly shows a trend of diminishing domination, exclusion, and discrimination. The Arabs began their life in Israel as a vanquished minority. As a result of the Arab defeat in the 1948 war and the mass exodus of Palestinians, a remnant of the Palestinian people stayed behind. These Arabs were left almost without elites, middle class, and functioning institutions. They mostly consisted of illiterate farmers and workers and lived in underdeveloped villages. Their family, social, cultural, and political ties with the Arab world were cut off. The authorities treated them as a disloyal minority, placed them under military rule, confiscated the bulk of their lands, and administered their affairs in a self-serving manner. The Arabs were excluded from Israeli institutions and mainstream, and could not and did not resist outright Jewish control.

More than four decades later, the Arab situation was much different. The Arabs are a working class minority with a sizable proportion on the middle and elite levels. Most live in private, high-standard houses in incorporated localities, which received the modern services of running water, electricity, paved roads, health care, education, and welfare. They enjoy all civil and political rights, including free press, the right to vote and run for office, and the freedoms of movement and association. They exercise these rights effectively by maintaining an impressive network of local and state-wide, independent organizations and by a recurrent use of extra-parliamentary politics, including demonstrations and general strikes. They have been conducting an intense struggle for peace and equality. The Arab protest and active opposition are a main factor in the virtual cessation of land expropriation and in the reduction of discriminatory policies. Furthermore, the Arabs have three predominantly Arab parties and a nationalist leadership that routinely deliberates and makes decisions on matters of wide concern. They also publicly support the intifada in defiance of the state's and the Jews' strenuous efforts to repress it.

To be sure, this appreciable change should not be interpreted as a satisfactory Arab situation in the early 1990s. In fact, Arab standards still fall much short of Arab aspirations, state promises, and Jewish achievements. Discriminatory policies against Arabs, though significantly softened over time, are still in effect. It is the headway made over the years in the spread (but still not the full institutionalization) of the norm of Arab-Jewish equality that nourishes the Arabs' keen sense of deprivation.

It is my contention that a proper explanation of the marked improvement in the status and condition of the Arab minority over the years must posit that the trend of change in the Jewish orientation toward the Arabs is a shift from intransigence to accessibility. If the contrary assumption of Jewish intransigence were correct, the positive change in the Arab status would have effectively been blocked by repression by the state and Jewish backlash.

Jewish accessibility consists of three components: inclusiveness, factionalism, and ambivalence. Inclusiveness implies the gradual shift from exclusion to inclusion of Arabs into Israeli society. Over the years Arabs have joined the labor market, the Histadrut, and the Jewish political parties, and they have increasingly used the same public facilities (transportation, hospitals, commercial centers, parks, beaches, cinemas) as the Jews. As a result, many Jewish institutions have already lost exclusivity, and many Jews have been finding themselves in growing contact with the Arabs. The Jews are becoming increasingly aware of the Arab presence, problems, needs, and demands. The concept "Israeli" is broadening to cover Arabs, as well. The Jews have been coming to terms with the reality of a permanent Arab minority living in Israel, and they realize more and more that concessions should be made in order to obtain Arab cooperation and quiet.

Factionalism of the orientation toward the Arabs is also taking shape. As Arab struggle intensifies, Arabs penetrate Jewish society, the Arab vote becomes the deciding force between a Likud and a Labor government, more Jewish concessions to Arabs are considered and granted, Jewish parties are forced to relate to Arab concerns and to form policies toward the Arab minority, and the Jewish public at large is compelled to rethink its views. In consequence, the Jewish parties and public are becoming more and more divided into five main orientations toward the Arabs. The "egalitarianists," close in orientation to the Rakah position, advocate de-Zionization of the state and full equalization of Arab and Jewish statuses. Following the lead of the Zionist left parties, the "conciliationists" favor equal rights and opportunities for Arabs while keeping Israel Jewish and Zionist. The "pragmatists" subscribe to the Labor Party approach, leaning toward dispensing concessions to the Arabs in order to keep them quiet and to preserve Jewish domination in less ostensible forms. On the other hand, the "hardliners" subscribe to the idea of the right-wing and radical right parties (the Likud, the religious parties, Tehiya, and Tsomet) that Jewish domination should be reinforced while respecting Arab civil rights. The "exclusionists" are predisposed to the Kach Movement, standing for pushing the Arabs out of Israel, disenfranchising them, or formalizing Jewish control over them. The political polarization between the right and left political camps tends to strengthen these differences among the Jewish orientations toward the Arab minority.

The Jews are also changing their orientation from negation to ambivalence toward Israeli Arabs. Jews' perceptions of the Arabs have become less stereotypical and negative, their attitudes less confident and categorical, their feelings more mixed and confused, and their accusations of Arabs more self-defensive and apologetic. The Jews have become less reluctant to examine Arab grievances and less prone to reject them outright. They are more willing to mix and associate with Arabs. At the same time, Jews have also become more fearful of Arabs' escalating demands of equality, solidarity with Palestinian nationalism, and the occasional involvement of some Arabs in sabotage. Although remaining quite discriminatory, state policies have become less so over time.

The contention that the Jewish shift away from intransigence was necessary for the improvement in Arab conditions over the years should be complemented by the parallel assertion that the positive change among the Jews could not have taken place if there were a true Arab radicalization. While Arab radicalization could have made Jews more alienated and intransigent toward the Arabs, Arab politicization has stimulated, rather, a favorable change in Jewish mind and behavior.

Arab politicization consists of three components: Israelization, factionalism, and militancy. Israelization refers to the Arab acquisition of bilingualism, biculturalism, habits of consumption, exposure to media, political culture, leisure spending, and other forms of thinking and behaving common in the wider Israeli society. It also entails the acceptance of Jews and Jewish standards as models of reference. It further implies the deep realization that the Arab fate and future are tied mostly to Israel than to anything else. Israelization occurs without identification with Israel and without accepting it as a Jewish-Zionist state. It proceeds independently of and parallel to Palestinization. It cannot be overemphasized, because it is a genuine innovation in the Arab orientation in the post-state period, unlike Palestinization, which is only a reassertion of a hitherto submerged identity.

Factionalism is also increasingly dividing the Arab population. The "accommodationists" are Arabs who accept Israel as a Jewish-Zionist state and seek piecemeal change through the use of persuasion and pressure from within the Zionist establishment. On the other hand, the "reservationists" pursue greater change by organizing independently in a party like the Democratic Arab Party and aspiring to participate in a government coalition. The "oppositionists" follow Rakah and the Progressive List for Peace in fighting from the outside as a permanent opposition advocating a two-state solution and equality. In contrast, the "rejectionists," following the ideology of the Sons of the Village Movement inside Israel and the Rejection Front outside the state, deny Israel's right to exist and endeavor to replace it by a Palestinian state. Despite the Arab political consensus on certain issues, the differences among these orientations are appreciable.

Militancy is evidenced in the Arabs' growing impatience with discrimination and privation and in their sustained struggle for change. It is reflected in the Arab use of extra-parliamentary, but legal means to advance Arab causes. Militant Arabs are willing to escalate protest and pressure without transgressing the bounds of the law. Rather than passively reconciling themselves to their predicament, they undertake to fight independently, peacefully, and rigorously for bettering their lot in Israeli society.

If, indeed, Arab politicization and Jewish accessibility characterize minority-majority relations, how can we account for the emergence of this pattern? The present application of the general models of internal colonialism, control, political economy, and modernization to Arab-Jewish relations do not provide an adequate explanation of such a historical trend. Neither can one find in the broad literature on comparative ethnic relations another suitable theory or model that can account properly for the Israeli case. For instance, since most Arabs live in the Galilee and Triangle, they seem, at first glance, to fit the category "a backward group in a backward region" in a scheme suggested by Horowitz for the comparative study of separatist ethno-nationalist movements (1985: 229-288). He draws on the historical evidence to show that this type of minority population (e.g., the Kurds in Iraq) is the most prone to secessionism and radicalism because it is institutionally discriminated against in both the region and the state. The Arabs of the Galilee and Triangle are not secessionist, however. At the same time, one can persuasively argue that, upon a closer examination, they do not really constitute "a backward group in a backward region." This is because the state drive to Judaize the Galilee and Triangle, through massive expropriations of Arab lands, Jewish settlements, and zoning policies, has successfully destroyed the Arab contiguity of these regions.

Rather than invoking the argument of uniqueness, I wish to stress certain developments in both the Palestinian people and Israeli ethnic democracy that have to be included in any satisfactory explanation of the relative quiet and the moderate positive change in Arab-Jewish relations.

The defeat of the Arab world in the 1948 war against Israel transformed the Palestinians into a diaspora people. Although they reside mostly among Moslem Arabs, diaspora Palestinians have kept their separate identity through a common memory of the 1948 catastrophe, the myth of redemption and return, a movement to liberate the lost land, and the resistance of most of the host societies to assimilate them. A clear distinction, however, has emerged over the years among the Palestinian core in the West Bank and Gaza Strip, those in the diaspora, and the Palestinians in Israel. With the passage of time, diaspora communities tend to accommodate themselves to life in their foreign habitats (Klausner, 1991: 219). This is especially true of the Palestinians in Jordan and the West, most of whom would probably not return to a future Palestinian state. The Arabs in Israel live in the homeland that the Palestinians would have to give up in order to reach a permanent settlement with Israel. This historical trend of divergence of interest, orientation, and fate among various Palestinian communities has contributed to the view that the Palestinians in Israel have a legitimately distinct and separate status within the Palestinian people.

The view of a separate status for Palestinians in Israel has strongly been reinforced by the historical shift of the Arab world, including the Palestinians, away from rejectionism which dates back to the 1920s. Until Sadat's peace initiative in late 1977, the Arab world rejected and fought against Israel. The Palestinians also have moved away from their traditional rejectionism during the last decade. The Palestinian moves in 1988 to declare the independence of Palestine, to renounce terrorism, to accept the United Nations resolution 242, and to acknowledge Israel's right of existence were significant steps forward. The message implied in the Palestinian endorsement of a two-state solution is that Israel is no longer rejected as a state, that the Arabs in Israel are not part of the peace settlement, and that they must come to terms with permanent minority status in Israel. Whereas in the 1970s the Palestinians embraced Israeli Arabs as full-fledged Palestinians, repudiated their Israeli identity, and called upon them to take part in the Palestinian resistance movement, they began in the late 1980s, paradoxically, to approve of Israeli Arabs as Israelis, not see them as full-fledged Palestinians, and expect them to serve primarily as a pro-PLO lobby in Israeli society. Some Palestinian leaders go a step further in counselling Israeli Arabs to accommodate themselves even with Israel's Jewish-Zionist character in the event a Palestinian state were to rise in the area.

Another central factor carving a separate status for Israeli Arabs is the firm, consistent policy of all Israeli governments to separate Israeli Arabs from other Palestinians. Israeli Arabs before 1967 were totally isolated from their people and were pressured to form a different identity. After 1967, the authorities discouraged and restricted contacts between Arabs on both sides of the Green Line. The two kinds of homeland Palestinians are kept apart by citizenship, military rule, position in the marketplace, educational system, knowledge of the Hebrew language, acquisition of certain Israeli culture patterns, and many other markers. In fact, joint Palestinian organizations across the Green Line are prohibited by law. Palestinian nationalism is still considered by Jews as illegitimate, the PLO is declared to be a terrorist organization, and the public display of identification with the PLO and contacts with its officials are legally defined as a crime. Although this Israeli policy has failed to instill a new, non-Palestinian identity into Israeli Arabs, it has rigidified the boundaries between them and the rest of the Palestinian people.

The cumulative impact of these forces has been to separate Israeli Arabs from other Palestinians, to stimulate their accommodation to Israeli society, and to legitimize their acceptance of minority status. Israeli Arabs respond by reconciling themselves to their life as a minority while keeping certain ties with and identity as Palestinians. Because of these influences and because Israeli Arabs do not want to appear as accomplices to the occupation, they are reluctant to conduct cultural and political activities with the Arabs on the West Bank and Gaza Strip. Furthermore, they chose not to participate in the intifada nor to express hostility against Israel during the Gulf War, although they sided with the Palestinian cause in both cases. They understand that they are not part of a two-state solution, though they strongly believe that all sides (the Palestinians, the Jews, and themselves) are bound to benefit from such a solution (Al-Haj, forthcoming).

The other key factor that could help explain the stability and improvement in Arab-Jewish relations is the democratization of Israeli ethnic democracy. Israel does not belong to any of the three types of democracies spelled out in the literature on comparative politics: majoritarian, consociational, and Herrenvolk (Smooha, 1990). The Anglo-Saxon majoritarian model does not apply because Israel is not a system, widely open to all groups and individuals for free and equal competition, irrespective of their national origin and political goal. Neither is it a consociational, binational society, because Arabs and Jews do not have equal status. Nor does it qualify as a Herrenvolk democracy, because Israeli Arabs are neither formally nor actually denied civil and political freedoms and rights. Israel is rather unique in the Western world to be an ethnic democracy; that is, a system that combines a genuine democracy for all with institutionalized dominance for one of its constituent groups. This is a democracy that accords the Jewish majority preferential status and builds Jewishness into its dominant language, institutions, public domain, holidays, heroes, symbols, emblems, and orientations. Furthermore, by law Israel is "the state of the Jewish people," not of citizens. This means that Jewish non-resident aliens who live abroad have more claim on the state than do Arab resident citizens.

Israel is doubly unique in the Western world, also, for having its ethnic democracy internationally recognized. The 1917 Balfour Declaration affirmed the Jews' rights to a homeland in Palestine. The British Mandate was chartered by the League of Nations in 1922 to develop a Jewish homeland in Palestine; and the United Nations adopted a resolution in 1947 that provided for the creation of a Jewish state in Palestine. All these international statements acknowledged Jewish rights to part of Palestine without denying Palestinian rights there. Even the 1975 United Nations resolution equating Zionism with racism did not negate Jewish rights to Israel within the pre-1967 borders, but it was motivated by the injustice of the post-1967 occupation. Israel within the Green Line is accepted by the world community as a Jewish state and the status of the Arab minority within it is considered neither as a cause for denying its claim to be a democracy nor subject to censure for the institutional discrimination of a national minority. The United Nations is reluctant to get involved in the protection of collective or minority rights, as distinguished from human, individual, civil rights, in order not to intervene in the internal affairs of state members (Ryan, 1990).

As in any ethnic democracy, there is an inherent contradiction between democracy and structured ethnic dominance. These are conflicting principles of the organization of states, one providing for equality for all and another for preference of a certain group. More specifically, a number of structural incompatibilities follow from this fundamental contradiction. First, individual rights cannot be fully equal, and certain restrictions are imposed on the minority. Second, the majority is bound to impose even greater restrictions on minority collective rights in order to curb the forces of binationalism (the transformation of ethnic to consociational democracy), autonomy, and secession. Third, there is a real problem of allowing the minority into the national power structure because full political participation might undermine institutionalized dominance. Fourth, the system suffers from insufficient loyalty and legitimacy. The majority and the state that acts on its behalf question the basic loyalty of the minority to the state. The discriminated minority cannot give full legitimacy and loyalty to the state as long as it cannot be fully equal in it and cannot unreservedly identify itself with its institutions, goals, and policies.

Ethnic democracies have their strengths and weaknesses. They have the great advantage of democracy itself as an effective, non-violent system for working out these contradictions and pursuing better compromises between minority demands and majority privileges. Compared with liberal democracies, they are, no doubt, low-rate democracies in terms of equality before the law, individual freedoms, and protection of rights. From a minority's point of view, they are even inferior to consociational democracies in their insufficient provision of collective, national rights. These third-rate ethnic democracies are also inflicted by a high level of political and ethnic intolerance as is the case of Israel (Shamir, forthcoming).

The Arab minority and Jewish majority face this set of problems, characteristic of ethnic democracies. The Arabs are not granted full individual rights, are denied the status of a national minority, and are subject to discriminatory policies. In response, they withdraw full loyalty and legitimacy from the state. The Jews do not consider the Arabs to be full, equal members of the society and distrust them. Since Israel can be neither fully democratic nor fully Jewish-Zionist, there is a continuous struggle between Arabs and Jews to test the limits of both democracy and Zionism. Whereas the Jews enjoy a definite lead in this fight, the Arabs can still score some gains in their drive for equality. Since Jewish groups are highly differentiated by their degree of commitment to democracy and Zionism, Arabs can, to some extent, count on the more liberal Jews in their effort to improve their position in society.

Israeli democracy as the arena for Arab-Jewish relations has both strengths and weaknesses. It is strong, viable, robust, and remarkably stable in managing the virulent internal conflicts and repeated external wars of survival. It is also distinguished by a low level of serious political violence (Lehman-Wilzig, 1990). On the other hand, its weaknesses are equally serious. Israel does not have a constitution and a bill of rights and, as a result, supplies insufficient protection to individual and minority rights. It has, instead, comprehensive legislation regarding internal security, the "Defense (1945 Emergency) Regulations," which can readily be misused to repress "illegitimate" opposition. The fact that Israel is in a state of war and the Arab minority is part of the external threat makes it easier to restrict Arab rights and opportunities. Another weakness is the overburdened, bottle-necked character of the Israeli system, which is unable to deal with the mounting problems and excessive demands raised by various groups (Horowitz and Lissak, 1989). In such a system, peripheral groups like the Arab minority tend to be slighted or even glossed over.

Despite the ever-present obstacles, Israel has since 1948 undergone an intense process of democratization. Comparison of the first decade of the state with the fourth shows Israel within the Green Line to be marked by much more of a competitive party system, changeover of governments, free press, an interventionist Supreme Court, a limited use of emergency regulations, controlled internal security services, and attention given to various non-dominant groups. Israeli Arabs benefit from the expansion of democracy, without which it is impossible to conduct a peaceful struggle. Democratization has not only enabled Arabs to engage in a sustained struggle without risking outright repression by the state but also has yielded partial gains. Democratization explains both the feasibility and partial success of the Arab struggle since the mid-1970s. Furthermore, the ongoing Arab struggle not only builds on the growing Israeli democracy, it also strengthens it further by any headway made.

It is the improvement in the two broad historical contexts of the encounter between Arabs and Jews in Israel that must be taken into account in explaining the prevailing patterns of Arab politicization and Jewish accessibility, rather than the patterns of Arab radicalization and Jewish intransigence postulated by the common models. These concepts are differently conceived of by Jews and Arabs. For many Jews, a radical or radicalizing Arab is one who rejects the Jewish-Zionist character of the state and calls for the formation of a Palestinian state in any area West of the Jordan river. Similarly, for many Arabs, an intransigent or a conservatizing Jew is one who insists on keeping Israel Jewish-Zionist and opposes the establishment of an independent Palestinian state. Many Jews invoke the idea of Arab radicalization in order to delegitimize the Arab struggle, whereas many Arabs use the idea of Jewish intransigence in order to validate their escalating demands and to present Jews in a bad light.

The approach guiding this study objects to these self-serving viewpoints and, instead, offers a stricter definition. The following principle is suggested as the guideline for the badly needed conceptual distinction: *acceptance of coexistence between the Arab national minority and the Jewish national majority in Israel as a democratic state within its pre-1967 borders.* Broadly speaking, Arab radicalism and Jewish intransigence are construed to be gross violations of this simple guideline, based on the conception of Israel as an open democracy that enshrines the fundamental right to dissent, not an ethnic democracy as incontrovertible fact. This narrow definition respects the right of both Arabs and Jews to disagree with the majority opinion of the other side. The acceptance or rejection of Zionism or Palestinian nationalism as blueprints for Israeli society constitutes neither Arab radicalism nor Jewish intransigence. The right to disagree in a democracy is accorded to both the minority and the majority, though it is restricted or even denied if pursued through coercion or exercised with the intention to destroy democracy or the state.

A few examples of what would and would not constitute Arab radicalism according to the definition suggested will demonstrate the utility of the principle. It would be radical for an Arab to reject Israel's right to exist as a state within the Green Line or to have it replaced by a Palestinian state. It would not be radical for an Arab to reject Israel as a Jewish-Zionist state or as a Greater Israel or to have it replaced by a binational state. It would be radical for an Arab to reject any minority status in Israel, but it would not be radical for an Arab to pursue a national minority status for the Arabs. It would be radical for an Arab to endorse or use illegal or violent means of struggle, to boycott Jewish persons or institutions, to define one's collective identity without reference to Israel, to seek secession from the state, and to see the future of the Arabs dissociated from Israel. It would not be radical for an Arab to endorse or use extra-parliamentary means of struggle, to define one's collective identity in Palestinian terms, to favor separate communities, to seek autonomy, or to support and promote non-rejectionist causes of Palestinian nationalism (nation-building, end of occupation, formation of a Palestinian state in the West Bank and Gaza Strip, and recognition of the PLO as a legitimate representative of the Palestinian people).

Similarly, some instances will clarify the concrete meaning of Jewish intransigence. It would be intransigent for a Jew to deny the right of Arabs to live as a minority in Israel, to call for their transfer from the country or for a limit on their fertility, and to deny them civil rights. It would not be intransigent for a Jew to support the idea of Israel as a Jewish-Zionist state in which the Arabs live as an ethnic but not as a national minority. It would be intransigent for a Jew to force Arabs to assimilate or to oppose their integration into Israeli institutions and public facilities. It would not be intransigent for a Jew to oppose Arab assimilation or to object to a process that would merge the two separate communities. It would be intransigent for a Jew to insist on the state's across-the-board preference for Jews, but it would not be intransigent to expect some preference in some areas. It would be intransigent for a Jew to object to any contact with Arabs, but not to intermarriage. It would be intransigent for a Jew to endorse sweeping restrictions on Arabs that are not necessary for national security or public safety, but it would not be intransigent to favor certain security-related restrictions. It would be intransigent for a Jew to treat Arabs as subversive, but it would not be intransigent to be suspicious of them and to oppose their Palestinian identity, their support for the PLO, and their solidarity with the intifada.

These distinctions are based on a narrow, restrictive definition of Arab radicalism and Jewish intransigence. According to them, in Israel today most Arabs would not qualify as radical and most Jews would not qualify as intransigent. On the other hand, proponents of the Arab radicalization thesis tend to apply a wide definition which includes militancy as part of radicalization and does not respect the Arab right to reject Israel's Jewish-Zionist character. By the same token, supporters of the Jewish intransigence thesis would castigate as intransigent Jewish insistence on keeping Israel as an ethnic democracy, with Jewish dominance and without full, equal rights to Arabs.

Response to Criticisms

In order to further clarify my approach and to distinguish it from other perspectives, I will try to answer certain criticisms raised against my analysis as presented in the previous volumes and various articles. My approach is particularly subject to misinterpretation and to attacks because it does not clearly side with either the Arab or Jewish cause and does not conform with the standard views on this loaded issue of Arab-Jewish relations. Hence, it is hard to pigeonhole and not to suspect its underlying assumptions and intentions. Its even-handedness, complexity, and ambiguity spring from a sustained effort to study and take into account the viewpoints of *both* Arabs and Jews, in contrast to the other approaches that mostly concentrate on the Arab minority without devoting equal attention to the Jewish majority.

The harshest criticism by far comes, as expected, from scholars working within the internal colonial perspective. In their critique of Israeli-Jewish writings on Palestinians in Israel, Haidar and Zureik conclude with regard to my work:

> His [Smooha's] analysis of Israeli society based on the concept of cultural pluralism puts him in the same camp as other Israeli researchers; to them, the Middle East conflict arises from cultural contradictions rather than the political issues of national rights and self-determination.
>
> In contrast to Smooha and others who conform to the mainstream approaches in Israeli social science, there is a minority of researchers who, despite their orientation, view the conflict as arising from two nationalisms rather than from a legitimate nationalism embodied in the Zionist movement colliding with an illegitimate one reflected in fragmented and disorganized Arab factions (1987: 81).

Since I do not belong to the political economy school, then in a dichotomous thinking I must have belonged to the pro-establishment school of cultural pluralism. Contrary to Haidar's and Zureik's sweeping attributions, I do not subscribe to cultural pluralism and I do hold to the views and fundamental assumptions I am accused of denying. My approach is based on the analysis of structural, intergroup conflicts over resources and values (ideology, state, territory, etc.) and on the premise that in the area West of Jordan a struggle has been underway for territory and national self-determination between two legitimate national movements. I always believed that the conflict can be settled only by territorial partition and a two-state solution (I stated this position in writing as early as 1974; Smooha, 1974). I see my work on Arab-Jewish relations as part of the study of the wider Palestinian-Israeli and Arab-Israeli conflicts. These national conflicts between Arabs and Jews within and outside the state of Israel have been exacerbated by the exclusionary nature of the dominant currents of both Zionism and Palestinian nationalism. But I do recognize and stress the implications for Arab-Jewish coexistence of both the positive change in the attitude of the Arab world toward Israel since the late 1970s and the opening up and the expansion of the democratic structure of Israeli society since the mid-1960s.

Some find my alternative thesis that the Arabs in Israel are neither radical nor radicalizing as untenable and unsubstantiated. Paradoxically, it strikes a nerve among some Arabs who read in this thesis a concealed message that the Arabs are successfully accommodating to Israel and identify themselves with it, and that Israel treats Arabs well and, therefore, should not adapt itself to them. For instance, Zureik detects such an accommodating slant in my interpretation of the 1976 survey findings and draws on them to demonstrate that "On almost every measure, Palestinians, who are Israeli citizens, perceive their situation to border on marginality and despair. Politically, they feel disenfranchised and reject the appropriateness of Zionism as an overarching ideology which governs the dominant sociopolitical institutions of society" (1987: 225-226). Rouhana (1991) also nicknames my approach as "an accommodation model" to expose its supposed overemphasis on Arabs' Israelization and their satisfactory adjustment to the Jewish state. Both Zureik and Rouhana contend that I am underplaying the Palestinian component and overstressing the Israeli element in Arab identity. Yet, I clearly do not say explicitly or implicitly that the Arabs are well-adjusted to Israel and the solution to the Arab-Jewish problem requires adaptation on their part only. My central thesis is that the Arabs are neither radical nor radicalizing according to my own definition of Arab radicalism. The thesis could be correct only if my definition of radicalism is accepted. I am trying to face the paradox of why Arab radicalism, as I define it, is limited despite the state's discriminatory policies and Jews' substantial ethnocentrism. I do not find an adequate answer to this paradox in

Zureik's internal colonialism, Rouhana's accentuated Palestinian identity, Lustick's system of control (which he has already abandoned), or in other formulations.

The Arab politicization thesis is criticized for its narrow definition of radicalism that excludes militancy. Many simply take any Arab opposition to the status quo as radicalism. For right-wing Jews, any objection to the Jewish nature of the state is radical. Furthermore, they demand of Arabs unqualified loyalty to the state, identification with its Zionist goals, and active army or civic service, and suggest to disenfranchise Arabs who refuse to meet these requirements. For others, voting for non-Jewish parties, general strikes, construction of illegal buildings (taken as a measure of delegitimation of the government, not actions taken out of lack of choice), and the formation of independent institutions (perceived as an alternative to state institutions, not responses to government inactions) are clear indicators of radicalism (Yiftachel, personal communication). Still, others interpret the survey findings as an evidence of radicalism. Soffer, for instance, considers as a manifest sign of radicalism the findings from the 1980 survey that 11% of the Arab public and 77% of the Arab activists in the rejectionist Sons of the Village Movement denied Israel's right to exist and that 7.5% and 61%, respectively, endorsed the use of violence. He then asks rhetorically: "What percentage of the residents of Catholic Ulster bear the brunt of carrying out the violence and terror in that area?" (1990: 818). Although Soffer grossly underestimates the proportion of the Catholics who withhold legitimacy from Ulster, he and others raise a legitimate objection to my conceptualization. I can only add that I personally find the conceptual distinction between radicalism and militancy to be very useful and the blanket, undifferentiated term of radicalism to be counterproductive.

A further objection to Arab politicization, advanced as an alternative to the Arab radicalization thesis, stems from the view of politicization as a stage in a long process of radicalization. This is a common criticism that concedes that Arab behavior has so far corresponded to the politicization thesis, but considers this as only a transition period that will eventually be followed by radicalization. Since my initial formulation of the Arab politicization thesis in the late 1970s, I have had to put up with the charge of naiveté and misunderstanding of the "deep" historical process. We social scientists do rather poorly in forecasting the future, but in view of the past experience, including the intifada that provides a hard test, this argument that Arab politicization is a step in Arab radicalization must be rejected. Of course, if Jews will substantially weaken, Israel will turn to a summary repression of Israeli Arabs, and Arab conditions will deteriorate, the Arabs will probably radicalize.

My rejection of the Jewish intransigence thesis and formulation of the alternative Jewish accessibility thesis also do not seem persuasive to reviewers such as Springborg (1990). Zureik claims that my "ahistorical approach fails to highlight the ideological rigidity of the Zionist state" (1987: 226). My conceptualization of the political system of the Jewish state as an ethnic democracy, the stress on the growing accessibility of Jews and Jewish institutions to Arabs, and the idea of continuing democratization of Israel would invite criticisms that I am offering a pro-establishment analysis and an apology for the status quo. Yet, contrary to stock Zionist (including left Zionist) thinking, I maintain that Israel's resilient ethnic democracy is a third-rate, non-Western democracy; Zionism and democracy are inherently contradictory; state discriminatory policies are a key factor in the political orientation of the Arabs in Israel; and Arab-Jewish coexistence would necessitate recasting of Zionism and of Israel's Jewish-Zionist nature, though without the need to dismantle them.

Methodological reservations are also made. Some doubt the utility of attitudinal survey data, compared to historical and structural accounts. Since I responded at length to these recurrent objections in the previous volume, it is enough here to reiterate that survey data are only one set of evidence and they should not and are not used as a substitute for institutional analysis. Others cast doubt on what Israeli Arabs are willing to tell pollsters, and Jewish ones in particular. Zureik makes this point and even goes as far as to show that Rouhana (1984), a Palestinian investigator, obtains more credible survey results than I did – Palestinian identity was more striking in his surveys than was in mine. Zureik, however, seems to be unaware of the fact that Rouhana's figures are much less representative than mine: they exclude Druzes and Bedouin (a quarter of the Arab population) and grossly over-represent the younger and more educated. His surveys also do not draw systematic, stratified samples of respondents from up-to-date, complete registers of the Arab population, but apply, rather, a less rigorous method based on listing of housing units and adults living in them. Before invoking the built-in biases in the investigator's background, differences in sampling should be considered. More generally, the common questioning of the validity of the Arab survey data stems from lack of appreciation of the viability of Israeli democracy and its spread to and internalization by Israeli Arabs.

Finally, my surveys provide a systematic, comprehensive, cross-time, and comparable information on Arab attitudes since 1976 and Jewish attitudes since 1980 toward Arab-Jewish coexistence. The methods, questionnaires, and findings of the surveys are reported in detail, and are, therefore, open to criticisms and alternative explanations. These survey data are pieces of evidence that researchers of Arab-Jewish relations can consider along with their own surveys or analyses.

The 1985 and 1988 Surveys

This volume reports the findings from the 1985 and 1988 surveys of Arabs and Jews. They are part of a long-term research project on Arab-Jewish relations that began in the mid-1970s and was designed to study the relations between the Arab minority and the Jewish majority within the Green Line. A central component of the project is the conduct of surveys of the two populations every 3-5 years in order to look into key issues dividing the two communities and to establish trends over time in the attitudes of both sides toward each other.

The previous surveys were conducted in 1976 and 1980. The pioneering 1976 surveys were based on a national representative sample of 656 adult Arabs and a sample of 148 adult Jews from two towns. The 1980 surveys drew on 1,140 interviews with adult Arabs and 1,267 adult Jews, representing the entire adult population of Israel within the pre-1967 borders. The surveys in 1980 also included 88 Arab and 90 Jewish public figures, representing three political streams in each population. The 1976 surveys were fully reported in *The Orientation and Politicization of the Arab Minority in Israel* (Smooha, 1984) and the 1980 surveys in *Arabs and Jews in Israel, Vol. 1* (Smooha, 1989).

The 1976 and 1980 surveys serve as baseline surveys for cross-time comparisons. The 1976 representative survey constitutes the base for the Arabs (from the sample we excluded youth under 18 who were included in the original sample and statistics), whereas the 1980 representative survey fulfills this purpose for the Jews.

The 1985 and 1988 surveys are comparable in methods to the 1976 and 1980 surveys, and, therefore, allow a direct comparison of the results. The 1985 surveys drew on interviews with 1,203 Arabs and 1,205 Jews, as well as 137 Arab and 144 Jewish public figures, representing four political streams in each population. The 1988 surveys consisted of 1,200 Arabs and 1,209 Jews, and did not include leaders. They were conducted in March-April 1988, namely, 4-5 months after the outbreak of the intifada.

These surveys were carried out according to common procedures. The 1976-88 Arab surveys were based on national samples from complete official voter rolls in a cross section of localities. Face-to-face interviews were administered by Arab interviewers at the respondents' homes, applying a standard questionnaire in Arabic. The 1980-88 Jewish surveys followed the usual practice, i.e., in this case, the interviewing of 1,200 adult Jews by Jewish interviewers through a standard questionnaire in Hebrew. The samples in these Jewish surveys were weighted according to age, education, and ethnic origin in order to correct biases (the population parameters were derived from the labor force surveys conducted by the Central Bureau of Statistics). The cooperation of the population was satisfactory.

Part Five (Appendixes) of this book provides details on the 1985-88 surveys. Appendix A discusses the methodology of the surveys, covering the procedures (measuring instrument, population and sampling, fieldwork, the leadership survey, and a special survey consisting of focused interviews), representativeness, reliability, and validity. The English translation of the 1985 questionnaire appears in Appendix B and that of the 1988 questionnaire in Appendix C. It is shown that the Arab surveys met the criteria of survey research and yielded results whose reliability and validity matched those of the Jewish surveys. Like all samples of 1,200 persons, the Arab and Jewish samples have an average sampling error of 3%.

Since the 1985 surveys included both rank and file and leaders, they constitute the core data for this volume, and the 1988 data are added to them. For this reason, the reported findings throughout the book refer to the 1985 surveys, if not otherwise indicated. Hence, tables without a cited source contain figures from the 1985 surveys. All the reported percentages, for all the 1976-88 surveys, ignore non-responses (don't know) and are adjusted accordingly (with a few exceptions, missing data do not exceed 3%).

A typical table, summarizing one or more items from the 1985 surveys, consists of ten columns of percentages, five for Arabs and five for Jews. These ten columns refer to the following groups:

1. *Arab public*. The 1985 sample consists of 1,203 adult men and women in the general Arab citizen population, including Druzes and Bedouin, and excluding Circassians and Palestinians across the Green Line.

2. *Establishment affiliated Arab leaders*. They include 32 Arab Knesset Members, heads of local councils, and top office holders in the Jewish parties.

3. *Unaffiliated Arab leaders*. They consist of 32 heads of local councils and members of the intelligentsia, who are at present politically independent, but in most cases used to be attached to the Zionist establishment.

4. *DFPE and PLP Arab leaders*. They include 41 heads of local councils, politicians, and intellectuals active in or affiliated with the two Arab-Jewish, but predominantly Arab, political bodies – the Democratic Front for Peace and Equality (DFPE – a front organization of the Communist Party) and the Progressive List for Peace.

5. *Sons of Village Arab leaders.* They consist of 32 activists in the rejectionist Sons of the Village Movement. These are mostly young men who do not hold political posts and are hardly recognized as leaders by the general Arab public. They represent, however, a distinct political stream in the Arab community.

6. *Jewish public.* The 1985 sample consists of 1,205 adult men and women in the general Jewish population, including members of kibbutzim and moshavim, but excluding settlers in the West Bank, Gaza Strip, and the Golan Heights.

7. *DFPE and PLP Jewish leaders.* These are 36 politicians and intellectuals active in or affiliated with the non-Zionist DFPE and PLP. They are marginal to Jewish politics but represent a distinct political stream and viewpoint.

8. *CRM and Mapam Jewish leaders.* These are 36 public figures from the Zionist left. They include Knesset Members, party officials, and intellectuals of the Citizens' Rights Movement (CRM), Mapam Party, and Shinui (Change).

9. *Labor Jewish leaders.* This group includes 40 leaders from the Labor Party, when it headed the national unity government. They consist of cabinet ministers, deputy ministers, Knesset Members, mayors, and intellectuals.

10. *Likud camp Jewish leaders.* They consist of 34 leaders from the Likud political camp – the Likud, Tehiya, and religious parties. They are mostly composed of Knesset Members and mayors.

The Arab and Jewish leaders represent the wide spectrum of views in Israel on Arab-Jewish relations. Two streams are missing, however. Leaders of the Islamic Movement were not included because at the time of the 1985 surveys they were not politically visible. Representatives of the Kach Movement were also not polled. They were hard to identify because of the giant shadow cast over them by the Kach leader, the late Rabbi Kahane.

I refer, throughout this volume, to the Arab population by the terms "Israeli Arabs," "Arabs in Israel," or just "Arabs." I am doing so primarily for the sake of clarity, namely, in order not to cause a confusion between them and the Arabs across the Green Line, whom I always address as Palestinians. By calling them "Israeli Arabs," I do not intend to deny their Palestinian identity. There are, nevertheless, other considerations in addition to clarity. First, the term "Israeli Arab" is not pejorative. Second, all Palestinians are Arabs. Third, the Arabs themselves are reluctant to change the names of their organizations from "Arab" to "Palestinian"; they keep the names "Arab Student Union" (instead of "Palestinian Student Union"), "The Committee for the Defense of Arab Lands" (instead of "The Committee for the Defense of Palestinian Lands"), and so forth. They resist the shift because they want to avoid ambiguity, to keep the distinction between themselves and other Palestinians, and not to antagonize the Jews and Jewish authorities that perceive Palestinian identity as subversive. Fourth, I do occasionally use the terms "Israeli Palestinians" and "Palestinians in Israel" in referring to Arabs in Israel, when the clarity of these terms is not likely to get lost by the context.

There are three substantive parts to the book (in addition to the methodological part). The first part deals with 13 key issues that divide Arabs and Jews. The second part uses these issues to construct a typology of Arabs and Jews according to their different orientations toward Arab-Jewish coexistence. Drawing on the survey data and a variety of non-quantative material, the third part analyzes trends over the years in Arab and Jewish orientations.

Part One

KEY ISSUES

2

Selecting the Key Issues

Of the numerous issues that divide Arabs and Jews in Israel, thirteen were selected for the 1980 survey and analyzed in Volume 1. They also served as the basis for the 1985 and 1988 surveys, on which Volume 2 focuses. These common, key problems are as follows:

1. *Ethnic stratification.* Do Arabs and Jews perceive inequality in Israel similarly or differently? Do they have similar or different status aspirations? Is Arab-Jewish inequality an issue dividing them? To what extent are Israeli Arabs resigned to their lower position in the class structure of Israeli society? To what extent are Jews prepared to place on the national agenda the achievement of Arab-Jewish equality?

2. *Cultural diversity.* To what extent do Arabs accept Israel's Western-oriented and Jewish culture or feel the strains of cultural dominance? Are Jews willing to promote institutional bilingualism and biculturalism as a means of accommodating Israeli Arabs?

3. *Legitimacy of coexistence.* Does each community recognize the legitimate presence of the other? Do Israeli Arabs acknowledge Israel's right to exist, and do they reconcile themselves to its Jewish-Zionist character? Are Jews receptive to having an Arab minority with full civil rights in their midst?

4. *Israeli-Arab conflict.* Is there an operative consensus among Jews on how to resolve the Palestinian question and do Israeli Arabs share it?

5. *Collective identity.* How widespread are various Palestinian versus Israeli concepts of identification among Israeli Arabs? Do Israeli Arabs and Jews agree on the definition of the Arab national identity?

6. *Institutional separation.* Do Israeli Arabs and Jews approve of the status quo of institutional separation, or does either side want greater integration?

7. *National autonomy.* Do Israeli Arabs claim the right to some sort of self-determination and, if so, what are its desired expressions (such as control over Arab institutions, regional self-rule, irredentism)? What degree or form of national autonomy is the Jewish public ready to grant Arabs?

8. *Group goals.* What goals are sought by Israeli Arabs and Jews vis-à-vis each other: exclusion, domination, equal opportunity, consociationalism (compromise and partnership), secession, non-sectarianism?

9. *Leadership credibility.* How much credibility do various local Arab leadership groups and the PLO enjoy among Israeli Arabs and Jews?

10. *Educational goals.* Do Israeli Arabs want Arab bilingualism, biculturalism, and Palestinian nationalism to become goals for Arab education? Do Jews consent to the educational goals desired by Israeli Arabs? What goals do both sides consider as suitable for Jewish education?

11. *Strategies for change.* Do Arabs and Jews concur on the legitimacy of the different means adopted to improve Israeli Arab conditions – parliamentary politics, extra-parliamentary politics, and extra-legal politics? Do Arabs feel that the means they employ are effective and their chances to effect change good?

12. *Ethnocentrism.* To what degree do Israeli Arabs and Jews show various forms of intolerance (stereotyping, mistrust, avoidance, and preferential treatment) toward each other?

13. *Deprivation and alienation.* How rampant are Israeli Arab feelings of being individually and collectively discriminated against and of being treated as outsiders? Do Jews see any basis for the sense of deprivation and alienation felt by Israeli Arabs?

Arab and Jewish opinions on these issues for the years 1985 and 1988 and trends for the 1976-88 period will be discussed in this part of the book (chapters 3-16).

3

Ethnic Stratification

Inequality in the distribution of resources and in access to opportunities, vital factors of intergroup relations, comprise as important a dimension in Arab-Jewish relations in Israel as in other deeply divided societies. Three aspects of this matter will be examined below: Do Arabs and Jews perceive inequality in Israel similarly or differently? Do they have similar or different status aspirations? Is Arab-Jewish inequality an issue dividing them?

Broadly speaking, Arabs and Jews view and accept Israel as a bourgeois, middle class, politically controlled, and achievement-based society. A majority of 62% of the Arabs and 70% of the Jews agree to the diamond-shaped, rather than pyramidal, description of social inequality in Israel, as "a majority of people are in the middle class with a small minority who are rich or poor" (Table 3.1). Many also find inequality in Israel to be on the increase. They see Israel as ruled much more by political-bureaucratic than by economic elites: cabinet ministers and leaders of political parties are considered by both sides as holding more influence than do big industrialists and top bankers (Table 3.2). These images of Israel are quite realistic.

The two communities also share the belief in the achievement ethos: 58% of the Arabs and 56% of the Jews regard hard work, education, and experience as the most important determinants of success in life, whereas factors unrelated to personal performance, such as connections and inheritance, are dismissed as irrelevant for personal progress (Table 3.3). Arabs, however, attach much more weight than Jews do (24.5% versus 5%) to "organizing and standing together as a group" because of their bad experience as a disadvantaged minority in a Jewish state. Yet both sides prefer the present system of private property to one of public ownership (Table 3.4).

Table 3.1 Shape and Trend of Social Inequality

	Arab Public	Jewish Public
Regard the following to be a better description of social inequality in the country		
A majority of people are in the middle class, with a small minority who are rich or poor	62.0	69.9
Most of the wealth is held by a small minority at the expense of the majority who are poor	38.0	30.1
Think that Inequality between rich and poor in the country in the past five years has		
Increased	64.9	48.4
Remained the same	25.2	37.3
Decreased	9.9	14.3

Source: The 1988 survey.

Table 3.2 Influentials

	Arab Public	Jewish Public
Persons perceived as having strong influence in society		
Cabinet ministers	83.6	76.8
Editors of the press, radio and television	78.6	72.0
Top commanders of the army	70.0	65.7
Leaders of political parties	69.6	76.0
Supreme court justices	62.1	55.3
Trade union leaders	54.9	53.7
Heads of religion	51.3	64.3
Big industrialists	48.4	51.1
Top bankers	36.1	49.3

Source: The 1988 survey.

Table 3.3 Determinants of Success in Life

	Arab Public	Jewish Public
The most important factor for achieving success in life		
Working hard for personal progress	33.6	23.9
Education	18.9	21.0
Experience	5.7	11.5
Organizing and standing together as a group	24.5	4.8
Connections	3.3	8.8
Religious belief[a]	7.0	–
Trustfulness[b]	–	7.5
Tricks	0.3	1.0
Luck	3.6	16.3
Inheritance	0.9	4.2
What one's parents taught oneself	2.2	0.9

[a]For Arabs only. [b]For Jews only.

Source: The 1988 survey.

There is, nonetheless, a sharp disagreement on the desirable role of government. While 62% of the Arabs prefer a government that intervenes through heavy taxation and other means to reduce social inequality in wages, housing, and education, 70% of the Jews would rather have a government that enables ambitious and hard-working people to get richer (Table 3.4). The Arabs, as a disadvantaged group, stand to gain more than do the Jews from any governmental effort to equalize the allocation of resources. It is generally true that self-interest prompts weaker segments of the population to support governmental intervention to decrease inequality. For instance, 68% of the Arabs with only primary education as compared to 54% of the Arabs with post-secondary education (among the Jews – 37% and 23%, respectively) are of this opinion. Political orientation also has some influence. Among the Arabs, the staunchest supporters of non-discriminatory policies are voters for the Communist-led Democratic Front for Peace and Equality (DFPE; 68% are in favor), whereas the least enthusiastic supporters are voters for the Progressive List for Peace (PLP; 53%). Among the Jews, the contrasting groups are voters for the populist Likud (36%) and voters for the elitist Shinui and Citizens' Rights Movement (CRM; 11%). When education and voting are combined, they produce the following proportions of endorsement of government intervention for lessening socioeconomic disparities: 73% of Arab voters for the DFPE with primary education versus 35% of Arab voters for the PLP with higher education; 48% of Jewish voters for the Likud with primary education versus 6% of Jewish voters for Shinui and CRM with higher education.

Table 3.4 Preferred Socioeconomic System

	Arab Public	Jewish Public
Would prefer		
Shops and factories owned by private businessmen who will work hard to make the business grow	68.9	80.7
Shops and factories owned by the government elected by the people	31.1	19.3
Would prefer		
All people should have the right to own property	76.6	84.8
The government should own all property and give it to the people to use	23.4	15.2
Would prefer		
A government which enables people who are clever and hard working to become wealthier than others	37.6	69.8
A government which tries to make all people as equal as possible in wages, housing and education, even if there is a need to impose heavy taxes	62.4	30.2

Source: The 1988 survey.

The socioeconomic aspirations of Arabs and Jews are high. Over half of both groups prefer to be self-employed to working as employees (Table 3.5). The attainment of this goal would require considerable relocation of manpower, since only a tenth of all persons in the labor force in Israel are self-employed (8.8% in 1988; Central Bureau of Statistics, *Statistical Abstract of Israel 1989*: 347). This bourgeois drive of the Israelis is further reflected in their definite preference for investing money won in a family.

Table 3.5 Bourgeois Aspirations

	Arab Public	Jewish Public
Preferred kind of work		
Owning a business where one can win a lot or lose a lot	52.9	51.1
Holding a job or office with good salary to rely on	47.1	48.9
Preferred way of spending money won in a lottery		
Investing in a big plant or business	39.3	16.2
Starting a small plant or business	33.2	28.0
Investing in a bank with good interest	8.4	24.9
Enjoying spending money on oneself or one's family	19.0	30.9

Source: The 1988 survey.

Most Israelis – 76.5% of the Arabs and 89% of the Jews – assign themselves to the middle or higher classes when asked to choose the stratum to which they belong (Table 3.6). To a certain degree, this echoes the middle-class structure of Israeli society, but to a larger extent it indicates the high status ambitions of the entire population. Even persons who hold manual or low-status jobs classify themselves as middle class or more. Among the lowest fifth on the occupational scale, for example, 75% of the Arabs and 86% of the Jews view themselves as part of the middle or upper strata. Since the proportion of Arabs in the working and lower class is at least twice as high, Arabs must cope much more with an undesirable socioeconomic status.

Table 3.6 Self-Classification into a Socioeconomic Level

	Arab Public	Jewish Public
Assign oneself to		
Upper class	0.9	2.0
Upper-middle class	8.8	19.7
Middle class	66.8	67.9
Lower-middle class	17.0	10.0
Lower class	6.5	0.9

Source: The 1988 survey.

The high status aspirations and, as a result, the frustrations of the Arabs are also manifested in their comparative groups. When they assess their socioeconomic achievements, 67% of the Arab public and 82% to 92% of the Arab leaders in 1985 compare themselves to Jews and Westerners (Table 3.7). This tendency of the Arab public was 72% in 1980, 67% in 1985, and 68% in 1988 (Table 3.8). The comparison to Jews is the established norm among Arabs in Israel, who reject comparisons both to Arabs in Arab countries and to themselves at an earlier period, which a good many Jews often suggest to them to make. Israeli Arabs insist on the same standards and entitlements common among their fellow Jewish citizens and would accept no less. They are not resigned to their fate as a working-class minority in a middle-class society and wish to be integrated, like the Jews, into the higher echelons and elites where their representation is presently meager.

Table 3.7 Arabs' Comparative Groups

	Arab Public	Estab. Affil. Arab Lead.	Unaffil-iated Arab Lead.	DFPE & PLP Arab Lead.	Sons of Village Arab Lead.
In assessing one's socioeconomic achievements today, comparison is made to					
Palestinian Arabs in Mandatory Palestine	11.7	6.9	3.2	5.1	9.1
Arabs in the West Bank and Gaza Strip	8.9	3.4	6.5	2.6	9.1
Arabs in Arab countries	11.0	3.4	3.2	0.0	0.0
Jews in Israel	60.7	75.9	77.4	84.6	68.2
Inhabitants of the Western world	7.7	10.3	9.7	7.7	13.6

Table 3.8 Arabs' Comparative Groups, 1976-85

	Arab Public		
	1976	1980	1985
In assessing one's socioeconomic achievements today, comparison is made to			
Palestinian Arabs in Mandatory Palestine	7.5	13.2	11.7
Arabs in the West Bank and Gaza Strip	4.3	5.6	8.9
Arabs in Arab countries	15.9	13.8	11.0
Jews in Israel	65.4	58.3	60.7
Inhabitants of the Western world	6.9	9.1	7.7

Arabs regard Israel as their country, expect it to uplift them, and enable them fully to fulfill their high socioeconomic aspirations. They see the socioeconomic gap separating them from the Jews as being large to medium, and most of the Jews agree with them, although they tend to underestimate it. The more leftist the person, the wider the Arab-Jewish gap looks to him. For instance, Jewish leaders who estimate the gap to be large constitute 86% of those affiliated with the DFPE or PLP, 67% of those on the Zionist left, 39.5% of Labor leaders, and only 6% of the leaders from the right-wing Likud camp (Table 3.9). The Jewish public rejects the Arab demand to treat the class discrepancy between the two communities as an urgent state goal; only the Jewish leaders in the leftist opposition accept this demand. Israel's shortage of resources and lack of commitment to Arabs (the latter is well evidenced in the survey in the attitude of those Jewish leaders associated with the ruling parties) leave little hope for closing the gap in the foreseeable future.

Table 3.9 Size and Urgency of Closure of the Arab-Jewish Socioeconomic Gap

	Arab Public	Estab. Affil. Arab Lead.	Unaffiliated Arab Lead.	DFPE & PLP Arab Lead.	Sons of Village Arab Lead.	Jewish Public	DFPE & PLP Jewish Lead.	CRM & Mapam Jewish Lead.	Labor Jewish Lead.	Likud Camp Jewish Lead.
Regard the present socioeconomic gap between Arabs and Jews as										
Large	51.1	48.4	78.1	100.0	87.5	35.0	86.1	66.7	39.5	6.1
Medium	39.9	48.4	18.8	0.0	6.3	48.6	13.9	24.2	47.4	57.6
Small	9.0	3.2	3.1	0.0	6.3	16.4	0.0	9.1	13.2	36.4
Consider the closure of the present socioeconomic gap between Arabs and Jews as an urgent state goal	* 86.5[a]	*	*	*	*	13.3 16.9[b]	100.0	76.5	48.7	11.8

*Not asked. [a]The 1980 survey. [b]The 1988 survey.

It is no wonder, therefore, that a majority of the Arabs, compared to only a minority of the Jews, feel discontented with their socioeconomic attainments and chances. Compared to only a quarter of the Jews, 71% of the Arabs believe that whatever one's personal efforts in Israel, one does not receive the education and job to which one is entitled, and 59% are afraid that the standard of living of their children might fall behind their own (Table 3.10).

Table 3.10 Perceived Chances for Social Mobility

	Arab Public	Jewish Public
Do not believe in getting the education and job one is entitled to whatever one's personal efforts are in Israel	71.0	25.4
Afraid that children might never enjoy as high a standard of living as one's generation used to have	59.2	24.0

Source: The 1988 survey.

In conclusion, the dual goal of the Arab struggle is equality and peace. The class dimension of the demand of equality is very divisive. The fact that the Arabs perceive social stratification in the same way as do the Jews and adopt high Israeli and Western standards testifies to their deep attachment to Israel; but it also exacerbates the sense of dissatisfaction with their inferior status. They feel that they do not receive what they deserve, and fear that their children may fare even less well. They reject their lower position in Israel's class structure and ethnic hierarchy and turn to the state for help. The Jews, on the other hand, benefit from their superiority and refuse to put the accomplishment of equality for the Arabs on the national agenda.

4

Cultural Diversity

Cultural diversity in Israel is characterized by Jewish dominance, accordance of the right to a separate culture to the Arab minority, acquisition of bilingualism and biculturalism by the Arabs, and Arab rejection of Jewish cultural dominance.

The status of the Arabs as a cultural minority is a source of tension between Arabs and Jews. The growing adoption of bilingualism by Israeli Arabs no doubt moderates the problem. In 1988, 74% of the Arabs were able to converse in Arabic and Hebrew and 67% could speak, read, and write in both languages (Table 4.1). In comparison, only 31% of the Hebrew-speaking Jews could speak Arabic (these were mostly Jews from Arab countries) and only 11.5% were fully literate in Arabic. While bilingualism in Arabic and Hebrew is on the rise among the Arabs, it is stable or even in decline among the Jews. It is high and has increased in all segments of the Arab population. Among Arab leaders and the new generation, especially young men who were educated in Israeli Arab schools and who work in the Jewish economy, it is almost universal (Table 4.2).

Table 4.1 Knowledge of Hebrew and Arabic, 1976-88

	Arab Public				Jewish Public		
	1976	1980	1985	1988	1980	1985	1988
Know how to speak Arabic	100.0	100.0	100.0	100.0	37.2	32.9	31.1
Know how to read and write Arabic	67.5	77.6	79.2	88.7	10.3	12.5	14.8
Know how to speak Hebrew	62.3	69.9	68.8	74.2	100.0[a]	100.0[a]	100.0[a]
Know how to read and write Hebrew	48.4	62.9	65.1	71.8	92.9	91.7	94.0
Know how to speak Arabic and Hebrew	62.3	69.9	68.8	74.2	37.2	32.9	31.1
Know how to read and write Arabic and Hebrew	47.7	62.7	64.1	71.3	10.3	12.1	14.1
Know how to speak, read and write in Arabic and Hebrew	47.6	60.6	60.3	67.2	8.1	9.6	11.5

[a]Since interviews with Jews for the survey were conducted in Hebrew only, all respondents obviously spoke Hebrew. It is estimated that about 85% of the Jews in Israel are Hebrew speakers.

Table 4.2 Arabs' Knowledge of Hebrew, 1976-88

	Arab Public			
	1976	1980	1985	1988
Speak Hebrew				
Total	62.3	69.9	68.8*	74.2*
Men	85.0	88.8	86.5*	86.3*
Women	39.7	50.4	47.6*	60.2*
Men, 18-25 years old	97.7	97.9	92.3*	91.8*
Women, 18-25 years old	66.6	70.7	68.1*	73.9*
Read and write Hebrew				
Total	48.3	62.9	65.1	71.8
Men	66.0	79.4	77.1	81.9
Women	30.6	46.0	50.6	60.0
Men, 18-25 years old	89.4	92.7	91.4	89.9
Women, 18-25 years old	59.9	73.1	76.7	80.7

*The phrasing of the question in 1985 and 1988 was more demanding than it was in 1976 and 1980.

Command of Hebrew is evident in the relatively high percentage of Arabs who read Hebrew newspapers – 53% of all Arabs and 74% of Arabs who are literate in Hebrew (Table 4.3). While Arabs read both Arabic and Hebrew newspapers, Jews do not read Arabic newspapers. Three quarters of the Arabs read newspapers, while the rest are either illiterate or literate persons who do not read newspapers at all (Table 4.4). Reading of newspapers is even higher among men, the better educated, persons under 35, and Christians. It rose from 47% in 1976, to 56% in 1980, to 61% in 1985, and to around 75% in 1988 (Table 4.5). During the same period, the proportion of Arabs reading both Arabic and Hebrew newspapers increased from 22% to 46.5%. Israeli Arabs read various newspapers, but in particular the two leading dailies – the Communist *Al-Ittihad* in Arabic and the independent *Yediot Aharonot* in Hebrew (Table 4.6). They also read Arabic local weeklies and the commercial *Al-Sinara* and listen to the Israeli Arabic radio station.

Table 4.3 Reading of Newspapers

	All Arabs	Arab Potential Users	All Jews	Jewish Potential Users
Readers of Arabic newspapers	68.5	77.2	*	*
Readers of Hebrew newspapers	53.3	74.2	89.2	94.9
Readers of Arabic and Hebrew newspapers	46.5	65.2	*	*

*Jews were not asked after 1980 whether they read Arabic newspapers. In the 1980 survey only 0.7% of all Jews and 8.2% of Jews who knew to read Arabic reported reading Arabic newspapers.

Source: The 1988 survey.

These high proportions of bilingualism and reading of newspapers reflect the growing Israelization of the Arabs. The increasing use of

Hebrew shows their considerable penetration into Israeli society, on which they heavily depend for public facilities, employment, and Israeli-related information. Their appreciable reading of newspapers and exposure to the electronic media also exhibit the Israeli Jewish peculiarities of high levels of media consumption and politicization.

Table 4.4 Arab Readers of Newspapers by Selected Population Groups

	Illiterate	Do Not Read News-papers	Read Arabic News-papers Only	Read Hebrew News-papers Only	Read Both
Total	10.9	14.3	21.6	6.6	46.5
Gender					
Men	5.7	11.7	15.2	10.5	57.0
Women	16.2	17.8	29.5	2.4	34.1
Education					
0-8	23.2	25.2	25.0	4.4	22.2
9-12	0.0	6.5	22.2	8.7	62.6
13+	0.0	0.0	7.0	7.7	85.3
Age					
18-25	3.4	11.4	24.0	8.3	52.9
26-35	1.9	13.9	20.4	8.1	55.7
36-45	13.1	17.3	19.9	3.1	46.6
46-55	26.1	18.3	21.7	6.1	27.8
56+	44.6	16.5	18.2	1.7	19.0
Community					
Druze	7.8	19.1	13.9	17.4	41.7
Northern Bedouin	23.8	15.9	14.3	14.3	31.7
Negev Bedouin	8.8	32.4	20.6	20.6	17.6
Non-Bedouin Moslem	11.5	13.9	23.6	5.0	46.1
Christian	6.3	9.1	20.6	1.1	62.9

Source: The 1988 survey.

Table 4.5 Arab Readers of Newspapers, 1976-88

	Arab Public			
	1976	1980	1985	1988
Classification by reading of Arabic and Hebrew newspapers				
Illiterate	32.2	22.5	20.0	10.9
Do not read newspapers	20.5	21.1	18.8	14.3
Read Arabic newspapers only	20.1	14.0	11.4	21.6*
Read Hebrew newspapers only	5.2	14.3	20.3	6.6
Read both Arabic and Hebrew newspapers	21.9	28.1	29.5	46.5*

*In the 1988 survey Arabs were asked whether they read any Arabic newspaper during the past week, whereas in the previous surveys they were asked whether they read any of the following: *Al-Ittihad*, *Al-Anba*, *Al-Thadamun*, or an East Jerusalem newspaper. Apparently there were Arabs in 1988 who read other Arabic newspapers, especially the commercial *Al-Sinara* which had become popular by 1988 (26.3% of all literate Arabs in 1985 reported reading it).

Table 4.6 Arabs' Exposure to Media

	All Arabs	Arab Potential Users
Read or listen to each of the following		
Al-Ittihad	41.0	49.9
Al-Thadamun	19.2	23.6
Al-Sinara	21.6	26.3
Al-Kuds	17.1	20.5
Yediot Aharonot	46.7	68.4
Maariv	24.4	35.6
Israeli Arabic radio	77.1	77.1
The Voice of Peace	26.8	26.8

Religious practices and beliefs also divide the two communities. Overall, Arabs are much less secular than Jews. The proportion of persons who define themselves as religious is 32% among the Arabs and 13% among the Jews (Table 4.7). Observance of religious practices is, however, much more widespread than self-classification indicates. Although a third of the Arabs consider themselves observant, 48% pray at least occasionally and 61% try hard to live according to the teachings of their religion. Similarly, whereas only 13% of the Jews in the study see themselves as religious, 25% do not travel on Sabbath, 37% attend synagogue from time to time or regularly, and 33% do their best to live according to Judaism. Religious beliefs, which are less demanding than practices, are more common. As many as 53% to 86% of the Arabs and 47% to 56% of the Jews believe in such fundamentals as life after death and the exclusive truthfulness of their own religion (Table 4.8).

Table 4.7 Religious Observance

	Arab Public	Jewish Public
With regard to the observance of religious tradition, one considers oneself as		
Very religious	10.4	1.5
Religious	21.4	11.5
Religious to some extent/ traditional	35.5	40.6
Not religious /secular	32.7	46.4
Frequency of prayer		
Regularly	24.3	9.1
Often	12.2	4.7
Sometimes	11.8	22.9
Hardly ever	16.6	26.9
Never	35.1	36.4
Attend regularly a house of prayer	35.9	20.3
Do not travel on Sabbath	–	24.8
Try hard to live one's daily life according to the teaching of one's religion	60.7	32.9

Source: The 1988 survey.

Table 4.8 Religious Beliefs

	Arab Public	Jewish Public
Believe in a life after death, where good people will be rewarded and bad people will be punished	80.5	47.8
Believe in some form of existence after death	65.6	55.2
Cannot be happy and cannot enjoy life without believing in a God	83.4	54.6
Believe that there are hidden forces of good and evil which may help or harm oneself	52.8	55.3
Convinced that one's own religion is the only true one	62.8	56.3

Source: The 1988 survey.

The proportion of religious persons in the general population differ enormously by religion, age, and education. It tends to be disproportionately higher among the Moslems, the older, and the less educated. While the religious are a minority in all four religions, in 1988 they constituted 13% among the Jews, 16.5% among the Christians, 25% among the Druzes, and 35.5% among the Moslems. Among the Moslems, 27% of the 18-34 years old, compared to 51% of those older than 34, are religious. Similarly, 24% of Moslems with 9 or more years of education as against 47% of those with 0-8 years of schooling are religious.

The trend in the observance of religion over the years is of much interest. Considerable public attention is devoted to the resurgence of religion in Israel, among both the Jews and Moslems. It is also true, however, that the bulk of the Israeli population originated from traditional societies and has been undergoing secularization. Assuming that the two countervailing processes are taking place simultaneously, the question is: to what extent has the recent return to religion slowed down, stopped, or even reversed the ongoing trend of attrition from religion? We find that secularization is still the dominant force in all four religions. There is a decline in the proportion of the religious, from 18% in 1980 to 13% in 1988 among the Jews (more generally, this decrease is estimated to be from 25% in the early 1960s to 15% in the early 1990s). During the 1976-88 period, the drop goes from 46.5% to 32% among the Arabs as a whole, from 38% to 16.5% among the Christians, from 36.5% to 25% among the Druzes, and from 50% to 35.5% among the Moslems (Table 4.9). Secularization, weathering the waves of return to religion, emerges from the data as the stronger force in all Israeli religions, and the Moslems come out as the least secular and least secularizing.

The general Arab population is not only more religious than the Jewish population, it is also experiencing a real tide of return to religion, mostly as a resurgence of Islam. In the 1985 survey, 18% of all Arabs, compared to 3% of all Jews, reported a personal return to religion in the past five years (Table 4.10). The internal differences are equally striking:

the rate of return to religion is only 6% among the Christians, 9% among the Druzes, 23.5% among the Moslems, 6% among Oriental Jews, and less than 1% among Ashkenazic Jews. In addition, 34% of the Arabs and 11% of the Jews reported the return to religion of an immediate family member (a sibling, a parent, a child, or a spouse). These figures, however, should not be interpreted as a measure of the surge of religious fundamentalism. Rather, return to religion in the study is a blanket category covering an increase in the religious observance of secularists, traditionalists, and observants.

Table 4.9 Religious Observance by Religion, 1976-88

	1976	1980	1985	1988
Consider oneself as religious or very religious				
Jews	–	17.6	13.1	13.0
Arabs – total	46.5	38.2	36.7	31.8
Christians	38.4	27.6	24.8	16.5
Druzes	36.5	51.3	27.6	25.2
Moslems	50.3	52.9	40.1	35.5

Table 4.10 Return to Religion by Religion and Ethnicity

	Arabs				Jews		
	Total	Christians	Druzes	Moslems	Total	Orientals	Ashkenazim
Report return to religion, during past five years, of the following							
Oneself	18.4	5.9	8.6	22.1	3.4	6.0	0.6
Sibling, parent, child, or spouse	33.7	8.7	36.2	38.1	11.2	15.8	5.6
None	47.9	86.0	55.2	39.7	85.4	78.2	93.8

The fact that attrition from religion is greater than return to religion can mostly be explained by the steady improvement in the standard of education in the general population. The percentage of persons with 9 or more years of schooling, who are known to be disproportionately non-observant, rose dramatically during the period of the surveys. To illustrate, among the Moslems, it increased from 18% in 1976, to 29% in 1980, to 40% in 1985, and to 51% in 1988.

Revival of religion in all four religious communities intensifies the divisions within and between them. Among the Arabs, this holds especially true for the Moslems. The religious Moslem in Israel before the rise of Islamic fundamentalism in the 1980s was conservative, maintained a traditional way of life, lived in a small village, had an apolitical and pragmatic approach, and cooperated with the authorities. On the other hand, the emergent new type of religious Moslem tends to be fundamentalist, nationalistic, activist, dwelling in an urban or a large community, and detached from the authorities. Unlike the passive, conforming, religious Moslem of the past, the new religious Moslem draws a sharp distinction between religious and non-religious lifestyles and people, and acts strenuously to spread religion and to take control over the community. Contrary to the common version of modernization theory, nationalism does not replace but rather reinforces religion in the life of the new religious Moslem. Yet for the time being, the new religious Moslem in Israel, unlike the Islamic fundamentalist in the West Bank and Gaza Strip, leads a pragmatic course, being careful not to antagonize his community or the authorities.

Although cultural change is a life necessity for Israeli Arabs, many feel ambivalence about it. This is evidenced, for instance, in the strong endorsement of large families, which are defined in Israel as consisting of four or more children. A majority of 70% of Arabs and 51% of Jews think that such large families are desirable (Table 4.11). These percentages are even higher among certain population groups: 84% among religious Arabs, 81% among Arabs with 0-8 years of schooling, and 85.5% among the Negev Bedouin; 86% among religious Jews, 62.5% among Jews with 0-8 years of schooling, and 65% among Oriental Jews. Although these figures are high, they indicate a retreat from the traditional norm of unrestricted fertility. As a matter of fact, there is a clear trend of a drop in birthrate among Israeli Arabs, including Moslems, during the 1980s (Eizenbach, 1989).

Table 4.11 Desired Family Size

	Arab Public	Estab. Affil. Arab Lead.	Unaffiliated Arab Lead.	DFPE & PLP Arab Lead.	Sons of Village Arab Lead.	Jewish Public	DFPE & PLP Jewish Lead.	CRM & Mapam Jewish Lead.	Labor Jewish Lead.	Likud Camp Jewish Lead.
Desired number of children										
1-2	6.8	3.2	6.3	10.0	10.7	7.4	52.9	16.0	3.2	0.0
3	23.0	19.4	28.1	27.5	21.4	41.9	35.3	52.0	38.7	24.1
4	34.7	51.6	37.5	40.0	39.3	31.8	11.8	32.0	48.4	34.5
5	16.5	12.9	21.9	12.5	17.9	8.3	0.0	0.0	3.2	24.1
6+	18.9	12.9	6.3	10.0	10.7	10.6	0.0	0.0	6.5	17.2

Moderate change is also evidenced in other family norms. Whereas 67% of the Arabs would abolish loyalty to the hamula and 50% would recognize a woman's right to choose a husband even against her parents' will, only 18% would allow a young, single Arab girl to have a boyfriend (Table 4.12). Arab leaders from all political streams hold much more liberal views than does the Arab general public, thereby sanctioning more change than the masses are willing to embrace.

Table 4.12 Arabs' Family Norms

	Arab Public	Estab. Affil. Arab Lead.	Unaffil-iated Arab Lead.	DFPE & PLP Arab Lead.	Sons of Village Arab Lead.
Loyalty to the hamula					
Retain as is	11.3	0.0	6.3	0.0	0.0
Modify	21.8	25.0	6.3	4.9	0.0
Abolish	66.9	75.0	87.5	95.1	100.0
Woman's right to choose a husband even against her parents' will					
Recognize	50.4	62.5	81.3	82.9	96.9
Have reservations	23.1	31.3	15.6	17.1	3.1
Deny	26.5	6.3	3.1	0.0	0.0
A young single Arab girl having a boyfriend					
Allow	17.7	18.8	29.0	63.4	84.4
Allow to some extent	27.2	37.5	29.0	34.1	15.6
Not allow	55.1	43.8	41.9	2.4	0.0

The trend of change in Arab family values came almost to a halt during the 1980s, probably as a result of the rise in Islam. To quote typical statistics, Arabs favoring a large family constituted 48% in 1976, 59% in 1980, 64.5% in 1985, but dropped to 59% in 1988 (Table 4.13). The forces of cultural change also appear weak in marriage patterns. Marrying within the extended family and within the same locality is very high in general, and exceedingly high among Arabs with large hamulas and among Bedouin (Table 4.14). The rates did not decline during the 1980s: hamula endogamy was 48% in 1976 and 46% in 1985 while locality endogamy was 76% and 75%, respectively (Table 4.15).

Table 4.13 Arabs' Family Norms, 1976-88

	Arab Public			
	1976	1980	1985	1988
Favor the abolition of hamula loyalty	43.4	64.8	66.9	*
Acknowledge a woman's right to choose a husband even against her parents' will	31.8	*	50.4	*
Allow a young single Arab girl to have a boyfriend	13.7	20.6	17.7	12.9
Think that an Arab family should have 4 or fewer children	48.1	58.9	64.5	58.7

*Not asked.

Apart from individual bilingualism and minimal biculturalism, which are prerequisites for coping, the majority of Arabs are reserved about or even opposed to serious adaptation to the Israeli modern, Western-oriented mainstream. First, they neither want modern values and practices to prevail in Israel nor see Jews as a model of modernity (Table

4.16). They are quite ambivalent toward modernity, which is associated in their mind with the hated ex-colonial, pro-Zionist, hedonistic, and permissive West.

Table 4.14 Arabs' Hamula and Locality Endogamy Rates by Size of Hamula and Community

	Hamula	Locality
Total	46.0	74.7
Number of hamula members living in one's locality		
Fewer than 100 persons	29.3	67.7
100-499	45.9	79.7
500-999	61.3	71.0
1,000 or more	65.6	82.8
Community		
Christian	20.2	67.3
Druze	37.9	89.0
Non-Bedouin Moslem	49.2	74.8
Bedouin	62.9	70.3

Table 4.15 Arabs' Hamula and Locality Endogamy Rates, 1976-88

		Arab Public	
	1976	1980	1985
Spouse (in the last marriage) is from same hamula	47.8	53.6	46.0
Spouse (in the last marriage) is from same locality	75.6	84.2	74.7

Table 4.16 Modern Values

	Arab Public	Estab. Affil. Arab Lead.	Unaffil-iated Arab Lead.	DFPE & PLP Arab Lead.	Sons of Village Arab Lead.	Jewish Public	DFPE & PLP Jewish Lead.	CRM & Mapam Jewish Lead.	Labor Jewish Lead.	Likud Camp Jewish Lead.
Modern values and practices should prevail in Israel										
In favor	32.8	32.3	37.9	65.0	50.0	63.0	74.2	84.8	77.4	36.0
Have reservations	37.7	61.3	48.3	32.5	50.0	23.9	22.6	15.2	22.6	52.0
Against	29.5	6.5	13.8	2.5	0.0	13.1	3.2	0.0	0.0	12.0
Arabs in Israel should learn modern values and practices from the Jews										
Yes	24.9	50.0	35.5	43.2	13.8	49.2[a]	*	*	*	*
Not certain	27.5	25.0	29.0	32.4	27.6	25.2[a]	*	*	*	*
No	47.6	25.0	35.5	24.3	58.6	25.6[a]	*	*	*	*

*Not asked. [a]1980 survey.

Second, the Arab public does not favor espousal of Jewish values and practices in addition to its own. Arab leaders understand the need for individual biculturalism better than the public, and, hence, a majority of them (except the rejectionist activists in the Sons of the Village Movement) endorse it for the Arabs (Table 4.17).

Third, the Arabs want Jews to be bilingual and bicultural and to create together with them new common values and practices (Table 4.17 and Table 4.18). From the Arab perspective, Jewish bilingualism and biculturalism imply paying respect to Arab culture, moderation of Jewish cultural exclusivity and superiority, and greater acceptance of Israeli Arabs by the Jews.

Table 4.17 Values of Individual Biculturalism

	Arab Public	Estab. Affil. Arab Lead.	Unaffiliated Arab Lead.	DFPE & PLP Arab Lead.	Sons of Village Arab Lead.	Jewish Public	DFPE & PLP Jewish Lead.	CRM & Mapam Jewish Lead.	Labor Jewish Lead.	Likud Camp Jewish Lead.
Hold that Arabs in Israel should adopt Jewish values and practices in addition to their own	29.5	67.7	53.1	66.7	26.7	35.6	46.4	66.7	58.8	38.5
Hold that Jews in Israel should adopt Arab values and practices in addition to their own	62.6	81.3	83.9	77.5	55.2	20.2	44.8	62.1	57.6	25.0

Finally, the Arabs reject Israel as Hebrew-speaking and Western-oriented, and wish to transform the state into a bilingual, bicultural, or even culturally Arabized state (Table 4.18). Some 71% of the Arab public and 90% to 100% of the non-rejectionist Arab leaders would like to see Arab culture as an integral part of Israel's national culture; but the first choice of over 90% of both these groups is that Israel will adopt a mixed or predominantly Arab culture.

There is not much in the patterns and attitudes of Jews to encourage the cultural accommodation of the Arabs. Only a minority of Jews are bilingual (Table 4.1 above) and bicultural. They support a greater use of Arabic, but stop short of making the state truly bilingual (Table 4.18). Most of them neither regard Arab culture as an important part of Israel's national culture nor favor the creation of new values and practices common to Arabs and Jews. They also insist on keeping Israel Western-oriented, with minimal incorporation of Arab cultural elements.

This Jewish posture is both strong and enduring. It has remained unchanged through the 1980s (Table 4.19). It is also sanctioned by the leadership, which shows greater consideration of Arab needs and desires than does the rank and file. For instance, although 67% of the liberal leaders of the Zionist left are willing to treat Arab culture as an important part of Israel's national culture and 93.5% favor the creation of new common values for both communities, only 25% of them endorse a mixed, Western-Arab culture for the state (Table 4.18).

It is clear that culture is a key divisive issue. The common cultural denominator for Arabs and Jews consists of the Hebrew language and a modern subculture. This is a must for the Arabs' well-being in Israel, and it is their forcible contribution to cultural Arab-Jewish coexistence. But beyond this common ground, discord looms large, involving the wider disagreement on the status of Arabs as a national minority in a Jewish state. The Jews desire Israel to be Jewish in language, heritage, and symbols and to be Western in values, practices, and life styles. They allow Arabs to preserve their own culture, which is stigmatized as backward, but expect them ultimately to adjust to Israeli life and institutions.

Table 4.18 Values of Institutional Bilingualism and Biculturalism

	Arab Public	Estab. Affil. Arab Lead.	Unaffil-iated Arab Lead.	DFPE & PLP Arab Lead.	Sons of Village Arab Lead.	Jewish Public	DFPE & PLP Jewish Lead.	CRM & Mapam Jewish Lead.	Labor Jewish Lead.	Likud Camp Jewish Lead.
Hold that Hebrew and Arabic should prevail equally in public and state institutions	*	*	*	*	*	16.6	80.6	42.4	20.5	0.0
Hold that the law should require all street and locality signs to be written in both Hebrew and Arabic	*	*	*	*	*	48.2	100.0	94.1	68.4	51.5
Hold that Arab culture should be treated as an important part of Israel's national culture	71.2	100.0	100.0	90.2	25.8	21.2	93.8	66.7	36.8	25.0
Hold that Jews and Arabs should together try to create new common values and practices in addition to their own	68.6	93.3	83.9	95.1	66.7	41.5	100.0	93.5	78.2	48.3
Type of culture desired for Israel										
Distinct Western culture	2.2	0.0	0.0	2.5	0.0	53.7	7.4	35.7	41.7	46.7
Western culture in which Arab elements are incorporated	5.6	3.4	9.7	5.0	0.0	17.8	14.8	39.3	44.4	23.3
A mixed culture consisting of Western and Arab elements	28.8	58.6	54.8	57.5	27.6	11.4	66.7	25.0	13.9	3.3
Arab culture in which Western elements are incorporated	27.8	37.9	22.6	25.0	41.4	2.8	11.1	0.0	0.0	0.0
Distinct Arab culture	33.8	0.0	12.9	10.0	6.9	0.4	0.0	0.0	0.0	0.0
Neither	1.9	0.0	0.0	0.0	24.1	13.9	0.0	0.0	0.0	26.7

*Not asked.

Table 4.19 Language and Culture Desired for Israel, 1980-88

	Arab Public			Jewish Public		
	1980	1985	1988	1980	1985	1988
Hold that Hebrew and Arabic should prevail equally in public and state institutions	92.2	*	*	24.3	16.6	20.1
Hold that the culture desired for Israel is an Arab culture in which Western elements are incorporated or is a distinct Arab culture	*	61.6	58.7	*	3.2	6.2

*Not asked.

The Arabs, on the other hand, feel themselves as part of a regional majority, are proud of their culture, and perceive advancing Westernization and biculturalism as a threat to their national culture. Hence, they aspire to reconstitute Israel's national culture so that Arab patterns will gain currency in Israel, or even predominate.

To conclude, although Israeli Arabs, as a non-assimilating minority, enjoy the right to a separate culture and identity, they endure their situation more as victims of cultural dominance than as beneficiaries of cultural pluralism. This predicament is bound to intensify at least among the growing section of the Arab population that has been turning to Islamic fundamentalism over the past decade.

5

Legitimacy of Coexistence

There are two facets to the legitimacy of Arab-Jewish coexistence. On the general and fundamental level, the question is whether Israeli Arabs agree to the very existence of Israel, and whether the Jews consent to the inclusion of Arabs in the state. On the more specific level, the question is whether Israeli Arabs assent to Israel as a Jewish-Zionist state, and whether Jews approve of the Arabs as a national minority with full civil rights.

It is evident that most Arabs and Jews acquiesce in each other's existence. Of the Arabs, 51% accept Israel's right to exist without reservation and 31% accept it with reservations; only 18% deny this right (Table 5.1). The Arabs have two major reservations about Israel: that it does not acknowledge the Palestinians' right to a state of their own in the West Bank and Gaza Strip, and that it does not extend full equality to Israeli Arabs. Despite these objections, over four fifths of the Israeli Arabs accede to Israel and to their being part of it.

Table 5.1 Arabs' Acceptance of Israel's Right to Exist

	Arab Public	Estab. Affil. Arab Lead.	Unaffil-iated Arab Lead.	DFPE & PLP Arab Lead.	Sons of Village Arab Lead.
Acceptance of Israel's right to exist					
Yes	51.4	96.9	90.6	85.4	0.0
Have reservations	31.0	3.1	9.4	12.2	48.4
No	17.6	0.0	0.0	2.4	51.6

With the exception of the openly rejectionist Sons of the Village Movement, all Israeli Arab political organizations accede to Israel's right to exist both officially and in practice. The non-rejectionist Arab leaders show greater acceptance of Israel than does the Arab public: 85% to 97% recognize Israel's right to exist without reservation, 3% to 12% have reservations, and 0% to

2% deny this right. On the other hand, the rejectionist activists in the Sons of the Village Movement repudiate Israel's legitimate existence.

The Arab firm acknowledgment of Israel's legitimacy as a sovereign state is strengthened by two related findings. From 1976-88, the proportion of Arabs who rejected Israel not only did not increase, it actually decreased, from 20.5% to 13.5% (Table 5.2). This drop came about despite Israel's war in Lebanon and the intifada, two events that adversely affected the Arab posture on Israel. Furthermore, a clear majority supporting Israel's existence prevails among all Arab population groups; the rejectionists are a minority, ranging from 0% (among Arab members of the Zionist parties) to 28% (among Arabs intending to vote for the Progressive List for Peace) (Table 5.3).

Table 5.2 Arabs' Acceptance of Israel's Right to Exist, 1976-88

	Arab Public			
	1976	1980	1985	1988
Acceptance of Israel's right to exist				
Yes	51.1	58.8	51.4	51.4
Have reservations	28.4	30.3	31.0	35.2
No	20.5	11.0	17.6	13.5

Table 5.3 Arabs' Rejection of Israel's Right to Exist by Population Groups

	% Rejecting
Less rejecting groups	
Aged 36-45 years	12.9
Druzes	2.7
Not affected by land expropriations	8.5
Have visited Jewish friends	11.7
Residents of mixed towns	12.1
Live in localities in which over 79% of the vote was won by Zionist parties	12.6
Members of Zionist parties	0.0
Voted for Zionist parties	5.3
Intend to vote for Zionist parties	4.2
More rejecting groups	
Aged 18-25 years	23.0
Non-Bedouin Moslems	21.4
Much affected by land expropriations	26.4
Have no Jewish friends	25.4
Residents of large local councils	23.3
Live in localities in which over 59% of the vote was won by the DFPE and the PLP	22.9
Members of Rakah	26.7
Voted for the DFPE in 1984	21.1
Voted for the PLP in 1984	24.2
Intend to vote for the DFPE	23.7
Intend to vote for the PLP	28.3

In the same vein, 51% of the Jews concur without any reservation in the existence of an Arab minority in Israel and 33% do so with reservations; only 16% totally reject the Arabs (Table 5.4). The Jews' reservations stem from their belief that most Arabs reject Israel. Except for the expressly rejectionist Kach Movement, no Jewish political organization disapproves of Arab-Jewish coexistence. The Jewish leaders in the survey are more approving of Arabs in Israel than is the public at large (leaders' rejection rates range from 0% to 6%, compared to 18% among the Jewish public). Rejection among the Jewish public has risen from 16% in 1985 to 19% in 1988, but it is doubtful if this small rise exists in all the major sections of the population. In fact, the rejectionists cannot claim the majority of any segment of the Jewish population: the proportion of rejectionists among various Jewish groups extends from 4% to 35% (Table 5.5).

Table 5.4 Jews' Acceptance of the Arab Minority's Right to Live in Israel, 1985-88

	1985					1988
	Jewish Public	DEPE & PLP Jewish Lead.	CRM & Mapam Jewish Lead.	Labor Jewish Lead.	Likud Camp Jewish Lead.	Jewish Public
Acceptance of the very existence of an Arab minority in Israel						
Yes	50.8	100.0	100.0	97.5	73.5	41.8
Have reservations	33.3	0.0	0.0	2.5	20.6	38.7
No	15.9	0.0	0.0	0.0	5.9	19.4

Table 5.5 Jews' Rejection of the Arab Minority's Right to Live in Israel by Population Groups

	% Rejecting
Less rejecting groups	
Aged 56+ years	11.2
Have higher education	6.1
Voted for CRM and Shinui in 1984	4.0
Voted for Labor in 1984	7.8
Residents of Jerusalem	13.4
Ashkenazim	9.2
More rejecting groups	
Aged 18-25 years	23.0
Have primary or less education	22.3
Voted for Kach, Tehiya, or the religious parties in 1984	35.2
Voted for Likud in 1984	21.3
Residents of development or immigrant towns	31.8
Orientals	20.7

Although Arab-Jewish coexistence is mutually agreed upon, its terms are vehemently disputed by both sides. The Arabs' negation of Israel and of their being a minority in it vary with the precise status they are accorded. The more clearly inferior their position in the state, the greater is their disapproval of it. Only 18% deny Israel's very right to exist in response to a general question, that did not spell out the Arab status in it as a minority (Table 5.1). Disapproval goes up to 29% in reaction to a question that defines the Arab position as "a national minority with full rights." It jumps to 45.5% following a question that refers to Israeli Arabs as just a minority and does not specify equality of rights (Table 5.6). Rejection reaches a peak of 62% when the Arabs are asked about Israel's right to exist as a Jewish-Zionist state, because they see themselves subordinated in this set-up (Table 5.7).

Table 5.6 Arabs' Resignation to a Minority Status in Israel, 1985-88

	1985					1988
	Arab Public	Estab. Affil. Arab Lead.	Unaffiliated Arab Lead.	DFPE & PLP Arab Lead.	Sons of Village Arab Lead.	Arab Public
Arabs in Israel should in principle resign themselves to the status of a national minority with full civil rights						
Yes	35.6	69.0	73.3	59.5	3.4	41.5
Have reservations	35.2	31.0	20.0	18.9	17.2	34.1
No	29.2	0.0	6.7	21.6	79.3	24.3
Resigned oneself to being a minority member in Israel today						
Yes	25.6	54.8	31.3	50.0	10.0	34.3
Have reservations	28.9	38.7	50.0	25.0	16.7	33.2
No	45.5	6.5	18.8	25.0	73.3	32.5

Table 5.7 Arabs' Acceptance of Israel as a Jewish-Zionist State

	Arab Public	Estab. Affil. Arab Lead.	Unaffiliated Arab Lead.	DFPE & PLP Arab Lead.	Sons of Village Arab Lead.
Acceptance of Israel's right to exist within the Green Line as a Jewish-Zionist state					
Yes	14.7	48.4	12.9	5.1	0.0
Have reservations	23.2	22.6	32.3	25.6	6.3
No	62.1	29.0	54.8	69.2	93.8
It is all right to use any means necessary to abolish Israel's Jewish-Zionist character					
Against	12.4	40.0	15.6	12.8	0.0
Have reservations	34.1	43.3	59.4	43.6	23.3
In favor	53.4	16.7	25.0	43.6	76.7

Arab objection to Israel and to a minority status in it is moderated to some extent by the drop in these objections between 1985 to 1988. Rejection of minority status with equality declines from 29% to 24%, and minority status without mention of equality diminishes from 45.5% to 32.5% (Table 5.6). Rejection is further softened by its smaller prevalence on the leadership level. For instance, 53% of the Arab public agrees that it is all right to use every necessary means to do away with Israel's Jewish-Zionist character; in contrast, the support for this view is only 17% among the leaders affiliated with the Zionist establishment, 25% among the unaffiliated leaders, and 44% among the leaders of the DFPE and PLP (Table 5.7). Rejection is of course overwhelming (77%) among the activists in the rejectionist Sons of the Village Movement.

By the same token, Jews' rejection of the Arab minority differs with the exact status conferred on the Arabs. While 16% of the Jews contest the very existence of an Arab minority in their midst (Table 5.4), 22% deny the existence of an Arab national minority with full rights (Table 5.8). Jewish rejection did not rise between 1985 and 1988 and is much lower among the leaders, including those of the Likud camp.

Table 5.8 Jews' Resignation to the Existence in Israel of an Arab National Minority with Full Civil Rights, 1985-88

	1985					1988
	Jewish Public	DEPE & PLP Jewish Lead.	CRM & Mapam Jewish Lead.	Labor Jewish Lead.	Likud Camp Jewish Lead.	Jewish Public
Resigned oneself to the Arabs' right to live in Israel as a national minority with full civil rights						
Yes	38.7	100.0	100.0	87.5	64.7	34.5
Have reservations	39.7	0.0	0.0	7.5	26.5	46.2
No	21.6	0.0	0.0	5.0	8.8	19.3

The heart of the dissension lies, however, in the Jews' insistence on the Jewish and Zionist nature of the state, even if this infringes on Arabs' civil or democratic rights. Two thirds of the Jewish public and a majority of Labor and Likud leaders would not allow an election list to participate in Knesset elections if it objected to Israel's Jewish-Zionist character (Table 5.9). In fact, an amendment to the election law, enacted in 1985, bars from participation in national elections any list that denies Israel as "the state of the Jewish people."

It is precisely this Zionist conception of the state that the Arabs negate. Israeli Arabs not only deny Israel's right to be Jewish-Zionist (Table 5.7), a third of them even deny Israeli Jews the status of a nation and two thirds view Zionism as racist (Table 5.10). With the exception of the Sons of the Village leaders, Arab leaders recognize Jews in Israel as a nation rather than as a mere religion. Yet the idea that Zionism is contaminated with racism is more widely scattered among the Arabs.

Table 5.9 Importance of Israel's Jewish-Zionist Character to Jews

	Jewish Public	DFPE & PLP Jewish Lead.	CRM & Mapam Jewish Lead.	Labor Jewish Lead.	Likud Camp Jewish Lead.
Maintain that Israel should strengthen or preserve as is its Jewish-Zionist character despite having an Arab minority	94.0	5.6	74.2	97.4	100.0
Believe that it is all right to use any means necessary to retain Israel's Jewish-Zionist character	64.3	0.0	6.1	28.2	50.0
Do not permit to run in the Knesset elections an election list that both accepts the principles of democracy and Israel's right to exist but opposes its Jewish-Zionist character	67.5	0.0	18.2	55.0	72.8

Table 5.10 Arabs' View of Israeli Jews as a Nation and of Zionism

	Arab Public	Estab. Affil. Arab Lead.	Unaffil-iated Arab Lead.	DFPE & PLP Arab Lead.	Sons of Village Arab Lead.
The Palestinian National Charter rules that Jews in Israel today are a religious community, not a nation					
Agree with the Charter	31.8	0.0	9.7	23.1	88.9
Disagree with the Charter	68.2	100.0	90.3	76.9	11.1
The UN General Assembly adopted the resolution that Zionism is a racist movement					
Agree with the resolution	65.3	16.7	44.4	87.5	96.9
Have reservations	22.5	33.3	44.4	10.0	3.1
Disagree with the resolution	12.2	50.0	11.1	2.5	0.0

The dispute over the Jewish-Zionist mission of the state is elucidated by an additional inquiry into self-classification on Zionism and into stands on the diverse Jewish features of the state. Whereas 86% of the Jews in 1988 defined themselves as Zionist as they understood this term, only 1% of the Arabs did so (Table 5.11). The fact that the Arabs are evenly divided between "non-Zionists" and "anti-Zionists" shows a significant drift away from the stiff rejectionist Palestinian position on Zionism since the early 1920s. When some of the Jewish-Zionist features of Israel are spelled out, an overwhelming majority of Jews, as against a negligible minority of Arabs (many of whom are Druze), endorsed each feature (Table 5.12). There is no consensus, however, among the Jewish leaders of Zionist parties. It is quite significant that most Jewish leaders of the Zionist left spurn the conception of Israel as a homeland only for Jews and oppose the state's preferential treatment of Jews. Also worth noting is the deep internal split among Jewish leaders from the Labor Party on the question of the Jewish state's giving preference to Jews over Arabs.

Table 5.11 Self-Classification on Zionism

	Arab Public	Jewish Public
According to one's own understanding and definition of what Zionism is, one defines oneself as		
Zionist	0.8	86.2
Non-Zionist	52.1	13.0
Anti-Zionist	47.1	0.8

Source: The 1988 survey.

Table 5.12 Endorsement of Israel's Features as a Jewish-Zionist State

	Arab Public	Estab. Affil. Arab Lead.	Unaffiliated Arab Lead.	DFPE & PLP Arab Lead.	Sons of Village Arab Lead.	Jewish Public	DFPE & PLP Jewish Lead.	CRM & Mapam Jewish Lead.	Labor Jewish Lead.	Likud Camp Jewish Lead.
Endorse each of the following features										
Israel as a homeland of Jews only	6.0	3.1	0.0	2.4	13.6	77.0	0.0	21.2	60.5	100.0
Retention of Jewish majority	18.7	53.6	33.3	0.0	0.0	97.7[a]	*	*	*	*
Law of Return (retain as is)	5.5	13.8	6.3	0.0	0.0	73.3[a]	*	*	*	*
Hebrew as the dominant language	2.4[a]	*	*	*	*	83.4	19.4	57.6	79.5	100.0
State's preferential treatment of Jews	3.4[a]	*	*	*	*	80.8	0.0	11.8	50.0	79.4

*Not asked. [a]The 1980 survey.

Since Jews are committed to both Zionism and democracy, the real issue is the choice to be made between the two ideologies when they collide. The Arabs who dismiss Zionism are obviously exempted from this dilemma. The Jewish public shows a preference of 58% to 42% in favor of Zionism to democracy (Table 5.13). The leaders are deeply divided on the issue: the left (both non-Zionist and Zionist) decides in favor of democracy (93%-100%), whereas the right-wing favors Zionism (81%). Labor is torn, with 45.5% preferring Zionism and 54.5% preferring democracy. Since Zionism in Israel today practically implies fewer rights and opportunities for the Arabs, it is no wonder that 51% of the Jews and 62% of the Arabs doubt whether Israeli Arabs can be equal citizens in

Israel as a Jewish-Zionist state and can identify themselves with such a state. The more refusing of Zionism one is, the more skepticism one evinces about the possibility that Israeli Arabs can be equal in and can identify with the Jewish state: the most pessimistic are Arab and Jewish leaders of the DFPE, PLP, and Sons of the Village Movement; and the most optimistic are Arab leaders who are tied to the Zionist establishment and Jewish Zionist leaders who usually believe that Zionism is inherently democratic and hence non-discriminatory.

Table 5.13 Possibility of Equal Status for Arabs in Israel

	Arab Public	Estab. Affil. Arab Lead.	Unaffiliated Arab Lead.	DFPE & PLP Arab Lead.	Sons of Village Arab Lead.	Jewish Public	DFPE & PLP Jewish Lead.	CRM & Mapam Jewish Lead.	Labor Jewish Lead.	Likud Camp Jewish Lead.
If the egalitarian-democratic character of the state stands in contradiction to its Jewish-Zionist character and a choice needs to be made between them										
Would prefer the egalitarian-democratic character	*	*	*	*	*	41.6	100.0	92.6	54.5	18.8
Would prefer the Jewish-Zionist character	*	*	*	*	*	58.4	0.0	7.4	45.5	81.3
Arabs can be equal citizens of Israel as a Jewish-Zionist state and can identify themselves with the state										
Yes	18.0	35.5	6.5	7.5	0.0	21.6	5.6	43.8	40.0	44.1
Possible	19.8	41.9	38.7	5.0	0.0	27.8	8.3	40.6	47.5	20.6
Doubtful	27.9	16.1	22.6	22.5	9.4	26.7	36.1	12.5	7.5	14.7
No	34.3	6.5	32.3	65.0	90.6	23.9	50.0	3.1	5.0	20.6

*Not asked.

The trend in the Arab attitudes toward the legitimacy of coexistence is clear. On the one hand, the Arabs continue to respect the political integrity of the state in its pre-1967 borders: as cited, disaffirmation of Israel's right to exist declined from 20.5% in 1976 to 13.5% in 1988 (Table 5.14). On the other hand, rejection of Zionism and the Zionist features of the state has remained unchanged or even increased a little during this period. For instance, 63.5% of the Arabs regarded Zionism as racist in 1976 and 70% did so in 1988. The Arab impatience with what they perceive as discrimination against them has grown over the years.

Table 5.14 Arabs' Rejection of Israel and of Its Features as a Jewish-Zionist State, 1976-88

	Arab Public			
	1976	1980	1985	1988
Reject Israel's right to exist	20.5	11.0	17.6	13.5
Reject Israel's right to exist within the Green Line as a Jewish-Zionist state	*	57.1	62.1	63.1
Disagree that Israel is the homeland of Jews only	*	94.9	94.0	91.9
Disagree that Israel within the Green Line should retain a Jewish majority	*	81.8	81.3	82.6
Favor the complete repeal of the Law of Return	63.4	60.8	71.9	*
Regard Zionism as racism	63.5	60.7	65.3	70.0
Believe that Arabs cannot be equal citizens in Israel as a Jewish-Zionist state and cannot identify themselves with it	69.6	51.6	62.2	67.0

*Not Asked.

The trend among the Jews, however, is not so evident. On certain questions they have become less rejecting of Arabs, while on others more so (Table 5.15). As a result, the overall picture is mixed but marked by a lack of a positive response to the Arab struggle for equality and peace. It is possible that different trends that counterbalance one another characterize different groups in the Jewish population.

Table 5.15 Jews' Rejection of Arabs as a Minority and Endorsement of Israel's Features as a Jewish-Zionist State, 1980-88

	Jewish Public		
	1980	1985	1988
Reject the Arab minority right to live in Israel	*	15.9	19.4
Definitely not resigned oneself to the Arabs' right to live in Israel as a national minority with full civil rights	*	21.6	19.3
Do not permit to run in the Knesset elections an election list that both accepts the principles of democracy and Israel's right to exist but opposes its Jewish-Zionist character	*	67.5	64.0
Hold that Hebrew should be Israel's only dominant language	75.7	83.4	79.6
Hold that Israel is the homeland of Jews only	74.6	77.0	76.3
Hold that Israel should prefer Jews to Arabs	83.9	80.8	73.8
Would prefer the Jewish-Zionist character of the state if it stands in contradiction to its egalitarian-democratic character	58.3	58.4	54.1

*Not asked.

In sum, Arabs and Jews acquiesce in coexistence; i.e., they accept both Israel and their own division into a minority and a majority. At the same time, they sharply disagree on the nature of the state, whose structures mold their relations and life chances. The Jews want Israel to be Jewish and Zionist, whereas the Arabs wish it to be democratic and binational, a state where they can enjoy full rights and escape the liabilities of a subordinate, minority status.

6

The Israeli-Arab Conflict

The discord between Israeli Arabs and Jews on the Israeli-Arab conflict is as deep and consequential as their disagreement on the Jewish-Zionist character of the state. The conflict involves a plethora of issues, but the surveys focus only on some of the most crucial ones.

It is rather surprising to find that for both sides the Israel-Egypt Peace Treaty is more acceptable than controversial. Most of the Zionist Jewish leaders and 58.5% of the general public accept the Peace Treaty without any qualification, and most Israeli Arabs endorse it at least partially (only 20% oppose it; Table 6.1). The massive support of the Arab public is granted despite the continued objection to the Treaty by the Israeli Arabs' dominant political forces – the DFPE, PLP, Sons of the Village Movement (in both their public statements and their survey responses), and certainly the PLO. The fact that backing for peace with Egypt has remained virtually solid and constant throughout the 1980-88 period reflects both the Israeli Arabs' great desire for peace and the gradual diminution of opposition to the Peace Treaty in the Arab world and among the Palestinians (Table 6.2).

Table 6.1 Israel-Egypt Peace Treaty

	Arab Public	Estab. Affil. Arab Lead.	Unaffiliated Arab Lead.	DFPE & PLP Arab Lead.	Sons of Village Arab Lead.	Jewish Public	DFPE & PLP Jewish Lead.	CRM & Mapam Jewish Lead.	Labor Jewish Lead.	Likud Camp Jewish Lead.
Stand on the peace treaty										
In favor	56.5	87.5	59.4	2.4	0.0	69.4	27.8	97.1	95.0	64.7
Have reservations	23.3	12.5	28.1	17.1	3.1	25.1	44.4	0.0	2.5	17.6
Against	20.2	0.0	12.5	80.5	96.9	5.6	27.8	2.9	2.5	17.6

Table 6.2 Israel-Egypt Peace Treaty, 1980-88

	Arab Public			Jewish Public		
	1980	1985	1988	1980	1985	1988
Stand on the peace treaty						
In favor	49.1	56.5	48.4	71.4	69.4	67.3
Have reservations	27.7	23.3	30.6	20.6	25.1	23.9
Against	23.2	20.2	20.9	8.0	5.6	8.8

Disagreement looms large on territorial issues. The Jews are internally divided on settlements in Judea and Samaria and on annexation (Table 6.3). About half wish to keep the present ceasefire borders and about half are willing to consider territorial concessions. Israel's post-partition borders, even according to moderate Jewish rank and file and leaders, will entail a significant part of the West Bank and Gaza Strip as well as East Jerusalem (Table 6.4).

Table 6.3 Jews' View of Settlements and Annexation

	Jewish Public	DFPE & PLP Jewish Lead.	CRM & Mapam Jewish Lead.	Labor Jewish Lead.	Likud Camp Jewish Lead.
Settlements in Judea and Samaria					
In favor	50.5	0.0	0.0	0.0	100.0
Have reservations	27.4	0.0	0.0	45.0	0.0
Against	22.1	100.0	100.0	55.0	0.0
Annexation of Judea and Samaria					
In favor of immediate annexation	41.2	0.0	0.0	0.0	43.8
In favor of future annexation	26.5	0.0	0.0	0.0	50.0
Against annexation	32.2	100.0	100.0	100.0	6.3

The existence of a positive Jewish attitude toward territorial compromise is reinforced by a number of indicators, however. First, support for the partition of Western Palestine has increased over the years – from 41.5% in 1980 to 49% in 1985 to 52.5% in 1988 (Table 6.5). Second, the proportion of Zionist leaders prepared to make a substantial withdrawal from the territories is becoming significant: 91% of the leaders from the Zionist left and 26% of the leaders from the Labor Party assent to a retreat to the pre-1967 borders with or even without modifications (Table 6.4). Third and most important, the clinging to the territories is less tenacious than it appears, even among the public at large. When asked about their reaction to a future government decision to withdraw from most areas of Judea and Samaria for a peace settlement, only about 20% of the Jews say that they would oppose the decision with all legal means (including demonstrations and strikes) and less than 5% would resort to violence (Table 6.6). Since the composition of the coalition government making such a fateful decision does not matter to them, a Labor Government should not feel more incapacitated to decide than should a national-unity government.

Table 6.4 Borders

	Arab Public	Estab. Affil. Arab Lead.	Unaffiliated Arab Lead.	DFPE & PLP Arab Lead.	Sons of Village Arab Lead.	Jewish Public	DFPE & PLP Jewish Lead.	CRM & Mapam Jewish Lead.	Labor Jewish Lead.	Likud Camp Jewish Lead.
Borders with which one is prepared to compromise in order to reach a peace settlement										
All of Mandatory Palestine, in which a new state will be established instead of Israel	13.1	0.0	0.0	2.5	71.0	0.8	0.0	0.0	0.0	0.0
1947 UN partition borders (the Galilee and Triangle not included in Israel)	19.2	0.0	18.8	17.5	25.8	2.1	0.0	0.0	0.0	0.0
Pre-1967 borders (the Galilee and Triangle included in Israel)	52.6	75.0	71.9	80.0	3.2	4.6	91.7	30.3	0.0	0.0
Present borders with certain modifications in favor of Israel	5.8	7.1	9.4	0.0	0.0	11.9	8.3	60.6	25.6	0.0
Present borders with a willingness to compromise also in Judea and Samaria	2.7	14.3	0.0	0.0	0.0	29.2	0.0	9.1	74.4	18.2
Present borders	6.6	3.6	0.0	0.0	0.0	51.3	0.0	0.0	0.0	81.8
Giving up East Jerusalem if this is necessary to reach a peace settlement										
In favor	*	*	*	*	*	4.1	100.0	45.2	15.0	0.0
Have reservations	*	*	*	*	*	12.5	0.0	29.0	25.0	3.0
Against	*	*	*	*	*	83.4	0.0	25.8	60.0	97.0

*Not asked.

The Israeli Arab outlook, however, stands in sharp contrast to the Jewish view. The Arabs totally reject settlements and annexation, and insist on a complete pullback to the pre-1967 boundaries. One third also go further in demanding that Israel should concede its territorial integrity; i.e., go back to the 1947 UN partition borders or be abolished altogether (Table 6.5). Although all the Sons of the Village leaders expectedly subscribe to this rejectionist view, it is meaningful that a quarter of both the unaffiliated leaders and the leaders of the DFPE and PLP follow suit, despite the fact that these parties accept the 1967 ceasefire borders as the basis for a peace settlement.

Table 6.5 Borders, 1976-88

	Arab Public			Jewish Public		
	1980	1985	1988	1980	1985	1988
Borders with which one is prepared to compromise in order to reach a peace settlement						
All of Mandatory Palestine, in which a new state will be established instead of Israel	11.8	13.1	11.9	1.1	0.8	1.1
1947 UN partition borders (the Galilee and Triangle not included in Israel)	26.3	19.2	17.6	0.3	2.1	1.8
Pre-1967 borders (the Galilee and Triangle included in Israel)	40.5	52.6	51.2	1.1	4.6	3.8
Present borders with certain modifications in favor of Israel	8.8	5.8	9.1	7.8	11.9	16.8
Present borders with a willingness to compromise also in Judea and Samaria	7.0	2.7	7.5	31.2	29.2	28.9
Present borders	5.5	6.6	2.7	58.5	51.3	47.5

Table 6.6 Jews' Readiness for Territorial Concessions

	A Decision Made by									
	A National Unity Government					A Labor Government				
	Jewish Public	DFPE & PLP Jewish Lead.	CRM& Mapam Jewish Lead.	Labor Jewish Lead.	Likud Camp Jewish Lead.	Jewish Public	DFPE & PLP Jewish Lead.	CRM& Mapam Jewish Lead.	Labor Jewish Lead.	Likud Camp Jewish Lead.
A reaction to a possible decision by the Government to withdraw from most areas of Judea and Samaria in return for a peace settlement										
Would act against the decision with all means, including violence	4.4	0.0	0.0	0.0	5.9	4.8	0.0	0.0	0.0	6.3
Would act against the decision with all legal means, including demonstrations and strikes	19.8	0.0	0.0	0.0	64.7	19.3	0.0	0.0	0.0	71.9
Would act against the decision mostly through persuasion and pressures	17.1	0.0	0.0	5.0	14.7	17.8	0.0	0.0	5.0	15.6
Would not act at all	41.6	2.8	0.0	2.5	11.8	41.9	2.8	0.0	2.5	6.3
Would act in favor of the decision	7.1	97.2	100.0	92.5	2.9	16.3	97.2	100.0	92.5	0.0

Arab-Jewish dissension over the Palestinian problem also abounds. The Jews are disunited, confused, and ambivalent on the fundamental issue of whether the Palestinians constitute a nation and whether they have a right to a state of their own (Table 6.7). But this internal split among the Jews marks a significant crack in the past total rejection of the various elements of the Palestinian right to self-determination, and respect for this right among leaders of the Zionist left and the Labor Party is quite impressive. No doubt, the most crucial question concerns an independent Palestinian state in the West Bank and Gaza Strip, to which all Israeli governments are vehemently opposed. While the objection holds for all the Likud camp leaders in the survey, it decreases markedly to 54% among the mainstream Labor Party leaders, diminishes to a minority of 12% among the CRM and Mapam leaders, and of course disappears altogether among the DFPE and PLP Jewish leaders (Table 6.8). The opposition of the Jewish public to a Palestinian state alongside Israel has fallen appreciably, from 77% in 1980 to 71% in 1985 to 54% in 1988 (Table 6.9).

Table 6.7 Jews' Recognition of the Palestinians' Right to Self-Determination

	Jewish Public	DFPE & PLP Jewish Lead.	CRM & Mapam Jewish Lead.	Labor Jewish Lead.	Likud Camp Jewish Lead.
Hold that the Palestinians today constitute a nation	30.4	100.0	97.1	73.0	36.7
Israel should recognize the Palestinians as a nation					
Yes	12.4	97.2	94.1	51.4	15.6
Only under certain circumstances	31.7	2.8	5.9	29.7	15.6
No	55.9	0.0	0.0	18.9	68.8
The Palestinians have the right to have a state that will include parts of the West Bank and Gaza Strip					
Yes	9.8	100.0	67.6	28.2	0.0
Have reservations	23.6	0.0	29.4	30.8	8.8
No	66.6	0.0	2.9	41.0	91.2

Israeli Arabs are settled on all these matters. For them, the Palestinians are and should be recognized by Israel as a nation, are entitled to a right to self-determination, should be allowed to establish a state in the West Bank and Gaza Strip, and should have the PLO acknowledged as their legitimate representative. All these demands are in line with a two-state solution; however, the additional call upon Israel to grant the Palestinian refugees of 1948 the right of repatriation has the effect of undermining Israel from within, a threat that makes the Jews utterly reluctant even to consider such a demand (Table 6.10). The refugees' right to choose between return or compensation is the official approach of all the Arab political streams that are not affiliated with the Zionist establishment. The Arabs are not intransigent on this demand, though, as shown by the majority who do not oppose conceding it if this is necessary for peace.

Table 6.8 Palestinian State in the West Bank and Gaza Strip

	Arab Public	Estab. Affil. Arab Lead.	Unaffiliated Arab Lead.	DFPE & PLP Arab Lead.	Sons of Village Arab Lead.	Jewish Public	DFPE & PLP Jewish Lead.	CRM & Mapam Jewish Lead.	Labor Jewish Lead.	Likud Camp Jewish Lead.
Favor the formation of a Palestinian state in the West Bank and Gaza Strip alongside Israel										
Yes	67.2	64.5	87.5	97.5	46.7	5.5	97.2	58.8	12.8	0.0
Only under certain circumstances	22.3	29.0	12.5	2.5	36.7	23.8	2.8	29.4	33.3	0.0
No	10.5	6.5	0.0	0.0	16.7	70.7	0.0	11.8	53.8	100.0

Table 6.9 Palestinian State in the West Bank and Gaza Strip, 1976-88

	Arab Public				Jewish Public		
	1976	1980	1985	1988	1980	1985	1988
Favor the formation of a Palestinian state in the West Bank and Gaza Strip alongside Israel							
Yes	74.7	64.0	67.2	76.5	5.7	5.5	11.6
Only under certain circumstances	15.7	19.8	22.3	17.4	17.8	23.8	34.0
No	9.6	16.2	10.5	6.0	76.6	70.7	54.4

The status of the PLO as the sole legitimate representative of the Palestinians is a clear issue dividing the two communities. Whereas Israeli Arabs follow other Palestinians in this regard, the Jews tend to be against but remain open for change (Table 6.11). The Jewish leaders in the center and on the left are more responsive to the PLO than is the public at large. In the 1988 survey, the Jews were asked if Israel should conduct peace negotiations with the PLO if it undergoes a basic change; that is, announces its recognition of the State of Israel and its willingness to stop terrorist actions completely. While 8% of the Jews accept the PLO as representative, 49.5% agree that Israel should talk to it if that organization changes fundamentally (Table 6.12). The endorsement of talks with a non-rejectionist, non-violent PLO varies with a person's political orientation – running from a third of the hardline Likud supporters to two thirds of the pragmatic Labor followers, to 90% of the conciliatory constituents of the small parties of the Zionist left.

Table 6.10 Recognition of Palestinians' Right of Repatriation

	Arab Public	Estab. Affil. Arab Lead.	Unaffil-iated Arab Lead.	DFPE & PLP Arab Lead.	Sons of Village Arab Lead.	Jewish Public	DFPE & PLP Jewish Lead.	CRM & Mapam Jewish Lead.	Labor Jewish Lead.	Likud Camp Jewish Lead.
Israel should recognize the Palestinian refugees' right of repatriation to Israel within the pre-1967 borders										
Yes	81.9	43.8	81.3	97.6	96.4	2.9	61.1	6.1	0.0	0.0
Only under certain circumstances	14.2	40.6	15.6	2.4	3.6	25.7	36.1	54.5	35.9	5.9
No	3.9	15.6	3.1	0.0	0.0	71.4	2.8	39.4	64.1	94.1
The Palestinians should give up the demand for the right of repatriation if this is necessary to reach a peace settlement										
Yes	25.9	61.3	31.3	9.8	0.0	*	*	*	*	*
Have reservations	37.0	29.0	43.8	31.7	6.3	*	*	*	*	*
No	37.0	9.7	25.0	58.5	93.8	*	*	*	*	*

*Not asked.

Table 6.11 Mutual Recognition of Israel and the PLO

	Arab Public	Estab. Affil. Arab Lead.	Unaffil-iated Arab Lead.	DFPE & PLP Arab Lead.	Sons of Village Arab Lead.	Jewish Public	DFPE & PLP Jewish Lead.	CRM & Mapam Jewish Lead.	Labor Jewish Lead.	Likud Camp Jewish Lead.
Israel should recognize the PLO as the Palestinians' representative										
Yes	81.6	51.7	80.6	100.0	84.0	4.2	97.2	41.2	2.5	0.0
Only under certain circumstances	14.1	41.4	19.4	0.0	4.0	21.1	2.8	55.9	52.5	8.8
No	4.2	6.9	0.0	0.0	12.0	74.7	0.0	2.9	45.0	91.2
The PLO should recognize Israel										
Yes	51.7	71.9	77.4	48.8	0.0	*	*	*	*	*
Only under certain circumstances	34.3	28.1	22.6	51.2	40.0	*	*	*	*	*
No	13.9	0.0	0.0	0.0	60.0	*	*	*	*	*

*Not asked.

It is, however, hard for the PLO to meet the Jewish conditions for change because of its long-standing tradition of rejectionism, double talk, and the use of terrorism. In mid-November 1988, half a year after the completion of the fieldwork for the last survey, the National Palestine Congress declared the Independence of Palestine, and its chairman immediately announced the PLO's recognition of Israel, acceptance of UN resolution 242, and renunciation of terror. The established Jewish leadership of the Likud and Labor parties dismissed these proclamations while the US moved to open a dialogue with the PLO. Surveys conducted within two years after these announcements showed that most of the Jews have remained unimpressed, simply have not believed the PLO, and, hence, have not dramatically increased their support for Israel-PLO talks.

Table 6.12 Jews' Willingness to Negotiate with the PLO If It Undergoes a Basic Change by Voting

	Jewish Public
Think that Israel should be ready to conduct peace negotiations with the PLO if the PLO undergoes a basic change, and it will announce its recognition of the State of Israel and its willingness to stop terrorist actions completely	
Total	49.5
Voters in the 1984 national elections for	
CRM, Shinui	90.0
Labor, Yahad, Ometz	65.0
Likud	34.4
Religious parties	33.9
Tehiya, Kach	41.4

Source: The 1988 survey.

Arab support for the PLO raises the very sensitive question of the right to use violence. Since Israeli Arabs regard the PLO as a liberation movement of the Palestinians – though not of Palestine – they would be expected to accede to its right to armed struggle. The survey findings reveal, in fact, that the Arabs' choice of "legitimate" Israeli targets is quite selective and far from complete (Table 6.13). Some 50% approve of the attacks carried out against the Israeli military outside Israel, but less than 30% concur with actions against the Israeli military within Israel. Over a third also favor strikes against the Jewish settlers, who are perceived as worse than Israeli soldiers. Nevertheless, when PLO violence is directed against Jewish citizens within the Green Line, the percentage in favor sinks to 8%. The Arab leaders draw the line between violence against Jewish civilians within the Green Line, which they negate, and violence against the army or any Jews in the occupied territories, which they sanction as part of the Palestinians' legitimate right to armed struggle. Only the activists in the Sons of the Village Movement express a larger proportion (23%) of consent to violence against Jewish civilians in Israel.

Table 6.13 Arabs' View of Actions Carried out by the PLO

	Arab Public	Estab. Affil. Arab Lead.	Unaffil-iated Arab Lead.	DFPE & PLP Arab Lead.	Sons of Village Arab Lead.
Favor actions carried out by the PLO against each of the following Israeli targets					
Soldiers and military bases in the West Bank, Gaza Strip, and outside Israel	50.3	10.7	40.0	94.7	100.0
Soldiers and military bases within the Green Line	28.7	6.9	15.4	66.7	88.5
Jewish settlers on the West Bank and Gaza Strip	34.5	4.0	7.7	86.5	82.8
Jewish citizens within the Green Line	7.9	0.0	0.0	0.0	23.1

Since the PLO is considered by the Jews to be a terrorist organization, the qualified Israeli Arab support for PLO violence would be labeled by Jews as subversive. Yet, the Jews themselves allow the bombing of PLO bases, which are usually located in civilian population concentrations, and even justify the part of Israel's War in Lebanon aimed at liquidating the PLO (Table 6.14). Furthermore, over a third of the Jews would authorize assaults against Palestinian civilians, whether in refugee camps, in the territories, or inside Israel, in retaliation for terrorist attacks. This implies Jewish endorsement of revengeful underground activities against innocent Arabs, including those who are Israeli citizens. The Jewish leadership, on the other hand, permits only state violence (in this case, bombing of PLO bases) and disqualifies all violence perpetrated by Jewish vigilantes.

Table 6.14 Jews' View of Actions against the PLO, the Palestinians, and the Arabs in Israel

	Jewish Public	DFPE & PLP Jewish Lead.	CRM & Mapam Jewish Lead.	Labor Jewish Lead.	Likud Camp Jewish Lead.
Favor each of the following actions					
Bombing of PLO bases	88.5	2.9	63.3	84.2	97.1
Bombing of refugee camps in retaliation for terrorist attacks	36.7	0.0	0.0	12.5	20.6
Terrorist actions by Jews against Arabs in the territories in retaliation for terrorist attacks	31.0	0.0	0.0	7.5	11.8
Terrorist actions by Jews against Israeli Arabs in retaliation for terrorist attacks by Israeli Arabs	36.1	0.0	0.0	2.5	8.8
Justify the part of Israel's War in Lebanon that aimed at liquidating the PLO in Lebanon	71.6	0.0	8.8	33.4	93.8

There are no indications in the 1980-88 surveys, however, of any rapprochement between the two sides on the Palestinian question (Table 6.15). The support of Israeli Arabs for the Palestinian cause has grown, while the Jews have become more open to the Palestinians but without actually having altered their basic stands. Still, there is a certain softening of the Jewish hardline posture on territorial concessions in the West Bank and Gaza Strip (Table 6.5 above).

Table 6.15 Recognition of the Palestinians as a Nation, Right of Repatriation, PLO, and Israel, 1976-88

	Arab Public				Jewish Public		
	1976	1980	1985	1988	1980	1985	1988
Hold that Israel should recognize the Palestinians as a nation	86.9	80.2	*	*	11.1	12.4	*
Maintain that Israel should recognize the Palestinian refuges' right of repatriation to Israel within the pre-1967 borders	84.8	78.0	81.9	76.8	5.8	2.9	5.5
Not opposed to Palestinians' renunciation of the right of repatriation if this is necessary to reach a peace settlement	*	63.2	63.0	69.3	*	*	*
Israel should recognize the PLO as the Palestinians' representative	*	67.8	81.6	81.6	3.0	4.2	7.9
The PLO should recognize Israel	*	51.7	51.7	54.9	*	*	*

*Not asked.

Israel's War in Lebanon also separates Arabs from Jews. The Jews are internally divided over the War, and an appreciable minority experiences its adverse effects on their attitude toward the state and Israeli democracy (Table 6.16). On the other hand, the Arabs totally reject the War because it is seen as directed against their own Palestinian people as well as the PLO, to both of whom they are firmly attached. Most Israeli Arabs feel its negative impact on their orientation toward Israel.

Beyond the separate issues, the polarity of views on the Israeli-Arab dispute can well be captured by four summary measures. The simplest one is an additive index in which a respondent can score from 0 to 14 points by giving "hawkish" answers to each of 14 questions. For instance, a person opposing the formation of a Palestinian state in the West Bank and Gaza Strip would score one point on this question, and a person subscribing to such a solution would score none. It was found that 70% of the Arabs are concentrated on the "dovish" end of the index (scoring 0-3 points only), whereas 62.5% of the Jews fall on the "hawkish" pole (11-14 points; Table 6.17). This distribution leaves only 30% of the Arabs and 35.5% of the Jews in the shared, broad middle ground (scoring 4-10 points).

The leaders of the two communities are even more divided than is the rank and file. To illustrate, as many as 54% of the moderate Arab leaders, who are affiliated with the Zionist establishment, and 68% of the unaffiliated Arab leaders join the extreme "dovish" Arab consensus. (The fact that only 37.5% of the activists in the Sons of the Village Movement are classified as "dovish" stems from their rejection of the general Arab agreement in favor of an independent Palestinian state alongside Israel.) All the Jewish leaders from the Likud camp (the Likud, religious, and radical right parties) fall in the "hawkish" category.

Table 6.16 Perceived Impact of Israel's War in Lebanon

	Arab Public	Estab. Affil. Arab Lead.	Unaffiliated Arab Lead.	DFPE & PLP Arab Lead.	Sons of Village Arab Lead.	Jewish Public	DFPE & PLP Jewish Lead.	CRM & Mapam Jewish Lead.	Labor Jewish Lead.	Likud Camp Jewish Lead.
Israel's War in Lebanon										
Strengthened the belief in a political (as opposed to a military) solution to the Palestinian question	55.0	84.4	75.0	64.1	9.4	34.4	77.8	76.5	67.5	8.8
Weakened the belief in Israeli democracy	67.7	46.9	71.0	69.2	56.3	35.9	60.0	45.5	41.0	21.2
Adversely affected the attitude toward the state	78.3	80.0	84.4	82.5	75.0	44.7	41.2	40.7	28.9	3.0

Table 6.17 Index of Hawkishness

	Arab Public	Estab. Affil. Arab Lead.	Unaffiliated Arab Lead.	DFPE & PLP Arab Lead.	Sons of Village Arab Lead.	Jewish Public	DFPE & PLP Jewish Lead.	CRM & Mapam Jewish Lead.	Labor Jewish Lead.	Likud Camp Jewish Lead.
0 Lowest	0.0	0.0	0.0	0.0	0.0	0.2	61.1	5.9	0.0	0.0
1	9.8	0.0	19.4	10.0	0.0	0.2	33.3	11.8	0.0	0.0
2	22.9	28.6	29.0	30.0	0.0	0.9	0.0	14.7	0.0	0.0
3	37.2	25.0	19.4	57.5	37.5	0.9	2.8	20.6	5.0	0.0
4	14.0	14.3	29.0	2.5	50.0	0.5	2.8	14.7	5.0	0.0
5	6.6	14.3	3.2	0.0	12.5	2.4	0.0	23.5	7.5	0.0
6	4.0	7.1	0.0	0.0	0.0	2.5	0.0	2.9	15.0	0.0
7	1.7	7.1	0.0	0.0	0.0	5.3	0.0	2.9	12.5	0.0
8	2.2	3.6	0.0	0.0	0.0	8.0	0.0	2.9	15.0	0.0
9	0.5	0.0	0.0	0.0	0.0	7.4	0.0	0.0	10.0	0.0
10	1.0	0.0	0.0	0.0	0.0	9.2	0.0	0.0	12.5	0.0
11	0.1	0.0	0.0	0.0	0.0	10.7	0.0	0.0	12.5	8.8
12	0.0	0.0	0.0	0.0	0.0	12.9	0.0	0.0	5.0	11.8
13	0.0	0.0	0.0	0.0	0.0	12.6	0.0	0.0	0.0	26.5
14 Highest	0.0	0.0	0.0	0.0	0.0	26.3	0.0	0.0	0.0	52.9

The second summary measure is based on answers to a question, in the 1988 survey, on the best overall solution to the Palestinian problem. The six options offered (the exact formulation of each appears in Table 6.18) can be broken down into three major alternatives: (a) unilateral Jewish domination without enfranchising the Palestinians on the West Bank and Gaza Strip (the first two answers in the Table); (b) a system with equal rights granted to Jews and Palestinians (the three middle answers); and (c) two states in the area West of the Jordan river (the last answer). The order of preference of these options is found to be reversed for Israeli Arabs and Jews: two states – 67.5% of the Arabs versus 18% of the Jews; one system with equal political rights – 30% versus 26.5%; and Jewish domination – 2% versus 56%. It is noteworthy that 56% of the Jews would prefer continued Jewish domination with a possibility of driving out those Palestinians who resist this role. (For findings of another survey, conducted in June 1989, on the acceptability, by Arabs and Jews, of various options for settling the Palestinian question, see Katz and Al-Haj, 1989; and Al-Haj and Katz, 1989.) Arab-Jewish discord on the Palestinian issue continues to be deep throughout the intifada, although both sides are increasingly in agreement that the status quo is no longer tenable. For instance, in a survey conducted in December 1990, only 2% of Arabs and 16% of Jews thought that the status quo was an acceptable option, as opposed to 98% and 17%, respectively, who felt the same about the solution of an independent Palestinian state (Al-Haj, forthcoming).

Table 6.18 The Best Solution to the Palestinian Problem in the Territories

	Arab Public	Jewish Public
Regard the following as the best solution for the problem of the Arabs in the territories		
The Jews will rule, and the Arabs in the territories who refuse to accept this, will have to keep quiet or leave the country	1.0	34.8
The Jews will rule, and the Arabs in the territories should accept what the Jews will decide	1.4	20.8
A single party, that will be open also to the Arabs in the territories, will rule without opposition	4.5	6.5
All people, including the Arabs in the territories, will vote for any party they like, and the winning party or parties will rule while other parties will be in opposition	9.8	12.0
All people, including the Arabs in the territories, will vote for any party they like, and parties will have to form a coalition government that will ensure a share of power for Jews, and for Arabs in Israel and the territories	15.8	8.0
Israel should withdraw, so that the Jews and the Arabs in the territories will live in separate states	67.5	17.9

Source: The 1988 survey.

The third summary measure consists of choices of the political body that offers the best solution to the Israeli-Arab conflict. The Arabs are divided into one third selecting the mainstream PLO, one third – PLP and Rakah, and one third – Zionist parties (Table 6.19). It is indeed remarkable that only 2% of the Arabs prefer the Rejection Front's idea of a Palestinian state instead of Israel, the favorite settlement in the eyes of the leaders of the Sons of the Village Movement, in the survey. In contrast, Jews are split into one half ("hardliners") choosing Kach, Tehiya, and Likud and one half ("compromisers") opting for Labor, CRM, and Peace Now. Once again, only a third of the Arabs and Jews share similar views.

Table 6.19 Political Body That Offers the Best Solution to the Israeli-Arab Conflict

	Arab Public	Estab. Affil. Arab Lead.	Unaffiliated Arab Lead.	DFPE & PLP Arab Lead.	Sons of Village Arab Lead.	Jewish Public	DFPE & PLP Jewish Lead.	CRM & Mapam Jewish Lead.	Labor Jewish Lead.	Likud Camp Jewish Lead.
Political body that offers the best solution to the Israeli-Arab conflict										
Kach	0.5	0.0	0.0	0.0	0.0	9.8	0.0	0.0	0.0	0.0
Tehiya, Gush Emunim	0.5	0.0	0.0	0.0	0.0	11.0	0.0	0.0	0.0	34.4
Likud	2.8	9.7	0.0	0.0	0.0	23.3	0.0	0.0	0.0	62.5
Labor	19.9	51.6	19.4	0.0	0.0	42.9	0.0	3.0	70.0	3.1
CRM, Peace Now	10.9	32.3	29.0	0.0	0.0	10.1	2.8	81.8	30.0	0.0
PLP	11.0	3.2	16.1	20.0	0.0	1.6	36.1	12.1	0.0	0.0
Rakah	23.1	0.0	25.8	67.5	0.0	0.6	58.3	3.0	0.0	0.0
PLO mainstream (Arafat)	29.2	3.2	9.7	12.5	17.2	0.4	0.0	0.0	0.0	0.0
Rejection Front	2.2	0.0	0.0	0.0	82.8	0.2	2.8	0.0	0.0	0.0

Since respondents tend to select a political body on grounds other than its solution to the Israeli-Arab conflict, the fourth and most appropriate way to summarize the discord is by classifying the respondents into existing ideological positions. In accordance with the major political and ideological streams prevalent at the time of the 1985 survey, six ideological positions were distinguished on the basis of the various issues and operationalized as follows:

1. *Tehiya.* To be classified as holding a Tehiya position, respondents must take all the following stands: (a) insist on retaining the post-June 1967 boundaries, (b) favor unrestricted Jewish settlement of Judea and Samaria, (c) approve of the immediate annexation of the territories, and (d) not favor (object to or have reservations about) the Peace Treaty with Egypt.

2. *Likud.* Persons are assigned to a Likud position if they agree with only the first two of the above four stands.

3. *Labor.* To be in the Labor position, respondents have to (a) accept territorial compromise but not a return to the pre-June 1967 borders, and (b) not favor unrestricted Jewish settlement of Judea and Samaria.

4. *Citizens' Rights Movement.* Respondents in this category (a) favor retreat to the pre-June 1967 borders with or without slight modifications

(including or excluding East Jerusalem), and (b) oppose unrestricted Jewish settlement of Judea and Samaria.

5. *DFPE and PLP.* To subscribe to this view, respondents should consent to all the following: (a) withdrawal to the pre-June 1967 borders, including retreat from East Jerusalem, (b) formation of a Palestinian state in the West Bank and Gaza Strip alongside Israel, and (c) Israel's recognition of the PLO as the legitimate representative of the Palestinians. The mainstream PLO stance is ambiguous, but Israeli Arabs and their established leadership believe that it is identical with that of the DFPE and PLP.

6. *Rejection Front.* Respondents are regarded as supporters of the Rejection Front position if they (a) favor the idea of a secular-democratic state in all of Palestine instead of Israel, or deny Israel's right to exist, and (b) hold that being part of a secular-democratic state is the only acceptable solution to the problem of the Arab minority in Israel.

These six ideological positions are nearly fully exhaustive of all views on the Israeli-Arab conflict. Hence, a failure to be classified indicates inconsistency, which is expectably appreciable among the rank and file. It was indeed found that 42% of the Arabs and 44% of the Jews in the survey are inconsistent in their overall view of the conflict (Table 6.20), but they do not differ from the consistent majority on each of the constituent stands. Inconsistency implies openness to change and is better than extremism. Among the Arabs, the ideological position of the DFPE and PLP is dominant, whereas that of the Rejection Front is adopted by only 7% of the population. Among the Jews, the approaches of the Likud and Labor camps enjoy nearly equal support; but 29% of the Jews consistently subscribe to the idea of Greater Israel. The main point, however, is that Arabs and Jews disagree sharply, and each side holds postures on the conflict that are rejected by the other.

Table 6.20 Distribution of Ideological Positions on the Israeli-Arab Conflict

	Arab Public (Including Inconsistent Position)	Jewish Public (Including Inconsistent Position)	Arab Public (Excluding Inconsistent Position)	Jewish Public (Excluding Inconsistent Position)
Ideological position				
Tehiya	0.0	7.6	0.0	13.5
Likud	1.2	21.2	2.0	37.8
Labor	2.2	21.4	3.7	38.0
CRM	4.5	5.4	7.7	9.6
DFPE and PLP	43.1	0.6	74.0	1.1
Rejection Front	7.3	0.0	12.6	0.0
Inconsistent	41.7	43.8	–	–

Although the ideological position in which the respondent is classified correlates with one's choice of the political body offering the best solution to the conflict, there is a significant discrepancy. Whereas 31% of the Arabs select the mainstream PLO and Rejection Front solutions, only 7% display a consistent, rejectionist stance. This means that an Israeli Arab who endorses the mainstream PLO view is not necessarily rejectionist but in most cases adheres to the Israeli Arab consensus on a two-state solution. It was also found that only one third of those categorized in the DFPE-PLP outlook actually choose the DFPE-PLP solution; one quarter opt for the PLO solution, but two fifths cite compromise solutions proposed by various Zionist parties (Table 6.21). By the same token, many Jews in the Likud ideological stand select the solutions identified with Tehiya, on the one hand, and with Labor on the other. This is also true of Jews holding the Tehiya viewpoint. Two fifths of the Jews in the CRM ideological position choose the Labor solution. These figures show that both sides are more ideologically moderate than what can be attributed to them on the basis of the political bodies they back.

Table 6.21 Ideological Position on the Israeli-Arab Conflict by Political Body That Offers the Best Solution to the Conflict

	Ideological Position							
							Rejec-	
				DFPE &	tion	Incons-		
	Total	Tehiya	Likud	Labor	CRM	PLP	Front	istent
Political body that offers the best solution to the Israeli-Arab Conflict								
	Arab Public							
Kach (Kahane's movement)	0.5	–	0.0	0.0	0.0	0.0	0.0	1.3
Tehiya, Gush Emunim	0.5	–	0.0	0.0	0.0	0.0	0.0	1.3
Likud	2.8	–	38.5	22.7	6.7	0.0	0.0	3.9
Labor	19.9	–	53.8	45.5	44.4	16.9	4.8	21.3
CRM, Peace Now	10.9	–	7.7	4.5	20.0	11.9	3.6	10.6
Progressive List for Peace	11.0	–	0.0	13.6	8.9	14.0	0.0	10.2
DFPE (Rakah)	23.1	–	0.0	9.1	4.4	32.2	25.0	16.5
PLO, Rejection Front	31.4	–	0.0	4.5	15.5	25.0	66.7	35.2
Total	100.0	–	100.0	100.0	100.0	100.0	100.0	100.0
N	1,104	0	13	22	45	479	84	461
	Jewish Public							
Kach (Kahane's movement)	9.8	16.9	13.0	0.0	0.0	–	–	13.2
Tehiya, Gush Emunim	11.0	45.4	19.9	0.0	0.0	–	–	5.9
Likud	23.3	22.7	38.9	8.9	0.0	–	–	25.5
Labor	42.9	13.2	25.7	75.4	42.1	–	–	42.8
CRM, Peace Now	10.1	1.8	2.5	15.6	56.3	–	–	6.5
Progressive List for Peace	1.6	0.0	0.0	0.0	1.6	–	–	3.3
DFPE (Rakah)	0.6	0.0	0.0	0.0	0.0	–	–	1.6
PLO, Rejection Front	0.6	0.0	0.0	0.0	0.0	–	–	1.2
Total	100.0	100.0	100.0	100.0	100.0	–	–	100.0
N	1,065	91	256	229	61	5	0	424

In sum, most Israeli Arabs favor a PLO-headed Palestinian state in the West Bank and Gaza Strip alongside Israel as a permanent settlement of the Palestinian question, whereas a minority of about one third demand more extreme solutions amounting to a partial or full disintegration of Israel. The Jews are internally divided on the issue of territorial compromise, but they are united in rejecting these two Israeli Arab views. As a result, Israeli Arabs are forced into the status of a dissident, untrustworthy minority on the most fundamental issue of the Israeli-Arab conflict.

Throughout the 1980s, this conflict remained the most important divisive issue and toward the end of the decade it was further exacerbated by the intifada and the Gulf War. The Arabs were on the side of the revolting Palestinians and the PLO-backed Iraq, to both of which positions Jews were strongly opposed. The Jews were particularly dismayed by the Arabs' use of these severe conflicts to register their dissent from the Jewish consensus and to reassert their fearsome Palestinian and pan-Arab affinities.

7

Collective Identity

Israel's Arabs are at once Israeli and Palestinian. They are Israeli in citizenship, which firmly links their rights, duties, and future to Israel; in their incorporation into various Israeli institutions, such as the economy, the political parties, the media, and the Histadrut; in their noticeable bilingualism and biculturalism; in their daily contacts with Jews; and in their acceptance of Israel as a state and of their being part of it. Yet, they are no less Palestinian in their ethnic and national origin; in their Arabic language and culture; and in their rejection of Zionism and of the Jewish views on the Palestinian issue. Given these undeniable forces, the question is how are the Israeli, Palestinian, and Jewish identities related? How central is national identity in the collective identity of Arabs and Jews? How do the Arabs in Israel conceive of themselves and how do the Jews see them? What kind of identity have the Arabs developed for coping with the strains in their complex identity and how have the Jews reacted to it?

Three types of relations among the components of a compound identity were found in the study of Jewish and Arab identity in Israel. These are mutual reinforcement, mutual exclusion, and independence. Mutual reinforcement best characterizes the relation between the Israeli and Jewish dimensions in the national identity of Israeli Jews because of Israel's Jewish majority and character. Yet, some tensions do exist and certain Jewish groups emphasize one element at the cost of the other (e.g., the ultra-orthodox stress Jewish identity, while secularists of the Zionist left underscore Israeli identity).

The literature on the identity of the Arabs in Israel unanimously points to mutual exclusion as a guideline for analyzing the interaction between the Israeli and Palestinian parts of the Arab identity. Peres and Yuval-Davis (1969) pioneered this line of analysis. They spoke of the Arabs' split identity and spelled out a number of coping mechanisms Arabs use, singling out compartmentalization as the main device. Hofman and Rouhana (1976) took this lead and demonstrated the precedence of the national to the civic aspect in the conflicted Arab identity. Rouhana (1991) updated and brought this approach to its extreme logic. He distinguishes among three layers of identity, of which the "shallow," instrumental layer (organizational participation, obedience to law, economic involvement) is reserved for the Israeli identity, the intermediate value stratum (style of life, political culture, status of women) is shared by both identities, and the deepest sentimental level (identification, loyalty, pride, willingness to represent and make sacrifices, attachment to symbols) is monopolized by the Palestinian identity. He claims that the Palestinian identity has become so overwhelming among the Arabs that the virtually empty and weak Israeli identity cannot possibly compete with it. He blames the defeat of the Israeli identity on the exclusionary nature of the Jewish state, which does not offer the Arabs the option to be Israelis. Rouhana concludes that the correct model for conceptualizing the identity of the "Palestinians in Israel" (for him, this is the only identity fitting the Arabs since the early 1980s) is the "accentuated Palestinian identity," overstressed at the expense of its failing Israeli rival. The Palestinian identity is also accentuated because it is still denied full expression.

In contrast to the mutual exclusion model of Israeli Arab identity that was formulated and applied by Peres, Hofman, and Rouhana, my model posits independence between the two primary components. Instead of stretching on a single continuum, the Israeli and Arab Palestinian identities extend on two separate, parallel, and independent continua. This means that an Arab can be high on both, low on both, low on one and high on another, or combine different doses of both. The rejectionists (e.g., followers of the Sons of the Village Movement) have a maximal Palestinian identity and a minimal Israeli identity, while the accommodationists (e.g., the Druzes) have a maximal Israeli identity and a minimal Palestinian identity. The Communists put equal emphasis on both identities, whereas the leading elite of the Progressive List for Peace gives more weight to the Palestinian dimension. Rather than being torn between the two internal forces, the "typical" Arab experiences the tension between the two identities as something imposed on him from the outside. The heart of the problem is the Jews' castigation of the Palestinian identity as illegitimate and subversive. The Arab predicament stems from the Jewish insistence on an "Israeli Arab" instead of an "Israeli Palestinian" identity for the Arabs in Israel.

Rouhana's thesis that the Arabs have developed an accentuated "Palestinian in Israel" identity is correct in its rejection of the assumption of a split Arab identity. He reaches this conclusion, not by switching to the model of independence, but rather by dwarfing the Israeli component. He is wrong in downplaying the importance of the instrumental and value levels of identity and in inflating the centrality of the emotional-symbolic level in the life of the Arabs of Israel. The first two levels determine not only the Arabs' daily life but also changes in their value system, fateful political decisions (e.g., non-participation in the intifada), and their future. It is true, however, that the Arabs do not identify themselves with Israel, but no researcher, commentator, or policymaker has ever claimed that they do.

With these ideas in mind, we can probe the importance of the different identities in the lives of Israelis. Eight to nine identities were presented in the 1988 survey, and the respondents were asked to indicate which was important and which was not. A majority of two thirds or more of both Arabs and Jews consider as important residence in the homeland, nationality, class, religion, status as a minority or a majority, and citizenship (Table 7.1). Two thirds of the Jews also view religious observance as significant but dismiss ethnic origin; less than half of the Arabs attach importance to religious observance and hamula membership.

Table 7.1 Importance of Self-Identities

	Arab Public	Jewish Public
Consider each of the following identities as important to oneself		
Residence in the homeland	97.7	94.0
Nationality (Arab nation/Jewish people)	87.9	93.7
Palestinian nationality	86.6	–
Socioeconomic stratum and lifestyle	83.9	89.1
Minority/majority status	79.7	88.5
Citizenship	68.7	96.3
Religion	67.5	86.5
Religious observance	49.3	68.6
Hamula	42.7	–
Ethnicity (Sephardic/Ashkenazic)	–	28.8

Source: The 1988 survey.

When each identity was evaluated separately, as was the case so far, most identities were found to be important, including non-national ones. Nevertheless, it is possible to establish the relative centrality of each identity by forcing respondents to choose the most important identity from a given list. This procedure also yielded a striking similarity between the Arab and Jewish first choices of identities (Table 7.2). Both sides chose nationality or nationality related identities and ignored other affiliations. The Arabs select Palestinian and pan-Arab nationality and residence in the homeland (Palestine), whereas the Jews opt for citizenship (in the Jewish state), Jewish people, Judaism (the Jewish faith, which is espoused only by Jews), and residence in the homeland (Eretz Israel). The wide gap between the 10% of Arabs and 37% of Jews selecting citizenship as their most cherished self-identity mirrors, on the subjective level, the true nature of Israel as a state of and for Jews, and hence as an object of strong identification for Jews and a country from which the Arabs are inevitably alienated.

Table 7.2 The Most Important Self-Identity

	Arab Public	Jewish Public
The most important self-identity (from the following)		
Palestinian nationality	34.5	–
Residence in the homeland	16.2	14.0
Religion	15.9	16.8
Nationality (Arab nation/Jewish people)	11.5	18.5
Citizenship	9.6	37.2
Socioeconomic stratum and lifestyle	6.2	7.8
Religious observance	2.5	0.6
Minority/majority status	2.4	4.5
Hamula	1.2	–
Ethnicity (Sephardic/Ashkenazic)	–	0.6

Source: The 1988 survey.

Although both Arabs and Jews are equally nationalistic, they differ widely in the expressions of their nationalism. For the Jews, the matter is relatively simple, thanks to the overlap between Jewish and Israeli identities. On the other hand, the Arabs have a dilemma of deciding between or combining Israeli and Palestinian identities. Whereas the Jews are sure of themselves as Israelis and Jews, only 45% of the Arabs think that the term "Israeli" fits themselves well, 51% feel that way about the term "Israeli Palestinian," but a majority of 68% consider the term "Palestinian" to be most appropriate (Table 7.3). During the 1976-88 period, a small decline took place in the appropriateness of Israeli identity as did a certain increase in the attractiveness of Palestinian identity (Table 7.4). The majority that considers the compound "Israeli Palestinian" identity as suitable is even larger among non-rejectionist Arab leaders than among the public at large (63%-87% versus 51%, Table 7.3). This is an indication of the direction from which the wind is blowing for most of the Arabs in Israel. An exception that confirms this rule is the activists in the Sons of the Village Movement, whose extremism is best evidenced, in their total rejection of Israeli and Israeli-Palestinian identities and in their absolute identification with Palestinian identity.

Table 7.3 Appropriateness of Terms of National Self-Identity

	Arab Public	Estab. Affil. Arab Lead.	Unaffil-iated Arab Lead.	DFPE & PLP Arab Lead.	Sons of Village Arab Lead.	Jewish Public	DFPE & PLP Jewish Lead.	CRM & Mapam Jewish Lead.	Labor Jewish Lead.	Likud Camp Jewish Lead.
Consider each of the following terms as an appropriate self-description										
Israeli	44.9	84.4	50.0	23.1	0.0	93.7	97.1	91.2	97.5	90.9
Israeli Palestinian/Jew	51.2	62.6	86.7	71.8	3.1	95.3[a]	*	*	*	*
Palestinian	67.6	53.2	64.5	100.0	96.9	**	**	**	**	**

*Not asked. **Not applicable. [a]The 1980 survey.

Table 7.4 Appropriateness of Terms of National Self-Identity, 1976-88

	Arab Public				Jewish Public		
	1976	1980	1985	1988	1980	1985	1988
Consider the term "Israeli" as an appropriate self-description	52.1	53.0	44.9	45.7	95.8	93.7	89.7
Consider the term "Palestinian" as an appropriate self-description	58.0	54.7	67.6	*	**	**	**

*Not asked. **Not applicable.

When forced to choose one of seven alternatives, 27% of the Arab respondents opt for "Palestinian in Israel," 22% – "Palestinian Arab," 21% – "Israeli Arab," and the remaining 30% is divided among the other four identities (Table 7.5). The three most popular identities represent three distinct options, and the other four choices can be reclassified into them. The identity "Israeli" naturally falls into the "Israeli Arab" category. The "Palestinian" tag corresponds well with the "Palestinian Arab" identity. The "Israeli Palestinian" label looks close to the "Palestinian in Israel." Since the "Arab" choice is neutral, devoid of an explicit Palestinian attachment, and unambiguously accommodating, it should be grouped with the "Israeli Arab" category.

The suggested categorization consists of three options: non-Palestinian Israeli (Israeli Arab, Israeli, Arab), Israeli Palestinian (Palestinian in Israel, Israeli Palestinian), and non-Israeli Palestinian (Palestinian Arab, Palestinian). It provides a choice between Israeli and Palestinian components, including the possibility of a synthesis. On the other hand, Rouhana, working with a model of mutual exclusion, argues for a dichotomy between Israeli and Palestinian identities and allows no synthetic choice. In his classification, the "Israeli Palestinian" identity is grouped with the non-Palestinian Israeli category, and the "Palestinian in Israel" identity is assigned to the non-Israeli Palestinian category. This dichotomy not only oversimplifies and distorts reality, it also serves as a tool for advancing the false claim that the Arabs have a predominantly non-Israeli Palestinian identity. The exclusion of Druzes and Bedouin from the survey statistics and the over-representation of the younger and more educated groups have the effect of further slanting the evidence in Rouhana's favor.

Table 7.5 Arabs' National Self-Identity as Chosen from Given Alternatives

	Arab Public	Estab. Affil. Arab Lead.	Unaffiliated Arab Lead.	DFPE & PLP Arab Lead.	Sons of Village Arab Lead.
Define oneself (from the following seven alternatives) as					
Israeli	5.3	0.0	0.0	0.0	0.0
Israeli Arab	21.1	59.4	25.0	0.0	0.0
Arab	5.7	0.0	0.0	0.0	0.0
Israeli Palestinian	11.7	28.1	28.1	15.0	3.1
Palestinian (Palestinian Arab) in Israel	27.0	12.5	37.5	72.5	12.5
Palestinian	7.6	0.0	0.0	2.5	18.8
Palestinian Arab	21.6	0.0	9.4	10.0	65.6

The survey findings do not lend support to Rouhana's dichotomous approach. A good part of his argument rests on a peculiar interpretation of the meaning of the identity "Palestinian in Israel." Rouhana maintains that any Arab who selects this identity from a seven-item menu makes a clearcut choice in favor of a Palestinian identity and against an Israeli identity. Yet, contrary to Rouhana's assertions, 70% of the Arabs choosing "Palestinian in Israel" as their identity also thought that the term "Israeli Palestinian" is appropriate for describing their identity; in contrast, only 24% of the Arabs choosing a "Palestinian" identity felt the same way. The fact that the term "Palestinian in Israel" belongs to the intermediate category and should not be lumped with the term "Palestinian Arab" can further be demonstrated by the sophisticated choices made by Arab leaders. The non-rejectionist DFPE and PLP leaders chose labels in the middle category: 72.5% selected "Palestinian in Israel" and 15%, "Israeli Palestinian." In contrast, the rejectionist activists from the Sons of the Village Movement opted for the extreme non-Israeli Palestinian categories: 66% preferred the term "Palestinian Arab" and 19%, "Palestinian." These and many other figures show that the notions "Palestinian in Israel" and "Israeli Palestinian" are closely related, representing a new, genuine identity that integrates the Israeli and Palestinian ingredients in the practical and spiritual lives of the Arabs in Israel.

Our three-way classification of the seven identity tags results in the following distribution: 32% of the Arabs prefer a non-Palestinian Israeli identity, 39% – an Israeli Palestinian identity, and 29% – a non-Israeli Palestinian identity. It is thus clear that the Israeli and Palestinian fundamentals are strong in the Arab mind and that the emerging identity combines both identities. That the Israeli Palestinian identity is indeed becoming predominant is well shown in the first choice of the rising non-extremist Arab leaders: 66% of the non-affiliated leaders and 97.5% of the leaders of the DFPE and PLP prefer to be Israeli Palestinians (or Palestinians in Israel). In contrast, 59% of the leaders affiliated with the Zionist establishment wish to remain Israeli Arabs, while 84.5% of the rejectionist leaders of the Sons of the Village Movement insist on being non-Israeli Palestinians.

Certain population groups are more attracted to a given category of identity than to others. The Druzes, Galilee Bedouin, persons not affected by land expropriations, and voters for Zionist parties lean more toward non-Palestinian Israeli identities (Table 7.6). On the other hand, Moslems in the Triangle and the central region and voters for the PLP are more disposed toward non-Israeli Palestinian identities. Most groups, and especially the leading non-Bedouin Moslems in the Galilee, Christians, the intelligentsia, and supporters of the Communist Party, adopt the synthesis embedded in the Israeli-Palestinian identity. Contrary to modernization theory, identity is not significantly shaped by age, education, or level of urbanization.

The ascendance of the balanced, informative Israeli Palestinian identity is further and best confirmed in the trend over time. During the 1976-88 period, it rose dramatically, from 12% to 40%, at the expense of a drop in the non-Palestinian Israeli identity from 55% to 33% and in the non-Israeli Palestinian identity from 33% to 27% (Table 7.7).

Arab national identity is a real issue separating Arabs and Jews. The Arab public and leaders (with the exception of those from the Sons of the Village Movement) wish to be counted as Israelis, like their fellow Jews, and to be identified as a special type of Palestinians rather than as Israeli Arabs (Table 7.8). The Jews are reluctant to fulfill these desires: only 45% consider the term "Israeli" to be applicable to Arab Israelis, too, and only 14.5% define Arabs in Palestinian terms. To comprehend Jewish objections, it must be recalled that most Jews experience the idea of a Jewish state as exclusionary and regard the rise of Palestinian nationalism as illegitimate and hostile. Jewish leaders, however, are more considerate of the Arabs than is the public at large: they view the Arabs as Israelis (even 67% of the right-wing leaders do so), and the leftists among them perceive the Arabs as Israeli Palestinians.

Table 7.6 Arabs' National Identity by Population Groups

	Non-Palestinian Israeli	Arab Public Israeli Palestinian	Non-Israeli Palestinian
Total	32.1	38.7	29.2
Community			
Druze	87.8	6.1	6.1
Christian	35.1	45.6	19.3
Northern Bedouin	48.8	35.4	15.9
Negev Bedouin	29.8	35.7	34.5
Non-Bedouin Moslem in the Galilee	22.1	47.1	30.5
Non-Bedouin Moslem in the Triangle	17.5	37.8	44.7
Non-Bedouin Moslem in the central region	25.0	32.9	42.1
Age			
18-25	29.1	37.3	33.6
26-45	33.5	40.2	26.4
46 or over	36.1	38.6	25.3
Education			
0-8	34.7	36.9	28.4
9-12	30.3	40.0	29.7
13 or more	25.2	46.3	28.5
Friendship and visiting terms with Jews			
Have no Jewish friends	26.3	36.6	37.1
Have Jewish friends but have not visited them	33.0	40.6	26.3
Have Jewish friends and visited them	37.7	39.4	22.9
Effect of land expropriations			
None	49.6	31.9	18.5
Some	25.8	39.6	34.5
Much	19.8	41.0	39.1
Voting in 1984			
Likud, or religious parties	80.0	14.5	5.5
Labor, CRM, or Shinui	50.2	34.4	15.5
DFPE (Rakah)	15.0	48.9	36.1
PLP	14.4	42.4	43.2

Table 7.7 Arabs' National Self-Identity as Chosen from Given Alternatives, 1976-88

	Arab Public			
	1976	1980	1985	1988
Define oneself (from the following alternatives) as				
Israeli, Israeli Arab, Arab	54.7	45.4	32.1	33.2
Israeli Palestinian, Palestinian in Israel	12.4	28.8	38.7	39.7
Palestinian, Palestinian Arab	32.9	25.7	29.2	27.1

Table 7.8 National Identity of the Arabs in Israel

	Arab Public	Estab. Affil. Arab Lead.	Unaffiliated Arab Lead.	DFPE & PLP Arab Lead.	Sons of Village Arab Lead.	Jewish Public	DFPE & PLP Jewish Lead.	CRM & Mapam Jewish Lead.	Labor Jewish Lead.	Likud Camp Jewish Lead.
When thinking of the term "Israeli," consider both Jews and Arabs	74.7	96.9	90.6	62.5	3.3	45.4	100.0	100.0	80.0	66.7
Define Arabs in Israel (from the following seven alternatives) as										
Israelis	2.3	0.0	0.0	0.0	0.0	3.3	2.8	8.8	2.5	0.0
Israeli Arabs	24.3	56.3	28.1	0.0	6.3	59.5	11.1	23.5	82.5	76.5
Arabs	6.8	0.0	0.0	2.5	0.0	22.8	0.0	0.0	2.5	17.6
Israeli Palestinians	11.1	25.0	28.1	10.0	3.1	2.1	41.7	44.1	5.0	0.0
Palestinians (Palestinian Arabs) in Israel	29.7	18.8	40.6	72.5	18.8	2.9	36.1	23.5	7.5	0.0
Palestinians	7.3	0.0	0.0	5.0	12.5	1.8	0.0	0.0	0.0	0.0
Palestinian Arabs	18.4	0.0	3.1	10.0	59.4	7.7	8.3	0.0	0.0	5.9

The Arab-Jewish chasm on what is the most adequate Arab identity has widened over the years. The absolute growth of Palestinian identities among the Arabs, from 54% in 1976 to 67% in 1988, is larger than the rise in the proportion of Jews recognizing them as Palestinians, which went from 7% to 16% (Table 7.9). The last figure – 16% of the Jews in 1988 who define Arabs in Palestinian terms – is deceptive, however, because many who so define the Arabs are right-wingers who convey their animosity toward the Arabs by condemning them as disloyal Palestinians.

Table 7.9 National Identity of the Arabs in Israel, 1976-88

	Arab Public			Jewish Public		
	1980	1985	1988	1980	1985	1988
Define the national identity of Arabs in Israel (from the following seven alternatives) as						
Israelis, Israeli Arabs, Arabs	46.0	33.4	33.2	91.7	85.5	84.4
Israeli Palestinians, Palestinians in Israel	29.8	40.8	43.9	3.4	5.0	7.1
Palestinian Arabs	24.2	25.8	22.9	5.0	9.5	8.5

The Arabs are keenly aware of their dual Israeli and Palestinian affinities: 55.5% feel that Arabs are more similar in lifestyle and daily behavior to Jews in Israel than to Palestinians in the West Bank and Gaza Strip, but 60% feel closer to the latter (Table 7.10 and Table 7.11). These figures disclose the dual Arab identity. The issue of cultural resemblance is also undecided and bewildering for the Jewish public and for Jewish and Arab leaders. There is no doubt, however, that the increase in Arab bilingualism and biculturalism, which draws Arabs and Jews nearer culturally does not weaken the strong national sentiment that Israeli Arabs feel toward their Palestinian brethren under Israeli occupation.

Table 7.10 Cultural Resemblance

	Arab Public	Estab. Affil. Arab Lead.	Unaffiliated Arab Lead.	DFPE & PLP Arab Lead.	Sons of Village Arab Lead.	Jewish Public	DFPE & PLP Jewish Lead.	CRM & Mapam Jewish Lead.	Labor Jewish Lead.	Likud Camp Jewish Lead.
Feel that the Arabs in Israel more resemble in style of life and daily behavior										
Arabs in the West Bank and Gaza Strip	44.5	40.0	47.8	71.1	82.8	58.8	45.5	56.3	48.4	52.2
Jews in Israel	55.5	60.0	52.2	28.9	17.2	41.2	54.5	43.8	51.6	47.8

Arabs' feelings of cultural resemblance and closeness are influenced by contacts with Palestinians and Jews. The ties with fellow Palestinians, though meaningful, are generally not common and are even less frequent than encounters with Jews. Only one quarter of the Arabs maintain ties with relatives living across the Green Line or in Arab countries, and less than two fifths pay social or business visits to the West Bank or Gaza Strip (Table 7.12). On the other hand, 74% of the Arabs meet Jews frequently or daily and 61% have Jewish friends (Table 7.13). Of course, for being a numerical and dominant majority, the Jews are less exposed to contact with Arabs (51% maintain some contact with Arabs and 24% also have Arab friends). Of particular significance, however, is the survey finding that the contacts, friendships, and visiting relations between Arab and Jewish leaders of all political streams are universal. This is due to the prevalence of mixed political parties and institutions where leaders from both communities regularly meet, cooperate, and discuss their differences. The open lines of communication on the leadership level are indeed frequently used to reduce interethnic tensions.

Table 7.11 Arabs' Feeling of Closeness

	Arab Public	Estab. Affil. Arab Lead.	Unaffiliated Arab Lead.	DFPE & PLP Arab Lead.	Sons of Village Arab Lead.
Feel closer to					
Arabs in the West Bank and Gaza Strip	60.4	41.7	78.3	90.9	100.0
Jews in Israel	39.6	58.3	21.7	9.1	0.0

Table 7.12 Arabs' Ties with Arabs outside Israel Proper

	Arab Public	Estab. Affil. Arab Lead.	Unaffil-iated Arab Lead.	DFPE & PLP Arab Lead.	Sons of Village Arab Lead.
Ties with relatives living across the Green Line or in Arab countries					
Have relatives there and maintain ties with them	23.6	35.5	43.8	39.0	40.6
Have relatives there but do not maintain ties with them	29.6	29.0	28.1	36.6	37.5
Do not have relatives there	46.8	35.5	28.1	24.4	21.9
Frequency of social visits to the West Bank and Gaza Strip					
Once or more a month	8.9	6.4	15.7	10.0	18.8
Several times a year	29.7	51.6	46.9	37.5	46.9
None	61.4	41.9	37.5	52.5	34.4
Frequency of business visits to the West Bank and Gaza Strip					
Once or more a month	12.5	3.2	9.4	7.5	6.3
Several times a year	23.2	22.6	31.3	10.0	9.4
None	64.3	74.2	59.4	82.5	84.4

Table 7.13 Interethnic Contact

	Arab Public	Estab. Affil. Arab Lead.	Unaffil-iated Arab Lead.	DFPE & PLP Arab Lead.	Sons of Village Arab Lead.	Jewish Public	DFPE & PLP Jewish Lead.	CRM & Mapam Jewish Lead.	Labor Jewish Lead.	Likud Camp Jewish Lead.
Frequency of interethnic contact										
Daily	34.8	78.1	71.9	48.8	46.9	14.5	47.2	20.6	37.5	15.2
Very often	11.0	18.8	18.8	39.0	21.9	13.2	44.4	50.0	35.0	30.2
Often	28.0	3.1	9.4	12.2	31.3	23.4	8.3	23.5	17.5	36.4
Almost never	26.2	0.0	0.0	0.0	0.0	49.0	0.0	5.9	10.0	18.2
Friendship and visiting terms with Jews/Arabs over the past two years										
Have Jewish/Arab friends and have visited them	34.7	90.6	87.5	87.8	62.5	10.1	88.6	70.6	77.5	63.6
Have Jewish/Arab friends but have not visited them	26.5	6.3	9.4	9.8	25.0	14.2	8.6	20.6	7.5	9.1
Have no Jewish/Arab friends	38.8	3.1	3.1	2.4	12.5	75.7	2.9	8.8	15.0	27.3

The trend in Arab-Jewish contacts is mixed, and not to the worse, despite the worsening conditions. On the one hand, the proportion of persons having friends from the other community rose from 61% in 1976 to 66% in 1988 among Israeli Arabs, and from 22.5% in 1980 to 26% in 1988 among Jews (Table 7.14). The percentage of Jews who visit

Arab homes also increased. On the other hand, the proportion of Arabs who visited Jewish homes during the same period decreased. In view of the growing difficulties in maintaining the relationship, the mixed trend can be interpreted as a real achievement. The Arabs have become increasingly dissatisfied with their situation and, as a result, critical of the Jews. They long to be unreservedly accepted by Jews as both equal Israeli citizens and members of the Palestinian people. In reaction, the Jews feel increasingly hard pressed to relax their strict criteria for the Arabs' full entry into Israeli society (an equal assumption of duties, acquiescence in the Jewish consensus on the character of the state and on the Palestinian question, and renunciation of Palestinian loyalties).

Table 7.14 Interethnic Friendship and Visiting Terms, 1976-88

	Arab Public				Jewish Public		
	1976	1980	1985	1988	1980	1985	1988
Friendship and visiting terms with Jews/Arabs over the past two years							
Have Jewish/Arab friends and have visited them	43.3	38.5	34.7	35.8	11.6	10.1	11.0
Have Jewish/Arab friends but have not visited them	17.9	27.9	26.5	30.0	10.9	14.2	14.6
Have no Jewish/Arab friends	38.7	33.6	38.8	34.3	77.5	75.7	74.4

A final, crucial indicator shedding light on the dilemma of Israeli versus Palestinian identity is where the Arabs see their future – in Israel or in an independent state to be established in the West Bank and Gaza Strip. Since most Arabs advocate the formation of a Palestinian state alongside Israel, it is possible that they would face the dilemma of whether to remain in the Jewish state or to move to the new Palestinian state. It is abundantly clear that most Israeli Arabs today are determined to stay, and have become even more determined over the years. In 1988, only 7.5% of the Arabs say they would move to a Palestinian state, 21% would consider moving, and a decisive majority of 72% would not; this compared to 14%, 28%, and 58%, respectively, in 1976 (Table 7.15). The Arabs are resolute in continuing to live in this country because of their ramified bonds with the Jewish state and their firm patrimonial ties with the land, the village, and the family house, all of which they regard as part of the Palestinian homeland and feel bound to preserve by their steadfast presence.

Table 7.15 Arabs' Willingness to Move to a Palestinian State, 1976-88

	Arab Public		
	1976	1980	1988
Willingness to move to a Palestinian state, if it were established alongside Israel			
Yes	14.4	8.3	7.5
Perhaps	27.7	18.1	20.7
No	57.9	73.6	71.8

To conclude, Jewish desires and apprehensions strain the Israeli and Palestinian components in the Arab identity. The Jews continue to fear the Israeli Arabs' relations with the Palestinians and expect them to dissociate themselves from their own people. For the Jews, Palestinian identity has remained subversive and, hence, irreconcilable with Israeli identity. On the other hand, the Arabs are simultaneously Israeli and Palestinian and have to settle these two elements in their identity. They blame the Jews for the contradictions they are forced to experience and believe that peace and harmony would be restored to their identity if the Jews would allow a Palestinian state in the occupied territories and agree to transform Israel into a non-Jewish state. As long as the Jews fail to do so, the Arabs are cornered into a painful dilemma over which they have no control. The Arabs attempt to cope with their predicament, not by abdicating the Israeli or Palestinian links, but rather by fashioning a new synthesis of the two. The rising Israeli-Palestinian identity is the most effective tool Israeli Arabs have devised in their strenuous efforts in the late 1970s to come to terms with the Jewish state, but the Jews have not responded favorably to this novel and growing identity.

8

Institutional Separation

Since both Arabs and Jews are non-assimilating groups, institutional separation should not be a major issue. The Arabs are granted the necessary institutional arrangements to insure their continuous separate existence. These include separate communities, schools, media, and religious-legal devices to discourage intermarriage. Yet, the integration of Arabs into all other walks of Israeli life is a declared and practiced policy of the state, to which policy Arabs subscribe.

The question concerns, therefore, the precise points of disagreement between Arabs and Jews who agree in principle on a mix of separation and integration. The nature of integration, not separation, is really the issue. The authorities seek integration mostly as a means of control lest Arab institutional separation is seized upon to promote national autonomy and be used as a solid base for radical struggle. On the other hand, the Arabs pursue integration primarily as a tool of equality; that is, as a way to avail themselves of the better opportunities in Jewish institutions. They also contend that if Israel is a true democracy, every Arab individual should enjoy the inalienable right to integration.

Arab-Jewish integration in the 1980s caused several controversies. One dispute was over contrived encounters between Arab and Jewish youth arranged by schools or summer camps. Objections were raised by rabbinical circles, especially because of the mixing of boys and girls and the eating of non-kosher food when the Jews are hosted by the Arabs. Jews also opposed Arabs' moving into Natzerat Illit (Upper Nazareth) in order to preserve its Jewish nature. On the other hand, the Arabs, suffering from a severe shortage of housing and seeking better facilities, felt fully entitled to open occupancy. Another frequently discussed matter was the lack of integration of the army; i.e., the exemption of Arabs from military service.

The surveys shed some light on the issue of integration. There is full agreement on the most fundamental question in Arab-Jewish relations; namely, that the desirable pattern is integration without assimilation. Both sides oppose intermarriage: according to the 1988 survey, 97% of the Arabs and 92.5% of the Jews are not willing to have their daughters marry men from the other community. Although not illegal, intermarriage in Israel is socially deviant, rare, and hard to manage in daily life. The demand for civil marriage and divorce is usually voiced by secular Jews in protest against religious coercion in the Jewish community, not out of intentions to legalize or legitimize intermarriage. The disqualification of intermarriage confirms that the Arab minority and Jewish majority are indeed non-assimilating and that social and cultural pluralism in Israel is voluntary in spite of the absence of a viable option of assimilation.

Like intermarriage, separation in residence and education is mostly voluntary and not a cardinal issue. Since, however, some integration is possible without fostering assimilation in these spheres, there is ample room for differences of opinion. The survey findings point to several trends. First, both sides are willing to allow much more integration than the little that prevails presently. Only 30% of the Arabs and 51% of the Jews approve of the near total residential separation splitting the two communities today (Table 8.1). Second, the Arabs are much more interested in integration than the Jews are prepared to permit: 72% of the Arabs, compared with 44% of the Jews, favor new mixed neighborhoods where Arabs and Jews who so wish will live together. Similarly, 79% of the Arabs, but only 48.5% of the Jews, assent to new elementary schools where Arabs and Jews who so wish will have their children study in mixed classrooms and in both languages. Despite the voluntary and partial nature of the suggestion, this endorsement by about half of the Jews of opening an integrated option in housing and schooling indicates a realization that Arab-Jewish coexistence requires some degree of integration. Third, the trend over the years among both Arabs and Jews clearly reveals an increasing desire for integration. The approval of separation of neighborhoods declined from 49% in 1976 to 30% in 1988 among the Arabs, and from 60% in 1980 to 51% in 1985 among the Jews (Table 8.2). And fourth, leaders, who better understand the benefits of greater integration for both groups, tend to favor it and to support new opportunities for closer contacts more than does the public at large. The Likud camp Jewish leaders, particularly the Orthodox among them, constitute a notable exception to this rule because of their reluctance to encourage any step that might eventually lead to assimilation.

The non-participation of the Arabs in the national security institutions (the military and secret services) is probably the most important issue in institutional separation. The official policy since 1948 has been to exempt the Arabs from compulsory army service, seemingly to save them from the possible agony of fighting other Arabs. Although the exemption inflicts on them a stigma of disloyalty and deprives them of numerous economic privileges accorded to army veterans and their families, Israeli Arabs have never challenged the arrangement. Since army service implies an unqualified allegiance to and identification with the state, the Arabs, rather, use their exclusion as a means of displaying their reservations about the Jewish state, their attachment to pan-Arab and Palestinian nationalism, and their protest against discrimination and restrictions. On the other hand, the Druzes, a small minority with a tradition of orienting itself to the ruling majority, adopted a reverse strategy in the late 1950s. They demanded to participate in the defense of the country and since then have employed the draft as a leverage in their fight for full admission and equality in Israeli society.

Table 8.1 Institutional Separation

	Arab Public	Estab. Affil. Arab Lead.	Unaffiliated Arab Lead.	DFPE & PLP Arab Lead.	Sons of Village Arab Lead.	Jewish Public	DFPE & PLP Jewish Lead.	CRM& Mapam Jewish Lead.	Labor Jewish Lead.	Likud Camp Jewish Lead.
Neighborhoods should be separate for Arabs and Jews										
Yes	30.3	9.7	9.7	4.9	22.6	51.2	0.0	8.8	35.1	65.6
Not certain	29.6	16.1	29.0	24.4	29.0	27.8	5.6	29.4	29.7	12.5
No	40.1	74.2	61.3	70.7	48.4	20.9	94.4	61.8	35.1	21.9
In favor of new mixed neighborhoods where Arabs and Jews who so wish will live together	72.0	87.5	93.5	95.1	84.4	43.6	97.2	94.1	84.2	48.5
In favor of new elementary schools where Arabs and Jews who so wish will have their children study in mixed classrooms and in both languages	79.3	90.3	90.6	82.1	77.4	48.5	100.0	100.0	89.7	39.4

Table 8.2 Institutional Separation, 1976-85

	Arab Public			Jewish Public	
	1976	1980	1985	1980	1985
Approve of the separation of Arabs and Jews in					
Schools	49.7	48.0	*	61.8	*
Neighborhoods	49.2	42.2	30.3	60.1	51.2
Political parties	36.5	30.4	*	42.6	*

*Not asked.

The question of the Arab draft has been raised by Jews from time to time. It is usually invoked in the context of fairness or inequity; namely, that the Arabs do not qualify for full rights unless they discharge full duties, including army service. Jews usually suggest that Arabs render some form of civil service as a substitute for the draft, as is the case with some Orthodox Jewish women who prefer to serve as teachers or medical aides than as soldiers. In late 1990, the minister in charge of Arab affairs made public a proposal to institute for Arab men a system of civil national service within and for the Arab localities. The stated purpose was to improve the quality of life in the Arab sector by the provision of free community services and to make Arabs equal to Jews in all the entitlements associated with army service. Nevertheless, the plan was dismissed on three grounds by the Supreme Follow-Up Committee: Arab draftees would relieve more Jews to repress the intifada, Arab volunteers in the Arab sector would release the government from its responsibility to invest there, and such a service was a kind of forced labor (*Haaretz*, January 7 and 10, 1991). Many Arabs see regular civil service as a ploy to expose them as objectors, who do not deserve equal rights, and as a premature, impractical scheme to enlist them long before the settlement of the Palestinian issue.

The questions presented in the survey in this regard were different for Arabs and Jews because it was assumed that the authorities, backed by the Jewish public, would play the role of initiator and policymaker while the Arabs would just react to the government's initiatives. An overwhelming majority of 85% of the Jews favor the status quo and would not impose compulsory military service on Arabs; moreover, 59% object to compulsory civil service for Arabs in lieu of the draft (Table 8.3). More significant, however, is the finding that 38.5% of the Jews favor either mandatory or voluntary military service by Arabs and 70% endorse either mandatory or voluntary civil service. These figures in favor of military or civil service are even higher among Jews who are generally more liberal, educated, or disposed to the Labor camp. For instance, 78% of the Jews who accept the Arabs' right to live in Israel as a national minority with full civil rights favor civil service by Arabs, whereas only 48% of the Jews who reject this right do so. These Jewish desiderata, which digress seriously from the status quo of the complete exemption of Arabs from any duty, reveal more of an openness to integration and equality than a pretext to deny Arabs equal rights and opportunities.

The suspicion that a government demand of Arab men to render some regular service may serve as an excuse to invalidate Arab claims for equality makes sense only for the radical right. The Tehiya, Tsomet, and Moledet parties call on Israeli Arabs to do service or to demote their citizenship status to permanent residence; that is, to give up the right to vote in the Knesset elections. Their hidden agenda is to deprive the Labor camp of Arab votes in order to prevent territorial compromises in Judea and Samaria. This rationale does not apply to the Jewish leaders in the survey, which includes some leaders from the radical right in the Likud camp. This hardline right-wing leadership group opposes military service by Arabs to the same degree as does the non-Zionist, left-wing, Jewish leadership group (62% versus 68%, respectively, Table 8.3). On the other hand, virtually all the Zionist left leaders, who sincerely believe in equality and integration between Arabs and Jews, endorse regular (military or civil) service by Arabs.

Table 8.3 Jews' Attitude toward Military or Civil Service by Arabs

	Jewish Public	DFPE & PLP Jewish Lead.	CRM & Mapam Jewish Lead.	Labor Jewish Lead.	Likud Camp Jewish Lead.
Military service by Arabs					
In favor of compulsory military service	14.7	11.8	2.9	10.3	11.8
In favor of voluntary military service	23.8	20.6	82.4	53.8	26.5
Against	61.5	67.6	14.7	35.9	61.8
Civil service in lieu of military service by Arabs					
In favor of compulsory civil service	40.9	15.2	41.2	57.5	58.8
In favor of voluntary civil service	29.1	36.4	44.1	37.5	32.4
Against	30.0	48.5	14.7	5.0	8.8

Since it is unlikely that Arabs will initiate a call for regular service, they were asked how they would react if such a service were instituted: 81% would advise their sons to refuse military service, and 50% to refuse civil service (Table 8.4). Given a choice between either duty, 7% would advise their sons to join the army, 43% to render civil service, and 50% to decline both options. The refusal to do any service varies considerably with population groups. The figure is 4.5% for the Druzes (who are presently subject to the draft), 32% for the Christians, 43% for the Bedouin, and 62% for other Moslems. It is 28% for Arabs with non-Palestinian Israeli identity, 52% for Arabs with Israeli-Palestinian identity, and 69% for Arabs with non-Israeli Palestinian identity. A total refusal is the position of the decisive majority of the Arab leaders of the DFPE, PLP, and the Sons of the Village Movement. On the other hand, most of the other Arab leaders would go along with civil, but not military, service by Arabs. Refusal also increased, apparently in response to the intifada, from 50% in 1985 to 63% in 1988.

Jewish and Arab attitudes toward military and civil service testify to a much greater willingness to have Arabs render some service, particularly of a civil type, than is usually assumed. It is worth considering the change both before and after the conclusion of a peace settlement. Despite the vocal opposition by representative Arab political bodies to proposals to introduce some form of regular service by Arabs, the survey data justify the immediate undertaking of a program that allows Arabs to volunteer for military or civil service. Such a program would meet the needs of at least that part of the Arab population seeking to obtain the primary gains of integration and would lessen Jewish mistrust. Once the Palestinian question is settled, however, the Arabs should be integrated fully into the state security institutions. In fact, the authorities and the Arab leadership concur on the full enlistment of the Arabs in the event of peace and do not regard the Jewish-Zionist character of the state as a legitimate ground for exclusion or refusal. Arab participation in Israel's security forces in peacetime would stimulate equality with Jews as much as the current non-participation induces inequality.

Table 8.4 Arabs' Attitude toward Military or Civil Service by Arabs

	Arab Public	Estab. Affil. Arab Lead.	Unaffil-iated Arab Lead.	DFPE & PLP Arab Lead.	Sons of Village Arab Lead.
Would advise one's son to refuse to serve if compulsory military service were imposed on Arabs	80.7	51.7	83.9	100.0	100.0
Would advise one's son to refuse to serve if compulsory civil service were imposed on Arabs	50.3	20.0	35.5	92.3	100.0
If a choice were given between military and civil service by Arabs, would advise one's son to					
Serve in military service	7.3	27.6	9.4	0.0	0.0
Serve in civil service	43.0	65.5	59.4	7.5	0.0
Refuse to serve	49.6	6.9	31.3	92.5	100.0

To sum up, Arabs and Jews agree on the need for greater integration between them, but disagree on its specific forms. The Arabs prefer more integration so as to increase their access to resources; Jews support more of the integration that promotes equal duties.

9

National Autonomy

Arabs and Jews are expected to be deeply divided over the question of national autonomy for the Arabs. Being a deprived, non-assimilating, and dissident minority and also being part of the rising Palestinian people and of the regional Arab majority, Israeli Arabs are disposed to seek a measure of self-determination within Israel. This predisposition is reinforced by persistent Arab-Jewish inequality and the failures to narrow this gap. The Jews, on the other hand, conceive of the Arab minority as a potential security threat and of Israel as the homeland of the Jewish people only. They are thus expected to reject Arab claims to autonomous expressions and institutions.

National minorities can have one of three forms of autonomy. The minimal form is "limited institutional autonomy," which refers to a high mobilization and to a network of separate, independent organizations. Yet, the minority possesses only a restricted degree of power, self-control, and state recognition. In the intermediate form, "extended institutional autonomy," the minority's rule over a variety of separate institutions is broad and publicly recognized. The maximal form is "territorial autonomy," by which the state accords to the minority control over a certain territory in which the minority constitutes a regional majority. Territorial autonomy for minorities exists only in federal states and takes such diverse forms as the French and Italian cantons in Switzerland, the province of Quebec in Canada, or one of the four levels of government in the Soviet Union – a republic, an autonomous republic, an autonomous region, and an autonomous area (Connor, 1984: 221). On the other hand, the two institutional, non-territorial forms of autonomy apply to minority members as individuals, irrespective of their place of residence.

How much autonomy do Israeli Arabs enjoy today? They have independent national leadership and a large number of independent organizations in all walks of life. Most Arabs live in incorporated localities, and elected Arab heads manage their local affairs. Three independent, predominantly Arab political parties represent Arab interests and outlooks on most issues, but there are no rejectionist, nationalist Arab parties. At the top of the Israeli Arab organizational structure stands the Supreme Follow-Up Committee, consisting of leaders from all political streams. It deliberates and makes decisions in all important matters of general concern to Arabs in Israel; from time to time it even declares and administers successful general strikes. The Committee maintains four subcommittees – for education, health, welfare, and sports. In 1990, it decided to appeal to the cultural attachés of the foreign embassies in Israel in protest of governmental discrimination in Arab education and it convened with the Egyptian ambassador for this purpose. Furthermore, the Health Subcommittee, following a pattern set by health organizations in the West Bank and Gaza Strip, signed a contract to receive direct financial aid from the European Community (Ha'etzni, 1990). The funds were used to establish and underwrite The Galilee Society for Health Research and Services in the village of Rama.

Although one should not underrate the value of the high level of Arab mobilization, it amounts to no more than a limited institutional autonomy. Israel is a highly centralized, unitary (non-federal) state that does not tolerate full autonomy by local governments or even voluntary associations and does not hesitate to intervene whenever a threat is posed to its central authority. Since the Arab minority is considered a menace to both Israel's national security and its Jewish-Zionist character, the authorities check the accumulation of power by Arab leaders and organizations, deny them official recognition, and curtail their freedom of action.

The Israeli Arabs' stand on the issue of autonomy is ambiguous and complex. First, the Arabs are dissatisfied with the small degree of autonomy they are presently allowed. Second, they desire more autonomy and probably want to gain "extended institutional autonomy." Third, for the time being, territorial autonomy appears to them remote, unrealistic, and counterproductive as an objective, and therefore unappealing.

To explain why the established Arab political leadership rejects the idea of territorial autonomy for Israeli Arabs, the wider context in which autonomy is seen should be examined. The term itself is usually used in Israel to refer to the autonomy plan option in the West Bank and Gaza Strip. The Likud offers the Palestinians, who demand a complete detachment from Israel and an independent state of their own, a limited territorial autonomy. The half-hearted offer is marred by various constraints to foreclose the development of autonomy into a sovereign state. In view of this usage and associated sensitivities, it is no wonder that the term "autonomy" has become the most loaded, explosive concept when applied to Israeli Arabs. In the minds of most Jews, including the more sophisticated leaders, it invokes an alarming equation of the supposedly loyal Israeli Arab citizens with the unruly Palestinians under occupation, subversion, unrest, and eventual secession. Since the Arab leaders are keenly aware of this fearsome meaning and connotation, they shy away from the word "autonomy" in order not to be labelled subversive, not to lose the support of liberal Jews, not to get stuck by an impractical demand, and not to dissipate the credibility of the Palestinian call for an independent state in the territories as a permanent settlement of the conflict.

In mid-1989, the idea of autonomy for Israeli Arabs was raised for public discussion by two Israeli Arab intellectuals, Bishara and Zaidani. Their viewpoint was that once the Palestinian question is settled, Israeli Arabs will have to face Israel alone. Since the Jewish state, by its very nature, cannot make them fully equal with Jews and identify with the state, Israel can and ought to compensate them with autonomy. Israel will not compromise, but rather consolidate, its Jewish character, political stability, and territorial integrity by providing the Palestinian minority with control over its institutions. Autonomy is advocated as the "Golden road" between two extreme, unrealistic alternatives to the Israeli Arabs' predicament – full integration and total separation. One of the two intellectuals promoting these ideas, Bishara, seems to favor an extended institutional autonomy while the other, Zaidani, proposes a full-fledged territorial autonomy (Ozacky-Lazar and Ghanem, 1990). Zaidani goes so far as to call for an intensive Arab campaign, employing continuous general strikes and even civil disobedience, to obtain territorial autonomy. Another Israeli Arab academic, Haidar, who teaches at Beir Zeit University as do Bishara and Zaidani, also strongly advocates national autonomy for the Arab national minority and the transformation of Israel into a binational state (O. Cohen, 1990).[1]

Despite their shared strategy of rejecting territorial autonomy and pushing for extended institutional autonomy while avoiding the loaded term altogether, Arab leaders differ in their approach to this question. The moderates justify autonomy on grounds of expediency; the militants resort to Palestinian nationalism. The review by Ozacky-Lazar and Ghanem (1990) makes these differences abundantly clear. The non-

[1]A symposium for debating the issue by senior representatives of all the political currents in the Arab sector was organized under the auspices of the Jewish-Arab Center at the University of Haifa. It was cancelled at the last moment by the administration in response to external pressures. The authorities feared that such a discussion might have conferred some legitimacy on an idea they frown upon as taboo (Segev, 1990).

partisan chairman of the Supreme Follow-Up Committee condemned the demand for (territorial) autonomy as illegal "secession" and saw it as contradictory to the struggle for equality. He also offered the following explanation for the setting up of the Follow-Up Committee and its subcommittees: "Since the Government fails to act in the area of health, we had to establish a Health Committee. It also does not do much in education, hence an Education Committee had to be created... We think that this is the Government's duty. Yet there is a great deal of discrimination between the Arab and Jewish sectors, so we act independently" (ibid.: 13). Knesset Member Darawshe accounted for his formation of the Democratic Arab Party, which was the only strictly Arab party in existence in 1990, as follows: "It [the Party] is neither a matter of ideology nor strategy. It is a tool to achieve our goals, a pressure group to affect decision making on political issues, as well. When we realize that there is no longer a need for this vehicle, we will transform it into an open Arab-Jewish party" (ibid.).

The view of the Irsraeli Communist Party combines pragmatic and nationalistic rationales in defending institutional autonomy for the Arabs. On the one hand, its genuine commitment to mixed organizations and to a joint Jewish-Arab struggle forces it to employ a vocabulary of expediency. To quote, Jubran, the editor of Al-Ittihad and a top leader of the Party: The Committee of Heads of Arab Local Councils "is a Committee to obtain concrete objectives. It does not stand as an antithesis to cooperation with Jews, but rather as a response to national discrimination. Had discrimination not existed, there would be no need for an association on a national basis.... When we attain equality, I do not want any framework in the state to be purely Arab or Jewish" (ibid.). While the platform of the Communist-led Democratic Front for Peace and Equality in the 1988 Knesset elections called for "the recognition of the Arab population as a national minority and guaranteeing it equal civil and national rights," it left these "national rights" vague and unspecified. On the other hand, the Communist Party also occasionally issues strong statements in favor of autonomous rights. For instance, the "Program for Equality of Civil and National Rights for the Arab Population in Israel," adopted by the Party in its 1985 convention, spelled out certain demands for autonomy. Among other things, it called for legal recognition of the Arab population as a national minority, full equality between Arabs and Jews in civil and national rights, and protection by law of the right of the Arab population to its lands (Israeli Communist Party, 1986: 89-90).

The PLP bases its rationale for extended institutional autonomy expressly on collective national rights. A plank in its 1984 platform for the Knesset elections read as follows: "The Palestinian minority in Israel is entitled to form its national, cultural, social, and political institutions (like the Committee of Heads of Arab Local Councils), as practiced in the best democratic states (e.g., Jews in Western countries)." The nationalistic wording of a similar clause in the Party's platform presented at its third convention, in July 1990, was even more explicit:

> Our Arab masses demand to implement their rights as a national minority, which is distinct nationally, culturally, and in way of life... We have to conduct our special life by forming cultural, social, and political institutions, to administer our own educational and cultural affairs, to launch an Arab university for strengthening our national Arab-Palestinian identity. We must manage the Waqf, the welfare services, to develop the villages and towns by subsidizing Arab agriculture and constructing industries in the Arab sector.

The head of the PLP, Knesset Member Mouhamad Mi'ari, declared in this regard: "I'm not the only one among my people who has despaired of the chance to achieve equality. We have despaired of Arab-Jewish cooperation.... Today I and many others have reached the conclusion that we must give up the demand for the unattained equality and call instead for self-rule" (Algazi, 1990).

The Islamic Movement is supposed to be the most susceptible group in the Israeli Arab population to extended institutional autonomy. In fact, it acts rigorously to create a fully autonomous network of Islamic organizations and services. Unlike other Arab organizations which depend for funding on external sources (the three predominantly Arab political parties receive monies from the state and many Arab voluntary associations raise funds abroad), the Islamic Movement derives its financial and other resources from the local community and invests them back in it. More importantly, institutional autonomy is the raison d'être of the Movement because its worldview revolves around a self-administered Moslem community and the idea that Moslems should be ruled by Moslems. Although the Movement is prudent not to make public its pro-autonomy inclination, the platform of the Islamic list for the local election in Kabul, a village in the lower Galilee, called for extensive autonomy for the Arabs.

The Sons of the Village Movement would support the broadest autonomy possible for the Arabs in Israel. A territorial autonomy would be the lesser evil if Israeli Arabs are forced to remain part of the Jewish state. This rejectionist Movement prefers a Palestinian state in all of the area of Mandatory Palestine or a Palestinian state in the West Bank and Gaza Strip that will continue the fight for the total liberation of Palestine.

The Israeli authorities attempt to contain the Arabs' endeavors to expand the limited autonomy they have already gained through continuous struggle. The authorities refuse Arabs the status of a national minority with collective rights. Jews fear that Arab national autonomy might turn into a firm power base for challenging Jewish dominance, might erode Israel's Jewish-Zionist character and transform it into a binational state, and might become a prelude to a separatist movement. Hence, the policy is to reinforce traditional divisions among the Arabs, to manipulate their separate institutions, to deny recognition to their independent and broadly-based organizations and leaders, and to undermine their territorial contiguity.

Jewish objections to Arab autonomous institutions are a matter of public record. In 1980, the government banned the convening of a Congress of the Arab Masses for fear of their building a mass power base and validating a claim to speak for the entire Arab population (*Haaretz*, December 2, 1980). Gur-Arye, then the Prime Minister's Adviser on Arab Affairs, expounded in a programmatic article his vehement opposition to the forming of the Supreme Follow-Up Committee composed of all Arab Knesset Members – pro-Zionist and Communist. He argued that the extremists take over such representative Arab bodies, civil demands are turned into nationalist claims, and extremism and confrontation with the authorities become inevitable (Gur-Arye, 1982). Gilboa, another Adviser on Arab Affairs, submitted in late 1987 a confidential document in which he warned the Government against Israeli Arab efforts to lay the foundations for autonomy much like the pre-1948 Jewish institution-building that led to Jewish statehood (*Maariv*, October 25, 1987). Another official explained: "The Supreme Follow-Up Committee and its subcommittees are no doubt increasingly perceived as a forum leading the Arabs in Israel, and actually seeking secession, like national institutions in the making" (quoted by Ha'etzni, 1990). This government official's conviction was well articulated in 1990 by Olmart, the Minister in Charge of Arab Affairs:

> I think that whoever speaks of autonomy means consolidation of the infrastructure that would bring about the secession of Israeli Arabs from the state. This is absolutely clear. There are today preparedness and desire for such a process on the part of the Arabs in Israel. In my opinion, this is the reason that we should not recognize the Arab Follow-Up Committee. The Committee strives to accord legitimacy to the idea of autonomy by its very dwelling on it. Hence, our stand on this matter must be firm and there should be absolutely no cooperation with all persons concerned (ibid.).

The policy to curb the Arab push for extended institutional autonomy is generally accepted by Jewish political parties and movements. A commentator in the Histadrut daily, *Davar*, voiced the suspicion of mainstream Labor thinkers that pro-autonomy Arabs are disguised separatists and rejectionists: "Those demanding autonomy do not represent, in the meantime, the majority of the Arab public, but there is a basis for the fear that they are the forerunners. Autonomy will not be their final destination. They will speak of the right to self-determination, the annexation of the Galilee and Triangle, the majority of whose inhabitants are Palestinian, to a Palestinian state, and finally we will have to struggle for Jewish autonomy in the Greater Palestinian state in all of Eretz Israel" (Landras, 1990). The Zionist left, despite its respect for Arab rights, is reserved about autonomy because it believes that the Arabs will generally benefit more from integration. At the same time it shows sympathy for certain demands. For instance, the Citizens' Rights Movement, in its platform for the 1988 Knesset elections, called for the government's recognition of the Committee of Heads of Arab Local Councils.

The survey findings confirm these observations. National autonomy presupposes the acquisition of national character and potential unity by the Arab minority. When asked about the extent and kind of internal divisions within the Arab minority, only 37% of the Arabs and 35.5% of the Jews perceive these divisions to be mainly religion and hamula (Table 9.1). This proportion among the Arabs dropped even further, to 23% in 1988. The majority sees the Arabs as a politically divided or not particularly divided national minority, capable of overcoming its traditional splits. Arab leaders downplay sectarian and kinship lines more than Jewish leaders do. Thus, traditional cleavages as a hindrance to national autonomy are to a large extent overcome.

Table 9.1 Perception of Internal Divisions among Arabs in Israel

	Arab Public	Estab. Affil. Arab Lead.	Unaffiliated Arab Lead.	DFPE & PLP Arab Lead.	Sons of Village Arab Lead.	Jewish Public	DFPE & PLP Jewish Lead.	CRM & Mapam Jewish Lead.	Labor Jewish Lead.	Likud Camp Jewish Lead.
Arabs in Israel are										
Divided mostly by religion and hamula	37.0	46.7	26.7	0.0	6.7	35.5	4.8	36.8	56.0	50.0
Divided mostly by political opinion	30.8	30.0	46.7	80.0	50.0	37.9	61.9	52.6	32.0	23.1
Not particularly divided	32.2	23.3	26.7	20.0	43.3	26.6	33.3	10.5	12.0	26.9

This generalization is valid despite the prevalence of covert rivalry among the Druzes, Christians, and Moslems. The civil war in Lebanon and Israel's involvement in it, the rise of the Islamic Movement in Israel and elsewhere, and the increasing pressure over limited resources in Arab localities have intensified friction among the Arab religious communities. Specific inquiries were made in the 1988 Arab survey in this regard. Arabs conceding the adverse effects on relations among the three religious communities of Islamic fundamentalism constitute 25%; of

Israel's War in Lebanon - 31%; and of competition for civil service jobs - 62% (Table 9.2).

A majority of Arabs and only a minority of Jews favor, without reservation, Arab control of existing Arab institutions. In the very important case of Arab education, Arab public support amounts to 71.5%, compared with 37% among the Jewish public; it is 70% to 82.5% among Arab leaders, compared with 26.5% to 42% among Zionist Jewish leaders (Table 9.3). A similar discord no doubt prevails with regard to the Waqf (Moslem endowments), which so far is managed by government appointees.

Table 9.2 Arabs' Perception of Factors Shaping Religious Divisions among Them

	Arab Public
Hold that Islamic fundamentalism in Israel adversely affects the relations among the Arab religious communities	24.7
Hold that Israel's War in Lebanon adversely affects the relations among the Arab religious communities	30.8
There exists competition for civil service jobs between the Arab religious communities in Israel	
To a great degree	14.2
To a considerable degree	18.5
To a certain degree	28.9
Almost none	38.4

Source: The 1988 survey.

Table 9.3 Arab Control of Arab Education

	Arab Public	Estab. Affil. Arab Lead.	Unaffiliated Arab Lead.	DFPE & PLP Arab Lead.	Sons of Village Arab Lead.	Jewish Public	DFPE & PLP Jewish Lead.	CRM & Mapam Jewish Lead.	Labor Jewish Lead.	Likud Camp Jewish Lead.
Arabs should control and manage their own system of education										
In favor	71.5	76.7	70.0	82.5	80.6	37.2	72.2	42.4	30.0	26.5
Have reservations	21.2	16.7	26.7	7.5	16.1	29.1	25.0	45.5	42.5	35.3
Against	7.3	6.7	3.3	10.0	3.2	33.7	2.8	12.1	27.5	38.2

Sharper disagreement between Arabs and Jews is noticeable in the formation of new, independent Arab organizations like an Arab university, Arab media, and an Arab trade union. From 85% to 88% of the Arabs and 23% to 26% of the Jews approve of these institutions (Table 9.4). Although controversy on the leadership level is also wide, it is noteworthy that Arab leaders are internally divided over the wisdom of setting up an Arab trade union because many believe in the unity of the proletariat and in the effective protection that the Histadrut extends to Arab workers. On the other hand, 51.5% of the leaders from the Zionist left support independent Arab media, and 54.5% an Arab university. Several requests to establish an Arab university in Arab Nazareth were turned down during the 1980s by the Council on Higher Education.

Table 9.4 Formation of Independent Arab Organizations

	Arab Public	Estab. Affil. Arab Lead.	Unaffil-iated Arab Lead.	DFPE & PLP Arab Lead.	Sons of Village Arab Lead.	Jewish Public	DFPE & PLP Jewish Lead.	CRM & Mapam Jewish Lead.	Labor Jewish Lead.	Likud Camp Jewish Lead.
Unreservedly in favor of forming each of the following as an independent Arab organization										
University	88.1	62.5	71.9	97.5	90.6	25.9	83.3	54.5	25.0	20.6
Mass media	86.1	31.3	54.8	81.1	87.5	23.4	68.6	51.5	18.4	11.8
Trade union	85.3	31.3	59.4	50.0	90.6	24.7	13.9	26.5	7.7	26.5

The gap between Arabs and Jews in their endorsement of independent Arab organizations has widened over the years. Arab support rose from 68%-70.5% in 1976 to 85%-88% in 1988, while Jewish support rose from 17%-22% in 1980 to 23%-25% in 1988 (Table 9.5).

Table 9.5 Formation of Independent Arab Organizations, 1976-85

	Arab Public			Jewish Public	
	1976	1980	1985	1980	1985
Unreservedly in favor of forming each of the following as an independent Arab organization					
University	70.5	71.0	88.1	22.1	25.9
Mass media	68.5	71.9	86.1	17.1	23.4
Trade union	68.4	63.1	85.3	19.0	24.7

The Israeli model for minority autonomy is certainly the successful minority of Orthodox Jews, who enjoy full control of a variety of institutions. Asked about this model, 65% of the Arabs, as against only 30% of the Jews, agree to have Arabs organize independently as do Orthodox Jews (Table 9.6). On the other hand, Jewish leaders show more enthusiasm about this possibility than do Arab leaders, perhaps hoping to coopt the Arab minority.

Autonomy also requires recognition of representative leadership. The Committee of Heads of Arab Local Councils is the most representative elected body in the Arab population (Al-Haj and Rosenfeld, 1990).

Although backed by most Arabs, it is denied recognition by the government. Perhaps on that account, 64% of the Jews do not even know of the Committee, and 75% of those familiar with it oppose its official recognition (Table 9.6). Jewish leaders are less opposed to the Committee than is the Jewish public because they better understand the necessity of dealing and negotiating with such an Arab political body that is as legitimate as parallel bodies in the Jewish sector, in particular the Committee of Heads of Development Towns.

Table 9.6 Independent Arab Organizing

	Arab Public	Estab. Affil. Arab Lead.	Unaffiliated Arab Lead.	DFPE & PLP Arab Lead.	Sons of Village Arab Lead.	Jewish Public	DFPE & PLP Jewish Lead.	CRM & Mapam Jewish Lead.	Labor Jewish Lead.	Likud Camp Jewish Lead.
Agree that Arabs should become organized independently, like Orthodox Jews, in order to advance their vital interests	65.0	37.6	48.2	33.4	64.0	29.7	50.0	61.3	39.5	54.8
Advocated position toward the Committee of Heads of Arab Local Councils										
Recognize the Committee	*	*	*	*	*	25.1[a]	100.0	90.0	51.4	34.6
Negotiate with it without recognizing it	*	*	*	*	*	32.4[a]	0.0	10.0	27.0	19.2
Ignore it	*	*	*	*	*	25.1[a]	0.0	0.0	16.2	42.3
Outlaw it	*	*	*	*	*	17.4[a]	0.0	0.0	5.4	3.8

*Not asked. [a]Based on the 35.7% of Jews who knew of the existence of the Committee.

The type of ethnic politics reflects enormously on the kind of autonomy extended to minorities, especially in countries like Israel where politics is central to the society. Five options regarding Arab politics were spelled out, and respondents were asked to choose the most desirable one:

1. Withdrawal: "No political party organization at all."

2. Integration: "To join existing Jewish parties as individuals with equal status."

3. Cooperative (or coalitionary) Arab parties: "To form Arab parties that can reach agreement or cooperate with the existing Jewish parties." The idea is to have independent Arab (or predominantly Arab) parties that are eligible for inclusion in government coalitions, like the non-Zionist, ultra-Orthodox Agudat Israel or Shas parties, but unlike the past election lists comprised of Arab dignitaries affiliated with Jewish parties. The Democratic Arab Party, which was founded in 1988 and which won one seat in the Knesset, can serve as a good example for such parties.

4. Oppositionist Arab-Jewish parties: "To belong to non-Zionist parties composed of Arabs and Jews." The Israeli Communist Party and the Progressive List for Peace are prime examples of this option.

5. Nationalist Arab parties: "To establish independent nationalist Arab parties." Such parties are perceived by the authorities as radical, rejectionist, or subversive. Arabs are keenly aware of the government's antagonism, particularly in view of the outlawing in 1965 of Al-Ard – the only attempt to set up a nationalist Arab party.

Arabs and Jews disagree on the most appropriate option for Arab politics: 86% of the Arabs favor independent Arab parties (the last three options), whereas only 47% of the Jews are ready to accept such organizations (Table 9.7). The disagreement, however, is wider, since 60% of the Arabs desire radical parties (the last two options), something only 13% of the Jews would tolerate. On the other hand, 53% of the Jews regard withdrawal or integration as the best options; only 14% of the Arabs embrace these methods. The single model that enjoys the widest agreement between Arabs and Jews is that of independent, cooperative Arab parties. In contrast, the model of nationalist Arab parties is the most disputed. In response to a separate, direct question, 58.5% of the Arabs, but only 15% of the Jews, favor the formation of nationalist Arab parties. The Arab leaders' preferences reflect the political streams to which they belong. For instance, most of those attached to the Zionist establishment prefer the integrationist model. It is interesting to note that only 30% of the rejectionist leaders from the Sons of the Village Movement opt for the boycott of Israeli national politics; most show realism by preferring oppositionist or nationalist parties. The first choice on the Jewish side is integration of the Arabs in Jewish parties; only the non-Zionist leaders advocate emulation of their own experience of mixed parties. There is also appreciable support among Jewish leaders for coalitionary Arab parties.

Looking at the trend over time of the most desirable form of Arab politics, we find several changes on both sides, which reduces the discord between them. Of utmost importance is the rise of cooperative Arab parties, from 4% in 1976 to 24% in 1988 (Table 9.8). On the other hand, the oppositionist and nationalist parties lost some Arab support during this period. This shows that the growing politicization of the Arabs intensifies their need and longing for power, which only coalitionary Arab parties can satisfy. Over the years, the Jews have increasingly come to understand that Arab integration in Zionist parties is not too realistic. Hence, their backing of this model dropped from 34% in 1980 to 20% in 1988, while their tolerance of non-Zionist oppositionist and nationalist parties rose from 9% to 20%.

Table 9.7 Independent Arab Political Parties

	Arab Public	Estab. Affil. Arab Lead.	Unaffiliated Arab Lead.	DFPE & PLP Arab Lead.	Sons of Village Arab Lead.	Jewish Public	DFPE & PLP Jewish Lead.	CRM& Mapam Jewish Lead.	Labor Jewish Lead.	Likud Camp Jewish Lead.
The most desirable type of political organization for Arabs today is										
To join existing Jewish parties as individuals with equal status	7.4	59.4	12.9	0.0	0.0	25.2	0.0	56.7	55.6	70.0
To form Arab parties that can reach agreement or cooperate with the existing Jewish parties	25.6	15.6	29.0	12.2	0.0	33.8	3.3	30.0	44.4	26.7
To belong to non-Zionist parties composed of Arabs and Jews	36.9	21.9	48.4	80.5	46.7	9.5	96.7	3.3	0.0	0.0
To establish independent nationalist Arab parties	23.2	3.1	9.7	4.9	23.3	3.7	0.0	10.0	0.0	0.0
No political party organization at all	7.0	0.0	0.0	2.4	30.0	27.7	0.0	0.0	0.0	3.3
Formation of an independent nationalist Arab party										
In favor	58.5	25.0	53.1	27.5	36.7	15.0	25.0	32.3	25.0	18.8
Have reservations	22.2	25.0	21.9	20.0	20.0	20.3	38.9	38.7	33.3	12.5
Against	19.4	50.0	25.0	52.5	43.3	64.7	36.1	29.0	41.7	68.8

Table 9.8 Independent Arab Political Parties, 1976-88

	Arab Public				Jewish Public		
	1976	1980	1985	1988	1980	1985	1988
The most desirable type of political organization for Arabs today is							
To join existing Jewish parties as individuals with equal status	6.6	15.1	7.4	5.8	33.7	25.2	19.9
To form Arab parties that can reach agreement or cooperate with the existing Jewish parties	3.9	28.6	25.6	24.4	32.7	33.8	35.1
To belong to non-Zionist parties composed of Arabs and Jews	41.4	31.4	36.9	33.6	5.6	9.5	11.9
To establish independent nationalist Arab parties	35.9	18.1	23.2	27.1	3.7	3.7	8.2
No political party organization at all	12.2	6.7	7.0	9.2	24.3	27.7	24.8
Formation of an independent national Arab party							
In favor	62.3	48.2	58.5	*	13.1	15.0	*
Have reservations	20.3	28.5	22.2	*	20.2	20.3	*
Against	17.4	23.3	19.4	*	66.7	64.7	*

*Not asked.

The most revealing indication of the willingness to integrate Arabs into Israeli society is to have them participate in coalition governments. This means having basic trust in the Arabs and allowing them to enter Israeli politics, negotiate, have an impact on decision-making, and receive their share of national resources. On this matter, 87% of the Arabs and 39% of the Jews approve of the Arabs' participation in coalition governments (Table 9.9). These figures are somewhat lower in the case of the possibility, created after the 1984 Knesset elections, of forming a Labor government supported by the DFPE and PLP. The strong Arab desire to be part of Israeli coalition politics is further evidenced in the willingness of 68% of the Arab respondents in the 1988 survey to vote for "a new, independent party that strives to participate in the coalition government in order to advance the interests of Israeli Arabs." The non-rejectionist Arab leaders approve of Arab inclusion in coalition governments, whereas most Jewish leaders of the mainstream Labor and Likud parties oppose cooperation with the DFPE and PLP, which they consider radical (as shown in the figures in Table 9.9).

Table 9.9 Arab Participation in Coalition Government

	Arab Public	Estab. Affil. Arab Lead.	Unaffil-iated Arab Lead.	DFPE & PLP Arab Lead.	Sons of Village Arab Lead.	Jewish Public	DFPE & PLP Jewish Lead.	CRM& Mapam Jewish Lead.	Labor Jewish Lead.	Likud Camp Jewish Lead.
Favor the participation in coalition government of existing or new political parties that truly represent the interests of Arabs in Israel	86.9	100.0	96.9	61.0	3.1	38.8	96.7	97.1	88.9	63.6
Favor in principle the possibility, created after the 1984 Knesset elections, of forming a Labor government supported also by the DFPE and PLP	72.7	83.9	93.3	67.5	6.2	23.2	96.4	96.9	34.2	2.9

The nascent possibility that arose in the aftermath of the 1984 elections to form a narrow Labor government dependent on the support of predominantly Arab parties gathered momentum in March 1990. At that time the Labor Party left the national unity government and even signed an agreement with the DFPE in this regard. The attempt was aborted by a lack of legitimacy, in the eyes of the Jewish public and the religious parties that were supposed to participate in the new Labor coalition, of a coalition that depends for its existence on Arab support. Both the attempt and the failure to establish, for the first time in Israel, a coalition government that included independent, oppositionist Arab members of the Knesset are equally significant. The survey figures and these political developments demonstrate the yearning of Israeli Arabs to be part and parcel of the Israeli mainstream as well as the reservations and apprehensions of the Jews with regard to such a possibility.

The Arabs' overwhelming longing to integrate into mainstream Israeli politics does not square well either with the explicit desire of 33% of them in 1980 and 34% in 1985 to obtain self-rule in the Galilee and Triangle (Table 9.10), with the 46% in 1985 and 40% in 1988 who disagree that these regions should remain integral parts of Israel, or with the 48% in 1985 who wish these areas to be ceded to a Palestinian state if one were established in the West Bank and Gaza Strip (Table 9.11). Since the Galilee and Triangle were designated for a Palestinian state according to the 1947 UN partition plan and since these regions comprise the residence of over 80% of Israeli Arabs today, the lingering Arab sentiment for self-determination should by no means be slighted. On the other hand, the absence of support, as shown in the surveys and in public statements, by the Israeli Arab leadership (except the rejectionist) for such nationalist demands together with staunch Jewish objections will effectively avert the transformation of this Arab hope into a political struggle.

Table 9.10 Regional Autonomy

	Arab Public	Estab. Affil. Arab Lead.	Unaffiliated Arab Lead.	DFPE & PLP Arab Lead.	Sons of Village Arab Lead.	Jewish Public	DFPE & PLP Jewish Lead.	CRM& Mapam Jewish Lead.	Labor Jewish Lead.	Likud Camp Jewish Lead.
Arab self-rule in the Galilee and Triangle										
In favor	34.0	3.2	19.4	42.1	61.3	9.7	9.1	12.1	0.0	2.9
Have reservations	35.1	19.4	32.3	15.8	12.9	29.4	45.5	18.2	7.7	11.8
Against	30.9	77.4	48.4	42.1	25.8	60.9	45.5	69.7	92.3	85.3

Table 9.11 Arabs' View of Irredentism

	Arab Public	Estab. Affil. Arab Lead.	Unaffiliated Arab Lead.	DFPE & PLP Arab Lead.	Sons of Village Arab Lead.
The Galilee and Triangle should remain as integral parts of Israel					
Agree	54.1	100.0	90.3	82.1	0.0
Disagree	45.9	0.0	9.7	17.9	100.0
If a Palestinian state were to be established, the Galilee and Triangle should be					
Integral parts of Israel	51.8	100.0	93.5	86.5	0.0
Parts of a Palestinian state	48.2	0.0	6.5	13.5	100.0

In conclusion, Arabs seek and Jews oppose national autonomy for the Arabs. Since the mid-1970s, the Arabs have been mobilizing, organizing, and gaining a measure of control over their separate institutions and communities. They find the "limited institutional autonomy" currently extended to them to be insufficient, and they want to expand it markedly. Most importantly, they act through three political parties that they dominate – 59% of the Arabs voted for these in 1988 – and that a majority consider the preferred way to ensure their independent status and influence in Israeli politics. The Supreme Follow-Up Committee serves as a top, representative, national, decision-making body; it has proven itself in taking numerous important resolutions and rallying the Arab population for general strikes and other protest actions. The Arabs' demands for autonomy include official recognition of the representative bodies they have formed, control of Arab education and the Waqf, and permission to open an Arab university. Although the call for territorial autonomy has been raised by a few Arab intellectuals, only a third of the Arab public wants self-rule in the Galilee and Triangle, and about half expresses a secessionist sentiment. Generally speaking, the Arabs pursue an officially recognized, broad status of a national minority, infusing a certain degree of binationalism into the state. The Jews insist on keeping Israel strictly Jewish and on confining Arabs to a standing of an ethnic, not a national, minority. This issue is bound to remain divisive for years to come because the manifestations of national autonomy are numerous and diverse; hence, the room for friction between the two sides is substantial.

10

Group Goals

Dominant and non-dominant groups may strive for convergent or divergent goals. Assimilation and egalitarian pluralism are the two most widespread goals common to minorities and majorities in democratic states, but both do not hold for Israel. Assimilation is not a common goal, simply because it is rejected by both Arabs and Jews. Egalitarian pluralism also cannot serve as a mutually accepted goal, because in a state of and for Jews it would amount to a denial of a superior status to the Jews. The Arabs are as prone to consent to such an aim as the Jews to oppose it.

With these tendencies in mind, it is possible to spell out six major goals that Arabs and Jews may pursue vis-à-vis each other. These overall objectives can rightly be conceived of as preferred solutions to their troubled relations or as policies to be adopted by the state toward Israeli Arabs.

Following is a list of the six group goals, a general definition of each goal, and the precise wording used in the survey questions to describe them:

1. *Exclusion.* This group goal is obviously relevant only to Jews who believe that the single solution to the Arab minority problem is that "Arabs will be forced to live outside Israel." Transfer of the Arab population from Palestine was a possibility raised by some Zionist leaders during the Mandatory period and has recently been revived by the late Rabbi Kahane's agitation. Although some extreme leaders may privately favor transfer of Israeli Arabs, none of the parties from the radical right advocates it. Even the Moledet Party calls for the voluntary removal only of the Palestinians from the West Bank and Gaza Strip, not of the Arab citizens of Israel.

2. *Domination.* Continued Jewish domination is also an option pertinent to Jews alone. It is expressed in ideas such as "increase in surveillance over Arabs" and "Arabs will live in Israel only if they are

resigned to their minority status in a state designed for Jews." It could be argued that in most cases, Jewish domination also underlies the ambiguous option of "continuation of the present policy" toward the Arab minority. Although the cornerstones of the official policy toward the Arabs are equality and integration, the actual practice is discrimination, denial of national autonomy, and Jewish domination (Smooha, 1982).

3. *Equal Opportunity*. This means "achievement of equality and integration with Jews" or that "Arabs will live in Israel as a national minority with full civil rights." The problem can be resolved by ensuring the Arabs individual civil rights and protection against discrimination.

4. *Consociationalism*. Rather than offering equal opportunity to Arabs as individuals, it is possible to furnish them with national autonomy, collective rights, or even partnership with the Jews. This solution is reflected in phrases like "allowing Arabs to get organized independently and become partners in state institutions," "Arabs will live in Israel as a national minority recognized by the state and enjoying proper political representation," and "granting Arabs a separate legal status like the autonomy offered to the Arabs in the West Bank and Gaza Strip."

5. *Secession*. Arabs may feel that their situation will be normalized only by repartition; i.e., through Israel's return to the 1947 UN partition borders, so that: "Arabs will live in a Palestinian state to be established in the West Bank, Gaza Strip, the Galilee, and Triangle." For Jews, retreat to the 1947 boundaries is unthinkable.

6. *Non-sectarianism*. Arabs may believe that the best solution is that they "will live in a secular-democratic state to be established in all of Palestine instead of Israel." Since this slogan of the Rejection Front implies the dismantling of Israel, Jews suspect it to be only a cover for replacing the Jewish state by a Palestinian state; in other words, non-sectarianism will amount to reverse Palestinian domination.

The surveys presented several combinations of these six suggested solutions to the Arab minority problem. On all the questions asked, Arabs and Jews are found to be deeply divided over their preferences. An overall glimpse into the disagreements emerges from the question that entails all six options (Table 10.1). The Arabs' order of priorities is consociationalism (31.5%), secession (24%), equal opportunity (23%), and non-sectarianism (16%); the Jews' preferences are domination (34%), equal opportunity (26%), exclusion (22%), and consociationalism (15%). A large Arab majority of 72% desires consociationalism, secession, or non-sectarianism, which a larger Jewish majority of 82% disfavors. The dissension is sharpest on the extreme possibilities: 41% of the Arabs as against only 4% of the Jews opt for secession and non-sectarianism; furthermore, 56% of the Jews compared to but 4.5% of the Arabs accept exclusion and domination.

Table 10.1 Solution to the Arab Minority Problem

	Arab Public	Estab. Affil. Arab Lead.	Unaffil-iated Arab Lead.	DFPE & PLP Arab Lead.	Sons of Village Arab Lead.	Jewish Public	DFPE & PLP Jewish Lead.	CRM & Mapam Jewish Lead.	Labor Jewish Lead.	Likud Camp Jewish Lead.
The most appropriate solution to the Arab minority problem										
Arabs will be forced to live outside Israel	1.0	0.0	0.0	0.0	0.0	21.9	0.0	0.0	0.0	3.0
Arabs will live in Israel only if they are resigned to their minority status in a state designed for Jews	3.5	3.1	0.0	0.0	0.0	33.9	0.0	0.0	12.5	66.7
Arabs will live in Israel as a national minority with full civil rights	23.2	53.1	23.3	15.8	0.0	25.8	45.5	63.6	62.5	27.3
Arabs will live in Israel as a national minority recognized by the state and enjoying proper political representation	31.5	43.8	66.7	73.7	0.0	14.7	54.5	36.4	25.0	3.0
Arabs will live in a Palestinian state to be established in the West Bank, Gaza Strip, the Galilee, and the Triangle	24.4	0.0	3.3	0.0	3.3	2.6	0.0	0.0	0.0	0.0
Arabs will live in a secular-democratic state to be established in all of Palestine instead of Israel	16.3	0.0	6.7	10.5	96.7	1.1	0.0	0.0	0.0	0.0

The controversies on the leadership level are equally striking. Among the Arab leaders, those affiliated with the establishment are split between equal opportunity and consociationalism; the unaffiliated and those belonging to the DFPE and PLP prefer consociationalism; while the rejectionists select non-sectarianism. In contrast, among the Jewish leaders, the non-Zionists fall between equal opportunity and consociationalism; a majority of those in the Zionist left and Labor choose equal opportunity; while most of the hardliners in the Likud camp wish to retain Jewish domination.

Arab-Jewish polarization on both the public and leadership is almost complete, as a majority of the Arabs disagree with a majority of the Jews on the goal that should direct their mutual relations. Between 1985 and 1988, however, a certain reduction in this polarization took place (Table 10.2). The proportion of Arabs selecting the extreme options of secession and non-sectarianism decreased from 41% to 31.5%, pushing up the option of consociationalism from 31.5% to 44%. Although a fifth of the Jews continued to pick exclusion, the proportion allowing consociationalism rose from 15% to 23%, pushing down the option of equal opportunity from 34% to 26%. A rise in realism among both sides is apparent despite the intifada.

Table 10.2 Solution to the Arab Minority Problem, 1985-88

	Arab Public		Jewish Public	
	1985	1988	1985	1988
The most appropriate solution to the Arab minority problem				
Arabs will be forced to live outside Israel	1.0	0.4	21.9	20.4
Arabs will live in Israel only if they are resigned to their minority status in a state designed for Jews	3.5	4.1	33.9	25.6
Arabs will live in Israel as a national minority with full civil rights	23.2	20.1	25.8	24.2
Arabs will live in Israel as a national minority recognized by the state and enjoying proper political representation	31.5	44.0	14.7	22.9
Arabs will live in a Palestinian state to be established in the West Bank, Gaza Strip, the Galilee, and the Triangle	24.4	16.5	2.6	5.1
Arabs will live in a secular-democratic state to be established in all of Palestine instead of Israel	16.3	15.0	1.1	1.8

This broad choice among the six options is completely hypothetical because exclusion, secession, and non-sectarianism are virtually unavailable. When respondents were offered only the other three realistic possibilities, the Arab-Jewish discord became even wider (Table 10.3). When limited to these non-extreme choices, about half of the Arabs chose equal opportunity (47%) and about half preferred moderate or substantial consociationalism (33% favored partnership in state institutions and 16%, full-fledged autonomy). The non-rejectionist Arab leaders lean more toward equal opportunity than does the public at large, whereas the overwhelming majority of the rejectionist Sons of the Village Movement desires consociationalism, especially "the autonomy offered to the Arabs in the West Bank and Gaza Strip." On the other hand, 70% of the Jewish public and 74% of the leaders from the Likud camp opt for the status quo of Jewish domination or for its reinforcement by increased surveillance. In contrast, the other Jewish leaders recognize the inadequacy of the present or even more hardline policy and endorse a policy of non-discrimination. The apparent agreement between most Arab and Jewish leaders on the goal of equal opportunity in this question probably stems from the vague and unattractive wording of the moderate consociational option ("allowing Arabs to organize independently and become partners in state institutions").

Table 10.3 Advocated Policy toward the Arabs in Israel

	Arab Public	Estab. Affil. Arab Lead.	Unaffiliated Arab Lead.	DFPE & PLP Arab Lead.	Sons of Village Arab Lead.	Jewish Public	DFPE & PLP Jewish Lead.	CRM& Mapam Jewish Lead.	Labor Jewish Lead.	Likud Camp Jewish Lead.
Policy that the state should adopt today toward the Arabs in Israel										
Increase in surveillance over Arabs	1.5	0.0	0.0	0.0	0.0	36.9	0.0	0.0	0.0	19.4
Continuation of the present policy	2.3	0.0	0.0	0.0	0.0	33.3	0.0	2.9	13.2	54.8
Achievement of equality and integration with Jews	47.2	71.0	65.6	62.5	13.6	19.8	62.9	70.6	86.8	19.4
Allowing Arabs to organize independently and become partners in state institutions	33.3	29.0	34.4	30.0	18.2	7.3	34.3	26.5	0.0	3.2
Granting Arabs separate legal status, like the autonomy offered to the Arabs in the West Bank and Gaza Strip	15.6	0.0	0.0	7.5	68.2	2.6	2.9	0.0	0.0	3.2

The support for consociationalism among both sides has been on the rise over the years. It went from 36% in 1976 to 47.5% in 1988 among the Arabs, and from 5% in 1980 to 17% in 1988 among the Jews (Table 10.4). The proportion of Jews advocating "an increase in surveillance over the Arabs" dropped from 43% to 34.5% during the 1980-88 period. The Arab-Jewish gap is still very wide despite some moderation among the Jews.

Table 10.4 Advocated Policy toward the Arabs in Israel, 1980-88

	Arab Public			Jewish Public		
	1980	1985	1988	1980	1985	1988
Policy that the state should adopt today toward the Arabs in Israel						
Increase in surveillance over Arabs	1.2	1.5	1.1	42.7	36.9	34.5
Continuation of the present policy	5.3	2.3	3.2	30.8	33.3	33.1
Achievement of equality and integration with Jews	59.7	47.2	48.3	21.2	19.8	15.3
Allowing Arabs to organize independently and become partners in state institutions	22.5	33.3	33.0	3.7	7.3	11.4
Granting Arabs separate legal status, like the autonomy offered to the Arabs in the West Bank and Gaza Strip	11.3	15.6	14.5	1.6	2.6	5.7

To pry further into the rationales for the divergent sets of preferences, a series of questions was posed regarding various modes of accommodation between national, religious, linguistic, and cultural groups. The respondents were asked to indicate whether they accept or reject each of the modes for accommodating the inter-group disparities in Israel. The majority of both Arabs and Jews agrees on democracy as a suitable means to hammer out group differences in Israel (Table 10.5). The most attractive form for the Arabs is consociational democracy: 79%, compared to 71% of the Jews, accept the idea that "all people will vote for any party they like, and parties will have to form a coalition government that will ensure a share of power for all major parties." This is the kind of accommodation instituted to manage the conflict between the Orthodox minority and non-Orthodox majority in Israel. Although non-religious Jews are disenchanted with this pattern, they concede its necessity and utility. For the Arabs, this is the best they can obtain in a Jewish state and they indeed aspire for inclusion in Israel's coalition governments (Table 9.9 in the previous chapter). By endorsing a method of non-consociational democracy (71% of the Arabs and 81.5% of the Jews agree to a winner-takes-all system, in which the losing parties remain in opposition), Israeli Arabs assume that their parties would be treated as legitimate candidates for coalition rather than forced into permanent opposition. The two sides also agree that partition is not an appropriate solution for Israel proper (only a quarter sees it as fitting).

Table 10.5 Accepted Options for Israel's Internal Divisions

	Arab Public	Jewish Public
Accept each of the following options for Israel's handling of its national, religious, lingual, or cultural divisions		
All people will vote for any party they like, and the winning party or parties will rule while other parties will be in the opposition	71.1	81.5
All people will vote for any party they like, and parties will have to form a coalition government that will ensure a share of power for all major parties	79.4	70.8
A single party, open to everyone, will rule without opposition	45.5	37.3
Agree that whether one likes it or not, when groups with different nationality, religion, language, or culture live in one country, one group will control another	28.7	54.4
The largest group will rule, and other groups should accept what it will be decided	16.8	64.8
One group will rule over other groups, and people who refuse to accept this will have to keep quiet or leave the country	10.5	43.1

Source: The 1988 survey.

Arabs and Jews sharply disagree, nevertheless, on domination. A small majority of Jews openly accept domination: 54% maintain that in a divided society "one group will control another," 65% think that "the largest group will rule and other groups should accept what will be decided," and 43% endorse the principle of offering the minority a choice between subordination and voluntary transfer. This strong orientation for majority dominance squares with the widespread conception of democracy as a system of majority rule. As a result, many Jews do not see any contradiction between domination by a majority and democracy.

When Arabs and Jews were asked to choose the best solution to the problem of the Arabs in Israel, the disputes in the final choices where no doubt shaped by their divergent outlooks. A majority (69%) of the Arabs as against a minority (40%) of the Jews opt for democracy (Table 10.6). Of the Arabs, 46.5% select consociational democracy and 12% consociational non-democracy compared to only 13% and 10%, respectively, of the Jews. On the other hand, 45% of the Jews, compared to but 2% of the Arabs, choose domination together with voluntary departure from the country. Yet, both sides realize that partition into two states is not a viable option for Arab-Jewish relations in Israel.

Table 10.6 The Best Solution to the Problem of Arabs in Israel

	Arab Public	Jewish Public
The best solution to the problem of Arabs in Israel (from the following six)		
All people will vote for any party they like, and the winning party or parties will rule while other parties will be in the opposition	22.5	27.0
All people will vote for any party they like, and parties will have to form a coalition government that will ensure share of power for Jews and Israeli Arabs	46.5	12.6
A single party, open to Jews and Israeli Arabs, will rule without opposition	11.6	9.9
The Jews will rule, and Israeli Arabs should accept what the Jews will decide	1.4	21.8
The Jews will rule, and Israeli Arabs who refuse to accept this will have to keep quiet or leave the country	1.4	23.6
The state of Israel within the Green Line (i.e., without the territories) should be divided up into two states between Jews and Israeli Arabs	16.6	5.1

Source: The 1988 survey.

There is another cardinal facet to the Israeli Arab minority problem. Is it a completely internal question or, rather, is it linked to the final settlement of the wider Palestinian issue? The authorities hold that it is an internal matter and not a component of the Palestinian issue. Paradoxically, this seems to be the emergent position of the mainstream PLO, Palestinian leaders in the occupied territories, and the Israeli Arab leadership. Their rationale is that the addition of Israeli Palestinian issues to the Palestinian agenda will intensify Jewish fears of irredentism and exacerbate the already overburdened Palestinian-Israeli conflict. On the other hand, the rejectionist Palestinians within and outside Israel tie all the issues together because, for them, historical Palestine in its entirety should be liberated.

These political considerations do not determine the thinking of rank and file Arabs, who look for rectification of the injustices they have endured. Hence, over two thirds of these Arabs, compared to a small minority of Jews, think that the solution of the Palestinian question should also include the settlement of land and other problems of Israeli Arabs (Table 10.7). Still, the Arabs object to adding to the peace agenda compensations for Jews from Arab countries for the property they left there. The positions taken by the Arab and Jewish publics thus reflect their rival interests.

Table 10.7 The Problem of Arabs in Israel and the Palestinian Question

	Arab Public	Jewish Public
The solution to the Palestinian question should include also the settlement of the land dispute between Israeli Arabs and the state		
Yes	70.3	15.6
Only under certain circumstances	18.5	35.3
No	11.2	49.1
Negotiation to settle the Palestinian question should include also a solution to other problems of Israeli Arabs		
Yes	67.0	18.8
Only under certain circumstances	18.4	35.7
No	14.6	45.5
Solution to the Palestinian question should include also compensations to Jews from Arab countries for the property they left there		
Yes	20.9	*
Only under certain circumstances	26.1	*
No	52.9	*

*Not asked.

Source: The 1988 survey.

To conclude, Arabs and Jews seek conflicting goals. A majority of the Arabs pursue greater opportunities and institutional, non-territorial autonomy, and a minority still hope for secession or for forming a secular-democratic Palestine in lieu of the Jewish state. Most Jews, on the other hand, are interested in continuing or even consolidating Jewish domination; some, though, are willing to extend more rights and institutional autonomy to the Arabs, whereas others are convinced that Arabs should be completely removed from Israel.

11

Leadership Credibility

Israeli Arabs need effective leaders in order to fight for their special interests, for equality, and for control of their own institutions and against discrimination. To be effective, these leaders must be credible to both Arabs and Jews. Arab leadership credibility is often an issue cutting across lines both within and between each community.

Some Arab political bodies are state-wide, all-inclusive, non-partisan organizations that address vital concerns, such as lands, civil equality, and education. Figuring prominently among these bodies are the Supreme Follow-Up Committee, the Committee of Heads of Arab Local Councils, the Committee for Defense of Arab Lands, and the Committee of Arab Students. Since the leaders of these organizations come from all of the major political streams in the Arab sector, they have the best chance of gaining the trust of a majority of the Arabs. This assumption is born out in the case of two of these organizations included in the surveys. An Arab majority of 71% considers the Committee for Defense of Arab Lands to be a true representative of the interests of the Arabs in Israel, and a majority of 63% thinks this about the Committee of Heads of Arab Local Councils (Table 11.1). A majority of leaders from all the four political streams in the study also approve of the credibility of these two organizations.

Is the PLO a true representative of the Arabs of Israel? This is a tricky issue. The PLO claims sole representation of all Palestinians, implying the Palestinian citizens of Israel, as well. On the other hand, the PLO and leaders on the West Bank and Gaza Strip have increasingly been moving to acknowledge the reality that the fate and future of Israeli Arabs are tied to Israel and that any demand to represent "the Palestinians of the inside," as Israeli Arabs are called by other Palestinians, would overburden the Palestinian-Israeli conflict with unnecessary hurdles. In Israel only the rejectionist Sons of the Village Movement stands for the absolute unity of the Palestinian people and the overall representation of the PLO. Non-rejectionist Arab leaders are keenly aware of the fact that in Israel the PLO is considered an illegal, terrorist organization, and thus they argue that the PLO speaks only for the Palestinians outside Israel. Seeing themselves as the legitimate spokesmen for the Arabs in Israel, these leaders regard the PLO as a genuine Palestinian leadership seeking peace with Israel according to the formula of a Palestinian state in the West Bank and Gaza Strip alongside Israel.

Table 11.1 Leadership Credibility

	Arab Public	Estab. Affil. Arab Lead.	Unaffiliated Arab Lead.	DFPE & PLP Arab Lead.	Sons of Village Arab Lead.	Jewish Public	DFPE & PLP Jewish Lead.	CRM & Mapam Jewish Lead.	Labor Jewish Lead.	Likud Camp Jewish Lead.
Consider each of the following bodies to be truly representative of the interests of the Arabs in Israel										
Committee of Heads of Arab Local Councils	62.7	74.2	90.3	92.7	71.0	61.4[a]	96.9	96.0	58.1	60.0
Committee for Defense of Arab Lands	70.7	56.6	78.2	85.4	81.3	*	*	*	*	*
Israeli Communist Party	45.8	6.3	42.0	75.6	43.8	44.3	88.2	26.7	16.2	15.6
PLP	35.5	25.8	40.0	29.2	0.0	48.5	57.1	44.8	28.6	21.9
Sons of the Village Movement	36.1	3.1	3.6	23.1	100.0	*	*	*	*	*
PLO	66.2	16.1	10.3	33.4	74.0	25.0	12.1	16.1	5.2	14.7

*Not asked.

[a]Based on the 35.7% of the Jews who knew of the existence of the Committee.

The question whether the PLO stands for Israeli Arabs or not came to the fore during the public discussion over the attempt to block the participation of the Progressive List for Peace in the 1984 elections to the Knesset. Before deciding the case of the PLP, the Central Elections Committee sought the advice of the security establishment. The leaders of the PLP were summoned for interrogation. The Minister of Defense presented his view that according to the PLP platform, the PLO represents Israeli Arabs and, hence, the PLP contains subversive elements. For this and other reasons, he recommended not to approve the PLP for participation in the elections. The Minister's inference was deduced from two statements made by the PLO and accepted by other Arab political bodies as well: (a) Israeli Arabs are part of the Palestinian people and (b) the PLO represents the Palestinian people. Since the second statement does not restrict the PLO's claim of representation to

Palestinians outside Israel, it follows that the PLP believes that the PLO represents the Palestinians in Israel too. Mi'ari, the head of the PLP, said in response: "The citizens of Israel who are Palestinian Arabs are represented by the State of Israel, by the Knesset, and by their election list. We are not a people, but rather citizens of the State of Israel. We are Palestinian in culture, family affiliation, and descent" (Ministry of Defence, 1984: 17). Yet, the ambiguity inherent in the PLO's representativeness probably influences the thinking of ordinary Arabs.

The Arab answers to the relevant question in the survey reflect these divergent inclinations. A majority of two thirds of the Arab public perceives the PLO as the true representative of the Arabs in Israel. While the activists in the Sons of the Village Movement also endorse this view, the other leaders do not (Table 11.1). Rather than conforming to a rejectionist ideology, the rank and file Arabs feel that the PLO embodies a just solution for the Palestinian problem. Since they project on the PLO their own outlook and desire that peace will come about by the formation of an independent Palestinian state alongside Israel, they see the PLO as representing them on the peace issue. This straightforward approach of the Arab public is also evidenced by the notion that the solution to the Palestinian question should also include the settlement of land and other disputes between Israeli Arabs and the state (Table 10.7 in the last chapter). The more sophisticated and responsible Arab leaders, however, who fear legal and other punitive Jewish reactions, shy away from such a suspect position.

It is state policy to deny Arab political bodies any official recognition. Most Jews are not even aware of the existence of the most representative Israeli Arab leadership – the Committee for Defense of Arab Lands and the Committee of Heads of Arab Local Councils. Yet, most of those in the Jewish public, including the leaders, who are familiar with these organizations, are willing to concede their representativeness (Table 11.1). As for the PLO, most Jewish rank and file and leaders view it as a terrorist organization, and, hence, not serving the Israeli Arab cause.

In contrast to Arab non-partisan organizations that enjoy the credibility of a majority of Israeli Arabs, partisan bodies can, of course, gain the trust of only a minority of the Arabs. These political parties and movements fall into three categories. The first one includes the Jewish-Zionist parties in which Arabs are integrated as members and voters, like Labor, Mapam, Citizens' Rights Movement, and Likud. The second category consists of the three predominantly Arab parties: the Democratic Arab Party, the PLP, and the Israeli Communist Party (or its front, the DFPE). The Islamic Movement and the Sons of the Village Movement constitute the last category of purely Arab movements that are either unwilling or unable to transform themselves into parliamentary Arab parties.

The expectation that these partisan bodies cannot gain the credibility of a majority of the Arabs was substantiated by the surveys. In the 1985 survey, the Israeli Communist Party (Rakah) was found to enjoy the trust of 46% of Israeli Arabs; the Progressive List for Peace – 35.5%; and the Sons of the Village Movement – 36% (Table 11.1). The confidence in these political bodies of Arab leaders, Jewish public, and Jewish leaders is also small. The partial credibility accorded to these organizations reflects deep internal divisions within the Arab community. The failure of Rakah, the best organized and the strongest party active in the Arab sector, to attain popular support is striking.

The credibility of Arab organizations has risen over the years. Among the Arabs, the credibility of the Committee of Heads of Arab Local Councils increased from 48% in 1976 to 79% in 1988, that of the PLO from 48.5% in 1980 to 66% in 1985. On the other hand, that of the Committee for the Defense of Arab Lands dropped from 80% in 1976, when the Committee was very active, to 71% in 1985, when it became inactive (Table 11.2). The Communist Party and the Sons of the Village Movement have kept their relative credibility. The Jews became more realistic and during the 1980s increased their acknowledgment of the credibility of Arab political organizations.

Table 11.2 Arab Leadership Credibility, 1976-88

	Arab Public				Jewish Public		
	1976	1980	1985	1988	1980	1985	1988
Consider each of the following bodies as truly representative of the interests of Arabs in Israel							
Committee of Heads of Arab Local Councils	48.0	55.3	62.7	78.8	41.9	61.4	52.3
Committee for Defense of Arab Lands	80.1	58.9	70.7	*	41.3	*	*
Israeli Communist Party (Rakah)	47.9	34.6	45.8	*	28.4	44.3	*
Sons of the Village Movement	*	40.2	36.1	*	*	*	*
Palestine Liberation Organization	*	48.5	66.2	*	20.6	25.0	*

*Not asked.

Further information about the Arab public's preferred leaders is provided by the 1988 survey. The Arab respondents were asked to name the two most preferred leaders, living in or outside Israel, for Israeli Arabs. When they were not given any names to choose from, their most favored leaders were PLO leaders, followed by Israeli Arab leaders from the Communist Party and then from Zionist parties (Table 11.3). These are the three most important forces for Israeli Arabs.

A list of 12 Israeli and non-Israeli Palestinian names, including the most prominent leaders of various parties and organizations, was then presented to the Arab respondents (see Table 11.4 for the complete list).

The final choices are revealing in a number of ways. First, Arafat, the head of the PLO mainstream, emerges as the most popular leader, while Abu-Musa, a leader of the Rejection Front, is ignored. This reconfirms the central role the PLO plays in the political life of Israeli Arabs of all political persuasions and also attests once more to their repudiation of the Rejection Front. Second, there is no Israeli Arab leader of an outstanding national stature who appeals to a majority or even to a significant minority of Israeli Arabs. The internal political factionalism is so deep that none receives more than 11% as a first choice or more than 18% as a second choice. Those leaders with limited appeal are Tubi and Zayad of the Communist Party and Darawshe of the Democratic Arab Party. Ibrahim Nimr Hussein, the non-partisan but pale Chairman of the Committee of Heads of Arab Local Councils, also belongs to this category. Mi'ari, the head of the PLP, draws some attraction, but only as a second choice. The broad choice that Arabs have among these leaders shows, once again, that the organizational base for the emergence of popular national leaders is diverse and no longer monopolized by the Communist Party. Third, all the other Arab leaders – of the Zionist parties, the Islamic Movement, and the Sons of the Village Movement – lack general appeal.

Table 11.3 Affiliation of Arabs' Most Preferred Leaders

	Arab Public	
	First Choice	Second Choice
Affiliation of the most preferred leaders of Israeli Arabs living in Israel or abroad (open-ended question)		
Jewish parties	18.0	24.1
Progressive List for Peace	5.1	10.5
Israeli Communist Party (Rakah)	17.5	25.6
Sons of the Village Movement	0.4	0.0
Non-partisan Israeli Arab organizations	5.3	9.1
Organizations in the West Bank and Gaza Strip	0.9	0.5
PLO mainstream	37.7	10.8
PLO Rejection Front	1.1	4.7
Other	14.0	14.7

Source: The 1988 survey.

Additional inquiries disclose the sound pragmatic basis of the mass support for the preferred Arab leaders. Nearly all Arabs perceive their chosen leaders as effective in promoting the interests of the Arab minority, and two thirds would not support a leader acting in an incomprehensible manner to them (Table 11.5). The "model leader" for the overwhelming majority is one who is concerned with the practical daily needs of Israeli Arabs, able to bargain and achieve reasonable compromises, and is not feared by the Jews (Table

11.6). These attitudes toward the present and desirable Arab leaders disclose a remarkable sense of realism and moderation on the part of Israeli Arabs.

Table 11.4 Arabs' Most Preferred Leaders

	Arab Public	
	First Choice	Second Choice
The most preferred Arab leader from the following		
Amal Nazr a-Din (Knesset member, Herut, Druze)	1.2	3.2
Zaydan Atshi (Knesset member, Shinui, Druze)	6.7	3.8
Mouhamad Wattad (Knesset member, Mapam, Moslem)	4.6	6.0
Ibrahim Nimr Hussein (Chairman of the Committee of Heads of Arab Local Councils, independent, Moslem)	8.8	11.3
Abdul Wahab Darawshe (Knesset member, head of the Democratic Arab Party, Moslem)	10.8	16.8
Kamel Daher (a top leader of the Progressive List for Peace, Moslem)	0.8	0.7
Mouhamad Mi'ari (Knesset member, head of the Progressive List for Peace, Moslem)	4.0	12.2
Tawfiq Tubi (Knesset member, the Arab leader of the Israeli Communist Party, Christian)	10.4	11.6
Tawfiq Zayad (Knesset member, Israeli Communist Party, Moslem)	8.6	18.0
Abdallah Darwish (a top leader of the Islamic Movement)	4.1	4.1
Yasir Arafat (head of the PLO mainstream, Moslem)	39.2	8.1
Abu Musa (leader of the PLO Rejection Front)	0.9	4.1

Source: The 1988 survey.

Table 11.5 Arabs' Trust of Their Most Preferred Arab Leaders

	Arab Public
Believe that one's most preferred Arab leader can be efficient in promoting the interests of Israeli Arabs	91.6
Would support one's most preferred Arab leader even if acting in a way one does not understand	34.9

Source: The 1988 survey.

Table 11.6 Arabs' View of Kind of Leader They Need

	Arab Public
Very important features of leader Israeli Arabs need now	
Concerned with the practical day-to-day needs of Israeli Arabs	90.1
Able to bargain and achieve reasonable compromises	84.0
Feared by Jews	34.0

Source: The 1988 survey.

To conclude, the Arab community in the 1980s had representative organizations that constituted a solid base for credible leadership. Prominent are the Committee of Heads of Arab Local Councils, the Committee for Defense of Arab Lands, and the external PLO representing all Palestinians on the peace front. Along with these widely based organizations, there are political parties and movements whose leaders command the trust and backing only of their followers. Arab leaders are supported for their genuine representation of Israeli Arab interests and potential or actual activity to further the daily needs of the Arab minority and to exact compromises from the authorities rather than for their rhetoric, charisma, and radicalism. This does not necessarily mean that Arab leaders affiliated with the Zionist establishment are favored over others, because the independent leaders have not yet proved themselves in the fight for peace and equality. The new, independent, militant Arab leaders replaced the previous coopted and traditional leaders but have failed to gain recognition from the authorities and the Jewish public at large. The Jews especially fear and deny legitimacy to credible Arab leaders who are grounded in representative Arab organizations and who possess the power to mobilize the entire Arab community in a struggle for its fundamental interests.

12

Educational Goals

The contribution of public education to Arab-Jewish coexistence has been questionable. Jewish schools devote limited attention to the teaching of the Arabic language, Arab history, Arab culture, and relations between Israeli Arabs and Jews. They also do not do much to inculcate democratic values, tolerance for diversity and disagreement, and respect for the right to protest and to dissent. The failure of the Ministry of Education and Culture to tackle the problem is accentuated by widespread expressions of intolerance among Jewish school youth. Jewish radical movements and parties emerged during the 1980s. They propagated such ideas as Jews have an exclusive, absolute right to Greater Israel, no Israeli government has the authority to disengage from the Land of Israel; the need to transfer Palestinian Arabs to other countries; and Israeli Arab citizens who refuse to render military or civil service should be disenfranchised. Furthermore, the late Rabbi Kahane introduced motions in the Knesset to institute legal segregation and discrimination between Arab and Jewish citizens and led crusades against Israeli Arabs.

The Ministry of Education and Culture initiated in the mid-1980s several programs to make up for part of the failure. They include contrived encounters between Arab and Jewish high school students to discuss democratic values and tensions in Arab-Jewish relations. Another program concerns the teaching in the eleventh and twelfth grades in the Jewish schools of courses on democracy, the Arab minority, and the Israeli-Arab conflict. The scale and effect of this activity are modest.

On the other hand, Arab schools are doing better. They teach Hebrew language and Jewish history, literature, and culture at a level that facilitates Israeli Arabs to become bilingual and bicultural. A gradual revision of the educational goals and curricula has been underway since the mid-1970s. The new curriculum includes significant reforms in the instruction of history, Arabic, Hebrew, and civics (Al-Haj, 1991: 127-134) and constitutes a break with the common, simple-minded approach of treating Arab education as a tool of Jewish domination (Mar'i, 1978). Of special importance is the new program in civics, which also includes discussions of the sensitive issues of civil rights, the Israeli-Arab conflict, and Israeli Arabs' links with the Arab world. A new civics textbook, issued in 1987, states that the Arabs are an integral part of the Palestinian people and takes up topics as touchy as land expropriations. The change in Arab education leaves, of course, much to be desired because it is restricted to parts of the school system and the curriculum. It certainly falls short of the objectives and criteria of the Arab leaders, educators, scholars, and the general public, who insist on complete parity with the Jewish sector.

One pertinent question concerns the national goals of education; i.e., the kind of person that the Israeli educational systems aim to produce. It is the official objective of Jewish education to make Jews proud of their heritage, to feel strong solidarity with the Jewish people, to love Israel as a Jewish state, and to be a devout Zionist; by contrast, official national goals for the separate Arab education system are still legally lacking. The practical, implicit aims of Arab education, however, are to make Israeli Arabs loyal to the Jewish state and to discourage Palestinian nationalism (the openness in the late 1980s in this respect is still limited to the upper classes of high schools).

The survey reveals marked disagreement between Arabs and Jews on the goals of Arab education: only 3.5% of the Arabs, compared to 53% of the Jews, want the Arabs to be educated to become loyal minority members of a Jewish state (Table 12.1). Since this is what the state is trying to do in practice, these figures indicate that the status quo is totally rejected by the Arabs but wins the approval of a substantial proportion of Jews.

A majority of 62% of the Arabs desire to have their children educated "to love Israel as the common homeland of its two peoples, Arab and Jewish." In the eyes of the Arabs, this objective implies that Israel is a binational, not a Jewish, state. Its acceptance by 42% of the Jews does not mean, however, Jewish endorsement of binationalism, but rather a desire to reduce Arab alienation from the Jewish state.

One third of the Arabs advocates Palestinian nationalism to guide Arab education. This target is entirely negated, of course, by the Jews, who regard Palestinian identity and nationalism as illegitimate and hostile to Israel.

The dispute among the leaders on this matter is even more striking than that between the publics at large. While 67% of the Jewish leaders from the Labor Party and 79% of the Jewish leaders from the Likud camp espouse the goal of a loyal Arab minority in a Jewish state, all the Arab leaders oppose the goal. The overwhelming majority of Arab leaders who are affiliated with the Zionist establishment or are non-partisan favor the common homeland goal; the DFPE and PLP Arab leaders are divided between education for a common homeland and Palestinian nationalism; and all the Sons of the Village Movement leaders insist on Palestinian nationalist education. Among the Jewish leaders, the non-Zionist left is split between common homeland and Palestinian nationalism, whereas the Zionist left prefers the goal of a common homeland.

Table 12.1 Alternative National Goals for Arab and Jewish Education

	Arab Public	Estab. Affil. Arab Lead.	Unaffiliated Arab Lead.	DFPE & PLP Arab Lead.	Sons of Village Arab Lead.	Jewish Public	DFPE & PLP Jewish Lead.	CRM & Mapam Jewish Lead.	Labor Jewish Lead.	Likud Camp Jewish Lead.
The most desirable goal for Arab education										
To be a loyal minority member in a Jewish state	3.5	6.5	0.0	0.0	0.0	53.2	0.0	15.6	66.7	78.8
To love Israel as the common homeland of its two peoples, Arab and Jewish	62.3	87.1	77.4	46.3	0.0	42.3	53.3	59.4	28.2	15.2
To be a member of the Palestinian people	34.3	6.5	22.6	53.7	100.0	4.5	46.7	25.0	5.1	6.1
The most desirable goal for Jewish education										
To be a loyal citizen	8.0	3.3	0.0	0.0	8.3	55.2	3.1	21.2	50.0	50.0
To love Israel as the common homeland of its two peoples, Arab and Jewish	81.3	93.3	93.5	82.5	45.8	23.2	96.9	69.7	34.2	5.9
To be a member of the Jewish people	10.7	3.3	6.5	17.5	45.8	21.6	0.0	9.1	15.8	44.1

The controversy over goals for Jewish education is even more pronounced: 81% of the Arabs favor the common homeland objective; that is, they intend to end Jewish exclusivity through binationalism. The Jews repudiate such a binational model of the Israeli Jew. Most of the 23% of the Jews who give this response have in mind a type of tolerant Jew who can better coexist with Arabs while remaining firmly committed to the idea of a Jewish-Zionist state. The leaders are similarly divided, with one notable exception. Paradoxically, 46% of the nationalists of the Sons of the Village Movement endorse the common homeland for Jews that they totally reject for Arabs. In the same vein, 97% of the Jewish leaders of the non-Zionist left and 70% of the Jewish leaders of the Zionist left side with the common homeland that smaller proportions of these leaders see fit for Arab education. The much greater endorsement of the goal of common homeland for Jewish education than for Arab education by Arab leaders and leftist Jewish leaders is based on the correct diagnosis that the present nationalistically oriented Jewish education needs softening and balance.

The disagreements between Arabs and Jews over the goals of both Arab and Jewish education continue to be contentious throughout the 1980s, but there was a significant increase in support for the goal of common homeland. For Arab education, support for this goal rose from 53.5% in 1976 to 58% in 1988 among the Arabs, and from 42% in 1980 to 49% in 1988 among the Jews (Table 12.2). For Jewish education, the rise was limited to the Jews – from 23% to 32% between 1980 and 1988.

Table 12.2 Alternative National Goals for Arab and Jewish Education, 1976-88

	Arab Public				Jewish Public		
	1976	1980	1985	1988	1980	1985	1988
The most desirable goal for Arab education							
To be a loyal minority member in a Jewish state	6.0	5.7	3.5	5.1	53.8	53.2	44.9
To love Israel as the common homeland of its two peoples, Arab and Jewish	53.5	64.8	62.3	58.2	42.0	42.3	49.2
To be a member of the Palestinian people	40.4	29.5	34.3	36.7	4.1	4.5	5.9
The most desirable goal for Jewish education							
To be a loyal citizen	*	11.9	8.0	13.5	56.9	55.2	49.2
To love Israel as the common homeland of its two peoples, Arab and Jewish	*	78.2	81.3	75.0	23.1	23.2	32.1
To be a member of the Jewish people	*	10.0	10.7	11.4	20.0	21.6	18.7

*Not asked.

Less dissension prevails on the matter of instruction of Arabic and Arab history in the schools. Since the Arabs accept bilingualism and biculturalism, they assent to the teaching of Hebrew and Jewish culture in their schools. They fully understand that these are prerequisites for their adaptation and progress in a society in which they constitute a lingual and cultural minority.

The Jews are less receptive of bilingualism and biculturalism for themselves than for the Arabs. The reason is that they assert themselves as a lingual and cultural dominant majority and want to keep Israel Jewish. Yet, their approval of the teaching of Arabic language and Arab history in Jewish schools is quite high. As many as half of the Jewish public, 47% of the nationalist leaders from the Likud camp, and 76% to 97% of other Jewish leaders favor the teaching of Arabic in Jewish schools at a level equal to English (Table 13.3). The approval of the teaching of Arab history is overwhelming – 73% among the Jewish public and 94% to 100% among the Jewish leaders. All these percentages much exceed the Jews' reserved position vis-à-vis bilingualism and biculturalism for the state and for themselves (compare Table 4.17 in chapter 4 with Table 12.3). This approval is motivated more by the lure of a measure of cultural enrichment and a benefit of expanded knowledge than by an understanding that Arab-Jewish coexistence in Israel requires Jews to be open to Middle Eastern culture and affairs.

Table 12.3 Instruction of Arabic and History in Schools

	Arab Public	Estab. Affil. Arab Lead.	Unaffil-iated Arab Lead.	DFPE & PLP Arab Lead.	Sons of Village Arab Lead.	Jewish Public	DFPE & PLP Jewish Lead.	CRM & Mapam Jewish Lead.	Labor Jewish Lead.	Likud Camp Jewish Lead.
Favor the teaching of Arabic in Jewish schools at a level equal to English even if this would require cutting down on other subjects	*	*	*	*	*	50.4	97.1	87.5	75.7	46.9
Favor the teaching of Arab history and culture in Jewish schools at a level that would equip any Jew with a good knowledge of Arab subjects	*	*	*	*	*	72.6	100.0	100.0	100.0	94.1
Favor the teaching of Jewish history and culture in Arab schools at a level that would equip any Arab with a good knowledge of Jewish subjects	85.1	100.0	100.0	97.6	96.7	*	*	*	*	*

*Not asked.

To conclude, the nationalist goals of education constitute an issue separating Arabs and Jews. While the Jews expect education to facilitate the adjustment of the Arabs to their status as a minority in a Jewish state, the Arabs are interested in education as a lever for shaping Israel and the Jews into binational molds.

13

Strategies for Change

As a disadvantaged minority in a democratic state, Israeli Arabs are expected to favor a struggle to better their conditions, to redress wrongs, to accomplish equality with Jews, and to advance the Palestinian cause. Several questions come to mind with regard to the intensity and issues of the Arabs' struggle: Do they regard democracy as an effective avenue for advancing their cause, or do they have to turn to extra-legal methods? What objectives are worth fighting for? Do they believe in their ability to affect change? Should they continue their struggle? The views of the Jews on some of these matters point to their preferred type of democracy and to their willingness to accommodate Arab demands.

The commitment to democratic values is common. Most Arabs and Jews approve of an open multi-party system, free press, politics of negotiation, avoidance of collective punishment, and prohibition of the use of violence by the opposition and government (Table 13.1). The only disagreement centers on preventive detention which is disapproved of by 65% of the Arabs but only by 38% of the Jews. Jewish endorsement of preventive detention is strongly influenced by the authorities' insistence on its vital importance for internal security, the amendments made to immunize it against misuse, and its exclusive use against Arabs.

Arabs have more faith in Israeli democracy as a useful tool for themselves than do Jews: 58% and 36.5%, respectively, believe that it is possible to improve the Arab situation considerably by the moderate democratic means of persuasion and pressure (Table 13.2). The percentage of those castigating parliamentary democracy as ineffective for Arabs is negligible. The adherence to democracy is much more widespread on the leadership level. Majorities ranging from 59% to 84% of non-rejectionist Arab and Jewish leaders place a high trust in parliamentary democracy for Arabs. Only the activists in the Sons of the freedom of action is curtailed and prospects of executing their extreme goals are nil. The Arabs' firm espousal of Israeli democracy is part of their political socialization in Israeli society, the relaxation of controls over them, and their experience that some change can indeed be generated through democratic struggle.

Table 13.1 Values of Political Democracy

	Arab Public	Jewish Public
Would prefer a regime of more than one party, each with its own plan for the country's future	68.7	62.7
Would prefer a government which allows newspapers to criticize the government and to enjoy freedom of expression	85.3	71.0
To protect national unity		
Approve of prosecution of political activists who use violence	58.2	93.9
Disapprove of preventive actions against opponents of the regime in order to prevent their activity ahead of time	64.8	37.8
Disapprove of collective punishment (punishing whole groups)	91.2	69.9
Disapprove of use of all military means irrespective of losses of human life	94.4	85.1
Approve of political solutions by negotiation	94.1	82.4

Source: The 1988 survey.

Table 13.2 Parliamentary Politics as a Strategy for Change

	Arab Public	Estab. Affil. Arab Lead.	Unaffil-iated Arab Lead.	DFPE & PLP Arab Lead.	Sons of Village Arab Lead.	Jewish Public	DFPE & PLP Jewish Lead.	CRM & Mapam Jewish Lead.	Labor Jewish Lead.	Likud Camp Jewish Lead.
The extent to which it is possible to improve the Arab situation by acceptable democratic means, such as persuasion and political pressure										
To a great extent	26.2	51.6	41.9	43.6	15.6	11.8	39.4	32.4	33.3	18.8
To a substantial extent	31.8	32.3	32.3	20.5	3.1	24.7	30.3	26.5	41.0	40.6
To a certain extent	33.1	16.1	19.4	35.9	31.3	47.4	27.3	32.4	17.9	28.1
To almost no extent	8.9	0.0	6.5	0.0	50.0	16.1	3.0	8.8	7.7	12.5

The tenacity of the belief in Israeli democracy is manifested in the trend over the 1976-88 period. We notice among both Arabs and Jews a strengthening of the faith in the feasibility of moderate, rather than appreciable, amelioration of Arab life through parliamentary politics (Table 13.3). Over the years this level of confidence has remained significantly higher among Arabs than Jews.

Table 13.3 Parliamentary Politics as a Strategy for Change, 1976-88

	Arab Public				Jewish Public		
	1976	1980	1985	1988	1980	1985	1988
The extent to which it is possible to improve the Arab situation by acceptable democratic means, such as persuasion and political pressure							
To a great extent	29.1	25.9	26.2	30.1	11.7	11.8	7.8
To a substantial extent	37.2	30.0	31.8	31.0	25.1	24.7	33.4
To a certain extent	17.4	26.6	33.1	28.3	44.3	47.4	42.1
To almost no extent	16.3	17.6	8.9	10.6	18.9	16.1	16.7

Arabs realize, however, that to score real gains, they must avail themselves of extra-parliamentary yet democratic politics. Arab majorities of 52% to 81% favor, without any reservation, the use of licensed demonstrations, general strikes, protest actions abroad, and boycotts of institutions or plants (Table 13.4). In contrast, only a minority of the Jews, ranging from 7% to 41%, assent to these tactics, thereby disclosing their unwillingness to extend to Israeli Arabs the right to meaningful, active protest. This Arab-Jewish dispute is also evident among the leaders, despite their shared and staunch commitment to democracy. The leaders agree that licensed demonstrations are all right for Arabs to hold, whereas boycotts are not desirable. On the other hand, the bones of contention are general strikes and protest actions abroad, sanctioned by most Arab leaders and repudiated by most Jewish leaders. It is noteworthy that even the leaders from the Zionist left, who pride themselves in fighting for equal civil rights for all, do not approve of these rigorous measures, because of the fear that they might degenerate into violence and damage Arab-Jewish coexistence.

Table 13.4 Extra-Parliamentary Politics as a Strategy for Change

	Arab Public	Estab. Affil. Arab Lead.	Unaffiliated Arab Lead.	DFPE & PLP Arab Lead.	Sons of Village Arab Lead.	Jewish Public	DFPE & PLP Jewish Lead.	CRM & Mapam Jewish Lead.	Labor Jewish Lead.	Likud Camp Jewish Lead.
In favor, without reservations, of each of the following means to improve the situation of the Arabs in Israel										
Licensed demonstrations	81.2	96.9	90.3	100.0	100.0	41.4	100.0	97.1	84.6	67.6
General strikes	61.2	34.4	54.8	97.5	100.0	10.3	91.7	42.4	13.2	6.1
Protest actions abroad	55.4	25.0	54.8	87.5	100.0	9.3	86.1	29.4	2.6	3.0
Boycotts of institutions or plants	52.1	9.4	22.6	40.5	90.6	6.7	65.6	26.5	7.9	0.0

Arab approval and Jewish tolerance of the Arab use of extra-parliamentary politics have increased over the years, but the wide Arab-Jewish disagreement has persisted. To cite the most crucial tactic, the proportion favoring the holding of Arab general strikes rose from 63% in 1976 to 74% in 1988 among the Arabs, and from 6% to 18% among the Jews (Table 13.5). Despite the growth in licensed demonstrations, general strikes and protest actions abroad by Israeli Arabs during the 1970s and 1980s, the Jews have continued to frown on them as threats to law and order and to stable Arab-Jewish relations.

Table 13.5 Extra-Parliamentary Politics as a Strategy for Change, 1976-88

	Arab Public				Jewish Public		
	1976	1980	1985	1988	1980	1985	1988
In favor, without reservations, of each of the following means to improve the situation of the Arabs in Israel							
Licensed demonstrations	*	75.5	81.2	*	44.2	41.4	*
General strikes	62.6	54.6	61.2	73.8	5.9	10.3	18.0
Protest actions abroad	63.7	51.9	55.4	67.1	8.8	9.3	16.8
Boycotts of institutions or plants	59.8	47.0	52.1	*	4.5	6.7	*

*Not asked.

A clear majority of Israeli Arabs cling to democracy and, therefore, oppose the employment of extra-legal means (Table 13.6). Yet, one tenth endorse without reservations and one quarter partially approve of resorting to unlicensed demonstrations and resistance with force. This is a significant minority of Arabs who seek a radical change and are disposed to adopt a radical strategy if need be. A substantial proportion of the leftist Arab and Jewish leadership condones unlicensed demonstrations because the police too often unjustifiably deny Arabs permission to demonstrate. Yet most of them stand against the use of violence to improve Israeli Arab conditions. The leaders of the Sons of the Village Movement are an exception, however, since they are distinguished by their very resistance to Israel's existence and Israeli authorities.

The trend over the years is consolidation of the Arab opposition to the use of violence. The Arab objection to resistance with force as a means to Israeli Arab progress rose steadily from 59.5% in 1976, to 70.5% in 1980, to 75% in 1985, and to 77% following the outbreak of the intifada in 1988 (Table 13.7). At the same time, the Arab support for unlicensed demonstrations declined from 17% in 1976 to 13% in 1988, while Jewish opposition decreased from 87% in 1980 to 78% in 1988. The Arabs well understand that turning to extra-legal politics will undermine their cherished and effective access to Israeli democracy.

Table 13.6 Extra-Legal Politics as a Strategy for Change

	Arab Public	Estab. Affil. Arab Lead.	Unaffiliated Arab Lead.	DFPE & PLP Arab Lead.	Sons of Village Arab Lead.	Jewish Public	DFPE & PLP Jewish Lead.	CRM & Mapam Jewish Lead.	Labor Jewish Lead.	Likud Camp Jewish Lead.
Unlicensed demonstrations as a means to improve the situation of the Arabs in Israel										
In favor	10.8	0.0	0.0	35.0	58.1	2.4	79.4	20.6	0.0	0.0
Have reservations	22.0	9.4	16.1	40.0	32.3	11.0	14.7	38.2	7.7	8.8
Against	67.2	90.6	83.9	25.0	9.7	86.7	5.9	41.2	92.3	91.2
Resistance with force as a means to improve the situation of the Arabs in Israel										
In favor	8.1	0.0	0.0	5.1	40.7	*	*	*	*	*
Have reservations	17.1	3.1	9.7	23.1	40.7	*	*	*	*	*
Against	74.8	96.9	90.3	71.8	18.5	*	*	*	*	*

*Not asked.

Table 13.7 Extra-Legal Politics as a Strategy for Change, 1976-88

	Arab Public				Jewish Public		
	1976	1980	1985	1988	1980	1985	1988
Unlicensed demonstrations as a means to improve the situation of the Arabs in Israel							
In favor	17.1	7.0	10.8	13.1	2.0	2.4	4.0
Have reservations	23.8	23.0	22.0	25.5	10.6	11.0	17.8
Against	59.1	70.0	67.2	61.4	87.3	86.7	78.2
Resistance with force as a means to improve the situation of the Arabs in Israel							
In favor	17.9	7.5	8.1	8.0	1.4	*	*
Have reservations	22.6	21.9	17.1	14.8	8.3	*	*
Against	59.5	70.5	74.8	77.2	90.3	*	*

*Not asked.

The unwavering commitment of Israeli Arabs to a democratic struggle is well evidenced in their selection of the most appropriate means for obtaining various goals. Extra-parliamentary politics receive the greatest backing, closely followed by parliamentary politics, while extra-legal politics appeal to a tiny minority only. When asked to choose the most suitable method of achieving each of eight important civil or national targets, 41% to 59% of the Arab respondents opt for holding demonstrations and strikes, 30% to 43% prefer persuasion and pressures, 4% to 15% pick "all means necessary, including violence," and 3% to 23% reject the target itself (Table 13.8). An overwhelming

Table 13.8 Arabs' View of Goals for the Struggle of Arabs in Israel

	Arab Public	Estab. Affil. Arab Lead.	Unaffiliated Arab Lead.	DFPE & PLP Arab Lead.	Sons of Village Arab Lead.
The most appropriate means of struggle that the Arabs in Israel should use with regard to each of the following possible goals					
Proper compensation for expropriated Arab lands					
All means, including violence	15.3	3.3	6.5	7.3	42.3
Legal means, including demonstrations and strikes	51.1	63.3	64.5	78.0	50.0
Persuasion and pressures	29.6	33.3	25.8	12.2	0.0
Not a target	4.0	0.0	3.2	2.4	7.7
Equal budgets to Arab and Jewish local councils					
All means, including violence	3.6	0.0	0.0	2.4	25.8
Legal means, including demonstrations and strikes	59.0	56.3	67.7	95.1	67.7
Persuasion and pressures	34.3	40.6	32.3	2.4	0.0
Not a target	3.1	3.1	0.0	0.0	6.5
A special punitive law against discrimination in employment, housing, etc., on religious or nationalist grounds					
All means, including violence	7.8	3.1	0.0	0.0	29.0
Legal means, including demonstrations and strikes	54.5	62.5	65.6	90.2	61.3
Persuasion and pressures	34.0	34.4	28.1	7.3	6.5
Not a target	3.7	0.0	6.3	2.4	3.2
Abolition of the special benefits to army veterans and to their families					
All means, including violence	4.4	3.1	0.0	0.0	34.4
Legal means, including demonstrations and strikes	41.4	43.8	50.0	75.0	50.0
Persuasion and pressures	30.8	31.3	34.4	17.5	6.3
Not a target	23.3	21.9	15.6	7.5	9.4
Repeal of the Law of Return					
All means, including violence	7.6	0.0	3.2	2.6	40.0
Legal means, including demonstrations and strikes	46.1	31.3	45.2	71.8	50.0
Persuasion and pressures	31.5	34.4	41.9	20.5	10.0
Not a target	14.8	34.4	9.7	5.1	0.0
Israel's recognition of the Arab refugees' right to repatriation					
All means, including violence	7.8	0.0	0.0	5.0	50.0
Legal means, including demonstrations and strikes	43.4	21.9	51.6	72.5	42.9
Persuasion and pressures	42.9	62.5	32.3	20.0	3.6
Not a target	5.9	15.6	16.1	2.5	3.6
The formation of a Palestinian state in the West Bank and Gaza Strip alongside Israel					
All means, including violence	8.9	3.1	0.0	9.8	58.3
Legal means, including demonstrations and strikes	42.5	21.9	45.2	73.2	29.2
Persuasion and pressures	40.0	56.3	51.6	14.6	4.2
Not a target	8.5	18.8	3.2	2.4	8.3
Israel's recognition of the PLO					
All means, including violence	7.7	0.0	0.0	4.9	36.0
Legal means, including demonstrations and strikes	40.9	22.6	45.2	75.6	36.0
Persuasion and pressures	42.7	61.3	45.2	17.1	12.0
Not a target	8.7	16.1	9.7	2.4	16.0

majority of the Arabs are committed to democratic procedures and stand out against a minority of radicals, who accept violence, and indifferent persons, who reject any concerted action. The Arabs regard all sorts of issues as worthwhile goals of their struggle, yet equal distribution of resources and non-discrimination (e.g., compensation for expropriated lands) command greater support than does either modification of Israel's character (e.g., the repeal of the Law of Return) or Palestinian causes (e.g., a Palestinian state). With the exception of those attached to the Zionist establishment, Arab leaders favor more intense means than does the public at large. The leaders realize that the Arabs must step up their struggle, while remaining within the bounds of law, in order to accomplish their collective goals.

The outbreak of the intifada made the Palestinian issues more urgent. The support for extra-parliamentary measures rose from 41% in 1985 to 48% in 1988 for fighting for Israel's recognition of the PLO, while that for equal budgets for Arab and Jewish councils remained unchanged – from 59% to 57% (Table 13.9). This modest and temporary rise in the salience of Palestinian problems falls much short of what one would have expected if the Palestinian dimension in the identity of Israeli Arabs were definitely predominant.

Table 13.9 Arabs' View of Goals for the Struggle of Arabs in Israel, 1985-88

	Arab Public	
	1985	1988
The most appropriate means of struggle that the Arabs in Israel should use with regard to each of the following possible goals		
Equal budgets to Arab and Jewish local councils		
All means, including violence	3.6	5.3
Legal means, including demonstrations and strikes	59.0	56.6
Persuasion and pressures	34.3	30.5
Not a target	3.1	7.7
Israel's recognition of the PLO		
All means, including violence	7.7	8.8
Legal means, including demonstrations and strikes	40.9	48.2
Persuasion and pressures	42.7	32.4
Not a target	8.7	10.6

A central component in any group struggle is a feeling of efficacy; namely, that the goals are valuable, the means are effective, and the chances to affect change are good. People are motivated for struggle by hope, not despair. The various facets of Arab efficacy investigated lead to the conclusion that Israeli Arabs carry out their continued struggle for peace and equality with a strong feeling of efficacy. This conclusion is based on the following indications.

First, most Arabs and Jews believe in the utility of collective action. For instance, 88.5% of the Arabs and 83% of the Jews agree that "ordinary people can make progress if they help each other"; but at the same time,

64% and 60%, respectively, feel that there is little that individuals, like the respondent, can do to improve the life of people in Israel (Table 13.10).

Table 13.10 Efficacy

	Arab Public	Jewish Public
Agree that ordinary people can make progress, if they help each other	88.5	83.4
Disagree that if one tries to change things, one usually makes them worse	79.1	78.3
Agree that there is little a person like oneself can do to improve the life of people in Israel	64.0	60.1

Source: The 1988 survey.

Second, most Arabs regard their political struggle as essential. To illustrate, 72% of them hold that their political goals are so important that any sacrifice on their part is worthwhile (Table 13.11). Yet the struggle does not justify the perpetration of violence and killing.

Table 13.11 Arabs' View of Intensity of Arab Struggle

	Arab Public
Agree that the political goals of Israeli Arabs are so important that any sacrifice is worthwhile, no matter how painful	72.3
Agree that violence and killing can never be justified, no matter how important the Israeli Arab struggle	59.0
Agree that unity among Israeli Arabs is more important even than loyalty to the state	69.3

Source: The 1988 survey.

Third, most Arabs desire the continuation of their struggle, although they understand well the limits of their power and, as a result, the modesty of their gains. A majority of 75% maintain that their struggle is proceeding well and must continue. On the other hand, 59% doubt whether they can fulfill the mission of their struggle in the face of superior Jewish power, and 70% agree that an open conflict with Jews will cause both sides to lose (Table 13.12).

And fourth, most Arabs see the current means of struggle as effective. Listed in descending order of effectiveness, these means are as follows: general strikes judged as effective by 81%; demonstrations – 79%; shutdowns of local councils – 79%; voting for the oppositionist DFPE and PLP lists – 65%; shutdowns of schools – 55.5%; voting for Jewish parties is considered effective by only 13% (Table 13.13). The contrast between these 13% in the 1988 survey and the 41% who actually voted for Jewish parties later that year is striking. It is indicative of the consistent trend of erosion in support for the Jewish parties, which is being expedited by a number of developments. The increasingly politicized Arabs feel more and more detached from the Jewish parties, from which they dissent on the key issues of peace and Zionism. Furthermore, voting for the Labor camp parties no longer yields handsome benefits, because of the entrenchment of the Likud Party, since 1977, as a permanent pillar of government coalitions.

Table 13.12 Arab Collective Efficacy

	Arab Public	Jewish Public
Agree that the strength of the Jews opposing Israeli Arabs makes it very doubtful whether Israeli Arabs will achieve the goals of their struggle	59.3	*
Agree that the gap in power between Jews and Israeli Arabs is such that no important change in power relations is possible for the long run	46.0	46.3
Agree that open conflict between Jews and Israeli Arabs will cause everyone to lose in the long run	69.6	77.3
Agree that the political struggle of Israeli Arabs is proceeding well and must continue	75.4	*

*Not asked.

Source: The 1988 survey.

Table 13.13 Arabs' Perceived Effectiveness of Means of Struggle

	Arab Public
Consider as good each of the following means of struggle that Israeli Arabs use to improve their situation in the country	
Voting for Jewish parties	12.6
Voting for the DFPE and PLP	64.6
Shutdowns of local councils	78.9
Shutdowns of schools	55.5
Demonstrations	79.3
General strikes	81.0

Source: The 1988 survey.

Several measures of involvement in the Arab struggle are available. Thus, 59% of the Israeli Arabs are willing to contribute time or money for a struggle (Table 13.14), 17% to 21% have taken part in protest activities (Table 13.15), and 10% have endured and 32.5% expect to endure privations as a result of expressing opinions or taking action to influence the present conditions of Arabs in Israel (Table 13.16). A majority of 61% took part in the first general strike in solidarity with the intifada as early as two weeks after it broke out. All these indicators of involvement are present, of course, a number of times more among the leaders, attesting to their overall militant and independent styles. This is also partially true of Arab leaders from the Zionist establishment. They usually join the common protest activities taken by the Arab population, but they are shielded from the privations experienced by the more radical Arab leaders.

Table 13.14 Arabs' Willingness to Contribute to the Struggle of Arabs in Israel

	Arab Public	Estab. Affil. Arab Lead.	Unaffil-iated Arab Lead.	DFPE & PLP Arab Lead.	Sons of Village Arab Lead.
Willingness to contribute own time or money for a struggle to change the present situation of Arabs in Israel					
Willing to contribute much	27.4	80.0	64.5	97.6	87.5
Willing to contribute some	31.5	13.3	22.6	2.4	9.4
Do not have time or money to contribute	22.9	0.0	0.0	0.0	0.0
Unwilling to contribute because it is not necessary	6.3	6.7	6.5	0.0	3.1
Unwilling to contribute	11.8	0.0	6.5	0.0	0.0

Table 13.15 Participation in Protest Actions

	Arab Public	Estab. Affil. Arab Lead.	Unaffil-iated Arab Lead.	DFPE & PLP Arab Lead.	Sons of Village Arab Lead.
Participated over the past two years in one or more demonstrations protesting the treatment of Arabs in Israel	17.6	48.4	59.4	95.0	96.9
Participated in 1985 in events commemorating Land Day	17.4	34.4	53.1	95.1	81.3
Participated in protest actions against Israel's War in Lebanon	20.9	67.7	71.9	92.5	100.0
Participated in the Peace Day strike (December 21, 1987)	61.4[a]				

[a]The 1988 Survey.

Table 13.16 Arabs' Experience and Expectation of Privations

	Endured Privations					Expected Privations				
	Arab Public	Estab. Affil. Arab Lead.	Unaffil-iated Arab Lead.	DFPE & PLP Arab Lead.	Sons of Village Arab Lead.	Arab Public	Estab. Affil. Arab Lead.	Unaffil-iated Arab Lead.	DFPE & PLP Arab Lead.	Sons of Village Arab Lead.
Privations endured or expected as a result of expressing opinions or taking action to affect the present conditions of Arabs in Israel										
Political harassment and economic suffering	3.5	0.0	16.1	56.1	60.0	21.0	0.0	17.2	29.3	41.4
Political harassment but no economic suffering	4.6	9.7	12.9	34.1	23.3	6.8	10.0	6.9	17.1	10.3
Economic suffering but no political harassment	2.3	0.0	6.5	0.0	3.3	3.7	3.3	10.3	2.4	0.0
Neither economic suffering nor political harassment	89.6	90.3	64.5	9.8	13.3	68.5	86.7	65.5	51.2	48.3

In sum, Israeli Arabs view Israeli democracy as a worthy instrument for promoting their special stake in peace and equality. They regard the extra-parliamentary methods of licensed demonstrations, general strikes, and shutdowns of local councils as the most effective means of struggle, and apply them skillfully and frequently. They also believe in the parliamentary steps of voting for predominantly Arab parties, persuasion, and pressure, but perceive them as less effective. Most importantly, they neither endorse nor turn to extra-legal or violent measures. They understand the limits of their ability to bring about change in a state of and for Jews but find enough room in it for reforms. It should be stressed that most Arabs support the incorporation of their independent parties into coalition governments. There is no doubt that were the system sufficiently open to admit Arabs, their participation in coalition politics could serve as a main road for improving their condition and Arab-Jewish coexistence.

The Jews are on the defensive about the intense Arab struggle. They acquiesce in the Arab use of parliamentary measures but oppose the resort to extra-parliamentary methods, fearing their deterioration into violence and instability. Since they wish to preserve their dominance, Jews object to the Arabs' adoption of strong means designed to produce immediate and meaningful modifications in Arab-Jewish relations. It must be emphasized, however, that the Jews do not react to the ongoing Arab struggle by outright repression, but rather by allowing it to proceed and granting it partial concessions.

Finally, the trend over the years is continued adherence to democracy as the sole vehicle of Arab struggle. Arabs have not despaired of Israeli democracy but rather have seized upon it to make some headway. The Arabs' struggle has shifted to extra-parliamentary means but has remained legal. The Jews have shown over time a little more tolerance toward this strong type of politics, but their fear of and opposition to it have persisted.

14

Ethnocentrism

Ethnocentrism refers to negative stereotyping, mistrust, avoidance, and denial of equal treatment to an ethnic group to a degree not justified by either reality or legitimate group goals. To illustrate, an image of all Arabs as primitive or of all Jews as racist is ethnocentric, but objection to intermarriage by either side is not ethnocentric, because both Arabs and Jews are non-assimilating groups.

Conditions in Israel stimulate considerable ethnocentrism among both Arabs and Jews. They include the Arab rejection of the Jewish character of the state, the Jewish suspicion that the Arabs side with Israel's enemies, mutual estrangement because of appreciable cultural differences and class and power disparities, intolerant religions, and strong ethnic nationalisms. These unrelenting forces aggravate Arab and Jewish ethnocentrism much beyond the personal prejudices common in minority-majority relations. Still, Arab and Jewish leaders should be expected to show considerably less ethnocentrism than the publics at large because of their greater commitment to democratic values, sophistication, education, and an ability to distinguish between defensible views and sheer intolerance.

Each side has its own stereotypes. For a majority of Arabs, most Jews do not care about self-respect and family honor, do not attribute any value to Arab life, are racist and exploitive (Table 14.1). On the other hand, a majority of the Arab leaders reject these sweeping, negative images of the Jews. Only the activists in the Sons of the Village Movement entertain such virulent perceptions, thereby revealing their extreme anti-Jewish feelings and rejectionism.

There is no clear trend of a change in Arab stereotypes. The proportion of Arabs who believe that Jews do not care about self-respect and family life dropped from 75% in 1980 to 65% in 1985; however, that of Arabs viewing Jews as exploitive rose from 69.5% to 73%, respectively

(Table 14.2). The tenacious Arab image of Jews as racist is connected with the continued attribution of discriminatory Zionism to Jews.

Table 14.1 Arabs' Stereotypes of Jews in Israel

	Arab Public	Estab. Affil. Arab Lead.	Unaffiliated Arab Lead.	DFPE & PLP Arab Lead.	Sons of Village Arab Lead.
Agree that most Jews in Israel					
Do not care about self-respect and family honor	64.9	26.7	32.1	28.6	57.7
Do not attribute any value to Arab life	65.6	21.9	43.3	45.9	96.6
Are racist	69.1	18.8	27.6	28.2	86.7
Are exploitive	73.1	18.8	45.2	27.0	79.3

Table 14.2 Arabs' Stereotypes of Jews in Israel, 1980-85

	Arab Public 1980	1985
Agree that most Jews in Israel		
Do not care about self-respect and family honor	75.2	64.9
Are racist	69.1	69.1
Are exploitive	69.5	73.1

Jews overall are less given to stereotyping than are the Arabs, but an appreciable segment perceives Arabs as incapable of reaching a Jewish level of development, as primitive, and as having no respect for Jewish life (Table 14.3). These negative evaluations stem from the Jews' own self-image as a culturally superior, modern people. The fact that these stereotypes are no longer so widespread is noteworthy; especially striking is their virtual absence among Jewish leaders and their feeble presence even among right-wing leaders.

Table 14.3 Jews' Stereotypes of Arabs in Israel

	Jewish Public	DFPE & PLP Jewish Lead.	CRM & Mapam Jewish Lead.	Labor Jewish Lead.	Likud Camp Jewish Lead.
Agree that most Arabs in Israel					
Will never reach the level of development Jews have reached	46.1	0.0	0.0	7.5	18.2
Are primitive	29.7	0.0	2.9	7.7	0.0
Do not attribute any value to Jewish life	55.6	0.0	9.7	10.3	26.9

There is little evidence to establish a trend in Jewish stereotyping over time. On the one hand, the proportion of Jews seeing Arabs as primitive declined from 38% in 1980 to 30% in 1985, but the idea that the Jews will always be ahead of the Arabs has remained unchanged at 44% to 46% (Table 14.4).

Table 14.4 Jews' Stereotypes of Arabs in Israel, 1980-85

	Jewish Public	
	1980	1985
Agree that most Arabs in Israel		
Will never reach the level of development Jews have reached	43.6	46.1
Are primitive	38.2	29.7

Another problem is mistrust. In view of the common hazards of life in Israel, it is no surprise that both sides feel that one must be very cautious and cannot trust the people who live and work around them (Table 14.5). Yet Arabs and Jews are quite discerning in the degree to which they trust various categories of people. As a rule, they trust family members and friends; about half also trust neighbors, townspeople, and coreligionists; but only a small minority trusts all Israelis. Against this background the 39% of the Arabs who trust Jews and the 54.5% of the Jews who trust Arabs constitute reasonable proportions. For instance, the 54.5% of the Jews who trust Arabs compares favorably with the 50% who trust other Jews from a different ethnic origin.

Table 14.5 Trust

	Arab Public	Jewish Public
Agree that one must be very cautious with people and that one cannot trust the people who live and work around oneself	75.6	69.4
Persons one trusts		
Family members	95.6	93.6
Friends	81.7	83.7
Neighbors	54.1	59.4
People from one's locality	50.2	44.5
People of one's religion/ethnic group[a]	52.0	49.8
People with the same work and life conditions as one's own	40.0	48.6
Jews/Arabs[b]	38.9	54.5
All citizens of the state	11.4	33.9

[a]For Arabs – Moslems, Christians, and Druzes; for Jews – Ashkenazim and Orientals (Sephardim).

[b]For Arabs – whether they trust Jews; for Jews – whether they trust Arabs.

Source: The 1988 survey.

Other inquiries disclose a high level of mistrust. A majority of 71% of the Arabs feel that it is impossible to trust most Jews, and 46% reject Israeli, non-Communist newspapers and broadcasts as trustworthy sources (Table 14.6). The Arab leaders hold a differentiating outlook: those affiliated with the Zionist establishment trust both the Jews and the Israeli media; those attached to the Israeli Communist Party and to the Progressive List for Peace trust Jews only; while the activists in the Sons of the Village Movement trust neither. The more intense the contact with Jews, the greater the Arab trust.

Table 14.6 Arabs' Mistrust of Jews in Israel

	Arab Public	Estab. Affil. Arab Lead.	Unaffiliated Arab Lead.	DFPE & PLP Arab Lead.	Sons of Village Arab Lead.
Agree that it is impossible to trust most Jews in Israel	70.7	9.4	30.0	18.4	85.7
Hold that the most trustworthy newspapers and broadcasts are					
Official, non-partisan Israeli newspapers and broadcasts	50.8	64.5	82.1	17.1	11.1
Israeli newspapers of the Jewish Left	5.3	32.3	3.6	9.8	7.4
Rakah newspapers	12.5	0.0	7.1	65.9	48.1
Non-Israeli newspapers and broadcasts from the occupied territories, Arab states or Europe	31.3	3.2	7.1	7.3	33.3

The level of Arab mistrust remained constant during the 1980s: about two thirds of the Arabs mistrust most Jews (Table 14.7). Israel's War in Lebanon and the intifada have not intensified Arab mistrust.

Table 14.7 Arabs' Mistrust of Jews in Israel, 1980-88

	Arab Public		
	1980	1985	1988
It is impossible to trust most Jews in Israel			
Agree	66.2	70.7	65.2
Disagree	33.8	29.3	34.8

Jewish mistrust is also substantial. A majority of 60% of the Jews do not trust most Arabs; 41% consider them to be highly dangerous and 42% somewhat dangerous to national security; 54% justify security restrictions on them; 41% favor a strong-arm policy toward them; and 37% want to step up surveillance over them (Table 14.8). In contrast to the public at large, Jewish leaders are rather guardedly trustful of the Arab minority; but the more tilted the political orientation toward the right, the greater is the mistrust. It is worth stressing, nonetheless, that Labor and Likud leaders agree that as long as the Israeli-Arab conflict persists, security restrictions on Arabs in Israel are fully or partly justified.

Table 14.8 Jews' Mistrust of Arabs in Israel

	Jewish Public	DFPE & PLP Jewish Lead.	CRM & Mapam Jewish Lead.	Labor Jewish Lead.	Likud Camp Jewish Lead.
Consider Arabs in Israel as a danger to national security					
To a great degree	16.6	0.0	0.0	0.0	3.0
To a considerable degree	24.0	0.0	2.9	0.0	21.2
To a certain degree	42.1	8.3	20.6	51.3	48.5
No	17.3	91.7	76.5	48.7	27.3
Agree that it is impossible to trust most Arabs in Israel	59.8	0.0	2.9	2.6	37.9
Favor an increase in surveillance over most Arabs in Israel	36.9	0.0	0.0	0.0	19.4
Consider as justified security restrictions on Arabs in Israel as long as the Israeli-Arab conflict persists					
Yes	54.1	0.0	2.9	21.1	47.1
To some extent	34.5	11.1	32.4	50.0	38.2
No	11.4	88.9	64.7	28.9	14.7
Strong-arm policy toward the Arabs in Israel					
In favor	41.3	0.0	0.0	0.0	24.2
Have reservations	35.9	0.0	2.9	27.5	45.5
Against	22.8	100.0	97.1	72.5	30.3

During the 1980s, the Jews became less distrustful and power-oriented toward Israeli Arabs despite the upswing in the perceived Israeli Arab security threat as a result of the intifada. To illustrate, the proportion of Jews in favor of an increase in surveillance over Israeli Arabs declined from 43% in 1980 to 34.5% in 1988 in spite of the rise, from 41% to 59%, during this period in the perception of Arabs as a serious danger to national security (Table 14.9). It appears that some of the Jews have become disenchanted with restrictions and punishments as effective means to pacify the Arab minority.

Mutual mistrust accounts for the attribution of more negative attitudes toward the other side. While 66% of the Jews believe that the Jews have reconciled themselves to the existence of the Arab minority in Israel and 70% believe that Jews do not hate Arabs, many fewer Arabs hold those beliefs to be so among the Jews; 42% and 46%, respectively (Table 14.10). This disagreement is even sharper among leaders. The moderate Arab leaders (those attached to Jewish parties or who are non-partisan) agree with the Jewish leaders that Jews accept Arabs as a minority and do not hate them, whereas the militant Arab leaders (those from the DFPE, PLP, and Sons of the Village Movement) evidently disagree.

Table 14.9 Jews' Mistrust of Arabs in Israel, 1980-88

Jewish Public	1980	1985	1988
Consider Arabs in Israel as a great or considerable danger to national security	40.9	40.6	58.8
Agree that it is impossible to trust most Arabs in Israel	65.9	59.8	60.0
Favor an increase in surveillance over most Arabs in Israel	42.7	36.9	34.5
Justifies, without any reservation, security restrictions on Arabs in Israel as long as the Israeli-Arab conflict persists	67.7	54.1	*
Favor, without any reservation, strong-arm policy toward Arabs in Israel	46.5	41.3	46.9

*Not asked.

Table 14.10 Perceived Jewish Acceptance of Arabs in Israel

	Arab Public	Estab. Affil. Arab Lead.	Unaffiliated Arab Lead.	DFPE & PLP Arab Lead.	Sons of Village Arab Lead.	Jewish Public	DFPE & PLP Jewish Lead.	CRM & Mapam Jewish Lead.	Labor Jewish Lead.	Likud Camp Jewish Lead.
Consider each of the following statements to be true for all or most Jews in Israel										
Reconciled themselves to the existence of an Arab minority in Israel	42.3	75.8	56.7	23.1	20.0	66.4	62.8	82.4	77.5	100.0
Hate Arabs	54.3	20.7	33.4	55.0	93.6	30.4	25.0	29.4	7.5	8.8

The Arab image of the Jews as rejecting Arabs became even more common in reaction to the strong Arab solidarity with the intifada. The proportion of Arabs seeing the Jews as accepting them as a minority shrunk further from 42% in 1985 to 27% in 1988; according to the Jews, in contrast, the decline went only from 66% to 51% (Table 14.11). The Arabs continue to feel much more Jewish distrust and rejection than the Jews apparently harbor or project.

By the same token, Jews consider Arabs to be more restive than the Arabs see themselves. Only 40% of the Jews regard all or most Arabs as being resigned to Israel's existence and only 17% view them as loyal to the state; much less than the 64% and 43%, respectively, of the Arabs who assess the situation this way (Table 14.12). Jews are split between the 60% who regard Israeli Arabs as being more loyal to the state than are the

Arabs in the territories and the 40% who doubt this. On the other hand, Arab and Jewish leaders share the appraisal that most Arabs are reconciled to Israel's existence, are loyal to the state, and do not feel hate or revenge toward Jews. Leaders are much less given to stereotyping and also more keenly aware of the adverse consequences of distorted group images. Although Jewish leaders conceive of the Arab minority as a security threat, they perceive the threat to be potential and limited to only a part of the Israeli Arabs.

Table 14.11 Perceived Jewish Acceptance of Arabs in Israel, 1985-88

	Arab Public		Jewish Public	
	1985	1988	1985	1988
Consider all or most Jews in Israel as reconciled themselves to the existence of an Arab minority in Israel	42.3	26.8	66.4	51.4

Table 14.12 Perceived Loyalty of Arabs in Israel

	Arab Public	Estab. Affil. Arab Lead.	Unaffiliated Arab Lead.	DFPE & PLP Arab Lead.	Sons of Village Arab Lead.	Jewish Public	DFPE & PLP Jewish Lead.	CRM & Mapam Jewish Lead.	Labor Jewish Lead.	Likud Camp Jewish Lead.
Consider each of the following statements to be true for all or most Arabs in Israel										
Reconciled themselves to Israel's existence	64.4	96.9	82.2	92.3	63.3	39.6	100.0	91.2	82.0	50.0
Loyal to Israel	43.0	90.6	65.7	76.3	10.0	17.1	83.9	85.3	65.8	26.5
Rejoice at Israel's suffering	31.2	6.3	3.3	12.8	72.4	43.4	3.2	5.9	0.0	29.4
Hate Jews	32.6	3.2	6.3	5.1	21.9	49.2	0.0	5.9	2.6	32.3
Engaged in spying against Israel	*	*	*	*	*	14.0	0.0	0.0	0.0	0.0
Agree that Arabs in Israel are more loyal to the state than are the Arabs in the territories	*	*	*	*	*	59.6	100.0	100.0	92.1	79.3

*Not asked.

A decline is observed in the attachment of the Arab minority to the state over the years. The Arabs regard themselves as having become less reconciled to Israel's existence (68% in 1980, but only 47% in 1988), less loyal, more resentful toward Jews, and more rejoicing at Israel's suffering (Table 14.13). The Jews are certainly aware of the increased Arab alienation but are right in their calculation that Israeli Arabs, despite their growing disaffection and unrest, are far more loyal to Israel than are their rebellious brethren on the West Bank and Gaza Strip.

Table 14.13 Perceived Loyalty of Arabs in Israel, 1980-88

	Arab Public			Jewish Public		
	1980	1985	1988	1980	1985	1988
Consider each of the following statements to be true for all or most Arabs in Israel						
Reconciled themselves to Israel's existence	68.2	64.4	47.3	*	39.6	33.4
Loyal to Israel	47.0	43.0	*	*	17.1	*
Rejoice at Israel's suffering	25.4	31.2	*	*	43.4	*
Hate Jews	28.6	32.6	*	*	49.2	*
Agree that Arabs in Israel are more loyal to the state than are the Arabs in the territories	*	*	*	*	59.6	61.8

*Not asked.

Avoidance is also appreciable, however, especially among the Jews. Jewish unwillingness for interethnic contact ranges, from 48% rejecting Arabs as coworkers, 62% as friends, 65% as schoolmates for one's children, to 75% as neighbors (Table 14.14). The Arabs' reluctance is smaller, yet significant, because as members of a subordinate minority they stand to gain more by interethnic contact. It is hard to estimate the exact size of the ethnocentric component in these avoidance patterns because, as willingly non-assimilating groups, Jews and Arabs are entitled to keep apart. Hence, the fact that 97% of the Arabs and 92.5% of the Jews in the 1988 survey showed an unwillingness to have their daughter marry a man of the other community should not be taken as evidence of extreme mutual intolerance and segregation; rather, it is an authentic, legitimate expression of a separate, religious, and national identity. The Arabs do not marry Jews as they do not marry Arabs of a different religion, and they do not desire to upset this centuries-old millet mores. Yet, it is clearly ethnocentric for Jews to refuse to have Arab coworkers and friends. That this is the case is confirmed by the considerable willingness of the norm-setting Jewish and Arab leaders to have various interethnic interactions that would boost integration without espousing assimilation between the two communities. A certain element of ethnocentrism is, however, also contained in the opposition of most right-wing Jewish leaders, some of whom are Orthodox and some secular nationalists, to selective mixing with Arabs in schools and neighborhoods.

Arab willingness to have contacts with Jews has intensified over the years despite the Jews' reluctance to open up. The proportion of Arabs unwilling to have Jews as friends dropped from 42.5% in 1976 to 34% in

1988 and as neighbors from 60% in 1976 to 52% in 1985; the unwillingness of the Jews has remained much higher and intact (Table 14.15).

Table 14.14 Willingness for Interethnic Contact

	Arab Public	Estab. Affil. Arab Lead.	Unaffiliated Arab Lead.	DFPE & PLP Arab Lead.	Sons of Village Arab Lead.	Jewish Public	DFPE & PLP Jewish Lead.	CRM & Mapam Jewish Lead.	Labor Jewish Lead.	Likud Camp Jewish Lead.
Willing to work in a place where Arabs and Jews work together	*	*	*	*	*	52.3	100.0	100.0	100.0	81.8
Willing to have Jews/Arabs as friends	63.4	96.9	100.0	95.0	81.3	38.4	100.0	100.0	95.0	81.8
Willing to have one's children (or children of one's close family) attend a mixed classroom	66.7	77.4	83.9	85.4	53.1	35.0	100.0	97.0	74.3	24.3
Willing to live in a mixed neighborhood	47.9	74.2	65.6	87.8	65.7	24.6	100.0	94.0	79.5	41.2

*Not asked.

Table 14.15 Willingness for Interethnic Contact, 1976-88

	Arab Public				Jewish Public		
	1976	1980	1985	1988	1980	1985	1988
Unwilling to have Jews/Arabs as friends	42.5	30.7	36.7	33.8	61.5	61.6	60.7
Unwilling to live in a mixed neighborhood	59.8	52.6	52.1	*	77.5	75.3	*

*Not asked.

It is, however, the predisposition of the Jews to deny Israeli Arabs equal treatment that most impedes Arab-Jewish coexistence An overwhelming Jewish majority of 81% maintains that Israel should prefer Jews to Arabs generally (Table 14.16). This is a controversial issue among the Jewish leaders, however. The leaders of the Likud, religious parties, and radical right hold and propagate the idea of a Jewish state that prefers Jews to Arabs – 79% adhere to this position in the survey. Labor leaders are evenly divided on this question. On the other hand, the endorsement of equal treatment by 88% of the Zionist left (and 94% of the non-Zionist left) is distinctive. Although there is a consensus on the idea of a Jewish-Zionist state, its precise meaning is highly disputed, and the provision of advantages to Jews is one of the cardinal bones of contention. The political division on this key issue attests to the right-wing bias toward the Jewish extreme and the left-wing slant toward the democratic extreme of the agreed-upon continuum of a Jewish-democratic state.

The unflagging Arab struggle for equality since the mid-1970s seems to bear some fruit, at least in terms of a certain reduction in the Jewish demand for preferential treatment. Jews favoring state preferential treatment of Jews constituted 84% in 1980 and 81% in 1985, but decreased to 74% in 1988 (Table 14.17). The decline from 68% in 1980 to 48% in 1988 of those calling for "considerable preference" is even more dramatic.

Table 14.16 Jews' Desire for Preferential Treatment

	Jewish Public	DFPE & PLP Jewish Lead.	CRM & Mapam Jewish Lead.	Labor Jewish Lead.	Likud Camp Jewish Lead.
The State of Israel should					
Prefer Jews to Arabs considerably	59.1	0.0	5.9	13.2	41.2
Prefer Jews to Arabs to some extent	21.7	0.0	5.9	36.8	38.2
Treat both equally	18.8	94.3	88.2	50.0	20.6
Prefer Arabs to Jews to some extent	0.4	2.9	0.0	0.0	0.0
Prefer Arabs to Jews considerably	0.0	2.9	0.0	0.0	0.0

Table 14.17 Jews' Desire for Preferential Treatment, 1980-88

	Jewish Public		
	1980	1985	1988
The State of Israel should			
Prefer Jews to Arabs considerably	67.6	59.1	47.9
Prefer Jews to Arabs to some extent	16.3	21.7	25.9
Treat both equally	15.8	18.8	25.5
Prefer Arabs to Jews to some extent	0.3	0.4	0.7
Prefer Arabs to Jews considerably	0.1	0.0	0.0

The Jewish expectation of state preferential treatment diminishes further when anchored in specific and concrete areas. Between 45% and 66% of the Jews expect preference in university admissions, employment, and social security benefits (Table 14.18). The Jewish leaders in the center and on the left insist on non-discrimination, whereas those on the right are split. Since these questions strictly pertain to equal opportunity for individuals, the stand of the Jewish public and right-wing in favor of preference is patently ethnocentric.

The Jewish public retreats further from the claim of a right to preferential treatment in the Jewish state when confronted with alternative principles of allocation of positions that in Western democracies are staffed on merit. The proportion of Jews demanding preference decreases in questions that mention merit and nationality as criteria of selection, in comparison to questions that mention only nationality: in admission to universities the drop is from 59% to 33% and in appointment to jobs in the civil service from 56% to 39% (compare Table 14.19 to Table 14.18). It is worth emphasizing that the Arabs favor recruitment according to performance and only 6% to 7% advocate proportional representation. Since Arabs in Israel face discrimination, they seek non-discrimination and do not dare to pursue affirmative action. Unlike the United States, affirmative action is not an acceptable option in Israel to rectify gross inequities in the representation of women, Oriental Jews and Arabs (Lerner, 1984). An official commission on reform in the civil service recommended that Arab representation be boosted by various measures of non-discrimination; it expressly decided against affirmative action as a policy (Committee on Civil Service, 1989: Vol. 2, pp. 313-314).

Table 14.18 Jews' Desire for Preferential Treatment in Selected Areas

	Jewish Public	DFPE & PLP Jewish Lead.	CRM & Mapam Jewish Lead.	Labor Jewish Lead.	Likud Camp Jewish Lead.
Favor preferential treatment of Jews in each of the following					
Admission to universities	65.8	0.0	6.1	18.0	58.8
Jobs in the civil service	65.2	0.0	3.0	15.4	55.9
Social security benefits	60.3	0.0	3.0	15.4	51.5
Layoffs during a state of unemployment	44.6	0.0	0.0	0.0	14.7

Table 14.19 Jew's Attitude toward Equal Treatment in Selected Areas

	Arab Public	Jewish Public
Kinds of persons that should be admitted to the universities		
Mostly Jews	0.9	32.8
The brightest persons, regardless if Jews or Israeli Arabs	90.5	57.4
Jews and Israeli Arabs according to their proportion in the population	5.8	5.6
Mostly Israeli Arabs	2.8	4.2
Kinds of persons that should get jobs in the civil service		
Mostly Jews	1.3	39.3
The brightest persons, regardless if Jews or Israeli Arabs	89.0	50.8
Jews and Israeli Arabs according to their proportion in the population	7.3	5.2
Mostly Israeli Arabs	2.4	4.7

Source: The 1988 survey.

Most Jews also disapprove of various measures designed to improve conditions for the Arabs by treating Arab institutions and localities the same way as the Jewish ones. Between 56% and 87.5% do not approve of such steps as equal budgets for Arab and Jewish local councils and schools or allocation of lands and funds to establish new Arab towns (Table 14.20). The Jewish leadership is as divided on this policy of non-discriminatory allocation to collectivities as on selection criteria of individuals. The left is consistent in its support for non-discrimination, Labor is ambivalent and internally split, while the right is mostly opposed to equal treatment.

Table 14.20 Jews' Disapproval of Measures to Improve Arab Conditions

	Jewish Public	DFPE & PLP Jewish Lead.	CRM & Mapam Jewish Lead.	Labor Jewish Lead.	Likud Camp Jewish Lead.
Jews reserved or opposed to each of the following measures to improve conditions for Arabs in Israel					
Proper compensation for expropriated Arab lands	56.2	0.0	11.8	17.9	8.8
Enactment of a special punitive law against discrimination in jobs, housing, etc., on religious or nationalist grounds	60.1	0.0	2.9	30.0	54.5
Extension to Arab schools of the same special assistance given to disadvantaged Jewish schools	63.8	0.0	8.8	21.1	53.0
Extension to Arab localities of the same special assistance given to Jewish development towns	77.6	0.0	15.1	67.6	79.4
Allocation of lands and funds to establish new Arab towns	87.5	13.9	35.5	55.2	91.2

The Jewish disapproval of a policy of non-discrimination did not change from 1980-85 (Table 14.21). The Jews are reluctant to renounce their superior access to opportunities and resources and feel that, as Jews, they are rightfully entitled to a variety of benefits.

Table 14.21 Jews' Disapproval of Measures to Improve Arab Conditions, 1980-85

	Jewish Public 1980	Jewish Public 1985
Jews reserved or opposed to each of the following measures to improve conditions for Arabs in Israel		
Enactment of a special punitive law against discrimination in jobs, housing, etc., on religious or nationalist grounds	75.2	60.1
Extension to Arab schools of the same special assistance given to disadvantaged Jewish schools	59.0	63.8
Extension to Arab localities of the same special assistance given to Jewish development towns	75.0	77.6
Allocation of lands and funds to establish new Arab towns	89.2	87.5

Furthermore, most Jews approve, with or without reservations, restrictions on Israeli Arabs that would increase discrimination between the two communities. A majority of three quarters of the Jews partly or fully endorse the outlawing of Rakah and the Progressive List for Peace, the seizing of any opportunity to encourage Arabs to leave the country, and the expropriation of Arab lands within the Green Line for Jewish development (Table 14.22). The Jewish leaders are, once again, divided on the issue. All oppose the outlawing of the Communist Party, which is as old as the oldest Jewish parties. But Labor and Likud leaders disagree on the political wisdom of declaring the PLP illegal, the need to continue expropriating Arab lands, and the propriety of pushing Arab citizens to resettle outside Israel.

Table 14.22 Jews' View of Restrictions on Arabs

	Jewish Public	DFPE & PLP Jewish Lead.	CRM & Mapam Jewish Lead.	Labor Jewish Lead.	Likud Camp Jewish Lead.
Outlawing of Rakah					
Agree	44.8	0.0	0.0	5.0	9.1
Have reservations	28.7	0.0	0.0	5.0	21.2
Disagree	26.5	100.0	100.0	90.0	69.7
Outlawing of the Progressive List for Peace					
Agree	41.7	0.0	0.0	10.3	51.5
Have reservations	31.5	0.0	0.0	10.3	21.2
Disagree	26.8	100.0	100.0	79.5	27.3
Israel should seek and use any opportunity to encourage Israeli Arabs to leave the state					
Agree	42.4	0.0	0.0	2.6	20.6
Have reservations	33.7	2.8	11.8	13.2	50.0
Disagree	23.9	97.2	88.2	84.2	29.4
Expropriation of Arab lands within the Green Line for Jewish development					
Agree	34.9	0.0	14.7	15.8	37.5
Have reservations	40.5	2.8	17.6	50.0	43.8
Disagree	24.6	97.2	67.6	34.2	18.8

During the 1980s, the Jews became less certain about their open support for imposing various restrictions on Arabs. For instance, Jews who favor without reservation the encouragement of Arabs to leave the state declined from 50% in 1980 to 40% in 1988 (Table 14.23). This is no doubt in response to the mounting condemnation of the idea of population transfer after Rabbi Kahane became a member of the Knesset in 1984.

As a result of the attempt to stop Kach candidates from running for the Knesset and the subsequent boycott of this movement, a majority of the Jews in the 1985 survey did not oppose the outlawing of Kach (Table 14.24). On the question of land expropriations, however, the Jews do not show consistency. Only 24% object to expropriating Arab lands within the Green Line for Jewish development, but 67% oppose expropriation of Jewish lands for Arab development (compare Table 14.23 to Table 14.24).

Table 14.23 Jews' View of Restrictions on Arabs, 1980-88

	Jewish Public		
	1980	1985	1988
Outlawing of Rakah			
Agree	51.7	44.8	44.8
Have reservations	25.8	28.7	33.3
Disagree	22.5	26.5	21.9
Israel should seek and use any opportunity to encourage Israeli Arabs to leave the state			
Agree	50.3	42.4	39.9
Have reservations	30.8	33.7	36.9
Disagree	18.8	23.9	23.2
Expropriation of Arab lands within the Green Line for Jewish development			
Agree	40.7	34.9	*
Have reservations	35.4	40.5	*
Disagree	23.9	24.6	*

*Not asked.

Table 14.24 Jews' View of Restrictions on Jews

	Jewish Public	DFPE & PLP Jewish Lead.	CRM & Mapam Jewish Lead.	Labor Jewish Lead.	Likud Camp Jewish Lead.
Outlawing of the Kach movement					
Agree	39.3	80.0	79.4	87.5	42.4
Have reservations	25.9	8.6	5.9	0.0	18.2
Disagree	34.8	11.4	14.7	12.5	39.4
Expropriation of Jewish lands for Arab development					
Agree	4.9	28.1	21.2	15.4	21.9
Have reservations	28.0	12.5	15.2	43.6	46.9
Disagree	67.1	59.4	63.6	41.0	31.3

Jewish ethnocentrism is at its peak in situations in which Jews are subordinate in status to Arabs. As many as 57.5% of the Jews are not prepared to accept an Arab as their personal doctor and 68%, as a superior in a job (Table 14.25). During the 1980s, they did not consistently become more tolerant (Table 14.26). The Jewish leaders show openness, and only those on the right are intolerant to some extent.

Table 14.25 Jews' Willingness to Accept Arabs of Superior Status

	Jewish Public	DFPE & PLP Jewish Lead.	CRM & Mapam Jewish Lead.	Labor Jewish Lead.	Likud Camp Jewish Lead.
Unwilling to have an Arab as one's own					
Personal doctor	57.5	0.0	2.9	7.5	30.3
Superior in a job	68.2	0.0	0.0	2.8	45.1

Table 14.26 Jews' Willingness to Accept Arabs of Superior Status, 1980-88

	Jewish Public		
	1980	1985	1988
Unwilling to have an Arab as one's own			
Personal doctor	65.0	57.5	*
Superior in a job	70.0	68.2	74.8

*Not asked.

Pure racism is a weaker element in Jewish ethnocentrism than is political intolerance. Thus 24% of the Jews would deny any Arab the right to vote (Table 14.27), but 38% to 72% would disenfranchise any person, a Jew included, whose loyalty to the state is dubious or any person who supports the formation of a Palestinian state in the West Bank and Gaza Strip alongside Israel. From a Jewish perspective, since most Arabs fall into this last category, Jewish objections to Arabs are grounded in intolerance of political critics, protesters, and dissidents, not in opposition to Arabs as such. These figures collaborate the main finding of other studies, that political intolerance in Israel is a focused phenomenon directed mostly against the dovish left (Sullivan, Shamir, Roberts, and Walsh, 1984).

The Jewish leadership's political tolerance stands in sharp contrast with the general public's political intolerance. Almost none of the leaders would deny Israeli Arabs the right to vote, but about a quarter of Labor and Likud leaders would disenfranchise people with questionable loyalty to the state and pro-PLO non-Zionists. At any rate, the stands of the leaders plainly confirm their firm commitment to democracy. This holds true, also, for right-wing leaders with the notable exception of the radical right.

The impact of the intifada is interesting. On the one hand, the growing polarization among the Jews lessened political intolerance. This is reflected in the decline in the proportion of Jews who would deny the franchise to non-Zionists who stand for two states for two peoples (Table 14.28). On the other hand, the unrest among Israeli Arabs during the intifada alarmed the Jews to the extent that support for the Arabs' disenfranchisement rose dramatically, from 24% in 1985 to 43% in 1988.

Table 14.27 Jews' Political Intolerance

	Jewish Public	DFPE & PLP Jewish Lead.	CRM & Mapam Jewish Lead.	Labor Jewish Lead.	Likud Camp Jewish Lead.
Favor the denial of the right to vote in national elections to each of the following citizen groups					
Arabs in Israel	24.1	0.0	0.0	0.0	2.9
Severe critics of government policy	37.7	0.0	0.0	0.0	0.0
Persons whose loyalty to the state is dubious	67.7	0.0	9.7	21.6	26.5
Zionists who support the formation of a Palestinian state in the West Bank and Gaza Strip alongside Israel	60.8	0.0	0.0	7.7	18.2
Non-Zionists who support the formation of a Palestinian state in the West Bank and Gaza Strip alongside Israel	72.0	0.0	3.0	23.1	28.1

Table 14.28 Jews' Political Intolerance, 1985-88

	Jewish Public	
	1985	1988
Favor the denial of the right to vote in national elections to each of the following citizen groups		
Arabs in Israel	24.1	42.8
Non-Zionists who support the formation of a Palestinian state in the West Bank and Gaza Strip alongside Israel	72.0	67.9

In sum, Arab and Jewish ethnocentrism is substantial. It is the cumulative result of a set of factors that inhibits Arab-Jewish coexistence. The ethnocentric and non-ethnocentric ingredients in these factors are, however, intertwined and hard to disentangle. To illustrate, it is difficult to ascertain how much of the Jewish distrust of Israeli Arabs is justified by the genuine intricacies and sensitivities of the Israeli-Arab dispute and by the "self-incriminating" admission of 57% of the Arabs who see only part of the Arab minority in Israel as loyal to the state. Also not clear is the amount of ethnocentrism in the Jewish unwillingness to have Arab children attend Jewish schools or Arab families live in Jewish neighborhoods in view of the common goal of separate coexistence.

Leaders are found to exhibit much less ethnocentrism than is the public at large, thanks to their greater sophistication and stronger commitment to democracy and equal treatment. Yet, Jewish leaders on the right, and particularly those on the radical right, are quite openly nationalistic and ethnocentric toward the Arab minority; they are also closer to the Jewish public in their attitudes than are other Jewish leaders. On the other hand, rejectionist Arab leaders reveal a virulent ethnocentrism that is not representative of the Arab public at large.

There is no consistent trend of change in the level of Arab and Jewish ethnocentrism since the mid-1970s, despite the growth of conditions conducive to a rise in ethnocentrism, including the Arab struggle for equality, the Arab challenge to Jewish dominance and the intifada, and, as a result, the increase in the belief that the Arabs are not reconciled to Israel's existence and that they pose a threat to national security. Ironically the failure of ethnocentrism to grow in a society in which mutual intolerance is prevalent and constantly reinforced should be interpreted as small solace.

15

Deprivation and Alienation

Since Israeli Arabs belong to the category of a subordinate, dissident, and non-assimilating minority, they are bound to feel deprived and alienated. How significant are these ill-feelings? Do Jews show understanding and sympathy?

At the heart of Arab discontent stands the conception of Israel as the state of the Jewish people, the bitter struggle between Israel and the Palestinian people, the state's discriminatory policies, the Jewish public's virulent ethnocentrism, and the persistent inequality between the two communities. The Arabs feel relative, not absolute deprivation. In fact, they have experienced steady improvement in civil rights, living standards, and integration into Jewish public institutions. They have not, however, become more satisfied, because they keep comparing themselves to the Jews; as a result, they feel grossly disadvantaged and discriminated against. The uncompromising demand for peace and equality is well evidenced in the recurrent demonstrations, shutdowns of local councils, and general strikes in protest of Israel's apparent intransigence on the Palestinian question and of the continuing civil and material inequalities between Arabs and Jews.

The Arabs have many grievances. The lengthy list relating to inequality includes unequal funding (of local councils, education, and development projects), lack of approved master plans for many localities, pending demolition injunctions for illegal housing units, disputed land holdings, the existence of forty unplanned, temporary communities that demand official recognition as permanent localities, and denial of certain benefits reserved to families whose members serve in the armed forces. Land expropriation is no doubt the most sensitive issue. In 1988, 58% of all Arabs and 75% of all land-owning Arabs reported having lands confiscated (Table 15.1). The Arab proportion reporting subjection to land expropriation increased from 57% in 1976 to 75% in 1988. This is due to two main developments: the takeover of certain Bedouin lands in the Negev needed for building new military airfields as a result of the retreat from the Sinai Peninsula in 1982, and the setting up in the Galilee of many Jewish settlements with jurisdiction over enclaves of unbuilt Arab lands. In the latter case, Arab lands were not technically confiscated, but, rather, lost much of their "Arab" value by their very annexation to Jewish localities. The mass immigration of Jews from the Soviet Union in late 1990 reinforced the Arabs' fear of further land losses.

Table 15.1 Arabs' Report of Land Expropriations, 1976-88

	Arab Public							
	All Arabs				Landowning Arabs			
	1976	1980	1985	1988	1976	1980	1985	1988
The extent of expropriations since 1948 of lands owned by oneself and one's brothers, parents, or sons								
Own no land	12.6	21.5	24.0	22.3	–	–	–	–
Own land but not expropriated	30.6	27.1	22.0	19.7	35.0	34.5	28.9	25.4
Some land expropriations	24.4	20.4	23.2	24.4	27.9	26.0	30.5	31.4
Much land expropriations	32.4	31.0	30.9	33.6	37.1	39.5	40.6	43.2

Most Arabs feel deprived: 87% hold that they do not enjoy equal job opportunities, 59% believe that Arab youth do not have reasonable chances of fulfilling their occupational aspirations, and 55% accuse the government of policies that widen the socioeconomic gap between Arabs and Jews (Table 15.2). These widespread feelings of deprivation are even stronger among Arab leaders, let alone the more radical among them from the Communist Party, the Progressive List for Peace, and the Sons of the Village Movement. On the other hand, except in the area of employment, where Jews concede inequality but not discrimination, only a minority of Jews share these Arab apprehensions. On the contrary, 84% of the Jews maintain that Israel does enough or too much for the Arabs. Leftist and Labor Jewish leaders disagree, but 89% of Likud and other right-wing Jewish leaders also think that Israel treats its Arab citizens well. Prime Minister Shamir spoke in this vein when he dismissed the public criticism against the government's decision to impose higher tuition fees on university students who are not army veterans. He declared that "Arab students feel too well in the universities" (*Haaretz*, May 19, 1987).

The perceived Arab deprivation has remained stable during the 1976-88 period (Table 15.3). The Arabs have not seen their deprivation increase or decrease over the years. The percentage of Jews conceding that the Arabs are a deprived sector in Israeli society has not risen either. This also means that the Arab-Jewish disagreement on the degree of Arab deprivation has remained wide.

Table 15.2 Perceived Arab Deprivation

	Arab Public	Estab. Affil. Arab Lead.	Unaffil-iated Arab Lead.	DFPE & PLP Arab Lead.	Sons of Village Arab Lead.	Jewish Public	DFPE & PLP Jewish Lead.	CRM & Mapam Jewish Lead.	Labor Jewish Lead.	Likud Camp Jewish Lead.
Hold that Israel does enough or too much for the Arabs	*	*	*	*	*	84.2	0.0	9.1	21.6	87.9
Hold that government policies widen the socioeconomic gap between Arabs and Jews	55.4	29.0	43.3	95.1	93.8	18.7	91.4	52.9	18.9	12.5
Hold that Arabs do not enjoy equal job opportunities or doubt if they do	86.7	90.6	96.9	100.0	100.0	59.9	100.0	97.0	85.0	50.0
Hold that Arab youth do not have reasonable chances of fulfilling their occupational aspirations	59.3	62.5	65.6	95.1	96.9	31.7	94.3	64.7	43.6	26.5

*Not asked.

Table 15.3 Perceived Arab Deprivation, 1976-88

	Arab Public				Jewish Public		
	1976	1980	1985	1988	1980	1985	1988
Hold that Israel does enough or too much for the Arabs	*	*	*	*	83.7	84.2	*
Hold that government policies widen the socioeconomic gap between Arabs and Jews	57.6	55.0	55.4	*	19.7	18.7	*
Hold that Arabs do not enjoy equal job opportunities or doubt if they do	83.2	79.0	86.7	*	50.3	59.9	*
Hold that Arab youth do not have reasonable chances of fulfilling their occupational aspirations	67.1	55.7	59.3	58.1	26.6	31.7	29.6

*Not asked.

When asked directly to assess the degree of their overall satisfaction with life as Arabs or Jews in Israel, only 29% of the Arabs and 8% of the Jews in the 1988 survey report dissatisfaction (Table 15.4). The Arabs feel less content with their lot in Israel than the Jews do, but they do not feel miserable. Only when they consider specific areas do the Arabs more readily notice their deprivation. For instance, 58% are dissatisfied with their Israeli citizenship and 71% are dissatisfied with local educational and cultural services (Table 15.5). Arab leaders, whose task is to articulate and to capitalize on Arab discontent, report even higher levels of dissatisfaction. On the other hand, Jews expectedly feel less dissatisfaction than Arabs do. For instance, only 31% of the Jews, compared with 71% of the Arabs, are dissatisfied with educational and cultural services. Although the more intense Arab dissatisfaction reflects poorer services, it also implies very high aspirations. A larger proportion of Arabs than of Jews feels that the present socioeconomic status of their families is worse than it was in the past five years (55% versus 47%) or even will be in the coming five years (51% versus 32%). This pessimism spills over to a sense of uneasiness with being an Israeli citizen because Arabs do not enjoy full civil benefits.

Table 15.4 Satisfaction with Life as an Arab/a Jew in Israel

	Arab Public	Jewish Public
Degree of satisfaction with one's life as an Arab/a Jew in Israel		
Very satisfied with life as an Arab/a Jew in Israel	6.8	21.3
Satisfied	28.9	47.9
Neither satisfied nor dissatisfied – in the middle	35.0	22.4
Dissatisfied	19.7	7.2
Very dissatisfied with life as an Arab/a Jew in Israel	9.6	1.2

Source: The 1988 survey.

Table 15.5 Dissatisfactions

	Arab Public	Estab. Affil. Arab Lead.	Unaffiliated Arab Lead.	DFPE & PLP Arab Lead.	Sons of Village Arab Lead.	Jewish Public	DFPE & PLP Jewish Lead.	CRM & Mapam Jewish Lead.	Labor Jewish Lead.	Likud Camp Jewish Lead.
Dissatisfied with being an Israeli citizen	57.9	37.5	56.2	65.8	100.0	*	*	*	*	*
Dissatisfied with educational and cultural services in one's place of residence	70.6	68.9	90.6	100.0	100.0	30.9	80.7	38.2	30.8	26.4
Feel that present socioeconomic status of one's family is worse than it was five years ago	54.6	29.0	46.9	63.4	65.6	28.5	47.1	18.2	10.0	26.5
Expect socioeconomic status of one's family in the next five years to be worse than it is today	51.1	7.1	44.4	62.5	51.6	31.8	70.8	30.0	21.6	0.0

*Not asked.

Over the years, Arabs feel increasingly more dissatisfied with life in Israel. Arab dissatisfaction with Israeli citizenship rose from 49% in 1976 to 62% in 1988, and disaffection with educational and cultural services increased from 61% in 1976 to 71% in 1985 (Table 15.6). This growth came despite the overall improvement in socioeconomic conditions during the 1980s.

Table 15.6 Dissatisfactions, 1976-88

	Arab Public				Jewish Public		
	1976	1980	1985	1988	1980	1985	1988
Dissatisfied with being an Israeli citizen	48.7	55.3	57.9	62.3	13.4	*	*
Dissatisfied with educational and cultural services in one's place of residence	60.6	64.9	70.6	*	35.2	30.9	*
Feel that socioeconomic status of one's family is worse than it was five years ago	*	*	54.6	35.5	*	28.5	14.7

*Not asked.

The Arabs' acute sense of deprivation is best reflected in their assessment of their own or their children's chances in life. A majority of Arabs, in contrast with a minority of Jews, believe their chances to be low. To illustrate, 71% of the Arabs, but only 25% of the Jews, feel that they do not receive the education and the job they deserve irrespective of their personal efforts; similarly, 59% and 24%, respectively, fear that their children might never enjoy as high a standard of living as they do (Table 15.7).

Table 15.7 Life Chances

	Arab Public	Jewish Public
Feel uncertainty and fear about one's future	67.7	50.8
Afraid that our children might never enjoy as high a standard of living as we used to have	59.2	24.0
Feel that whatever one's personal efforts are in Israel, one will not get the education and job one is entitled to	71.0	25.4
Disagree that Israeli Arab youth have a reasonably good chance of reaching their goals in life	67.0	28.6

Source: The 1988 survey.

It is no wonder, therefore, that Arabs are slow to acknowledge the privileges that have accrued to them by living in Israel. They were asked to indicate whether certain developments were good or bad and whether they enjoyed or suffered from them. Seven changes in Arab life in Israel were presented; among them, social security benefits, transformation of the status of Arab women, and democracy. From a Jewish perspective, all of these changes are good things that happened to the Arabs during the period of the state, and for which Israel should receive full credit. The Arabs agree that the changes were good, but the proportion of those who think that these benefits are, in fact, enjoyed by Arabs ranges from 34% to 60% (Table 15.8). The two lowest percentages related to democracy and a rise in the standard of living (37% and 34%, respectively). Once again, underlying Arab appraisals is a sense of inequality with Jews; the result is that many Arabs are displeased with their achievement because it falls below the high Jewish standard. In a peculiar way, Arab dissatisfaction betrays the depth of Arab Israeliness.

Table 15.8 Arabs' View of Good Things They Enjoy in Israel

	Arab Public	Estab. Affil. Arab Lead.	Unaffil-iated Arab Lead.	DFPE & PLP Arab Lead.	Sons of Village Arab Lead.
Hold that Arabs in Israel enjoy today each of the following good things					
Social security benefits	60.3	84.4	64.5	60.0	29.6
Increase in the standard of education and culture	51.7	77.4	45.2	32.5	11.1
Greater equality among the Arabs themselves than formerly	51.4	76.7	56.7	57.1	54.2
Change in the status of women	47.0	80.0	56.7	55.0	25.0
Opportunity to develop and modernize	41.0	54.8	44.4	42.9	15.4
Democracy	37.3	75.9	54.8	30.0	4.0
Rise in the standard of living	33.8	71.4	48.1	31.3	13.6

In view of their intense sense of deprivation, the Arabs' feelings of social and cultural alienation are relatively moderate. Only a minority of 36% says it would feel more at home in an Arab country than in Israel, and only 22% feels quite alien here because of its different way of life (Table 15.9). This remarkable lack of social and cultural alienation from Israel is further evidenced by the fact that Arab leaders are not more alienated than is the public at large (Table 15.9) and that the rise, during the 1980s, in feelings of this kind of alienation is not significant (Table 15.10).

Feelings of political and nationalist alienation between Arabs and Jews are considerable, however. A majority of 57% among the Arabs, compared to 41% of the Jews, would either rejoice at or justify an action in which a member of their community killed, on nationalist grounds, a person from the other group (Table 15.11). With the notable exception of the rejectionist activists in the Sons of the Village Movement, the leaders of both sides reject these feelings of detachment. Although the intifada did not affect the Arab level of nationalist alienation (57% in 1985 and 58% in 1988), it did dramatically increase Jewish alienation, from 41% in 1985 to 76% in 1988 (Table 15.12). These figures point to a great deal of pent-up nationalist animosity in the two communities.

Table 15.9 Arabs' Feeling of Alienation

	Arab Public	Estab. Affil. Arab Lead.	Unaffil-iated Arab Lead.	DFPE & PLP Arab Lead.	Sons of Village Arab Lead.
Feel at home more in					
An Arab country	35.7	0.0	7.4	8.8	45.0
Israel	64.3	100.0	92.6	91.2	55.0
Feel alien in Israel in style of life, practices, and values					
To a great degree	7.4	0.0	6.3	4.9	36.7
To a considerable degree	14.9	6.5	12.5	17.1	43.3
To some degree	52.7	54.8	56.3	48.8	10.0
Do not feel alien	25.0	38.7	25.0	29.3	10.0

Table 15.10 Arabs' Feeling of Alienation, 1980-88

	Arab Public		
	1980	1985	1988
Feel more at home in an Arab country than in Israel	*	35.7	41.1
Feel quite alien in Israel in style of life, practices, and values	22.3	24.2	*

*Not asked.

Table 15.11 Detachment

	Arab Public	Estab. Affil. Arab Lead.	Unaffil-iated Arab Lead.	DFPE & PLP Arab Lead.	Sons of Village Arab Lead.	Jewish Public	DFPE & PLP Jewish Lead.	CRM & Mapam Jewish Lead.	Labor Jewish Lead.	Likud Camp Jewish Lead.
Feeling about an action in which an Israeli Arab/Jewish citizen killed a Jewish/Arab citizen on nationalist grounds										
Rejoice and justify action	8.3	0.0	0.0	0.0	8.7	8.5	0.0	0.0	0.0	0.0
Rejoice but do not justify action	3.6	0.0	0.0	0.0	4.3	10.6	0.0	0.0	0.0	0.0
Sadden but justify action	45.2	18.8	22.6	20.0	65.2	22.2	0.0	0.0	2.6	6.5
Sadden and do not justify action	42.9	81.3	77.4	80.0	21.7	58.6	100.0	100.0	97.4	93.5

Table 15.12 Detachment, 1985-88

	Arab Public		Jewish Public	
	1985	**1988**	**1985**	**1988**
Feeling about an action in which an Israeli Arab/Jewish citizen killed a Jewish/Arab citizen on nationalist grounds				
Rejoice and justify action	8.3	5.6	8.5	8.8
Rejoice but do not justify action	3.6	3.4	10.6	9.7
Sadden but justify action	45.2	48.6	22.2	57.3
Sadden and do not justify action	42.9	42.4	58.6	24.2

To conclude, Israeli Arabs feel highly deprived and nationalistically detached from the Jewish state, but progressively Israelized and, hence, not quite culturally and socially alienated from Israeli society. The Jews, on the other hand, do not lend credence to Arabs' feelings of deprivation and feel nationalistically detached from them; this was especially so during the first year of the intifada.

16

Issues as a Measure of Arab-Jewish Dissension

Beyond the agreement and disagreement between Arabs and Jews on each of the issues of coexistence, it is useful to construct a single overall quantitative measure that sums up the differences of opinion between and within the two sides. The issues selected for inclusion in the summary measure refer to the state's character, Arab national identity, the Palestinian question, and the means of Arab struggle. These matters constitute the core of the Arab-Jewish discord. With minor exceptions, all the items included in the "index of dissension" were presented to the Arabs in all the four surveys, conducted between 1976 and 1988, and to the Jews in the three surveys between 1980 and 1988. For each item, a score of 0 was assigned to a stand conforming with the dominant consensus, and a score of 1 to a dissenting view.

The following seven representative stands were taken to indicate dissent from the dominant consensus:

1. Regard Zionism as racism.[1]

2. Do not regard Israel as a homeland for Jews only.[2]

3. Define the collective identity of Israeli Arabs in Palestinian terms.

4. Agree to the establishment of a Palestinian state in the West Bank and Gaza Strip alongside Israel.

5. Hold that Israeli Arabs should politically organize in nationalist Arab or non-Zionist mixed parties.

[1]Jews were not asked this question, but it is safely assumed that had they been, they would have objected to equating Zionism with racism. Only Jewish leaders active in the Communist Party and the Progressive List for Peace may be an exception to this rule.

[2]Arabs were not asked this question in the 1976 survey, but it is presumed that they would have given the same answers as they did in the ensuing 1980-88 surveys.

6. Approve of the use of Arab protest actions abroad as a means of struggle to improve conditions for Israeli Arabs.

7. Approve of the use of Arab general strikes as a means of struggle to improve conditions for Arabs.

The index well distinguishes between Arabs and Jews. It reveals overwhelming consensus among the Jews: 95% of the Jewish public and 95% to 100% of Labor and Likud camp leaders score a total of 0 to 2 points (Table 16.1). Leaders from the Zionist left moderately dissent, and leaders from the non-Zionist left strongly dissent from the Jewish consensus.

Table 16.1 Index of Dissension

	Arab Public	Estab. Affil. Arab Lead.	Unaffil-iated Arab Lead.	DFPE & PLP Arab Lead.	Sons of Village Arab Lead.	Jewish Public	DFPE & PLP Jewish Lead.	CRM & Mapam Jewish Lead.	Labor Jewish Lead.	Likud Camp Jewish Lead.
Degree of acceptance of Jewish versus Arab consensus[a]										
0	0.3	3.1	0.0	0.0	0.0	47.9	0.0	2.9	42.5	84.8
1	4.9	12.5	3.2	0.0	0.0	34.2	0.0	17.6	40.0	12.1
2	8.6	28.1	3.2	0.0	0.0	13.1	0.0	17.6	12.5	3.0
3	12.5	15.6	9.7	0.0	0.0	3.3	2.8	32.4	2.5	0.0
4	15.3	21.9	22.6	0.0	6.5	1.1	0.0	11.8	2.5	0.0
5	21.4	12.5	35.5	10.0	32.3	0.2	5.6	17.6	0.0	0.0
6	22.2	3.1	19.4	35.0	45.2	0.1	38.9	0.0	0.0	0.0
7	14.9	3.1	6.5	55.0	16.1	0.0	52.8	0.0	0.0	0.0

[a]A scale ranging from fully accepting Jewish consensus (0) to fully accepting Arab consensus (7).

The index unequivocally demonstrates Arab dissidence. Opposing the status quo, with scores of over 2 points on the index, are 86% of the Arab public, 56% of the Arab leaders affiliated with the Zionist establishment, 94% of the non-partisan Arab leaders, and 100% of the Arab leaders from the Communist Party, the Progressive List for Peace, and the Sons of the Village Movement. The Arabs reject the solid Jewish consensus on vital issues of Arab-Jewish coexistence.

Arab dissent constitutes a basis for an Arab consensus, on the one hand, and for Arab factionalism, on the other. The three pillars of the Arab consensus are equality, peace, and legal struggle. More specifically, Israeli Arabs seek a status of a minority equal to Jews in Israel as a non-Zionist and non-Jewish state, pursue peace in the form of a Palestinian state in the West Bank and Gaza Strip, and use extra-parliamentary means in their democratic struggle for equality and peace.

Arab internal factionalism, at the same time, centers on the extent to which Arabs dissent from the Jewish consensus and on significant variations in the Arab consensus. The Arabs are widely divided on the index: 14% (0-2 points) conform , 28% (with 3-4 points) dissent to some extent, 43% (with 5-6 points) deviate moderately, and 15% (with 7 points) show strong dissidence. The activists in the rejectionist Sons of the Village Movement score less on the index than do the leaders of the non-rejectionist DFPE and PLP because they reject the Arab consensus on a Palestinian state in part of Palestine. More generally, the Arabs are split among themselves over key issues, such as the balance between Palestinian and Israeli national identity, acceptance of a Palestinian state on the West Bank and Gaza Strip, the use of extra-parliamentary or illegal means, and the most appropriate type of political organization.

Although not reflected in the index, there are significant differences among the Jews in their orientation toward the Arabs. The overarching contention, from which many disagreements stem, is the relative emphasis to be placed on Israel's Jewish-Zionist character versus democracy.

The trends during the 1976-88 period disclose substantial continuity, with certain change. The orientation of both sides has remained basically the same and distinctly different. Dissent (defined as 3-7 points on the index) increased, however, from 83% in 1976 to 92% in 1988 among the Arabs, and from 4% in 1980 to 10% in 1988 among the Jews (Table 16.2). The change among the Arabs means growth in militancy rather than rejectionism; among the Jews, it implies a sharpening of the attitude of the Zionist left, probably in response to the emergence in the 1980s of the radical right as a significant force.

Table 16.2 Index of Dissension, 1976-88

	Arab Public				Jewish Public		
	1976	1980	1985	1988	1980	1985	1988
Degree of acceptance of Jewish versus Arab consensus[a]							
0	0.0	0.6	0.3	0.2	52.9	47.9	38.2
1	5.1	7.9	4.9	2.5	33.9	34.2	34.3
2	11.8	12.8	8.6	5.7	9.6	13.1	17.1
3	11.9	13.5	12.5	8.6	3.0	3.3	6.3
4	12.1	17.2	15.3	15.1	0.5	1.1	2.7
5	13.4	18.2	21.4	21.2	0.2	0.2	1.2
6	25.2	17.8	22.2	28.2	0.0	0.1	0.2
7	20.3	11.9	14.9	18.5	0.0	0.0	0.0

[a]A scale ranging from fully accepting Jewish consensus (0) to fully accepting Arab consensus (7).

The Arab-Jewish discord is perceived as both salient and manageable. An Arab majority of 83% and a Jewish majority of 63.5% in the 1988 survey considered Arab-Jewish differences to be the most important when compared with the differences between poor and rich, religious and non-religious Jews, and Sephardic and Ashkenazic Jews (Table 16.3). Still, 65% of the Arabs and 60% of the Jews believe that despite the recent conflicts between Arabs and Jews in Israel, quiet and mutual cooperation can still be achieved. The intifada has intensified Arab-Jewish tension, but it has not disrupted coexistence.

Table 16.3 Comparing Arab-Jewish Relations with Other Group Relations

	Arab Public	Jewish Public
Consider the most important differences in Israel today to be between		
Poor and rich	9.4	14.4
Religious and non-religious Jews	5.5	15.7
Sephardic and Ashkenazic Jews	1.8	6.3
Israeli Arabs and Jews	83.2	63.5
Feel that despite the recent conflicts between Arabs and Jews in Israel, quiet and cooperation between them can still be achieved	65.0	59.9

Source: The 1988 survey.

We conclude the part of the book dealing with key issues. The plural nature of Israeli society is, throughout, abundantly evident in the recurrent divergences in the mutual attitudes of Arabs and Jews and in their views concerning the character of the state. Since the Jews determine the national consensus, the Arabs appear as dissident; but in the Arabs' eyes, the Jews look intransigent. The deep division between the two sides, however, is mitigated by the differences of opinion within each side. We now turn to the matter of internal factionalism.

Part Two

TYPOLOGIES

17

Studying Orientation Types

The study of orientation types among both Israeli Arabs and Jews in the 1985-88 surveys closely follows the rationale and method set forth in the 1980 survey. This continuity is required for cross-validating the typologies in the 1976-80 surveys and for monitoring changes in the types over the years.

The assumption that inter-communal differences are as important as intra-communal differences provides the rationale for studying types. Our detailed examination (in Part One) of the differences between the stands of Arabs and Jews on key issues of coexistence tends to overstress sharp divergences and polarity. In fact, it is shown that on the crucial ideological questions – namely, equality (as related to the nature of Israel as a state) and peace – the two communities are polarized. Along with this polarity, however, both Arabs and Jews differ appreciably among themselves on how to relate to the other group. The classification of the general public into various types according to the major orientation toward the other side shifts the focus from polarization between minority and majority to the internal factionalism within each side. The studies of the *inter* and *intra* differences complement and shed light on each other.

The method selected for the identification and classification of types is based on the premise that in democratic, but deeply divided societies, there is a rough correspondence between the factionalisms on the mass and elite levels. Leaders emerge to articulate the views and interests of a certain segment of the population; at the same time, leaders with rival ideologies compete for the support of different population groups. For this reason, the use of political streams as a criterion for distinguishing between leaders applies to the general public, as well. An orientation type can thus be operationalized as a subscriber to the views of one of the political streams prevalent in the community. Hence, four orientation types were defined to correspond to the four political streams (or groups of leaders) discerned in each community. The empirical data determine the proportion of the population that falls into each type and the percentage of the unclassified (those who have different or inconsistent viewpoints). This method of constructing a typology is superior to the "blind" procedure of building a numerical scale and assigning arbitrary cutoff points to separate one type from another. The method that identifies distinct types according to a predefined set of attitudes yields much clearer, more meaningful, and socially relevant types than does the continuous scale technique.

As a handy tool for examining the internal differences in orientation of the minority and majority, the typologies present a more accurate and complex picture of the positions of each side than does just a study of the key issues dividing the two. The typologies are also useful for de-stereotyping the populations, revealing the emergence of concurring segments from the two sides, and monitoring the stages of inter-group conflict and the point at which conflict-management becomes feasible.

The next chapter is devoted to the classification of the Arab population into four orientation types and to their correlates and determinants. The analysis proceeds with a similar chapter on Jewish types. These two chapters are followed by concluding remarks on several implications of the two typologies.

18

Arab Orientation Types

Arab orientation types are classified according to their attitudes toward the state, the Jewish majority, and their status as a minority. Four types were discerned in correspondence with the four major political streams in the Arab sector in the mid-1980s. The *accommodationist* type follows the Zionist establishment. The *reservationist* type is politically independent but steers a middle course between the Zionist establishment and permanent opposition to the regime. The *oppositionist* type is in tune with the critical posture of the Israeli Communist Party and the Progressive List for Peace. The *rejectionist* type goes as far as accepting the radical ideology of the Sons of the Village Movement.

This classificatory scheme leaves out three positions. One is that taken by the fundamentalist Islamic Movement. Although this movement has been active since the early 1980s, it moved to the political foreground only during the municipal elections of February 1989. It is, however, a new and uncrystallized perspective, and, therefore, it is not at all clear whether it is a variant of the rejectionist orientation.

Another political party emerged for the Knesset elections in November 1988. This was the Democratic Arab Party, founded and led by Abdul Wahab Darawshe, who had broken away from the Labor Party early that year. Darawshe has explicitly charted the route of the party as independent of the Zionist establishment, yet capable of cooperating with it. He intends to make the party a potential coalition partner and to escape the destiny of the Israeli Communist Party and the PLP as permanent opposition parties. It is too early to tell whether the Democratic Arab Party has succeeded in speaking for the reservationist type or whether it will in time become another variant of a permanent oppositionist party.

Another orientation that is popular among minorities in democratic societies and even among Israeli Jews hailing from different countries of origin, the idea of the amalgamation of exiles, is hardly to be found among Israeli Arabs. Such an "egalitarian" orientation would stand for Israel as an open, democratic society where nationality is privatized and Arabs and Jews are free to mix and intermarry. Since Israeli Arabs wish to preserve their separate national existence and Jews also would not allow them to assimilate, the egalitarian orientation is untenable and is not a real option for the Arab population at large. It is, in fact, hard to find an Arab ideological or political group that advocates such a position.

Constructing the Typology

The four Arab orientation types above were identified by the following questions in the 1980-88 surveys:

1. *Accommodationist type*. Arabs who conform in their views to the Zionist establishment are considered accommodationist. They believe that by accepting the Jewish consensus and working through the system, they can best extract concessions from the Jews.

Arabs were classified as accommodationists if they met 4-6 of the following conditions on which Jews agree: (1) accept Israel's preservation of a Jewish majority, (2) accept Israel's right to exist as a Jewish-Zionist state, (3) oppose protest abroad as a means of struggle to improve the Arabs' situation in Israel, (4) oppose general strikes, (5) favor the Israel-Egypt Peace Treaty, and (6) do not endorse the Arab refugees' right of repatriation to territory within the Green Line.

2. *Reservationist type*. Many Arabs find themselves sandwiched between the Zionist establishment, on the one hand, and the oppositionist Communist Party and the PLP, on the other. They have reservations about both, but do not wish to antagonize either. They reason that change can best be effected by organizing independently and negotiating with, rather than opposing, the authorities. Since the reservationists are still not crystallized organizationally, politically, or ideologically, their views are ambivalent and ambiguous. These rising, non-partisan Arabs, on which the emergent Democratic Arab Party counts and wishes to mobilize, attempt to take an independent middle course between the two powerful rival establishments in the Arab sector – the governing-Zionist and the oppositionist-anti-Zionist.

Arabs were placed in the reservationist orientation if they took 4-6 of the following moderate stands: (1) do not deny Israel's right to exist as a Jewish-Zionist state, (2) do not agree that Zionism is racism, (3) do not endorse protest abroad, (4) oppose unlicensed demonstrations, (5) do not oppose the Israel-Egypt Peace Treaty, and (6) concede or consider conceding the Arab refugees' right of repatriation in return for a peace settlement.

3. *Oppositionist type.* The ideology and politics of the Israeli Communist Party and PLP serve as a guide to this Arab type. Both accept Israel as a state but oppose its Zionist character.[1] Since their views clearly fall outside the Jewish consensus, they are not taken into consideration by the Jews as political allies or as potential coalition partners. Oppositionist Arabs, like supporters of the DFPE and PLP, are convinced that only by challenging the Zionist establishment from the outside can they alter Israeli society.

To belong to the oppositionist type, Arabs have to assent to 4-6 of the following opinions: (1) deny Israel's right to exist as a Jewish-Zionist state, (2) hold that Zionism is racism, (3) endorse protest abroad, (4) do not oppose unlicensed demonstrations, (5) do not endorse the Israel-Egypt Peace Treaty, and (6) oppose or have reservations about conceding the Arab refugees' right to repatriation.

4. *Rejectionist type.* Followers of the Sons of the Village Movement and the Progressive National Movement are certainly rejectionist. These Arabs totally negate Israel and desire to replace it with a secular-democratic or a Palestinian state in the entire area of Palestine. Some less radical Arabs reject the status of an Arab minority in a Jewish state and want to include the Galilee and Triangle, where most Israeli Arabs live, in a future, independent, Palestinian state. These rejectionist Arabs are not committed to the democratic process, and they endorse partly or fully the use of extra-legal means of struggle.

Rejectionist Arabs are identified by holding 4-6 of the following views in the survey: (1) deny Israel's right to exist, (2) oppose the recognition of Israel by the PLO, (3) endorse unlicensed demonstrations, (4) endorse the use of violence, (5) favor either a Palestinian state in all of Mandatory Palestine or Israel's withdrawal to the 1947 UN partition resolution borders, and (6) favor either a secular-democratic state instead of Israel or a Palestinian state that includes the Galilee and Triangle.

[1]Both parties had to disguise and blur their position on Zionism in 1988, by issuing contradictory and elusive statements, in order to qualify for participation in the 1988 Knesset elections. According to the amendment to the Election Law passed in July 1985 any election list that denies Israel as the state of the Jewish people may not take part in elections to the Knesset. The PLP was nearly disqualified on the grounds of violating this law. It was finally approved by the Central Elections Committee by a 19:18 vote which was confirmed by the Supreme Court by a 3:2 vote.

Evaluating the Typology

This set of definitions managed to classify 88% (1,058 of 1,203) of the Arab sample in 1985 and 90% in 1988 (compared to 89% in 1980), a high percentage in view of the inconsistency of opinions expected of rank-and-file Arabs and non-responses. The typology satisfies several reliability checks. It correlates highly (r=0.67 in 1985, compared to r=0.71 in 1980) with an empiricist typology based on a simple, additive index. The two typologies yield a similar incidence of types and more or less identical findings with regard to inter-type differentiation and prediction.

The typology also passes initial tests of validity. The distribution into 11% accommodationists, 39% reservationists, 40% oppositionists, and 10% rejectionists is meaningful. The split between the 50% "moderates" and 50% "militants" in the typology is similar to the division between the 49% of Arabs who voted in the 1984 Knesset elections for Jewish parties and the 51% who voted for the DFPE and PLP.

The distribution into types is also significant in other respects. Each of the accommodationist and rejectionist types amounts to only about one tenth of the Arab population. Of course, espousal of certain accommodating and rejecting opinions far exceeds 10%, but there is insufficient convergence of various attitudes to increase the two consistent, extreme types. The real division, therefore, is in the broad middle between the reservationists and the oppositionists, who are otherwise unequal in political power and ideological sophistication. While the reservationists lack an ideological and organizational base, the oppositionists behave as if they were the Arabs' exclusive establishment. The future has much in store for the politically untapped reservationist segment in the Arab sector. The Democratic Arab Party aspires to fill this gap although it is not clear if it can do so.

Most important, the typology passes the critical validity test of distinguishing very well among the four Arab leadership groups included in the 1985 survey. Despite the internal heterogeneity in views usually found among leaders belonging to the same political stream, 97% of the Arab leaders affiliated with the Zionist establishment fall into the accommodationist and reservationist categories, 86% of the unaffiliated leaders conform to the two middle types (a plurality being reservationists), 87% of those affiliated with the DFPE and PLP are classified as oppositionists, and 100% of the activists in the Sons of the Village Movement and the Progressive National Movement fit the rejectionist category (Table 18.1). This close fit, found in both the 1980 and the 1985 studies, which included leaders, shows that these types are real, authentic political types, rather than straw men.

Table 18.1 Arab Orientation Types

	Arab Public	Estab. Affil. Arab Lead.	Unaffiliated Arab Lead.	DFPE & PLP Arab Lead.	Sons of Village Arab Lead.
Orientation type					
Accommodationist	11.3	46.7	13.8	0.0	0.0
Reservationist	38.9	50.0	48.3	12.8	0.0
Oppositionist	39.8	3.3	37.9	87.2	46.9
Rejectionist	9.9	0.0	0.0	0.0	53.1
Total	100.0	100.0	100.0	100.0	100.0
Number of cases	1,058	30	29	39	32

Test of significance for leaders only: Chi-square=134.31869 d.f = 9 p<0.0000.

Differences in Views, Identity, and Behaviors

The authenticity and usefulness of the typology are best demonstrated by the significant differences among the types on various issues of coexistence, national identity, and behaviors related to Arab-Jewish relations. Each type stands, therefore, for a distinct set of characteristics. The data show that the 1985 and 1988 typologies are as handy, parsimonious, and discerning tools as the 1980 typology.

Table 18.2 reproduces the political views used in building the typology of the four Arab types. The differences among them are as sharp in 1985 as in 1980. For instance, Arabs opposing any resort to general strikes constituted 85% of the accommodationists, 17% of the reservationists, 4% of the oppositionists, and 2% of the rejectionists in 1985 (79%, 20%, 4%, and 0% in 1980). Similarly, those denying Israel's right to exist as a Jewish-Zionist state constituted 8.5%, 41%, 85%, and 93% of the four types in 1985 (18%, 31%, 87%, and 91% in 1980).

Disagreement among the Arab types prevails in other issues related to Arab-Jewish coexistence (Table 18.3). To illustrate from the civic area, 13% of the accommodationists, 30% of the reservationists, 46.5% of the oppositionists, and 79% of the rejectionists in 1985 (15%, 39%, 45%, and 73% in 1980) rejected Jews as a comparison group for assessing their own socioeconomic achievements. By the same token, 12%, 41.5%, 79%, and 90% in 1985 (9%, 42.5%, 79%, and 95.5% in 1980) felt dissatisfied with being Israeli citizens. Finally 8.5%, 39%, 64%, and 85% in 1985 would have advised their own sons to refuse military or civil service if such a duty were imposed on Israeli Arabs. (In response to a related question in 1980, 34%, 48%, 73%, and 85%, respectively, expressed opposition to compulsory military or civil service for Arabs.) The Arab types are similarly distinguished in 1988.

Table 18.2 Arab Orientation Types by Constituent Components

	Accommo-dationists	Reserva-tionists	Opposi-tionists	Reject-ionists
Total	11.3	38.9	39.8	9.9
Accommodationist orientation				
Accept Israel's preservation of a Jewish majority	78.6	16.9	8.7	3.8
Accept Israel's right to exist as a Jewish-Zionist state	66.1	15.6	4.6	1.9
Oppose protest abroad by Israeli Arabs	82.4	23.2	2.6	2.9
Oppose general strikes by Israeli Arabs	84.7	17.3	3.6	1.9
Favor Israel-Egypt Peace Treaty	97.5	70.3	29.9	16.2
Do not endorse the Arab refugees' right of repatriation	66.9	21.7	7.9	3.9
Reservationist orientation				
Do not deny Israel's right to exist as a Jewish-Zionist state	91.5	58.8	14.9	6.7
Do not agree that Zionism is racism	66.9	61.6	9.8	12.4
Do not endorse protest abroad by Israeli Arabs	87.4	72.3	12.0	17.3
Oppose unlicensed demonstrations by Israeli Arabs	94.9	86.8	46.5	22.3
Do not oppose Israel-Egypt Peace Treaty	99.2	96.6	64.1	39.1
Concede or consider conceding the Arab refugees' right of repatriation for a peace settlement	87.4	89.3	44.8	37.9
Oppositionist orientation				
Deny Israel's right to exist as a Jewish-Zionist state	8.5	41.2	85.1	93.3
Hold that Zionism is racism	33.0	38.4	90.2	87.6
Endorse protest abroad by Israeli Arabs	12.6	27.7	88.0	82.7
Do not oppose unlicensed demonstrations by Israeli Arabs	5.1	13.2	53.4	77.6
Do not endorse Israel-Egypt Peace Treaty	2.5	29.7	70.1	83.9
Oppose or have reservations about conceding the Arab refugees' right to repatriation	38.7	66.8	90.1	88.3
Rejectionist orientation				
Deny Israel's right to exist	0.8	6.8	17.8	83.8
Oppose the recognition of Israel by the PLO	5.9	3.0	12.4	80.0
Endorse unlicensed demonstrations by Israeli Arabs	1.7	1.0	12.2	62.1
Endorse the use of violence by Israeli Arabs	1.7	1.2	5.8	59.6
Favor a Palestinian state in all of Mandatory Palestine, or Israel's withdrawal to the 1947 UN partition resolution borders	8.5	22.1	34.9	84.1
Favor a secular-democratic state instead of Israel, or a Palestinian state that includes the Galilee and Triangle	6.8	28.8	49.6	94.1

Types differ in national identity so appreciably that identity can serve as a substitute for orientation. This generalization has remained true despite the growing spread of Palestinian identity among all Arabs in Israel. Throughout the 1980s, the various types continued to differ in their choice between Israeli and Palestinian identity. As a rule, the more militant the type, the more Palestinian (or less Israeli) is the self-identity.

Table 18.3 Arab Orientation Types by Selected Attitudes

	Accommo-dationists	Reserva-tionists	Opposi-tionists	Reject-ionists
Reject Jews as a comparison group for assessing one's socioeconomic achievements	12.9	29.6	46.5	68.9
Desire Israeli culture to be Arab	39.2	56.6	69.2	79.8
Hold that Arabs should not in principle resign themselves to the status of a national minority with full civil rights	5.1	21.7	35.0	60.6
Think that Arabs cannot be equal citizens of Israel as a Jewish-Zionist state and cannot identify themselves with the state	25.2	49.0	79.6	87.7
Favor PLO actions against Israeli soldiers and military bases in the West Bank, Gaza Strip, and outside Israel	11.0	30.7	72.2	85.0
Feel that Israel's War in Lebanon weakened own belief in Israeli democracy	29.1	59.5	79.1	88.2
Hold that the PLO and the Rejection Front offer the best solution to the Israeli-Arab conflict	3.7	18.0	41.3	71.0
Feel closer to Arabs in the West Bank and Gaza Strip than to Jews in Israel	13.5	50.5	76.3	93.2
Agree that neighborhoods should be separate for Arabs and Jews	21.7	26.0	31.4	57.7
Would advise own son to refuse military or civil service if such a duty were imposed	8.5	38.6	63.9	84.8
Hold that the best political organization for Arabs is the formation of independent Arab nationalist parties	2.5	16.3	25.8	58.1
Think that if a Palestinian state were to be established, the Galilee and Triangle should be parts of it	10.9	36.1	58.6	93.1
Consider the PLO as truly representative of the Arabs in Israel	21.1	57.2	80.9	88.3
Hold that Arab education should be Palestinian in its goal	1.7	17.5	48.9	84.6
Advocate the use of violence, strikes or demonstrations in order to repeal the Law of Return	22.1	46.7	65.3	73.8
Feel that it is impossible to trust most Jews in Israel	41.2	60.1	81.8	90.4
Believe that most or all Jews hate Arabs	28.8	43.1	64.6	89.5
Believe that most or all Arabs hate Jews	20.3	20.7	40.3	71.6
Unwilling to live in a mixed neighborhood	31.6	53.1	52.7	77.2
Hold that Arab youth do not have reasonable chances of fulfilling their occupational aspirations in Israel	27.5	47.2	76.7	75.3
Think that Arabs in Israel are deprived of the benefits of democracy	23.1	49.0	69.6	72.8
Feel dissatisfied with being an Israeli citizen	11.8	41.5	78.9	90.4
Would feel more at home in an Arab country than in Israel	3.4	25.8	45.8	80.8
Would rejoice or justify an action in which an Israeli Arab killed a Jew on nationalist grounds	30.3	52.5	64.0	83.2

This trend is precisely what is found in the 1980-88 studies. To illustrate, 89% of the accommodationists in 1985 considered the term "Israeli" as an appropriate self-description, but only 25% so perceived the term "Palestinian"; the respective proportions in 1980 were very similar – 94% and 16% (Table 18.4). The rejectionists felt exactly the opposite – 9% and 94% in 1985, and 6% and 94% in 1980. These figures show continuity over the years in the capacity of types to differentiate between identities. That Palestinization of self-identity has become a reliable expression of orientation is evident in the differences in choice by type of most fitting self-description. The correlations between orientation and the chosen self-identity were 0.52 in 1985 and 0.53 in 1980. As many as 81% in 1985 (88% in 1980) of the accommodationists opted for non-Palestinian Israeli identities (Israelis, Israeli Arabs, Arabs); the reservationists were divided between 42% (61%) who defined themselves as non-Palestinian Israelis and 40% (26%) as Israeli Palestinians (or Palestinians in Israel); the oppositionists were split between 51% (38%) who saw themselves as Israeli Palestinians and 36% (40%) as non-Israeli Palestinians (Palestinians, Palestinian Arabs); the latter figure compared with the 80% (82%) of the rejectionists who regarded themselves as non-Israeli Palestinians.[2] More generally, although the Israeli and Palestinian components of national identity are accepted by the Arabs, the types continue to differ markedly on which of the two components receive more emphasis.

Table 18.4 Arab Orientation Types by National Self-Identity

	Accommo-dationists	Reserva-tionists	Opposi-tionists	Reject-ionists
Consider each of the following terms as an appropriate self-description				
Israeli	88.9	59.7	25.9	8.9
Israeli Palestinian	34.2	59.4	51.0	22.3
Palestinian	24.8	54.9	84.5	94.2
Define oneself as				
Israeli, Israeli Arab, Arab	80.8	42.4	13.0	5.8
Israeli Palestinian, Palestinian in Israel	15.0	39.8	50.7	14.4
Palestinian, Palestinian Arab	4.2	17.8	36.3	79.8

The types also continued to differ in their behavior later in the 1980s as they had earlier. Compared with the more moderate types, the more militant types read more Arabic or oppositionist newspapers, were less likely to have Jewish friends, paid more social visits to the residents of the West Bank and Gaza Strip, and maintained more frequent ties with relatives across the Green Line or in Arab countries (Table 18.5). The militancy of the oppositionist and rejectionist types was also evident in their greater participation in protest activities and their greater suffering as a result.

[2]The association between types and national self-identities in 1988 remained strong despite a slight decline. The correlation is 0.48. As many as 83% of the accommodationists selected non-Palestinian Israeli identities; of the reservationists 50.5% opt for non-Palestinian Israeli identities and 34% for Israeli Palestinian identities; the oppositionists are split between 51% who saw themselves as Israeli Palestinians and 32% as non-Israeli Palestinians; lastly, 73% of the rejectionists defined themselves as non-Israeli Palestinians.

Table 18.5 Arab Orientation Types by Selected Behaviors

	Accommo-dationists	Reserva-tionists	Opposi-tionists	Reject-ionists
Newspapers read				
An Arabic newspaper	18.3	32.8	54.5	50.9
Al-Ittihad	10.6	31.6	56.1	54.5
Al-Thadamun	8.9	15.9	24.8	28.0
Al-Kuds	10.5	15.4	20.7	21.0
Contacts				
Have Jewish friends	75.8	63.3	58.1	43.8
Have paid social visits to the West Bank or Gaza Strip during the past year	19.2	33.5	46.7	51.0
Maintain ties with relatives in West Bank, Gaza Strip or Arab countries	14.3	17.8	25.7	40.2
Party membership				
Member of a Jewish political party	9.2	3.2	1.7	0.0
Member of Rakah or PLP	0.0	1.2	5.4	6.8
Voted in the 1984 elections for				
Jewish parties	91.3	64.6	22.0	8.8
PLP	3.3	13.9	17.5	33.3
DFPE	5.4	21.4	60.5	57.9
Protest activities				
Participated in 1985 in events commemorating Land Day	1.7	5.2	32.3	40.6
Have demonstrated in past two years in protest of treatment of Arabs	3.3	7.1	30.3	34.9
Have suffered privations (economic loss or political harassment) resulting from protest on behalf of Arabs	0.8	4.5	18.3	20.4

Most pertinent, however, are the divergences in voting in the 1984 Knesset elections, when there was a choice between Zionist and non-Zionist lists. The proportion voting Zionist was 91% among the accommodationists, 65% among the reservationists, 22% among the oppositionists, and only 9% among the rejectionists. In a way, these figures directly validate the entire typology, which is based on the political splits in the Arab sector.

Determinants

A regression analysis shows, indeed, that of a battery of factors, community and effect of land expropriations are the two best predictors of Arab orientation (Table 18.6). If voting is introduced, however, it is certainly the single most powerful predictor of all. Since the typology is designed to capture political currents, it is no wonder that voting is strongly associated with orientation.

Table 18.6 Regression Analysis of Predictors of Arab Orientation Index

	N	r	R	Beta
The three best predictors, excluding voting behavior				
Community status (Druze/other)	1,203	0.33	0.33	0.27060*
Effect of land expropriations	906	-0.30	0.40	-0.23246*
Age	1,177	-0.11	0.42	-0.12363*
The three best predictors, including voting behavior				
Voting (Jewish/non-Jewish parties)	822	0.53	0.53	0.44644*
Effect of land expropriations	906	-0.30	0.56	-0.14073*
Community status (Druze/other)	1,203	0.33	0.58	0.15202*

*Statistically significant at 0.0000 level.

Apart from community, the various types do not come from markedly different social backgrounds. The majority (69%) of the accommodationists are Druzes, Christians, and Bedouin whereas most (82%) rejectionists are non-Bedouin Moslems (Table 18.7). On the other hand, age, education, and size of locality, which correlate with level of modernity, seem to make limited to little difference. For instance, 52% of the accommodationists, 60% of the reservationists, 67% of the oppositionists, and 69% of the rejectionists in 1985 were under the age 36; 12.5%, 9%, 12.5%, and 8%, respectively, had at least some college education.

Table 18.7 Arab Orientation Types by Social Background

	Accommodationists	Reservationists	Oppositionists	Rejectionists
Total	11.3	38.9	39.8	9.9
Age				
18-25	32.8	32.9	43.6	50.5
26-35	19.3	27.5	23.1	18.6
36-45	24.4	19.1	16.4	13.4
46-55	13.4	10.9	9.6	10.3
56+	10.1	9.7	7.2	7.2
Education				
0-8	61.7	60.9	52.0	56.9
9-12	25.8	30.0	35.5	35.3
13+	12.5	9.1	12.5	7.8
Size of community				
15,000 persons or more	15.0	26.0	33.3	24.8
10,000-14,999	1.7	6.8	13.5	23.8
5,000-9,999	38.3	26.9	26.1	25.7
Under 5,000	45.0	40.3	27.0	25.8
Community				
Druze	42.5	10.4	3.3	1.0
Bedouin	14.1	17.5	10.2	11.5
Christian	12.5	13.6	15.9	5.7
Non-Bedouin Moslem	30.8	58.5	70.5	81.9

It is clear, therefore, that the orientation of Israeli Arabs toward Jews and the state is shaped largely by how the Arabs are treated. Those who are less discriminated against (namely, Druzes and members of families not affected by land expropriations) are more likely to be moderate, irrespective of their age, education, and level of individual modernism. This general finding, from which may be inferred the importance of policy toward Arabs as a determinant of their orientation, runs counter to public and some scholarly expectations that single out the young, urban, and better educated as the most militant. This conclusion is derived from the 1976-80 studies and is confirmed by the 1985-88 data.

19

Jewish Orientation Types

Although most political parties in Israel lack a clear, or, indeed, any policy toward the Arab minority, they differ on both their orientation toward Israeli Arabs and questions that are undoubtedly relevant to Arab policy. A party's approach toward the Arab minority is evidently shaped by its stands on four wider, cardinal matters: Israel's Jewish-Zionist character, reservation about democracy, control over the occupied territories, and the role of religion in the state.

Table 19.1 contains a classification of all the parties in 1988 on these four ideological issues as well as on orientations toward Israeli Arabs. To facilitate comparability, a four-point scale was used, ranging from a score of 0 to mark the least liberal (most particularistic or nationalistic) stand to 3 to indicate the most liberal (most universalistic or cosmopolitan). Scores are impressionistically assigned to each party according to its platform for the 1988 Knesset elections, pronouncements of its leaders, and its record of activities. Parties that take similar positions are grouped together, and the listing in the table is in a descending order of liberalism.

Several points stand out. First, stances on the various issues tend to correlate highly and to make a logically consistent configuration. Hence, the total score assigned to each party is meaningful and can serve as a criterion for ranking or measuring the distance between the parties. Second, the Israeli political spectrum is very wide indeed, reflecting the plural nature of society and politics. There are parties on both extremes of the continuum as well as a range of parties in the middle. Third, the two largest parties constitute the political center, where Labor occupies a slightly left-of-center position and Likud a slightly right-of-center standing. Since its ascendance to power in 1977, the Likud has gradually shifted to the center and lost its distinct right-wing posture. Fourth, along with the broad variation, there exists a bifurcation of parties into Labor and Likud camps. The Labor camp includes the small parties of the Zionist left but keeps the non-Zionist parties on its left margin. By the same token, the Likud camp includes the religious parties but keeps the radical right on its right margin. Overall, the Labor camp is more open for mitigating Israel's Jewish-Zionist character, more committed to democracy, more compromising on land for peace, and more reserved about the incorporation of Jewish religion into the public domain.

Table 19.1 Classification of Political Parties, 1988

	Israel's Jewish-Zionist Character	Demo-cracy	Terri-tories	Role of Religion in State	Total Score	Orientation toward Israeli Arabs
Israeli Communist Party, Progressive List for Peace	3	3	3	3	12	Egalitarianist
Democratic Arabic Party	2	3	3	2.5	10.5	Egalitarianist
Citizens' Rights Movement, Mapam, Shinui	2	3	2.5	2.5	10	Conciliationist
Labor Party	1	2	2	1.5	6.5	Pragmatist
Likud Party	0.5	1.5	1	1	4	Hardline
Agudat Israel, Shas, Degel Hatora	1	1.5	1.5	0	4	Hardline
National Religious Party	0.5	1.5	1	1.5	3.5	Hardline
Tehiya Party, Tsomet Party	0	1	0	1	2	Hardline
Moledet	0	0.5	0	1	1.5	Hardline
Kach Movement	0	0	0	0	0	Exclusionist

Key to Codes in Table:

Israel's Jewish-Zionist character: 0. Strengthen; 1. retain as is; 2. reduce; 3. abolish.

Democracy: 0. Abolish; 1. reduce; 2. retain as is; 3. strengthen.

Territories: 0. Annex; 1. retain as are; 2. compromise; 3. withdraw.

Role of religion in state: 0. Strengthen; 1. retain as is; 2. reduce; 3. abolish.

Each party is also classified into one of five orientations toward Israeli Arabs, yielding five possible types: egalitarianists, conciliationists, pragmatists, hardliners, and exclusionists. Egalitarianists stand for opening up society by free mixing, doing away with relations of dominance, and striving for complete equality between the subordinate and dominant groups. Conciliationists accept minority members as equals and are ready to make certain changes in the social structure to promote ethnic equality. Pragmatists support relations of dominance but would make certain concessions necessary for preserving this relationship. Hardliners seek to reinforce their dominant position without making concessions to the minority. Exclusionists are supremacists, who desire to do away with minority-majority statuses through the total removal of the minority from the country.

Overall, five party clusters roughly correspond to five orientations: the non-Zionist, predominantly Arab parties lean toward an egalitarianist orientation; the small left Zionist parties propagate a conciliationist orientation;

the Labor Party promotes a pragmatist orientation; the Likud, religious, and radical right parties assume a hardline orientation; and the Kach Movement disseminates an exclusionist orientation toward Israeli Arabs.

There is no Jewish political party (or Jewish ideological movement of significance) that advocates an egalitarianist orientation because Israeli Jews are as non-assimilating as are Israeli Arabs. Egalitarianism would imply de-Judaization and de-Zionization of Israel and its recasting into either a secular-democratic state, in which Arab and Jewish statuses would be privatized, or a binational state, where Arab and Jewish parity would be instituted without the guarantee of a Jewish majority. Only the Israeli Communist Party, Progressive List for Peace, and Democratic Arab Party espouse a perspective that comes close to egalitarianism; but as non-Zionist parties, they receive little support from Jews. In fact, only 0.4% of the Jews in the 1985 survey reported voting for the DFPE and PLP in the 1984 Knesset elections, and only 0.2% of the Jews in the 1988 survey expressed an intention to vote for one of these lists in the 1988 Knesset elections. Hence, the Jewish leaders affiliated with the non-Zionist left are actually devoid of a Jewish following.

For these reasons, the typology of the Jewish general public to be described below excludes the egalitarianist as a distinct type.

Constructing the Typology

The four Jewish orientation types were spelled out in the 1980-88 surveys as follows:

1. *Conciliationist type.* The most liberal Zionist Jews in Israel insist on guaranteeing Arabs full civil rights, equality, and integration into Israeli society, while keeping the state both Jewish and Zionist. They do not see any contradiction between Zionism and democracy, but would prefer democracy in most cases when a contradiction did develop. They criticize Israel's policies toward Israeli Arabs and advocate new policies that aim at compensating for past injustices and advancing Arab-Jewish equality and integration without assimilation. The conciliationists are close in outlook to the small, leftist Zionist parties.

Jews in the survey who subscribed to 4-6 of the following views were classified as conciliationist: (1) see Israel as a common homeland for Arabs and Jews; (2) hold that the state should not prefer Jews to Arabs; (3) endorse the love of Israel as the common homeland of Arabs and Jews to be the goal of Jewish education; (4) consider the closing of the socioeconomic gap between Arabs and Jews to be an urgent, important state goal; (5) feel that the state does too little for the Arabs in Israel; and (6) oppose the idea that Israel should seek and use any opportunity to encourage Israeli Arabs to leave the country.

2. *Pragmatist type.* At the heart of the pragmatist orientation is the Labor Party's position vis-à-vis Israeli Arabs. During the first three

decades of statehood, the governing Labor Party instituted a policy of control over Arabs while extending them civil rights, development funds, jobs outside their places of residence, and incorporation into Jewish institutions (e.g., the Histadrut). It still acts on the assumption that if a proper mix of inducements and sanctions were applied, Arabs would maintain law and order and contribute to the well-being of the state, even if they did not identify with it. Another belief is that as long as the Israeli-Arab conflict persists, there will be no solution to the Arab problem; hence, practical arrangements should be made to reconcile the promise of equality and integration with the pressing needs of national security and continued construction of the Jewish state.

To be placed in the category of the pragmatist type, Jews in the survey had to endorse 4-6 of the following stands: (1) advocate the present policy toward the Arab minority or a policy of greater equality and integration between Arabs and Jews; (2) do not endorse a strong-arm policy toward the Arabs in Israel; (3) consider the closing of the socioeconomic gap between Arabs and Jews to be an important – but not necessarily urgent – state goal; (4) do not feel that the state does too much for the Arabs in Israel; (5) believe that it is possible to improve the Arab situation to a great or substantial degree by such acceptable democratic means as persuasion and political pressure; and (6) do not endorse the outlawing of Rakah.

3. *Hardliner type*. According to the hardline viewpoint, which is represented by the Likud Party, the Arabs should be granted rights and opportunities to the extent that they demonstrate resignation to minority status in a Jewish-Zionist state and discharge all their civil duties. At present, they are denied full equality because they identify themselves with the hostile Arab world, neither serve in the army nor render civil service, and behave in ways that raise doubts about their loyalty to the state. For this reason, surveillance and restrictions over the Arab population must be continued and even increased.

The hardliners were identified by their support of 4-6 of the following opinions: (1) prefer the Jewish-Zionist character of the state to democracy if the two conflict; (2) advocate a strong-arm policy toward the Arabs in Israel; (3) feel that it is impossible to trust most Arabs in Israel; (4) consider Arabs in Israel to be a certain or substantial danger to national security; (5) consider the closing of the socioeconomic gap between Arabs and Jews as neither an urgent nor important state goal; and (6) advocate the outlawing of Rakah.

4. *Exclusionist type*. Jews who believe that the Arabs should either unreservedly submit to Jewish rule or leave the country fit the exclusionist type. They perceive the very presence of Arabs in the Jewish state to be Israel's defect and liability. They feel that Jews have exclusive right to the land, the state, institutions, resources, and opportunities, and

that the existence of an Arab minority, especially one that is not loyal, impairs Israel's exclusivity, mission, and integrity. These views resemble, but fall short of, the Kach ideology because they fail to call openly for the Arabs' organized emigration, disenfranchisement, subordination, and forced segregation, and for the establishment of a Jewish theocracy.

The questionnaires for the 1980-88 surveys did not include enough questions for adequate identification of the exclusionist type. It was necessary, therefore, to resort to just three items for making this categorization. Jews were categorized as exclusionist if they accepted all of the following views: (1) advocate the idea that Israel should seek and use any opportunity to encourage Arabs to leave the state; (2) totally oppose having an Arab as their superior in a job; and (3) feel that the state does too much for the Arabs in Israel.

Evaluating the Typology

Analysis of the questionnaire responses shows that 86% (1,035 of 1,205) of the Jewish sample in 1985 and 81% in 1988 (compared to 85% in 1980) falls into one of the four orientation types, thus demonstrating the relevance and comprehensiveness of the typology. This achievement in classifying the overwhelming majority of rank-and-file Jews left only 14% unclassified in 1985 because of their holding other sets of views, inconsistency, or non-response.

The preconceived, predetermined typology further proves its reliability through its strong association (r=0.77 in 1985 compared to r=0.72 in 1980) with another kind of typology, which was constructed by applying cutoff points to an empirical, additive index. The two typologies also correspond to each other in their distribution of and differentiation among the four types.

The validity of the 1985 typology is evident in the close fit between the division into types and political divisions in the Jewish public. The distribution of types into 9.5% conciliationists, 36% pragmatists, 35% hardliners, and 19% exclusionists is very significant. It yields a split of 45% "liberals" and 55% "illiberals" on the Israeli Arab question that corresponds to the bifurcation of the Jewish public into 48% who voted for the Labor camp in the 1984 Knesset elections and 52% who voted for the Likud camp.[1] The typology is also in line with the well-known asymmetry between the Jewish extreme types: the proportion of exclusionists is twice that of conciliationists.

[1]The 48:52 Labor camp/Likud camp ratio in 1984 was computed only for Jewish voters; excluded were the Arab votes for these camps, the votes for the DFPE and PLP, and the votes cast for election lists that failed to win a seat in the Knesset.

The typology is further validated by its potency in distinguishing among four Jewish leadership groups. It succeeds well in classifying 100% of the Jewish leaders active in the DFPE and PLP as well as 79% of the Jewish leaders in the Citizens Rights Movement, Mapam, and Shinui as conciliationists (Table 19.2). The typology is also quite satisfactory in categorizing 65% of Labor's Jewish leaders as pragmatists and 35% as conciliationists. On the other hand, it also places 66% of the Jewish leaders of the Likud, religious parties, and Tehiya as pragmatists and only 25% as hardliners. The disproportionate categorization of leaders from the Likud camp as pragmatic is probably due to the genuinely moderating impact of their experience as a governing party since 1977.

Table 19.2 Jewish Orientation Types

	Jewish Public	DFPE & PLP Jewish Lead.	CRM & Mapam Jewish Lead.	Labor Jewish Lead.	Likud Camp Jewish Lead.
Orientation type					
Conciliationist	9.5	100.0	79.4	35.0	3.1
Pragmatist	35.9	0.0	20.6	65.0	65.6
Hardliner	35.4	0.0	0.0	0.0	25.0
Exclusionist	19.2	0.0	0.0	0.0	6.3
Total	100.0	100.0	100.0	100.0	100.0
Number of cases	1,035	36	34	40	32

Test of significance for leaders only: Chi-square=100.39485 d.f.= 9 p<0.0000.

All these methodological tests that the four fold typology passed, in both the 1980 and 1985 surveys, which also included leaders, show that it yields a rather useful, meaningful, and realistic set of types among the Jewish population.

Differences in Views and Behaviors

The 1985-88 surveys confirmed the appreciable differences in views and behavior among the types found in the 1976-80 surveys. We are thus assured that the Jewish population falls into distinct orientation types toward the Arabs in Israel.

The four Jewish types are, of course, well distinguished on all the views incorporated as components of the typology itself. In the 1985 survey, for example, 88% of the conciliationists, 25% of the pragmatists, 12% of the hardliners, and 5% of the exclusionists saw Israel as a common homeland for Arabs and Jews (Table 19.3). On the other hand, 1%, 19%, 54%, and 100%, respectively, endorsed the idea that Israel should encourage Israeli Arabs to leave the country.

Table 19.3 Jewish Orientation Types by Constituent Components

	Concilia-tionists	Pragma-tists	Hard-liners	Exclu-sionists
Total	9.5	35.9	35.4	19.2
Conciliationist orientation				
See Israel as a common homeland of Arabs and Jews	87.8	24.9	12.1	5.3
Hold that the state should not prefer Jews to Arabs	86.0	22.7	8.9	1.8
Endorse the love of Israel as a common homeland of Arabs and Jews as a goal of Jewish education	72.4	24.3	17.5	9.0
Consider the closing of the socioeconomic gap between Arabs and Jews as an urgent, important state goal	65.1	15.2	4.1	6.5
Feel that the state does too little for the Arabs in Israel	72.5	21.0	5.6	0.0
Oppose the idea that Israel should seek and use any opportunity to encourage Israeli Arabs to leave the state	90.1	28.6	12.5	0.0
Pragmatist orientation				
Advocate the present policy or a policy of greater equality and integration between Arabs and Jews	77.1	83.4	41.0	15.9
Do not endorse a strong-arm policy toward the Arabs in Israel	96.7	93.6	30.5	19.3
Consider the closing of the socioeconomic gap between Arabs and Jews as an important (but not necessarily urgent) state goal	92.8	69.3	16.4	19.5
Do not feel that the state does too much for the Arabs in Israel	98.4	91.7	69.5	0.0
Believe that it is possible to improve to a great or substantial degree the Arab situation by acceptable democratic means	58.7	55.7	24.5	25.5
Do not endorse the outlawing of Rakah	91.2	84.4	31.5	24.3
Hardline orientation				
Would prefer the Jewish-Zionist character of the state to democracy if they conflict	11.7	42.9	83.5	82.2
Advocate a strong-arm policy toward the Arabs in Israel	3.3	6.3	69.5	80.6
Feel that it is impossible to trust most Arabs in Israel	17.2	30.1	89.1	94.6
Consider Arabs in Israel as a certain or substantial danger to national security	48.0	65.8	81.6	51.5
Consider the closing of the socioeconomic gap between Arabs and Jews as neither an urgent nor important state goal	7.2	30.7	83.6	80.5
Advocate the outlawing of Rakah	8.8	15.6	68.5	75.5
Exclusionist orientation				
Advocate the idea that Israel should seek and use any opportunity to encourage Israeli Arabs to leave the state	11.3	18.9	53.8	100.0
Are totally unwilling to have an Arab as one's superior in a job	5.0	26.3	54.3	100.0
Feel that the state does too much for the Arabs in Israel	1.6	8.3	30.5	100.0

These marked differences extend virtually to all questions of coexistence. To cite just a few findings from the 1985 survey, 14% of the conciliationists, 35.5% of the pragmatists, 64% of the hardliners, and 83% of the exclusionists held that neighborhoods should be separate for Arabs and Jews; 15%, 42%, 76%, and 95%, respectively, were unwilling to have Jewish friends; 2%, 5%, 29%, and 68%, respectively, favored disenfranchisement of Israeli Arab citizens; and 1%, 5%, 21%, and 72%, respectively, maintained that the most appropriate solution to the Arab minority problem is to force them out of Israel (Table 19.4).

Table 19.4 Jewish Orientation Types by Selected Attitudes

	Concilia-tionists	Pragma-tists	Hard-liners	Exclu-sionists
Total	9.5	35.9	35.4	19.2
Hold that Jews should not adopt Arab values and habits in addition to their own	26.3	37.7	59.8	78.8
Oppose a law requiring all street and locality signs to be written in both Hebrew and Arabic	21.9	39.8	59.6	81.9
Reject the very existence of an Arab minority	1.0	3.9	15.4	49.2
Maintain that Israel should strengthen its Jewish-Zionist character despite having an Arab minority	29.7	52.2	73.8	84.5
Do not believe that Arabs can be equal citizens in Israel as a Jewish-Zionist state and can identify themselves with the state	36.6	39.9	55.9	80.6
Favor immediate annexation of Judea and Samaria	9.7	21.3	55.2	71.8
Hold that neighborhoods should be separate for Arabs and Jews	14.2	35.5	63.8	83.1
Oppose the establishment of an Arab university	35.7	38.3	54.6	65.2
Oppose the possibility that Arabs organize independently, like Orthodox Jews, in order to advance their vital interests	34.1	59.8	79.8	89.3
Hold that the most appropriate solution to the problem of Arabs in Israel is				
To live in Israel as a national minority recognized by the state and enjoying proper political representation	36.8	20.5	8.6	1.6
To live in Israel as a national minority with full civil rights	52.4	42.8	15.0	1.2
To live in Israel only if they are resigned to their minority status in a state designed for Jews	4.5	28.6	50.7	25.3
To force them out of Israel	1.0	5.3	21.2	71.9
View most Arabs in Israel as primitive	10.8	13.8	39.7	56.6
Do not consider Arabs in Israel to be more loyal to the state than are the Arabs in the territories	16.1	25.1	49.6	61.4
Unwilling to work in a place where Arabs and Jews work together	5.9	27.8	59.6	86.4
Unwilling to have Arab friends	14.6	41.8	75.7	94.8
Favor preferential treatment of Jews in admission to universities	4.8	54.3	79.3	91.9
Hold that Arabs should be fired first in a state of unemployment	2.3	20.4	58.5	87.6
Oppose giving proper compensation for expropriated Arab lands	3.3	17.2	44.4	61.8
Favor the disenfranchisement of the Arabs in Israel	1.8	5.1	28.7	67.7
Rejoice or justify an action in which an Israeli Jew killed an Israeli Arab citizen on nationalist grounds	6.7	24.8	52.1	73.4

Jewish types in 1985-88 also continued to differ in behavior toward Israeli Arabs as they did in 1976-80. Although 76% of all the Jews in the 1985 study did not have Arab friends, this is to some extent more true of the more illiberal types: 64% of the conciliationists, 70% of the pragmatists, 79% of the hardliners, and 84% of the exclusionists (Table 19.5). These figures reveal, nevertheless, that even liberal Jews lack meaningful contacts with Arabs, and that much of their tolerance is an abstract openness rather than a concrete experience.

Table 19.5 Jewish Orientation Types by Selected Behaviors

	Concilia-tionists	Pragma-tists	Hard-liners	Exclu-sionists
Do not have Arab friends	63.4	72.0	75.6	86.7
Voting in the 1984 national elections for				
CRM, Shinui, PLP, DFPE	31.3	9.6	2.2	1.2
Labor (including Yahad and Ometz)	60.1	64.7	32.9	23.8
Likud	6.2	20.9	48.6	47.8
Religious parties	2.3	2.9	6.1	8.6
Tehiya, Kach (Kahane's list)	0.0	1.8	10.2	18.7

More crucial is the continued divergence among types in voting behavior. Of the conciliationists, 60% voted in the 1984 Knesset elections for Labor and 31% for the Citizens' Rights Movement, Shinui, PLP, and DFPE; of the pragmatists, 65% voted Labor and 21% Likud; of the hardliners, 49% voted Likud and 32% Labor; and of the exclusionists, 48% voted Likud, 24% Labor, and 19% Tehiya and Kach (Table 19.6). The real differences between the types are much greater than those reflected in these figures because of the bifurcation of Israeli politics. To illustrate, 91% of the conciliationists in 1984 cast their vote for the Labor camp as against 75% of the exclusionists who voted for the Likud camp.

Table 19.6 Regression Analysis of Predictors of Jewish Orientation Types

	N	r	R	Beta
All predictors, including voting				
Voting in the 1984 national elections (Labor camp/Likud camp)	860	0.46	0.46	0.34732*
Education	1,016	-0.30	0.51	-0.19880*
Visiting terms with Arabs	984	-0.13	0.53	-0.11474*
Ethnic origin (Oriental/Ashkenazic)	896	-0.34	0.54	-0.11107*
Religious observance	1,026	-0.30	0.54	-0.06539*
All predictors, excluding voting				
Ethnic origin (Oriental/Ashkenazic)	896	-0.34	0.34	-0.22427*
Religious observance	1,026	-0.30	0.40	-0.18119*
Education	1,016	-0.30	0.43	-0.18660*
Visiting terms with Arabs	984	-0.13	0.45	-0.12665*

*Statistically significant at 0.0000 level.

Determinants

These behaviors, with regard to friendship (or being on visiting terms) with Arabs and voting, both influence and are influenced by orientation types. They were included in the 1985 survey within the set of the five most important factors known from the 1980 survey to predispose or reinforce liberal or illiberal orientations among Israeli Jews.

Table 19.7 Jewish Orientation Types by Social Background

	Concilia-tionists	Pragma-tists	Hard-liners	Exclu-sionists
Total	9.5	35.9	35.4	19.2
Age				
18-25	16.2	14.1	24.1	25.4
26-35	31.7	26.2	24.9	26.1
36-45	19.4	18.4	16.2	14.1
46-55	6.2	13.6	9.5	15.5
56+	26.4	27.7	25.3	18.9
Education				
0-8	7.3	20.5	29.9	33.6
9-12	30.4	42.2	51.5	53.7
13+	62.3	37.2	18.6	12.6
Religious observance				
Religious	2.4	4.0	14.3	22.9
Traditional	14.1	23.8	41.0	39.7
Secular	80.8	70.8	41.1	36.5
Other	2.7	1.4	3.6	0.9
Ethnic origin				
Oriental	24.2	36.2	62.4	74.3
Ashkenazic	75.8	63.8	37.6	25.7
Father's country of birth				
Israel	9.6	8.8	5.0	6.2
Yemen	0.8	2.0	7.8	14.4
Morocco	5.3	5.1	15.9	13.1
Algeria, Tunis, Libya	2.7	2.8	4.6	8.9
Syria, Lebanon, Egypt	0.8	2.4	5.7	4.2
Iraq	6.0	8.8	12.0	17.5
Turkey, Greece, Bulgaria	5.4	8.1	6.4	4.3
Rumania	10.4	9.7	10.0	6.2
Soviet Union	9.9	10.2	5.4	4.4
Poland	13.1	19.7	13.7	10.6
Germany	14.4	6.2	1.7	0.0
Other	21.6	16.2	11.7	10.2

When all the five variables are regressed on orientation types, all are found to be statistically significant and together to account for 29% of the variance on the typology (R=0.54; Table 19.6; the explanatory power of these predictors was smaller in 1980: 24% of the variance, R=0.49). The variables were ranked in the following order of predictive power:

1. Voting (explains 21% of the total variance)
2. Education (explains an additional 5%)
3. Being on visiting terms with Arabs (an additional 2%)
4. Ethnic origin (Oriental/Ashkenazic) (an additional 1%)
5. Religious observance (an additional 0.3%).

If voting is excluded, on the grounds that the types are constructed to approximate political orientations, a change in the order of the predictive power of the four other factors is evident. The two best predictors are ethnicity and religious observance, jointly explaining 16% of the total variance on orientation. Education and visiting terms with Arabs account for an additional 4%.

The difference between 1980 and 1985 in the predictive power of the five factors is of limited significance. The reason is that all of them are intercorrelated and indicative of a political subculture that, in turn, is associated with voting. It is hard to disentangle one from another. For instance, since religious observance is tied with voting for religious parties and the latter is part of voting, it is difficult to separate the effects on orientation of religious observance and voting.

Jewish types thus differ appreciably in their social background. The conciliationists tend to be university educated, secular, Ashkenazic, and to predominate among German Jews (Table 19.7, see above). The pragmatists are disposed to be more educated and less religious than the average, and to be Ashkenazic. On the other hand, the hardliners are inclined to be undereducated, religious, Oriental, and disproportionately Moroccan. The exclusionists are mostly religious and Oriental, with an extreme overrepresentation of Yemenite and Iraqi Jews.[2]

[2]Types are not distinguished by age (r=0.06) and gender (r=0.03), however.

20

Implications of the Typologies

Do the implications deduced from the analysis of the 1976-80 typologies hold true for the 1985-88 typologies? The first implication, that factionalism within each of the communities is genuine and appreciable, is still valid. The internal divisions continue to be strikingly similar in the number and relative size of the four types. On each side, there are two large middle types and two small extreme ones. With the exception of the rejectionists, Arabs share in common the acceptance of Israel, insistence on equality, and a two-state solution to the Israeli-Palestinian dispute. They disagree, however, on the extent of their rejection of Israel's Jewish-Zionist character and on the means of struggle. With the notable exception of the exclusionists, the Jews are willing to have an Arab minority in their midst, but are internally divided on their demands of the Arabs and on the amount of equality they are prepared to extend to them.

The second implication, that there is a significant asymmetry between the two typologies, is no longer correct. By the end of the 1980s, the parallels between types and political parties were as incomplete among Arabs as among Jews. Both communities lack the egalitarianist type as a social, mass-based phenomenon; i.e., there are only a few Arabs or Jews who favor democratic pluralism to the extent of free mixing, loss of identity, and assimilation. In the aftermath of the disqualification of the Kach Party from participation in Knesset elections, a new symmetry was introduced, since the extreme types on both sides, Arab rejectionists and Jewish exclusionists, became devoid of a representative party in the Knesset. It was also less true after 1988 that Arab reservationists lack an ideological and political base, because the new Democratic Arab Party, which split from the Labor Party in 1988, aspires to provide such a base and to enter a Labor coalition.

The third implication, that genuine internal factionalism in the two communities started to soften Arab-Jewish polarity, continues to be true. Both factionalisms have begun to exercise a positive impact on Arab-Jewish coexistence. They have a certain destereotyping effect. The Arabs are increasingly conscious of the fact that the Jews are neither uniform in views nor united in actions against them; the same holds for the Jews. The growing mutual awareness of the other's internal diversity and discord enables increasing numbers of Arabs and Jews to seek understanding, cooperation, and alliance with segments congenial to them on the other side

The development of cross-communal alliances holds, of course, for the conciliationist and pragmatist Jews in the Labor camp and for the overwhelming majority of the non-rejectionist Arabs. The Zionist left parties at the end of the 1980s had become much more considerate and solicitous of Israeli Arabs, and they also won a greater share of the Arab vote than ever before. The Labor Party, despite losing Arab support in the 1988 elections, is also increasingly aware of the importance of the Arab vote and of the dependence of any future Labor government on the backing of the predominantly Arab parties. Alarmed by this possibility, the Likud has made a number of attempts to delegitimize possible alliances between Labor and the three predominantly Arab parties (Lustick, 1990).

At the same time, internal factionalisms have failed to undermine Arab-Jewish polarity on key issues of coexistence. Arabs continue to be a dissident minority with which the Labor establishment feels uneasy; it is fearful of the political risks involved in making concessions to this minority or accepting them as members of a coalition. (The failing attempt in 1990 to form a narrow Labor coalition with the support of Arab Knesset Members will be discussed in chapter 22.)

Part Three

TRENDS

21

Trends among Arabs

The Six Day War was the watershed in Arab-Jewish relations as in many other areas in Israeli life. Yet there is a controversy on whether Arab-Jewish coexistence has worsened since then. In the next two chapters, evidence bearing on the historical trends among Arabs and Jews will be examined in detail.

As introduced and elaborated upon in chapter 1, the radicalization and politicization perspectives provide alternative hypotheses on the political developments among Israeli Arabs. According to the former view, the Arabs have increasingly become more alienated from and hostile toward the state and Jews; according to the latter, they have only been exercising their rights to fight for peace and equality.

The politicization thesis makes a crucial distinction, overlooked by the radicalization thesis, between radicalism and militancy. Radicalism is a struggle that presents a challenge to the territorial and political integrity of the state and may also use extra-legal measures. Militancy is a more moderate fight that lacks such radical excesses and keeps its goals and means within democratic bounds. While the radicalization perspective hypothesizes a trend toward an increase in both militancy and radicalism, the politicization perspective predicts a rise only in militancy.

These two theses will be examined by looking into the Arab political response over the years in the following spheres: orientation (political attitudes toward the state and Jewish majority), leadership, voting, and protest.

Orientation

It seems that during the decade prior to the 1967 War, most Israeli Arabs were undergoing a process of reconciliation with life as a minority in Israel. Such reconciliation was reinforced by growing cultural and social contacts with the Jews, isolation from the Arab world, and a sense of powerlessness. This tendency toward accommodation bordered on passivity and a "wait and see" attitude. Since many Arabs skirted the issues, the orientation types were much less clearly defined before 1967. The militancy that took place thereafter caused a contraction of the extreme accommodationist and rejectionist types, and the concomitant growth to majority of the reservationist and oppositionist types. As some Arabs became more and more militant, most were then forced to take stands and to fashion a more general orientation. As a result, more distinct types emerged, disagreeing among themselves more consistently on the issues.

It is impossible to test these observations, however, for the lack of quantifiable data for the 1950s and 1960s. Precise comparisons could be made only for the 1976-88 period because the first representative survey of Arabs was conducted in 1976.

The comparability of the 1976-88 Arab surveys makes it possible to examine trends for this period. Straightforward comparisons can be made between either summary measures or separate questions by repeating the same representative sampling, questions, and typology construction.

The best way to ascertain a trend in Arab orientation is by comparing the distributions of orientation types in the four surveys. Since the 1980-88 typology, presented earlier, cannot be reproduced, because not every question appeared in the 1976 survey, a variant was constructed, drawing on identical items included in all the surveys and following exactly the same procedures. The operational definition of each orientation type follows:

1. Arab respondents who concurred on all the following views were classified as accommodationists: (1) consider the term "Israeli" as an appropriate self-description, (2) oppose protest actions abroad as a legitimate means of struggle, and (3) oppose the use of general strikes.

2. Arabs subscribing to the following opinions fell into the reservationist type: (1) do not agree that the Zionist movement is racist, (2) do not endorse protest actions abroad, and (3) oppose unlicensed demonstrations.

3. Arabs were regarded as oppositionists if they took the following stands: (1) agree that the Zionist movement is racist, (2) favor protest actions abroad, and (3) do not oppose unlicensed demonstrations.

4. Arabs espousing the following outlooks were categorized as rejectionists: (1) deny Israel's right to exist, (2) endorse unlicensed demonstrations, and (3) do not oppose the use of violence in the struggle to improve conditions for Israeli Arabs.

This typology correlates very highly (r=0.78) with the more widely based typology for the 1985 survey. Its reliability is further shown in its full coverage of the Arabs surveyed (98% – 4,118 of 4,199 – of the Arabs included in the four samples were classified into one of the four types).

The comparison of the distribution of the Arab types during the 1976-88 period reveals a complex picture rather than any single linear trend (Table 21.1). First, there is a drop in the percentage of the oppositionist and rejectionist types from 1976 to 1980, probably reflecting both the diminishing impact of the first Land Day general strike in 1976 and the accommodating effect of the peace treaty between Israel and Egypt. After 1980, the two moderate types, the accommodationist and the reservationist, steadily declined in response to the alienating Israel's War in Lebanon in 1982 and the repression of the intifada in 1988. Second, the simultaneous decline of the accommodating type and the rise of the oppositionist type from 1985 to 1988 show a clear trend of growing militancy under the influence of the intifada. Third, throughout the entire period, the rejectionist type did not increase and it even slightly decreased, from 13.5% in 1976 to 10% in 1988, testifying to the lack of growth in Arab radicalism. Fourth, as a result of the contraction of the extreme accommodationist and rejectionist types, the two middle types rose from 73% in 1976 to 83% in 1988.

Table 21.1 Arab Orientation Types, 1976-88

	Arab Public			
	1976	1980	1985	1988
Arab orientation types				
Accommodationists	13.1	15.3	12.7	7.2
Reservationists	29.5	39.1	36.2	31.1
Oppositionists	43.9	39.9	40.3	51.9
Rejectionists	13.5	5.7	10.8	9.8
Total	100.0	100.0	100.0	100.0
Number of cases	607	1,133	1,190	1,188

Chi-square = 104.90012 d.f. = 9 $p < 0.0000$.

Two conclusions can be derived from these findings. One, there has been a rise in Arab militancy (or a decline in accommodation) over the years, confirming the assertions made by both the radicalization and politicization perspectives. The other conclusion is that a rise in Arab rejectionism is absent, thus affirming the prediction of the politicization perspective and refuting the forecast of the radicalization perspective. These initial conclusions are further tested below by applying specific measures of militancy and rejectionism.

Let us first look into measures of a rise in militancy. Table 21.2 presents selected militant attitudes for the 1976-88 period. They have in common all the elements of dissent from the Jewish national consensus, including rejection of Israel's Jewish-Zionist character and endorsement of firm means of struggle, institutional autonomy, Israeli Palestinian identity, and a two-state solution to the Palestinian question. Yet none of these attitudes is rejectionist in the sense of negating the very existence and territorial integrity of the state. Of the eleven questions in the table, ten show a rise in militancy. To illustrate, during the 1976-88 period, the view that Zionism is racist rose from 63.5% to 70%, dissatisfaction with Israeli citizenship from 49% to 62%, and approval of general strikes from 63% to 74%.

Table 21.2 Arabs' Selected Militant Attitudes, 1976-88

	Arab Public			
	1976	1980	1985	1988
Favor the repeal of the Law of Return	63.4	60.8	71.9	*
Agree that Zionism is racist	63.5	60.7	65.3	70.0
Dissatisfied with Israeli citizenship	48.7	55.3	57.9	62.3
Consider the Committee of Heads of Arab Local Councils truly representative of Arabs in Israel	48.0	55.3	62.7	78.8
Favor the establishment of an Arab university	70.5	71.0	88.1	*
Favor protest abroad to improve Arab conditions	63.6	51.9	55.4	67.1
Favor general strikes to improve Arab conditions	62.6	54.6	61.2	73.8
Define oneself as an Israeli Palestinian or a Palestinian in Israel	12.4	28.8	38.7	39.7
Define Arabs in Israel as Israeli Palestinians or Palestinians in Israel	**	29.8	40.8	43.9
Favor the formation of a Palestinian state in the West Bank and Gaza Strip alongside Israel	74.7	64.0	67.2	76.5
Think that Israel should recognize the PLO	*	67.8	81.6	81.6

*Not asked. **This category was not offered.

To obtain a summary measure of militancy, an additive index of seven items, of those in Table 21.2 that appeared in all the four surveys, was constructed. A score of 1 was assigned to endorsement of any of the following stands: Zionism is racist, dissatisfaction with Israeli citizenship, recognition of the Committee of Heads of Arab Local Councils, Arab protest abroad, Arab general strikes, self-identity as an Israeli Palestinian (or Palestinian in Israel), and a Palestinian state on the West Bank and Gaza. This cumulative index, ranging from 0 to 7, indicates a clear rise in militancy over the years (Table 21.3). Arabs scoring 6-7 points on the index increased from 19% in 1976, to 22% in 1980, to 27% in 1985, and to 39% in 1988. The mean score was 3.9, 3.9, 4.2, and 4.7, respectively. The test of analysis of variance detected no increase between 1976 and 1980 (the various indicators show either stability or decline), but did reveal statistically significant increases in the years from 1980-88 (Table 21.4).

Table 21.3 Arab Militancy Index, 1976-88

	Arab Public			
	1976	1980	1985	1988
Militancy index				
0 Lowest	3.8	3.6	2.4	1.0
1	7.9	8.8	6.0	4.2
2	12.7	12.6	10.7	6.1
3	10.0	15.6	12.4	11.0
4	19.2	19.2	21.7	16.5
5	27.7	18.2	20.0	22.4
6	16.8	16.6	19.5	27.0
7 Highest	2.0	5.3	7.3	11.8

Table 21.4 Analysis of Variance of Arab Militancy Index by Year of Survey

	Arab Public			
	1976	1980	1985	1988
Number of cases	581	1,097	1,164	1,178
Mean	3.9280	3.8541	4.1959	4.7182
Standard deviation	1.7469	1.8281	1.7543	1.6587
One-way analysis of variance D.f. (between)=3 d.f.(within)=4,016 F=53.4738 p<.0000				
Multiple comparison test				
1980				
1985	*	*		
1988	*	*	*	

*Significant at 0.05 level according to Scheffe's test.

The same procedure was repeated for measures of rejectionism. Table 21.5 displays selected rejectionist attitudes that negate Israel's right of existence, its territorial integrity, compliance with the law, or the continued affiliation with the state and with Jews. The trend emerging from these questions can best be illustrated by the following proportions: Arabs denying Israel's right to exist amounted to 20.5% in 1976, 11% in 1980, 18% in 1985, and 13.5% in 1988; Arabs favoring the use of violence to improve Arab conditions were 18%, 7.5%, 8%, and 8%, respectively. There is a drop between 1976 and 1980 as against stability to a moderate increase thereafter. There is no overall rise in rejectionism over the years, not even in 1988 in reaction to the intifada.

A 0-7 point scale of rejectionism, based on 7 of the items in Table 21.5, was built. One point was accorded to endorsement of each of the following stances: denial of Israel's right to exist, Arab conditions cannot be improved by acceptable democratic procedures, approval of unlicensed demonstrations, endorsement of the use of violence, self-identity as non-Israeli Palestinian, a Palestinian state in all of Mandatory Palestine (including the Galilee and Triangle), and unwillingness to have Jewish friends. Arabs scoring 5-7 on the rejectionism index constituted 11% in 1976, 5% in 1980, 6% in 1985, and 7% in 1988 (Table 21.6). At the same time, the proportion of Arabs with no rejectionism (scoring 0-1) rose dramatically, from 36% in 1976, to 52% in 1980, to 56% in 1985, and to 60% in 1988. The test of analysis of variance demonstrates a significant decrease in the rejectionism index from 1976 to later years, but stability for the 1980-88 period (Table 21.7).

Table 21.5 Arabs' Selected Rejectionist Attitudes, 1976-88

	Arab Public			
	1976	1980	1985	1988
Deny Israel's right to exist	20.5	11.0	17.6	13.5
Do not believe in the possibility of improving Arab conditions by acceptable democratic means	16.3	17.6	8.9	10.6
Favor unlicensed demonstrations to improve Arab conditions	17.1	7.0	10.8	13.5
Favor use of violence to improve Arab conditions	17.9	7.5	8.1	8.0
Define oneself as a Palestinian or a Palestinian Arab	32.9	25.7	29.2	27.1
Define Arabs in Israel as Palestinians or Palestinian Arabs	**	24.2	25.8	22.9
Endorse a Palestinian state in all of Mandatory Palestine instead of Israel or including the Galilee and Triangle	58.7	38.1	32.3	29.5
Would move to a Palestinian state in the West Bank and Gaza Strip if it were established	14.4	8.3	*	7.5
Unwilling to have Jewish friends	42.5	30.7	36.7	33.8

*Not asked. **This category was not offered.

Table 21.6 Arab Rejectionism Index, 1976-88

	Arab Public			
	1976	1980	1985	1988
Rejectionism index				
0 Lowest	13.9	25.4	26.6	33.0
1	22.5	26.8	29.4	27.4
2	21.2	22.8	17.6	17.2
3	17.3	13.7	12.8	9.4
4	14.5	6.0	7.1	5.9
5	5.9	3.4	4.5	3.9
6	4.5	1.4	1.6	2.2
7 Highest	0.2	0.4	0.3	0.9

Table 21.7 Analysis of Variance of Arab Rejectionism by Year of Survey

	Arab Public			
	1976	1980	1985	1988
Number of cases	589	1,112	1,179	1,178
Mean	2.3315	1.6646	1.6599	1.5289
Standard deviation	1.6561	1.4831	1.5512	1.6254
One-way analysis of variance D.f. (between)=3 d.f.(within)=4,054 F=36.6293 p<.0000				
Multiple comparison test				
1980	*			
1985	*			
1988	*			

* Significant at 0.05 level according to Scheffe's test.

Taken together, all these figures lend credence to the analysis set forth by the politicization perspective, according to which Arab militancy is expected to rise but without increasing the level of rejectionism. Manifestations of rejectionism are relatively small, considerably smaller than manifestations of militancy, and even the intifada has not pushed rejectionism up.

Additional clues as to the general trend can be gleaned from an examination of the changes in the orientation of selected Arab population groups. Contrary to the radicalization thesis, the trend is far from being uniform or linear. The Druzes and Northern Bedouin have become much less accommodating over the years, Christians have not changed much, Negev Bedouin lost much of their rejectionism, and the non-Bedouin Moslems have become more militant but not more rejectionist (Table 21.8). Education by itself does not make much difference. Public misconceptions aside, Arabs with post-primary schooling not only do not differ in orientation from those with only primary or no education, but also have remained the same over the years (Table 21.9). When combined with other factors, however, education produces a special effect. For instance, Arabs who are 46 years old or older, have 0-8 years of schooling, and live in localities of fewer than 5,000 inhabitants have lost their rejectionism, whereas the contrasting group (i.e., 18-35 years old, possessing 13 or more years of schooling, and living in localities of 5,000 or more) have kept their above-average rejectionism (Table 21.10). Women and older men have become less rejectionist but more oppositionist.

Several factors can be suggested to account for the trend in Arab orientation. The greater moderation in the 1980 survey, compared to the 1976 survey, could be a result of one or a combination of three new

Table 21.8 Arab Orientation Types by Community, 1976-88

	Arab Public				
	Accommodationists	Reservationists	Oppositionists	Rejectionists	N
Druzes					
1976	34.8	40.6	24.6	0.0	55
1980	41.3	41.3	16.5	0.9	109
1985	42.2	37.1	19.0	1.7	116
1988	23.7	44.7	22.8	8.8	114
Northern Bedouin					
1976	30.2	42.8	20.6	6.4	44
1980	33.3	44.4	16.7	5.6	54
1985	15.9	47.6	26.8	9.8	82
1988	9.5	34.9	46.0	9.5	63
Negev Bedouin					
1976	2.1	21.4	48.1	28.4	32
1980	8.2	42.5	39.7	9.6	73
1985	9.5	39.3	38.1	13.1	84
1988	0.0	50.0	50.0	0.0	34
Christians					
1976	9.3	30.6	49.8	10.3	115
1980	13.8	42.4	40.4	3.4	203
1985	11.0	40.1	42.4	6.4	172
1988	9.2	29.5	56.6	4.6	173
Non-Bedouin Moslems					
1976	10.0	26.5	47.3	16.2	361
1980	11.0	37.0	45.2	6.8	694
1985	8.4	33.6	45.0	13.0	736
1988	4.5	28.5	55.5	11.6	804

Table 21.9 Arab Orientation Types by Education, 1976-88

	Arab Public				
	Accommodationists	Reservationists	Oppositionists	Rejectionists	N
Primary education					
1976	13.3	28.6	43.9	14.2	469
1980	16.8	40.7	36.7	5.8	762
1985	14.2	38.5	37.5	9.9	678
1988	7.8	34.4	50.0	7.8	540
Secondary education					
1976	15.5	36.9	38.0	9.6	94
1980	13.4	36.5	44.0	6.1	277
1985	10.1	36.0	42.6	11.4	378
1988	6.5	29.8	52.1	11.6	493
Post-secondary education					
1976	7.1	20.9	56.9	15.0	42
1980	7.5	34.4	53.8	4.3	93
1985	13.1	26.2	48.4	12.3	122
1988	7.6	23.6	56.3	12.5	144

factors: the waning of the radicalizing effect of the 1976 Land Day strike, the fear of the Likud government, and the Israel-Egypt Peace Treaty. The greater militancy in the 1985-88 survey, compared to the 1980 survey, could be attributed to the diminution of these moderating factors and the addition of three new unsettling elements: the return to religion, Israel's War in Lebanon, and the intifada.

The dramatic increase in Israeli Arabs' return to religion during the 1980s did have some effect on orientation. Although 18% of all respondents in the 1985 Arab survey said that they had returned to religion during the past five years, 22% of the Moslems as against only 5% of the Christians did so (Table 21.11). Return to religion is higher among rejectionist women (33%) and highest among rejectionist Moslem women (36%). When it takes a fundamentalist twist, it tends to alienate Arabs from Jews. Return to religion, more specifically a rise in Islamic fundamentalism, may explain part of the rise in rejectionism of certain groups among the Moslem majority.

Table 21.10 Arab Orientation Types by Selected Population Groups, 1976-88

	Arab Public				
	Accommo-dationists	Reserva-tionists	Opposi-tionists	Reject-ionists	N
Women					
1976	10.5	27.3	44.0	18.2	306
1980	15.1	43.0	36.2	5.6	549
1985	12.5	36.1	40.9	10.5	543
1988	5.9	31.1	53.5	9.6	492
46-55 years old					
1976	8.7	34.0	40.1	17.1	69
1980	14.8	48.7	32.2	4.3	115
1985	14.7	43.4	35.7	6.2	129
1988	7.0	39.5	45.6	7.9	114
18-35 years old, 13+ years of schooling, living in localities of 5,000+					
1976	0.0	22.7	62.8	14.5	24
1980	4.4	31.1	60.0	4.4	45
1985	4.8	17.7	56.5	21.0	62
1988	5.3	15.8	59.2	19.7	76
46+ years old, 0-4 years of schooling, living in localities of fewer than 5,000					
1976	9.5	38.9	43.3	8.4	49
1980	24.7	40.4	29.2	5.6	89
1985	18.1	45.8	30.1	6.0	83
1988	6.1	43.9	50.0	0.0	66

Table 21.11 Arab Orientation Types by Return to Religion, 1976-88

	Arab Public			
	Accommodationists	Reservationists	Oppositionists	Rejectionists
Returned to religion in past five years				
Total	13.9	19.6	16.2	25.0
Women	14.7	17.4	13.6	33.3
Moslem women	22.5	21.3	16.0	35.9

For the Arabs, Israel's War in Lebanon was also an alienating force. In their eyes, it was the only war that Israel fought against the Palestinians, not against the Arab countries. Its declared goal, to liquidate the PLO, was considered utterly illegitimate. Also totally rejected was the War's hidden intention, to consolidate Israel's control of the West Bank and Gaza Strip through successful disintegration of the Palestinians in the Diaspora. Arabs who in the 1985 survey had reported adverse effects of the War on their attitudes toward the state were more militant than the average (Table 21.12).

Table 21.12 Arab Orientation Types by Experienced Impact of Israel's War in Lebanon

	Arab Public			
	Accommodationists	Reservationists	Oppositionists	Rejectionists
Feel that Israel's War in Lebanon adversely affected one's attitude toward the State of Israel	50.3	76.4	86.2	88.1
Feel that Israel's War in Lebanon weakened one's belief in Israeli democracy	38.1	63.1	76.7	83.2
Took part in protest against Israel's War in Lebanon	6.6	11.0	27.9	45.7

The intifada had a similar impact. The more militant the orientation, the more adverse was the effect of the intifada on the attitude toward the state. The intifada's adverse effect ranged from 51.5% among the accommodationists to 86% among the rejectionists (Table 21.13). There is no doubt that the intifada contributed to the increase in the militancy level of the Arabs, but apparently not to rejectionism.

Table 21.13 Arab Orientation Types by Experienced Impact of the Intifada, 1988

	Arab Public			
	Accommodationists	Reservationists	Oppositionists	Rejectionists
Feel that the events in the territories that began on December 9, 1987 adversely affected one's attitude toward the State of Israel	51.5	68.9	85.0	68.2

Source: The 1988 survey.

These developments well explain the growing moderation of the Christians during 1976-85. The protracted civil war in Lebanon and the rise in Islamic fundamentalism exposed the vulnerability of the Christians as a minority among Arabs both in the Arab world and in Israel. The intifada, however, has shifted a significant proportion of the Christians from the reservationist to the oppositionist type.

To conclude, the data from the four surveys display a rise in militancy over the years, but do not disclose any trend of radicalization or growth in rejectionism and extremism among Israeli Arabs.

Leadership

The conditions following Israel's establishment were not conducive to the nurturing of an independent Arab leadership. First, the mass Arab exodus from Western Palestine left those who remained virtually without national and organizational leaders. Second, the contraction of the Arab class structure, as a result of the massive departure of the upper and middle classes, deprived Arabs of an elite from which a new public leadership might be recruited. Third, the reservoir for leadership was further drained by the fact that the Arabs who stayed behind were disproportionately less urban, less educated, and more accommodating than the "leavers." Fourth, the Arabs had to face the predicament of being a vulnerable population as they abruptly ceased to be a majority and became a suspected minority. Lastly, in addition to the hardships of disorientation and psychological readjustment, Israeli Arabs were faced with problems of sheer economic survival and a dearth of basic services after the collapse of their major institutions in 1948.

The huge vacuum created by the war was quickly filled by the Jewish authorities. To control the Arab minority, military government was imposed, including demarcation of closed areas, travel restrictions, detentions, curfews, and close surveillance. Proletarization, which made the Arabs economically dependent on the Jews, further inhibited the emergence of an autonomous elite. Less visible, but no less effective, was the conscious policy of cultivating a dependent leadership and of discouraging non-accommodation (Lustick, 1980).

Two major sub-types of accommodating leadership were singled out and promoted. These were the notables and the functionaries. The notables were hamula heads or other village strongmen. They were informally recognized, and their traditional intermediary role ("*wasta*") between the villagers and the outside world was partially retained. Underlying the support given the hamula elders by the authorities was the desire to curb Arab nationalism and to facilitate Jewish domination; it was supposedly easier to control tradition-bound, small, and local collectivities than to contain frustrated, nationalistic, Westernized individuals.

Together with the retention of traditionalist hamula elders, a new leadership cadre was recruited. Separate departments for Arab affairs were established in various government ministries, in the Histadrut, and in the major political parties. They aimed to gather information, to monitor developments, to intercede, to appease, to administer, and to win the votes of the Arab minority. These Jewish-headed Arab departments enlisted Arab functionaries to staff low-ranking positions and to do the work in the field. The most important public figures in this category are today Arab Knesset Members affiliated with the Zionist parties, pro-establishment heads of Arab local authorities, Arab high-ranking officials in the Histadrut, and Arab representatives of the Labor and Zionist left parties.

The Arab leadership in the 1950s and 1960s had all the characteristics of an effectively controlled minority. First, being selected, appointed or maintained by the Jews, it was accountable to the Jewish authorities rather than to the Arab masses; further, it derived its power over Arabs by mediating the exchange of Arab loyalty and supplying manpower, lands and votes for protection and benefits. Second, it was compromising, and it reconciled itself to minority status and encouraged Arabs to accept this condition in a Jewish-Zionist state. Avoiding protest and extra-parliamentary politics, it worked through the system to improve conditions for Arabs. Third, it was totally ethnic, dealing only with Arabs or Arab affairs; it lacked any ambition to achieve influential posts in Israeli society as a whole or to have a say in state or Jewish matters. Not aspiring even to general leadership, it was satisfied with the secondary rank afforded by minority leadership. Fourth, it was devoid of qualities that a minority in the process of socialization into the Israeli political culture might hold in high regard: formal education, ideological articulateness, statesmanship, personal example, assertiveness, and balanced accountability to minority and majority.

At the same time, an independent national Arab leadership could not establish itself. The Al-Ard group, composed of professionals, writers, and other nationalist elements, was blocked by the authorities because of its rejectionist orientation. The remaining leaders of the Arab National League, the Arab Communist Party of the 1940s, joined Maki (the Jewish Communist Party) in 1949. These militant leaders, the most prominent among whom were Emil Habibi, Tawfiq Toubi, Saliba Hamis, and Emil Tuma, could not gain wider acceptance in the Arab sector as long as they were Maki functionaries within a party remaining under tight Jewish control.

During the first two decades, the initial obstacles to independent non-accommodationist leadership substantially diminished. After overcoming the early psychological and existential hardships, the Arabs took the road of politicization. Concomitantly, their class structure gained greater depth and complexity with the rise of a sizable middle stratum of intelligentsia, self-employed professionals, and businessmen, who soon became available for recruitment as public leaders.

Growing politicization and the expanding pool of qualified persons produced a number of changes in the leadership of the 1970s. First, a considerable decline took place in the standing of dependent leadership as hamula elders lost much of their power and functionaries lost much of their credibility and following. Second, some of the veteran leaders managed to retain influence by becoming more independent of the Zionist establishment, more responsive to Arab needs, and more militant. Third, there was a marked rise in independent leadership. Finally, the new leaders possessed better qualifications than their predecessors, being younger, better educated, more articulate, more ideological, and less opportunistic.

By the mid-1980s, the factionalization of the Arab leadership into four major types paralleled and shaped a similar differentiation among the population at large, as revealed in the surveys. The Jewish parties and the Histadrut provided a solid organizational base for a new breed of accommodationist Arab leaders, who were far removed from the traditional, coopted elders and notables. Nouwaf Matsalha of the Labor Party, the top Arab leader in the Histadrut who became a Knesset Member in 1988, best represents this new breed of Arab leaders.

Many unaffiliated leaders have also come to play an active role. Some used to be associated with the Jewish parties; others have chosen to be non-partisan because they distrust both the Zionist and Communist establishments. Nimr Ibrahim Houssein, the mayor of Shefaram and chairman of the Committee of Heads of Arab Local Councils, is a typical leader of this stripe. He tries to retain an independent posture and at the same time to be acceptable to both the Jewish establishment and its Arab opposition. Knesset Member Abdul Wahab Darawshe is one who casts himself into a model of this emergent, reservationist Arab leader. His innovative style is well evident in his stated goal to make the new Democratic Arab Party (DAP), which he founded and which gained one Knesset seat in 1988, eligible for inclusion in coalition governments and to make Israeli Arabs a fully legitimate pressure group within the Israeli political system and sharers of national power.

The Israeli Communist Party (Rakah) and the Progressive List for Peace provide a broad base for oppositionist leaders. Rakah operates directly and through many front organizations, the most prominent among these being the Democratic Front for Peace and Equality (DFPE). The rise of the PLP in 1984 introduced yet another variant. Unlike the

Rakah leadership, PLP leaders are nationalist, not bound by Communism, Soviet hegemony, or hardcore secularism. Because of their ideology and tactics, however, both the PLP and DFPE are rejected by the Zionist establishment and find themselves in permanent opposition. On the other hand, employing the same leadership style and appealing to the same Arab constituency, the two groups compete intensely, and the hostility between them is fierce.

The emergence of the Sons of the Village Movement and the Progressive National Movement as successors to the outlawed Al-Ard Movement has brought with it new rejectionist leaders. They operate only in certain localities and in every university because the authorities do not let them set up statewide organizations. In fact, an attempt to form a national coordinating body was declared illegal in early 1981. During the 1980s, the Sons of the Village Movement split into a number of factions, and its leaders have faded from the public view and are less influential.

At the same time, a new kind of leader has developed in conjunction with the rise in Islamic fundamentalism. These Islamic leaders are well organized in certain villages, maintain numerous self-help community projects, and publish several periodicals. Fortified with their contributions to the well-being of local residents, they won an impressive victory in the 1989 local elections, capturing the chairmanship of five localities, including the city of Um al-Fahem in the Triangle and the Bedouin town of Rahat in the Negev (Paz, 1990).

It is too early to tell about the political orientation of the new Islamic leaders. Rejectionism is one possibility that has alarmed the authorities and the Jewish majority. The Islamic movement actually started as rejectionist in the early 1980s, and some of its activists were convicted and sentenced on charges of sabotage (Mayer, 1989). Any influence of the Hamas of the Gaza Strip and the Islamic Jihad Movement of the West Bank would activate and reinforce a rejectionist predisposition. Rejectionism would entail negation of Israel's Western, Jewish, and Zionist features, repudiation of the Moslem minority status in a Dahimmi-ruled society, and a desire to replace the Jewish with an Islamic state. Delegitimation of Israel is expressed by the Islamic fundamentalists' boycott of Knesset elections as both voters and candidates. Furthermore, their clashes with the atheist, anti-clerical Communists; with the secularist, nationalist adherents of the Sons of the Village Movement; and with the non-practicing Moslems and Christian rank and file are already evident (Friedman, 1987).

The other option is to develop a religious alternative to the secularist Communists and PLP backers. As another oppositionist orientation, Islamic fundamentalism would mean joining the Israeli Arab consensus on a two-state solution to the Palestinian question, acceptance of Israel as a state and the status of minority for the Arabs, a struggle for equal rights and opportunities, and full participation in Knesset elections. Like other oppositionists, the fundamentalists would remain in permanent opposition to the regime. The political cleavage between them and other oppositionists, however, would be reflected in the shaping of the public domain, community institutions, and individuals' way of life by Islam. If they take this route, they would duplicate the split between Orthodox and non-Orthodox Jews and act much like the ultra-Orthodox parties. This means that they would segregate themselves into separate communities, attempt to pass religious local by-laws, build non-coed schools, and use their political power to extract financial and other concessions from local and national power centers.

It is more likely that Islamic fundamentalism would develop along oppositionist lines because of Israel's special conditions and influences. On the one hand, Islamic rejectionism would lead to subversion and to effective repression by the authorities. On the other hand, in a free country like Israel, non-rejectionist Islam would enjoy the chance of open competition with other forces and, hence, of scoring gains. The odds, therefore, favor an oppositionist style. In fact, Sheikh Abdallah Darwish, the most outstanding leader of the Islamic Movement, declared in late 1989 his intention to establish an Islamic party that will run for the next Knesset elections. Since this is a very divisive issue and he represents only one faction of the Movement, it remains to be seen how much support he will receive.

To overcome this appreciable factionalism, a "Supreme Follow-Up Committee" was formed in 1984 to deliberate and decide matters of common interest to all Arabs in Israel. This committee consists of every elected Arab public figure from all political parties and movements: Knesset Members, members of the Executive of the Committee of Heads of Arab Local Councils, members of the top governing bodies of the Histadrut, and representatives on the board of the School Teachers' Association. Although Druze leaders do not participate, the Supreme Follow-Up Committee is, nonetheless, the most representative Arab body ("the Arab parliament in Israel"). It is this committee that usually calls for general strikes and issues nationalist statements. Through this body the Arab leadership, despite internal splits, has demonstrated its ability to reach consensus and concerted action on questions of civil rights and equality and to exert firm control of the Arab population, as evidenced by the peaceful nature of the mass strike in June 1987 and several other general strikes thereafter (Mansur, 1987).

All the features of Arab politicization are to be found in these changing patterns of leadership. The Israelization of the new leaders of every type is reflected in their growing resemblance to Jewish leaders in background, political culture, and style (e.g., younger age, more educated, verbally fluent, and ideologically committed). With the exception of the rejectionists, they endeavor to enter, rather than abstain from, Israeli politics as an organized interest group and to avail themselves fully of all avenues opened to them by Israeli democracy.

Factionalism is also quite substantial. By the late 1980s, accommodationist Arabs were represented by leaders affiliated with the Zionist establishment, reservationist Arabs by the new DAP, oppositionist Arabs by both the Communist Party and Progressive List for Peace, and rejectionist Arabs by activists in the Sons of the Village Movement. The Islamic Movement is also contributing a new style, still crystallizing, and hovering between the oppositionists and rejectionists.

Israelization and factionalization have channeled the Arab leadership into militancy rather than radicalization. All types of Arab leaders in the 1980s are more militant than were their pre-1967 counterparts; they are, by and large, not coopted, insistent on Arab rights, and prepared to voice protest; they also try hard to reconcile their Palestinian and Israeli ties and loyalties. As a whole, Arab leaders want to be an integral, equal part of Israeli society and politics.

This basic non-rejectionist orientation of Israeli Arabs and their leaders presents a considerable challenge to rejectionists who are truly extremist and hostile to Israel. Increasingly, they find themselves dissenting from the Israeli Arab consensus and isolated from both Arabs and Jews. To their great dismay, they are also realizing that their ideology and politics of confrontation run counter to the historical shift of Palestinian nationalism and the PLO away from rejectionism and toward accommodation with Israel. This is the reason that the Sons of the Village Movement has been undergoing a deep crisis, splitting, and becoming less rejectionist since the mid-1980s. These are also the forces that are deterring the Islamic fundamentalists from turning rejectionist.

Voting

In the 1988 national elections, Arabs accounted for 347,039 of the 2,894,267, (i.e., 12%) eligible voters in Israel. Since 85% of these Israeli Arabs live in wholly Arab localities (the remainder live in predominantly Jewish towns), it is possible to trace Arab voting behavior with considerable assurance.

Within certain limitations, the Arab vote reflects the underlying trend in Arab opinion, as demonstrated by the correlation between the reported voting in the survey and the attitudes toward Jews and the State of Israel. Arab voting choices, however, are restricted in two crucial ways. One is the conspicuous absence of an independent, Arab national party, owing in no small measure to countermeasures taken by the authorities, who fear such a party would serve as a source of unrest and as a potential stronghold of Palestinian nationalism. An attempt by the radical Al-Ard Movement to form a national Arab party in the early 1960s was finally declared illegal by the courts in 1965. Arabs who are oppositionist or rejectionist in orientation are not offered the option of voting for a radical, Palestinian national party.

Also missing before 1988 was an independent, integrationist, Arab or Arab-Jewish political party that could fit into the mainstream of Israeli coalition politics. Rakah and the PLP are considered outside the national consensus and, therefore, ineligible for membership in coalition governments. Unlike non-Zionist religious Jews, who can support the ultra-Orthodox parties, accommodationist and reservationist Arabs lacked before 1988 the option of voting for a predominantly Arab party that would fight for their equality, take part in coalition politics, and extract meaningful concessions while maintaining a low profile on Zionism and on the Palestinian question. This situation changed in 1988 with the formation of the DAP, which tries to play this role. The Arab voters in 1988 and in the early 1990s still do not have the choice of an independent integrationist Arab party, because the new DAP has not as yet performed this function.

Arab voters in Knesset elections can choose among three types of election lists: Zionist parties, Arab lists affiliated with the Zionist parties (until 1981), and non-Zionist, predominantly Arab parties. Of the 6-8 Zionist parties that appeal to the Arab vote, the Labor Party is by far the most important. Arab lists are headed by dignitaries associated with Jewish parties; whereas the Communists (Maki, Rakah, or DFPE), the PLP (since 1984), and the DAP (since 1988) constitute the non-Zionist, predominantly Arab parties.

Analysis of the Arab vote for the entire 1949-88 period reveals the following patterns (R. Cohen, 1985 and 1989; Gal, 1989; and Landau, 1989 provide the main figures cited here): First, Arab participation in Knesset elections is very high although lower than the Jewish rate. In 1988, 73% of the eligible voters in Arab localities, compared to 80% of the eligible voters in Jewish localities, voted.[1] This high participation signifies the Arab desire to take part in and influence, rather than abstain from, Israeli politics. If fact, even the PLO usually urges Israeli Arabs not to stay away,

[1]The Jewish rate is, in fact, much higher because an appreciable proportion of Jewish non-voters are abroad permanently as emigrants (but their names continue to appear in the register of voters prepared by the ministry of the Interior) or temporarily as tourists or sojourners. This is much less true of Arab non-voters.

but to vote for the non-Zionist lists, and in 1988 even called on them to vote for any party (including Zionist parties) that stood for a two-state solution. The call of the Sons of the Village Movement to boycott elections is not taken seriously by the Arab public at large.

There has been, however, a slow but steady decline in the Arab participation rate since the peak of 85% in the 1959 elections. Furthermore, the Arab voting rate since 1965 has been lower than the national average. The drop is probably a direct outcome of the heightened politicization of the Arabs, reflecting their frustration at the narrowness of voting choices compared with the wide range available to Jewish voters. With the emergence of the PLP and DAP, Arab participation went on the rise, from its record low of 70% in 1981 to 73-74% later. It seems that three kinds of Arab potential voters abstain from voting for lack of a viable option: secular rejectionists, fundamentalist Moslems, and reservationists who are still not sure that the DAP is indeed an integrationist Arab party.

Second, there has been a consistent drop since 1959 of Arab votes for Arab lists affiliated with the Zionist establishment (from 58.5% in 1959 to 13% in 1981) (Table 21.14). All these Arab lists were defeated in 1981 and none ran thereafter. This total disappearance is partly explained by the significant degree of Israelization that has come to mark Arab voting behavior (Al-Haj and Yaniv, 1983). Like the Jews, the Arabs now vote for modern ideological parties rather than for traditional ethnic lists. The change also marks a real erosion in control -the hamulas and notables can no longer be depended on to deliver the Arab vote en bloc.

Table 21.14 Arab Vote in Knesset Elections, 1949-88

	1949	1951	1955	1959	1961	1965	1969	1973	1977	1981	1984	1988
Jewish lists	26.1	28.9	26.6	30.2	32.0	33.1	29.7	27.1	27.9	48.9	48.6	41.7
Affiliated Arab lists	51.7	54.8	57.8	58.5	45.5	40.8	41.0	36.0	21.5	13.2	-	-
Communist lists	22.2	16.3	15.6	11.3	22.5	23.1	29.5	36.9	50.7	37.9	33.2	33.8
Progressive List for Peace	-	-	-	-	-	-	-	-	-	-	18.2	13.6
Democratic Arab Party	-	-	-	-	-	-	-	-	-	-	-	10.9

Third, equally noteworthy is the fact that there has been a steady substantial rise in the Arab vote for non-Zionist lists. It soared from 16% in 1951 to 23% in 1965, to 37% in 1973, and to 51% in 1977. It then dropped to 38% in 1981 but rose steadily thereafter to 51% in 1984 and to 58% in 1988 (Table 21.14). This dramatic rise in the non-Zionist vote testifies to the unrelenting trend of the waning dependence of Israeli Arabs on the Jews and Israeli authorities and in their growing militancy.

The division of the Arab vote into Zionist and non-Zionist is also the best behavioral indicator of Arab factionalism. In the absence of truly integrationist and rejectionist Arab parties, voting is inescapably less differentiated than is orientation. Voting Communist or Zionist does not necessarily imply acceptance of those parties' ideological points of view: in fact, the overwhelming majority of Arab voters reject both. Voting for the Zionist lists is, rather, an expression of moderation, of a willingness to come to terms with the system; on the other hand, a vote for the DFPE, PLP, or DAP is a show of militancy, of a challenge to the system from the outside. Both kinds of voting behavior are, thus, equally ideological; they reflect the Arab voter's overall attitude to Arab-Jewish relations.

Fourth, the distribution of the Arab vote among the various parties is also highly significant. Until 1984, the non-Zionist Arab vote was monopolized by the Communist Party, but in 1988 it was divided between 34% DFPE (led by the Communists), 14% PLP, and 11% DAP. The Communists have actually been on the decline since 1977, when they won 51% of the Arab vote. Their claim to be the Arab political establishment is no longer valid. Their position was further undermined by the victory of the Islamic Movement in the 1989 local elections, by the sweeping changes in Eastern Europe late that year, and the eventual demise of the Communist Party in the Soviet Union in the aftermath of the abortive coup d'état there in August 1991. The fate of the Labor Party among the Zionist parties was similar to the weakening of the Communist Party in the Arab sector. It also lost its dominance and declined from 29% of the Arab vote in 1984 to 17% in 1988. The beneficiaries of the Labor Party's loss among the Arabs are the small Zionist left parties (the Citizens' Rights Movement, Mapam, and Shinui), whose sensitivity to the problems of the Arab minority and the support lent to them by Arabs have steadily risen during the 1980s.

Furthermore, the Arab vote has become increasingly important over the years because of the bifurcation of Israeli politics. While the Jewish vote is divided almost evenly between the Labor and Likud camps, the Arab vote is distributed at a ratio of 9 to 1 in favor of the Labor bloc. The Likud, religious parties, and radical right together receive only 10% of the Arab vote. As a result, Arab voters help to prevent the Likud bloc from gaining a political majority. The more they go to the polls, the less are the chances of the Likud to form a winning coalition. This new reality underlies the hostility of many politicians in the Likud camp toward Israeli Arabs. There were many expectations and speculations that the Arab vote in the 1988 elections would be decisive in preventing the Likud from forming a government. The 6 seats won by the DFPE, PLP, and DAP together fell too short of blocking a Likud-headed unity government, a disappointment for many in the Labor camp. Two reasons were given to the poor Arab achievement: the lower Arab participation vote and the failure of any of the three predominantly Arab parties to sign a vote surplus agreement because of the animosity among them (Diskin, 1989). It is estimated that the Arabs lost 2-3 seats, precisely the number that could have turned around the making of a coalition government.

Israeli Arabs clearly prefer Labor to Likud. In the 1988 survey, 61% of the Arabs versus 37% of the Jews favored a Labor government, 7% versus 40% a Likud government, and 32% versus 23% a national unity government. While Jews were evenly split on the issue, the Arabs were 9 to 1 in favor of a Labor government.

Fifth, a detailed examination of election returns reveals significant, long-lasting differences in the voting preferences of different localities and communities. The vote for the DFPE and PLP is disproportionately higher among non-Bedouin Moslems, Christians, and residents of Arab towns, urban localities, and large villages; but it is considerably lower among the Druzes, the Bedouin, and residents of small villages. Although the Arab vote for the two oppositionist lists in 1988 averaged 47%, it was 59% in localities with a Christian majority, compared to 15% in localities with a Druze majority; it was 63% in Arab towns, compared to 17% in small villages and 5% among Bedouin tribes (Table 21.15). It is worth noting the remarkable success of the DAP in 1988 among the Bedouin tribes (it captured 42% of their vote), thus pointing to the middle-of-the road character of this party and to the growing militancy of the Bedouin. The poor showing of the Likud is also conspicuous, even where it did best: compared to obtaining 7% of the Arab vote nationally, the Likud won 19.5% in predominantly Druze localities, 13% among Bedouin tribes, and 12.5% in small villages. The Likud does better than its low average among population groups that contain a small proportion of Israeli Arabs. These divergent voting patterns reflect both differences in official policy toward the various communities and localities and also the political orientations of the latter.

Sixth, the non-Zionist lists have proven less effective in the elections to the Histadrut and to local councils than in elections to the Knesset, but the gap has been closing over time. The Communists (or DFPE) won 20% of the Arab vote to the Histadrut convention in 1965, 31% in 1969, 27% in 1973, 30% in 1977, 32% in 1981, and 35% in 1985. The vote for the DFPE and PLP together in the Histadrut elections of 1985 totalled 45%, compared to 51% in the Knesset election the year before; the joint Arab list (DFPE, PLP, and DAP) to the Histadrut won 33% of the Arab vote in 1989, much less than the 58% they had gained together in the 1988 Knesset election. The Zionist parties have a special advantage in the

Histadrut because among its Arab electorate, in contrast to the Arab voters to the Knesset, there is an over-representation of the economically dependent (wage earners who are employed by Jews, fewer self-employed and employers) and of the less urbanized (inhabitants of smaller villages, including the Druzes).

Table 21.15 Arab Vote in Knesset Elections by Type of Locality and Community, 1988

	Likud	NPR	Labor	CRM, Mapam, Shinui	ADP	PLP	DFPE	Other
Total	6.6	2.9	17.2	10.7	10.9	13.6	33.8	4.3
Religious community								
Localities with a Druze majority	19.5	9.0	28.2	18.8	1.8	0.6	14.6	7.5
Localities with a Christian majority	4.2	3.3	16.9	12.3	1.4	11.5	47.2	3.2
Mixed and Jewish towns	6.1	1.6	21.6	10.2	8.6	9.3	37.9	4.7
Type of Locality								
Arab towns	2.2	1.8	12.5	8.3	9.6	14.7	48.4	2.5
Urban Arab localities	4.6	2.2	14.8	9.9	9.6	16.7	39.5	2.7
Large Arab villages	8.3	4.6	18.2	8.6	10.0	14.5	30.1	5.7
Small Arab villages	12.5	4.6	21.9	16.6	19.2	4.1	13.1	8.0
Bedouin tribes	12.8	1.3	18.6	7.9	41.7	1.1	4.3	12.3

Source: Gal, 1989; Diskin, 1989 (for Bedouin tribes only).

Although Rakah wins fewer votes still in local elections, the increase in its Arab support has, nonetheless, been dramatic. Arab local politics are usually dominated by hamula, local, or Zionist-affiliated lists. The Communist penetration has, therefore, been slow and difficult. In 1969, Communist lists participated in 16 of the 33 Arab local elections and won 8% of the vote. In 1973, they took part in 16 of the 37 Arab local elections, and their share dropped to 7%. The turning point occurred after the 1973 war, when the Communists joined forces with other groups (the young, university graduates, but also, sometimes, hamulas) to form the DFPE, which won a remarkable victory in Nazareth in 1975. In the 1978 local elections, the DFPE ran in 32 of the 51 Arab councils in which elections were held and received 26% of the vote; in 1983, contesting 32 of the 46 councils, it gained 24% of the vote. Of even greater significance was the triumph of DFPE candidates in 17 of the 51 direct-balloting elections for heads of local councils, which took place for the first time in Israel in 1978; 14 of the 46 heads elected in 1983 represented the DFPE.

Since 1984, the Communists have, however, been losing their momentum in local elections as elsewhere. This is evidenced by the results of the direct elections of the 47 heads of Arab local councils in 1989: 17 independents, 13 DFPE, 2 PLP, 4 DAP, 3 Labor, 2 Likud, 1 CRM, and 5 Islamic Movement. These outcomes show that neither the Zionist parties nor the Communists have either control of or a majority in Arab local governments.

The large increase in Arab voting for non-Zionist lists clearly reflects a growing politicization (Rouhana, 1986), which is particularly evident in the declining support for the Zionist establishment. The proportion of Arabs voting for non-Zionist, predominantly Arab lists (DFPE, PLP, and DAP) during the 1969-85 period rose from 8% to 24% in local elections, 20% to 45% in Histadrut general elections, and 29.5% to 51% in Knesset elections.

These and other figures are also indicative of the Arabs' firm attachment to Israel. The high voting turnout (73% in the 1988 Knesset election) demonstrates their strong desire to integrate into Israeli society and politics; a moderate decline in turnout suggests growing impatience with their limited voting choice, especially the absence of an integrationist Arab party prior to 1988 and the lack of experience with the DAP, which aspires to play this role. Israelization is further reflected in the phasing out of the non-ideological, traditional election lists and in the heightened ideological nature of the conflict between non-Zionist and Zionist parties. In a way, the political experience of Israeli Arabs is similar to that of the Oriental Jews in that both groups have gradually liberated themselves from Labor Party hegemony; having become freer Israeli citizens, they have shifted their voting to the opposition (for the non-Zionist Arabs, this has come to mean Rakah, the PLP, and DAP; for the Zionist Orientals, the Likud camp).

These same figures demonstrate a growing factionalization. There is an increasing split between voting for non-Zionist and Zionist parties and particular parties within each of these categories. Like Jewish voters, Arab voters who vote Zionist have to choose between the Likud and Labor blocs. The majority of the Arabs who opt for non-Zionist parties have to decide among the DFPE, PLP and DAP. These choices, no longer limited to Knesset elections, are becoming available in Histadrut and local elections. Factionalization, however, is far from running its full course because of the lack of a nationalist Arab party and a state-wide Islamic party and the short public record of the DAP as an integrationist party.

The shifting Arab vote implies intensified militancy rather than radicalization. This is abundantly clear even in voting for Zionist lists. Jewish parties can no longer take the Arab vote for granted; on the contrary, they must present a good record in minority affairs, face up to rising Arab expectations and demands, increase Arab political representation, and compete with their non-Zionist rivals.

The majority vote for the predominantly Arab parties should not be interpreted as a drift away from Israel and the Jews. To substantiate this view, an account of the character and activities of these three small parties is required.

Although its constituency is essentially Arab, Rakah is an Arab-Jewish party in both ideology and leadership (Rekhess, 1986; Dotan, 1991). Its mixed composition fits the Communist ideology of coexistence, in which the constituent national groups should be represented. The Jewish presence in the party is also calculated to ensure a certain immunity against harassment by the authorities. Rakah is an orthodox Marxist class party, for which nationalism is secondary; as a follower of Moscow, it remained until 1990 impervious to the spirit of Eurocommunism. Like other Communist parties in the Western, "bourgeois" democracies, however, it abides by the rules of parliamentary procedures, though resorting at times and selectively to lawful mass action.

The Communist Party enjoys a legal basis as a result of its recognition (following the lead of the Soviet Union) of the UN resolution on the partition of Palestine in 1947 and because, until 1967, it called for that resolution's implementation. After the 1967 war, however, Rakah extended its recognition of Israel to the borders of June 4, 1967, including those territories originally set aside in the 1947 resolution for the proposed Palestinian state but occupied and annexed by Israel during the War of Independence. It has consistently endorsed the right of the Palestinians to self-determination (during the 1950s, it even demanded the extension of this right to the Arabs of Israel).[2] Today it advocates the formation of a Palestinian state on the West Bank and Gaza Strip; it views the PLO as the representative body of the Palestinians but dissociates itself from the PLO's National Charter and unequivocally condemns any act of terrorism.

Its recognition of Israel's right to exist within the pre-1967 borders and its commitment to parliamentary politics render Rakah an opposition party, not a resistance movement. It employs normal democratic methods in its attempt to reverse Israel's "imperialist" foreign policy and to transform the state into a de-Zionized, Communist society.

The increased support for Rakah among Israeli Arabs over the years reflects their difficult and partial incorporation into Israeli society as well as their massive shift from moderate passivity to militant activism. As

[2]The 13th Congress of the Israeli Communist Party confirmed the report of the party's secretary-general, who said: "The just solution for the problem of Eretz Israel and for the question of Israeli-Arab peace requires that Israel recognize the right to self-determination, including secession, of the Arab people in Eretz Israel, including that part living in Israel" (Israeli Communist Party, 1959: 29).

Rakah itself articulates an essentially oppositionist ideology, it has both exploited and promoted this trend.

Until the appearance of the PLP in 1984, the Communist Party served as the major political outlet for protest against the Zionist establishment and its policies. It is wrong, however, to regard Arab support for Rakah as merely a protest vote and unrelated to its ideology. Disregarding its Communist stance, Arabs closely and critically follow the policies of the party on Arab issues both within and outside Israel, and refrain from supporting it when they find its stands objectionable. A case in point was the sharp drop in the Arab vote for the Communist Party in the 1959 national elections as a result of its opposition to Egypt's popular president, Gamal Abdul Nasser, who had taken anti-Communist actions. In the absence of a national Arab party, many militant Arabs vote for Rakah because, of all the existing parties, it comes closest to representing their own views on Israel. By voting Communist, they do not intend simply to register a protest against the Zionist establishment; rather, they seek to express their agreement with Rakah's analysis of the unequal status of the Arab minority in Israel, with its proposed solution to the Israeli-Arab conflict, with its recognition of their Palestinian identity and ties, with its view of their future linked to Israel, and with its consistent struggle for equality and peace.[3]

Thus, the main function of Rakah is to integrate Arabs into Israeli society as oppositionists, providing them with ideology and leadership. This acts as a barrier to large-scale radicalization and accommodation alike. Rakah's non-accommodationist and non-rejectionist position finds expression in many areas, but it suffices to mention only a few. Many Arabs enter Israeli politics through Rakah. Because it is the only party in the fullest sense (with party organization, ideology, membership, press, and ongoing activities) operating in the Arab sector, it introduces Arabs into a modern political culture and incorporates them into the political system. Yet Rakah, ostracized and stigmatized as anti-Israel by the Jewish public, blocks real political integration for Arabs and institutionalizes their political isolation and impotence. Its efforts to break this quarantine by forming the DFPE with non-Communist Jewish and Arab circles have so far failed.

Rakah's position on the critical issue of Israel's legitimacy has important implications for the standing of Arabs in Israel. It encourages

[3]Ginat (1986) offers a different interpretation for the Rakah and PLP Arab vote. He sees it as a protest vote solely because Israeli Arabs feel only solidarity with the Palestinians but lack Palestinian identity and ties. According to Ginat, Arabs are not now and are not becoming Palestinian because Palestinization means rejection of Israel.

them to accept Israel's right to exist, on the one hand, and not to recognize Israel as a Jewish-Zionist state, on the other hand. Hence, it reinforces the Jewish image of Arabs as anti-Israel. While taking a staunch stand against Zionism and branding it as imperialist and racist, Rakah moderated its stand during the 1980s by distinguishing between left and other brands of Zionism and also between the Jewish and Zionist character of the state. But these ambiguous distinctions are usually lost on the Jewish public, for whom they are intended. Overall, Rakah hampers Arab reconciliation with Israel's Zionist ideology and features.

The Palestinian question is another example. Rakah is a strong proponent of the Palestinian cause. It urges Israeli withdrawal from the occupied territories and the establishment there of a Palestinian state under PLO rule. This plan is labeled extremist by Jews; consequently, its dissemination by Rakah deepens the alienation between Arabs and Jews. On the other hand, because this plan is to apply only to the non-Israeli Palestinians in the occupied territories and abroad, it effectively contributes to the Israelization of the Arabs. Rakah stresses the Palestinian past of the Arabs in Israel, but not a Palestinian present or future. According to its platform and pronouncements, the non-Israeli Palestinians have the right to self-determination, but the Arabs in Israel do not; the Palestinian state on the West Bank and Gaza Strip is envisioned for the Palestinians in these territories and in the diaspora, not for Israeli Arabs; the PLO represents the Palestinians, not Israeli Arabs (Rakah does).

Rakah maintains that Israeli Arabs are part and parcel of Israel and should seek solutions for their problems within this state. In fact, Rakah is instrumental in the dissociation of Israeli Arabs from the Palestinians, although it proclaims the reverse. It aims to turn Israeli Arabs into a well-integrated Palestinian minority in Israeli society, acting as a strong pressure group in Israeli politics on behalf of Israeli Arabs and the Palestinian people in general.

This oppositionist rather than rejectionist position on Arab-Jewish coexistence is shared equally by the PLP. The PLP differs markedly from Rakah in being non-Communist, not oriented toward Moscow, democratic, less hostile to religion, and more fully devoted to Palestinian nationalism. It, too, is a mixed Arab-Jewish party that is engaged in the hard task of reconciling the double commitment of a majority of Arabs to both Israel and the Palestinian people. A systematic comparison of DFPE voters with PLP voters in the survey detected no difference in their views.

The DAP resembles Rakah and the PLP in being a non-Zionist, independent, predominantly Arab party, devoted to a two-state solution and to Arab-Jewish equality; however, it differs markedly from them in several respects. First, it is exclusively Arab rather than Arab-Jewish. It does not have Jews among its members and leaders; nor does it appeal to Jewish voters. Its leaders claim that a vote for the DAP is a one-hundred percent vote for the Israeli Arabs' cause in electing only Arab representatives and in representing only Arab interests. The critics argue that the ethnic composition of the party is very divisive and counterproductive. Furthermore, the actual social base of DAP is Arab Moslem; it includes almost no Christians and Druzes, though that may change.

Second, the DAP also differs from Rakah and PLP in self-styling itself as a reservationist rather than an oppositionist party. It aims to escape the dead end of permanent opposition faced by the two other parties and to become the first Arab party eligible for government coalitions. Its stated goal is to shift Arab politics from protest to participation in decision-making. This objective is accepted by a majority of Arabs; 66% of the Arabs in the 1988 survey were willing to vote for "a new, independent Arab party that strives to participate in the coalition government in order to advance the interests of Israeli Arabs." The middle-of-the-road position of the DAP is also reflected in the former affiliation of the bulk of its leaders and voters with Jewish parties, especially Labor. Darawshe himself served as a Knesset Member for the Labor Party and broke away from it in protest against the repression of the intifada by the Labor Defense Minister, Rabin. Most of the DAP's voters are Arabs fed up with Labor but too moderate to support the DFPE and PLP (Reiter, 1989).

Third, unlike Rakah and the PLP, which put the Palestinian question at the top of their agenda, the first priority of the DAP is Arab-Jewish equality, though endorsing the Israeli Arab consensus on Palestinian nationalism. The redistributive thrust of the DAP is more acceptable to Jews and Jewish parties than is the Palestinian nationalism of the other oppositionist Arab-Jewish parties. This is the reason that no attempt was made to stop the DAP from participating in the Knesset elections in 1988, whereas such an action was taken against the PLP in both the 1984 and 1988 elections.

In conclusion, voting non-Zionist (DFPE, PLP, or DAP) does not mean rejection of Israel; rather, it represents, first, a protest against the policies and practices of the Zionist establishment; second, a demand for full equality, for participation, and for recognition of the Arabs' Palestinian identity; and third, a desire to achieve a comprehensive peace settlement by establishing a PLO-led Palestinian state on the West Bank and Gaza Strip next to Israel.

Protest

Accommodation rather than protest characterized the Arab response in the period prior to 1967. The Arabs did not resist the sudden transformation of their status into an alien minority in a Jewish-Zionist state, manifested among others by massive land expropriations, the military government, and other forms of differential treatment. They became resigned, instead, to their fate and waited passively for a better future. The limited struggle for Israeli Arab rights was led by liberal Jews, who enjoyed the democratic freedoms that, in part, were temporarily denied to the Arabs.

Arab protest was not, however, entirely absent. It was expressed in the refusal to accept the meager compensation offered for confiscated lands, the frequent breaches of military restrictions, the abortive attempt to form a national movement (Al-Ard), and the emergence of literary works (poetry and short stories) critical of the state.

After 1967, the Arab response shifted from accommodation to protest. Such protest has become so common that it is now very difficult to imagine Arab politics without it. Its contemporary importance is clearly evident in the new forms and patterns that have come to prevail.

First, protest has become a standard strategy for change. Arabs are no longer passive and compliant; they are willing to act and to struggle. Moreover, they accept the need for protest to effect change. This is true of Arabs of all orientations, even the accommodationists protest within the Zionist establishment and take part in the overall Arab protest.

Second, protest has become Arabized. Before 1967, protest on behalf of Arabs was undertaken mostly by Jews; but since then, Arabs have become the dominant force. Jews are still, of course, involved in protest related to Israeli Arab issues, but Arabs predominate.

Third, protest has become pervasive. It is concerned with education, lands, housing, budget allocations, agriculture, employment, the occupied territories, and foreign affairs. Most important, civil rights protest has acquired a national dimension. For example, the struggle against land expropriation is seen as involving not only the defense of personal property but also the national right of the Arab minority to keep its collective property. Turned into a national issue, land losses have become a great concern to all Arabs, including those who do not own land and those whose land has not been confiscated.

Fourth, protest has become organized. During the 1970s, many Arab organizations were formed to promote Arab interests through direct action or protest. They included, for instance, the Committee of Heads of Arab Local Councils, the Sons of the Village Movement, the Progressive National Movement, the Islamic Movement, the Committee for Bedouin

Rights and Lands in the Negev, as well as the Committee for Defense of Arab Lands. Protest is increasingly coordinated to involve representatives from all the political streams and to extend beyond local and sectional concerns to regional and statewide issues.

Fifth, protest has become diverse in its means and forms. In addition to the use of the standard parliamentary measures of verbal protest and voting, Arabs have turned since the 1970s to extra-parliamentary and even extra-legal methods. Mass demonstrations and general or partial strikes have become common. During the pre-intifada period, three landmark general strikes deserve mention: the first, on March 30, 1976 (Land Day) was directed against land expropriations in the Galilee; the second, on September 22, 1982, arose in spontaneous response to the Sabra and Shatilla massacre; and the third, on June 24, 1987 (Equality Day) was called to protest inequality, discrimination, and insufficient development funds (especially for education and local services).

Use of serious violence, though still comparatively minor, has also gained in significance and is occasionally resorted to by both the Arab protestors and the police. Between 1967 and 1971, 400 Arabs were convicted of sabotage or collaboration with the enemy. Although this wave of terrorism subsided, convictions of Israeli Arabs for membership in terrorist organizations or for involvement in terror continue to be reported in the press from time to time (for one wave of arrests, see, e.g., Dar, 1979). Substantial notoriety has been attached to several cases in which Jews (a male soldier in the Triangle, a female soldier, and a 15-year-old boy from Haifa) were murdered by Israeli Arabs, apparently motivated by nationalistic sentiments; those incidents enraged many Jews.[4] Although seldom pressed in courts, charges are repeatedly made by anonymous sources in the Jewish National Fund and the police accusing nationalist Israeli Arabs of starting fires in the national forests (*Haaretz*, July 7, 1987).

Other extra-legal actions of political protest for some Israeli Arabs include painting walls with slogans, raising the Palestinian flag in public places, shouting calls for liberation during demonstrations (the most common phrase is "We will liberate the Galilee with our spirit and blood") and singing nationalist songs at weddings.

[4]The case of the Haifa boy is still not finally settled in the public mind. Although convicted for committing the murder and believed to be motivated by nationalism (Tal, 1985), the accused Israeli Arabs continue to claim innocence (Gvirtz, 1990). Their appeal to the Supreme Court and a plea to reopen the case were finally denied (*Haaretz*, August 26, 1991). Yet, doubts concerning the evidence that led to the conviction have lingered on.

The shift from passive accommodation to active protest is an essential component of the rising Arab politicization. Yet, despite its dramatic growth, Arab protest has remained predominantly non-violent and within the bounds of democratic processes. It amounts to less than one might have predicted given the pervasive inequality and institutionalized discrimination and the depth of the issues dividing Arabs and Jews.

Paradoxically, most Arabs express their "Israeliness," not rejection or extremism, in acts of protest. The realization that they are here to stay as a permanent minority in the Jewish state prompts them to fight for equality and improved conditions by using Israeli democracy to achieve this goal. This struggle is part of the broader process of the democratization of the state – the expansion of individual rights and the rise of disadvantaged groups. Hence, any headway in pushing the Arab cause will advance Israeli democracy by reducing Arab-Jewish inequality and widening the national consensus.

To a significant degree, Arab protest derives from the fact that the Arabs are not part of Israeli democracy in the fullest sense. Because they neither constitute a strong pressure group within the Zionist establishment nor are organized in integrationist political parties that participate in routine coalition politics, they lack the necessary negotiating power that is the essence of the Israeli political system. As a result, Arabs are forced to turn to, and to over-employ, extra-parliamentary mass politics. The Equality Day strike of June 21, 1987 is a case in point. For months the organizers' efforts to obtain more funds for Arab local councils failed; they waited in vain until the last moment for a real move on the part of the government. The strike, therefore, was the only resort left. Disadvantaged Jewish groups, on the other hand, use less extra-parliamentary means because they have better access to Jewish parties.

A study by Lehman-Wilzig (1991) of public, extra-parliamentary protest in Israel for the 1949-86 period confirms and elaborates on the above observations. He shows that "in most respects the evolution and character of Israeli Arab protest are markedly similar to that found among Israel's Jews: regarding its periodic chronology, the factors underlying increasing protest, the rank order of issues protested, and the more recent turn to circumventing the official system through alternative self-help" (ibid.: 23). The differences between the protest of the two communities are, however, not less significant. There is a time lag in the take-off point: the 1970 Black Panther protest on class and ethnic issues among the Jews, compared to the 1976 Land Day strike for the Arabs. Being on the geographical, political, and ideological periphery of the country, the Arabs have to intensify their protest in order to receive the attention of the media and the response of the authorities. For this reason, events classified as "violent" (usually mild attacks against persons and property) are twice as frequent among the Arabs as among the Jews: 26% versus 14%. Similarly, although the Arabs constitute only 15% of the population, large protest events with a thousand or more Arab participants constitute 28% of all protest events as against only 15% among the vastly larger Jewish sector. With regard to issues, 47% of the Arab protests and 32% of the Jewish protests were "social" (such as discrimination, education, services, and land), and 44% and 29%, respectively, "political" (such as war and peace and parties). The recent trend to turn to grassroots self-help (most notably, the community services undertaken by the Islamic Movement and the Jewish Shas Party) as an alternative action for dealing with the privations causing the protest, is also more intense among the Arabs.

Lehman-Wilzig concludes that the Arabs' public protest reveals their deep Israelization and that "the process of Palestinization has not yet become the dominant trend in the Israeli Arab community" (*ibid*: 19). They do not simply copy Jewish patterns but rather have internalized the Israeli democratic culture and have acted according to the rules of the democratic game. Still, it is doubtful, Lehman-Wilzig warns, whether Israeli Arabs will continue to abide by the rules if the state keeps on violating the basic democratic values of equality before the law and of non-discrimination vis-a-vis Israeli Arabs.

The Role of the Intifada

The Israeli Arab response to the intifada can serve as a good test of the relative validity of the competing radicalization and politicization theses. If radicalization is the dominant trend, Israeli Arabs should be expected to join the intifada, or at least to show a significant increase in rejectionism and use of violence against Israel.

Contrary to the warnings of various commentators and widespread Jewish fears, Israeli Arabs did not join the intifada even three years after its eruption. A quick comparison of Arab life in the territories and in Israel would readily substantiate this hard fact. The intifada is a popular uprising, involving daily clashes with the army and settlers, throwing of stones and Molotov cocktails, curfews, demolitions of houses, mass arrests and detentions, deportations, hundreds of wounded and dead, killing of collaborators, popular committees running villages and small towns, and communiques issued by the clandestine Unified National Command. None of these distinct occurrences exists in the Israeli Arab localities in the Galilee, Triangle, or Northern Negev. Also absent from Israeli Arab lives is the severe disruption of the daily routine, including frequent absenteeism, closures of schools, very limited shopping hours, common interruptions of basic facilities (water, electricity, gas, telephone), and an appreciable decline in the standard of living. One also does not find among Israeli Arabs the social changes associated with the intifada: the ascendance of youth and young adults to leadership, the sudden improvement in the status of women, the considerable expansion of the activities of voluntary associations, and a boost in institutional autonomy. The symbolic expressions of living under an emergency situation that is found among the rebellious Palestinians are also lacking among Israeli Arabs who continue to hold big family celebrations and to be oblivious to specific dates in Palestinian history. Finally, Israeli Arabs do not accept for themselves the goals of the Palestinian struggle: dissociation from Israel and becoming part of an independent Palestinian state.

The March-April 1988 survey, conducted when Arab rage was high, revealed a low level of and a lack of increase over time in rejectionism. For instance, only 13.5% of the Arabs rejected Israel's right to exist and only 8% endorsed the use of violence to improve Arab conditions, and these figures did not increase compared to the 1976-85 period (Table 21.5 above). The proportion of rejectionists has also remained around a tenth of the Arab population and has not increased over the years (Table 21.1 above).

The most pertinent indicator of rejectionism is, however, illegal activity, which did increase significantly as a result of the intifada. There are no good statistics on this sensitive matter, however. We do not know how many Israeli Arabs are involved and what their outlooks and motivations are. The available figures refer to violations within the Green Line (excluding Arab Jerusalem and the Golan Heights), but an unknown number was perpetrated by Arabs from the West Bank and Gaza Strip. According to these official statistics, acts of sabotage went up from 69 in 1987 to 238 in 1988, but dropped to 187 in 1989, an average annual increase of 308% (Table 21.16). The Minister responsible for Arab Affairs further disclosed that the 187 severe acts carried out in 1989 consisted of incidents involving 91 arsons, 28 petrol bombs, 17 explosives, 8 stabbings, 8 violent assaults, 6 shootings, and 3 hand-grenade attacks (*Knesset Proceedings*, December 4, 1990). More frequent but less grave were nationalist subversive acts, which rose from 101 in 1987 to 507 in 1988 but declined to 353 in 1989. In that last year, they included these incidents: stone-throwing (119 cases), writing anti-Israeli or pro-PLO slogans (104), hoisting of the Palestinian flag (92), roadblocks (15), destruction of state emblems (14), laying of false explosives (4), and unclassified incidents (5). In addition, the number of subversive or terrorist cells detected by the Israeli secret service, the *Shin Bet*, rose from 2 in 1987 to 15 in 1988, and to 20 in 1989. These cells were composed of scores of youth who used or planned to use terrorism.

Table 21.16 Security Violations Perpetrated within the Green Line, 1987-89[a]

	1987	1988	1989
Type of security violation			
Acts of sabotage	69	238	187
Nationalist subversive acts	101	507	353
Subversive cells detected	2	15	20

[a]Excluding East Jerusalem and the Golan Heights; effective date in 1989 is November 15.

Source: *Proceedings of the Knesset*, December 4, 1989 (Minister Olmart's statement).

Nevertheless, the overall volume of security violations by Israeli Arabs throughout the first three years of the intifada remained low. In a population that is firmly united against Israel's handling of the intifada and a tenth of which is rejectionist, the reported figures show rather low involvement. It is unrealistic to expect Israeli Arabs, especially those who are generally rejectionist and particularly enraged by the repression of the intifada, not to take any move. In his presentation of the above figures, the Minister correctly concluded that "the majority of the Arab citizens in the State of Israel are law-abiding and loyal to state laws. These acts [security violations] are committed by an extremist minority and are handled by the security branches." Most significantly, the Israeli Arab leadership as a whole does not condone and even condemns security violations by Arabs. For instance, the organizing committees of demonstrations and general strikes forbid the display of the Palestinian flag despite popular identification with it.

Rather than taking part in the intifada and turning rejectionists en masse, Israeli Arabs register their strong solidarity with the intifada and against the Israeli policy of putting it down. By 1988, they had also become more politicized and militant, probably also as a result of the intifada. The 1988 survey clearly indicates a high rise in militancy, as reflected in an increase in dissatisfaction with Israeli citizenship, in Palestinian identity, and in endorsement of general strikes (Table 21.2 above). The oppositionists increased their share of the population from 40%-44% in 1976-85 to 52% in 1988 (Table 21.1 above).

The Israeli Arab solidarity with the intifada is strong and open. Actually Israeli Arabs are unique in being the only large group of citizens in Israel to do so. Non-Zionist Jewish leftists who side with them on this issue are marginal to Israeli politics. Certain Jews from the Zionist left feel sympathy with the intifada and welcome it as a catalyst of the peace process, but they keep their feelings private and take part in the clampdown. Hence, the public support given by Israeli Arabs to the intifada is an important omen of their militancy on a vital matter on which they have a clearcut stand.

Israeli Arabs express their support for the intifada by mass demonstrations and strikes. From December 1987 to April 1990, they held five general strikes, compared to only 11 during the pre-intifada period (1976-87). The first strike in the series, the Peace Day strike held on December 21, 1987, came as a great shock to the Jewish public. Jewish cars were stoned on several occasions, clashes with the police occurred in the mixed towns as well as in Nazareth, the main road connecting the Triangle with the Jezreel Valley was temporarily blocked; policemen had to employ force to disperse the crowds and some of them were wounded. This strike, whose exclusive theme was the nationalist identification with the intifada served as an eye-opener for the Jews, who at that time did not comprehend the real meaning of the uprising. Solidarity with the intifada continued to be a message in subsequent strikes.

Israeli Arabs also lent political and material support for the intifada. Arab Knesset Members appeared in certain demonstrations and funerals held in East Jerusalem, visited detention camps, and tried to intercede on behalf of some Palestinians. During the first two years, $2.5 million were collected in the Arab sector and extended as relief (foodstuffs, clothes, bedding, and medications) to the rebellious Palestinians.

This level of lawful and unlawful support of the intifada fell short of what Israeli Arabs could have done. They can and do avail themselves of democracy for fighting for their own and broader Palestinian causes. They are allowed to register their protest effectively without resorting to violent means. It is to their advantage to strengthen the democratic process. A major disruption of democracy by any group in Israel, let alone by Israeli Arabs, would endanger their position in society and provide pretexts for imposing further restrictions on them.

Furthermore, Israeli Arabs are not called by other Palestinians to take part in the intifada or to undermine Israel. The Palestinian resistance in the early 1990s is based on a division of labor among the three segments of the Palestinian people: those under occupation conduct the intifada, those in the diaspora engage in international politics and diplomacy, and those in Israel serve as a peace lobby within Israel (Klein, 1989). The role assigned to Israeli Arabs is thus grounded on the assumption that they are Israelis and, as such, should take advantage of their political rights and familiarity with the Jews for advancing Palestinian objectives.

This moderate peaceful role in the Palestinian strategy has been confirmed by the PLO on a number of occasions. In 1988, the PLO called on Israeli Arabs to go to the polls and support any party that accepted the principles of land for peace and an international conference as a framework for negotiations. The first and main strike that took place on December 21, 1987, was apparently cleared and coordinated with the PLO

(Schiff and Ya'ari, 1989: 128). After the downfall of the national unity government in March 1990, the three predominantly Arab parties backed the abortive attempt to form a narrow Labor government.

Faisal Al-Husseini, the top Fatah leader in the West Bank, goes even further. In his many public appearances, he legitimizes the role Israeli Arabs have played in the intifada; namely, to explain the two-state solution to the Jews and to dispatch relief to the territories. If they join the intifada, Husseini reasons, they would reinforce the Jews' fear that any concession made to the Palestinians in the West Bank and Gaza Strip is a step in the demise of the state. He then counsels Israeli Arabs: "You must forget the dreams of the past. You will not be citizens of Palestine. Your battle must be to attain full equal rights in Israel. National aspirations can only be realized in the Palestinian state, not in the State of Israel" (Be'er, 1990: 26). He angers many Israeli Arabs by drawing a telling corollary from this rationale; i.e., that Israeli Arabs should accept Israel not only as a state but also as a Jewish state.

The intifada has, therefore, the paradoxical impact of further Israelization of the Arab citizens along with deepening their Palestinization. The Israeli dimension in their lives has been reinforced by the growing acceptance of Israel by non-Israeli Palestinians and by the Palestinian consensus that Israeli Arabs should stay away from the intifada and play, rather, a role corresponding to their Israeli status. By not participating in the intifada and by performing the lobbying function, they have reaffirmed their Israeli identity.

In conclusion, Israeli Arabs have passed the hard test of the intifada. Their loyalty to the state has remained firm and the Israeli component in their identity has not eroded. The long-term process of politicization has continued even in this trying period in the post-1967 history of Arab-Jewish relations in Israel.

22

Trends among Jews

The Jewish intransigence and accessibility perspectives provide alternative hypotheses regarding the change in the Jewish orientation toward the Arab minority. The dominant intransigence perspective posits that since the Six Day War, Jews have become increasingly alienated from and hardline in their position toward Israeli Arabs. It is believed that the Jews are partly reacting to what they perceive as the radicalization of Israeli Arabs, who have adopted a Palestinian identity, have supported the PLO, and have demonstrated deep solidarity with the intifada. The other contributory factors to the Jewish resistance to change are assumed to be the continued Arab challenge of Jewish vested interests and dominance; the steady growth in Jewish hawkishness; the rise to power of the Likud and of Oriental Jews, who concur on hostility against Arabs; the creeping annexation of the territories, which has blurred the distinction between Arabs on either side of the Green Line; and the erosion of Israeli democracy.

In contrast, the accessibility thesis suggests that rather than responding by intransigence and backlash, the Jewish public, authorities, and institutions have increasingly, though reluctantly, become more accessible and, to some extent, even more responsive to Israeli Arabs, whose major orientation is to join and to participate in the system and not to undermine it. Since the mid-1960s, Israel proper has been experiencing a real growth in democracy, manifested by the elimination of military administration over Arab areas in 1966, the shift of controls from citizen to non-citizen Arabs after the 1967 war, the expansion of the freedom of the press, the rise of numerous protest groups, and the replacement of a dominant party politics by a competitive two-camp politics in 1977. Within this solid democratic framework, the Arab minority is waging a struggle for better rights and opportunities, and the Jews are forced to liberalize. The Jews are switching from rejection of Arabs to ambivalence toward them. They are less given to stereotyping Arabs, more discerning in their perception of the differences among Arabs, more cautious in their statements about Arabs, and more defensive with regard to Arab rights and criticisms. Although feeling a threat to their dominance and security, Jews more and more realize that Israeli Arabs are here to stay and that their accommodation into the system would necessitate more meaningful Jewish concessions.

The intransigence and accessibility approaches disagree on the three main trends among the Jews: an increase versus a decrease in inclusiveness, factionalism, and negation. The accessibility perspective objects to the appraisal of the intransigence perspective that the Jews have become more exclusionary toward the Arabs, more homogeneous in their views and treatment of the Arabs, and more negative in their orientation. It hypothesizes, rather, that the Jews are increasingly inclusive, polarized, and ambivalent toward Israeli Arabs.

In contrast to the plethora of material relating to trends in the orientation of Israeli Arabs toward Arab-Jewish coexistence, the data regarding trends in the orientation of Jews toward the Arab minority are meager. The question of the Jews' attitudes and behavior toward their fellow Arab citizens has never been of much concern to the Jews. Hence, it remains marginal in the growing literature dealing with the ideological and political change that Israel and the Jewish majority have undergone since the Six Day War. To illustrate, there is an impressive growth over the years in the support for the right-wing parties at the expense of Labor and the left-wing parties (Table 22.1). Yet, it would be wrong to infer a growth in Jewish animosity toward Israeli Arabs from this drift toward the right-wing. It is possible that the right-wing parties distinguish among different kinds of Arabs and that their hostility toward Israeli Arabs has not necessarily risen. Direct evidence of Jewish attitudes and practices toward the Arab citizens of Israel is necessary.

In view of the scant material and confounding developments, the following analysis is inescapably explorative. Only data on the attitudes and behavior of the Jewish public at large and the Jewish establishment toward the Arab minority will be considered. Three types of evidence will be examined: attitudinal change as measured in our three comparable 1980-88 surveys, change in the public pronouncements and actions, and policy change.

Table 22.1 Results of Knesset Elections by Political Camp, 1949-1988

	1949	1951	1955	1959	1961	1965	1969	1973	1977	1981	1984	1988
Labor bloc												
Labor parties	53.4	54.5	52.6	56.1	52.7	55.0	49.7	42.7	26.0	36.6	34.9	30.0
Other	4.1	3.2	4.4	4.6	–	3.8	3.2	5.8	2.4	3.5	8.4	8.6
Religious bloc	12.2	11.9	13.8	14.6	15.4	14.0	14.8	12.1	13.9	11.8	11.4	15.3
Likud bloc												
Herut, Liberals	16.7	22.8	22.8	19.7	27.4	21.3	24.8	30.2	33.4	37.1	31.9	31.1
Other	–	–	–	–	–	–	1.2	–	1.9	3.9	4.0	7.0
Radicals												
Communists	3.5	4.0	4.5	2.8	4.2	3.4	2.8	3.4	4.6	3.4	3.4	3.7
Other	–	–	–	–	–	1.2	2.4	2..1	1.6	0.4	1.8	2.7
Other	10.1	3.6	1.9	2.2	0.3	1.3	1.1	4.3	16.2	3.6	4.0	1.6

Source: *Statistical Abstract of Israel 1989*, No. 40, 1989, pp. 549-551.

Attitudinal Change

Before the mid-1960s, the Jewish majority was detached from internal Arab affairs. The Arabs lived on the fringe of Israeli society, were placed under military rule, and were administered by Jewish officials associated directly or indirectly with Mapai, the ruling party. Lack of concern, estrangement, and exclusion characterized the Jewish orientation toward the suspected Arab minority. Differences between the political parties toward Israeli Arabs were, however, evident in the nature of their opposition to the military government in Arab areas. The opposition of the General Zionists and Herut Party, the two right-wing parties, to the abolition of the military administration was primarily propelled by the desire to undercut the hegemony of Mapai, which captured the Arab electorate through direct control. On the other hand, the objections of Ahdut Haavoda and the Progressive Party, to Mapai's left, indicated greater sensitivity to Arab rights. Protection of Arab rights was also a primary consideration for Mapam, a Zionist leftist party, and for the non-Zionist Communist Party. The last two were mixed Arab-Jewish parties, committed to Arab-Jewish cooperation, but dominated by Jews. It is doubtful, nonetheless, whether the objections to the treatment of Israeli Arabs on the part of the elites of the political opposition were motivated by a genuine concern for equal individual and national rights for the Arabs and whether their democratic spirit actually filtered down to the Jewish masses.

In terms of the classification of Jews into four orientations, it seems that their distribution in the general population during the pre-1967 period was tilted toward the illiberal exclusionist and hardline types. The exclusionist type drew popular support from the anti-Arab atmosphere following the 1948 war and the uncompromising desire to have a Jewish state with as few Arabs as possible. The hardline type was the most predominant because it characterized both the largest ruling party (Mapai under Ben-Gurion) and the main right-wing opposition party (Herut under Begin). The conciliationist type was also significant, however, because the Jewish constituency of both Mapam and the Communist Party during the 1950s was appreciable. The weakest type at the time was probably, and paradoxically, the pragmatist.

It is impossible to test this hypothesis concerning the relative incidence of the various Jewish types because of the absence of detailed, comparable surveys, before 1980, of the attitudes of the Jewish population toward the Arab minority. The three 1980-88 surveys of the Jewish population, however, provide some data for establishing trends for the 1980s.

The items and methods used for constructing the Jewish typology, which is fully reported in Part Two, are the same for the three surveys. The typology is based on the following fourteen statements which are representative of the various issues in Arab-Jewish relations:

1. View of Israel as an exclusively Jewish or a common homeland for Arabs and Jews.

2. The goal for Jewish education is the love of Israel as an exclusively Jewish or a common homeland for Arabs and Jews.

3. Israel should or should not prefer Jews to Arabs.

4. The closing of the Arab-Jewish socioeconomic gap is or is not an urgent, important state goal.

5. Israel does too little, enough, or too much for the Arabs in Israel.

6. Israel should or should not seek and use any opportunity to encourage Arabs to leave the country.

7. Endorsement of the present policy or of a policy of greater equality and integration as the best solution for the Arab minority problem.

8. Endorsement or rejection of a strong-arm policy toward the Arabs in Israel.

9. Belief or disbelief in the possibility of improving Arab conditions through the use of common democratic procedures of persuasion and political pressure.

10. Endorsement of or objection to the outlawing of Rakah.

11. Preference for the Jewish-Zionist character of the state to democracy when they conflict or the other way round.

12. Trust or mistrust of most Arabs in Israel.

13. Perception of Arabs in Israel as a substantial or negligible danger to national security.

14. Unwillingness or willingness to have an Arab as one's superior in a job.

On the basis of these statements when put as questions, a typology is constructed that includes 85% of the sample cases in 1980, 86% in 1985, and 81% in 1988. Contrary to the intransigence thesis, the distribution in the three surveys did not show any increase in the illiberal types. While the exclusionists kept their strength of 22%, the hardliners dropped from 37% in 1980 to 30% in 1988 (Table 22.2). At the same time, the pragmatists rose from 33.5% to 37%, and the conciliationists from 8% to 11%.

Table 22.2 Jewish Orientation Types, 1980-88

	Jewish Public		
	1980	1985	1988
Jewish orientation types			
Conciliationists	7.7	9.5	10.9
Pragmatists	33.5	35.9	37.4
Hardliners	36.7	35.4	30.1
Exclusionists	22.2	19.2	21.6
Total	100.0	100.0	100.0
Number of cases	1,081	1,035	979

Chi-square=17.90596 d.f.=6 p=0.0065.

This overall moderation in the Jewish orientation toward Israeli Arabs stands in apparent contradiction to the rise of the right, radical right, and the quasi-fascist Kach movement during the 1980s. When a further scrutiny of the sources of change was made through an analysis of variance test, it became clear that the supporters of the Labor and left-wing parties liberalized during the decade, whereas the supporters of the Likud and religious parties did not (Table 22.3). A closer check revealed that the decline in the illiberal types took place among most Jewish population groups: those with low and those with higher education; religious and secular; Oriental and Ashkenazic Jews (Table 22.4). The political polarization among the Jews is, nevertheless, evident in the amount of decrease in the illiberal types: the drop is dramatic among voters for the small, Zionist left-wing parties and Labor, but is moderate and even reversed among voters for the religious parties, Tehiya, Kach, and Likud. The contrast between Labor and Likud voters demonstrates this point well: the proportion of hardliners and exclusionists declined from 55% in 1980 to 35% in 1988 among Labor voters, while it rose from 68% to 74%, respectively, among Likud voters.

Rather than signaling intransigence and the spread of extremism, these findings confirm the assumption that internal Jewish factionalism concerning Israeli Arabs is appreciable and deepening. Furthermore, the trend toward a heightening political polarization in Israeli society is spreading to issues involving the Arab minority.

Table 22.3 Analysis of Variance of Jewish Orientation by Year of Survey and Voting

	Total	Jewish Public 1980	1985	1988
Means and number of cases				
Year of survey	2.65	2.74	2.58	2.63
	(2,328)	(849)	(790)	(688)
Voting in the last Knesset elections				
DMC, CRM, Shinui, Mapam	1.93	2.10	1.81	1.66
	(246)	(131)	(61)	(55)
Labor	2.39	2.61	2.33	2.30
	(928)	240)	(390)	(298)
Likud	2.99	2.94	3.00	3.06
	(934)	(379)	(296)	(260)
Religious parties	3.13	3.17	3.02	3.16
	(219)	(100)	(43)	(76)

Analysis of variance

Source of variation	Sum of Squares	D.F.	Mean Square	F	Significance of F
Year of survey	6.373	2	3.186	4.838	0.008
Voting	346.270	3	115.423	175.238	0.000
Interaction	20.405	6	3.401	5.163	0.000
Explained	378.355	11	34.396	52.221	0.000
Residual	1,525.508	2,316	0.659		
Total	1,903.863	2,327	0.818		

A more detailed examination of the change in specific attitudes during the 1980s demonstrates stability or even a certain softening, rather than hardening, of the Jewish position toward Israeli Arabs. To illustrate, between 1980 and 1988, the proportion of Jews with intransigent stands reduced from 76% to 55% among those opposing the use of general strikes by Arabs and from 50% to 40% among those feeling that Israel should encourage Israeli Arabs to leave the country (Table 22.5). As against this overall trend on most of the questions, a significant rise from 24% to 43% took place during the 1985-88 period in the percentage of the Jews who would deny Israeli Arabs the right to vote in national elections. This Jewish backlash was in response to the intensified agitation, by the right-wing camp, against the possibility that the Arab vote would decide the 1988 Knesset elections in favor of a "selling-out" Labor government.

Table 22.4 Jewish Orientation Types by Selected Population Groups, 1980-88

	Year	Conciliationists	Pragmatists	Hardliners	Exclusionists	N
Education						
Primary	1980	3.6	22.9	37.3	36.2	338
	1985	2.7	29.5	41.9	25.8	255
	1988	3.9	39.8	31.8	24.4	217
Post-secondary	1980	15.0	49.3	26.4	9.2	247
	1985	20.8	47.5	23.2	8.6	287
	1988	21.2	42.0	21.9	14.8	282
Religious observance						
Religious	1980	2.8	17.4	47.7	32.1	128
	1985	2.0	12.9	45.4	39.7	114
	1988	0.0	28.4	41.6	30.0	116
Secular	1980	14.8	43.3	27.1	14.8	445
	1985	13.9	46.7	26.5	12.9	561
	1988	20.7	43.6	23.9	11.8	456
Ethnic origin						
Oriental	1980	3.7	24.3	39.3	32.7	491
	1985	4.7	25.7	42.9	26.7	459
	1988	5.4	28.7	35.6	30.3	470
Ashkenazic	1980	11.0	40.2	36.3	12.5	486
	1985	15.4	47.7	27.2	9.7	437
	1988	13.7	45.1	25.4	15.9	366
Voting in the last Knesset elections						
DMC, CRM, Shinui, Shelli	1980	20.1	52.6	24.5	2.8	131
	1985	36.3	49.7	10.8	3.1	61
	1988	41.0	52.0	7.0	0.0	55
Labor, Yahad, Ometz	1980	11.3	33.9	37.9	16.9	240
	1985	12.4	52.2	25.7	9.8	390
	1988	15.7	49.2	24.8	10.3	298
Likud, Shlomtzion	1980	2.9	29.0	39.3	28.8	379
	1985	1.7	22.3	50.2	25.9	296
	1988	3.3	22.7	39.0	35.1	260
Religious parties	1980	0.8	17.9	45.1	36.2	100
	1985	4.3	21.3	42.9	31.5	43
	1988	0.0	19.8	44.8	35.4	76
Tehiya, Kach	1985	0.0	8.4	46.7	45.0	66
	1988	0.0	14.2	48.3	37.5	30

There is no doubt that the intifada has had an adverse effect on Jewish attitudes toward Israeli Arabs. When asked in April 1988 about the effect of the Peace Day strike (the general strike of Israeli Arabs on December 21, 1987) in solidarity with the intifada, the ratio of negative to positive effect for the Jewish general population was 30% to 11% (Table 22.6). The ratio varied considerably from one type to another: 13% to 14%

among conciliationists, 26.5% to 14% among pragmatists, 33% to 9% among hardliners, and 37% to 9% among exclusionists. This differential impact of the intifada points to the broadening split among Jews over their orientation toward Israeli Arabs. Data on the later 1987-90 period reveal the continued adverse influence of the intifada on the Jewish public's support for equal political rights for Arabs (Yuchtman-Ya'ar and Peres, 1991: 23). According to a survey taken in July 1990, 68% of the Jews felt that the Arab loyalty to the state has declined since the outbreak of the intifada; in comparison, 65% of the Arabs felt that Arab loyalty has not changed (Al-Haj, forthcoming).

Table 22.5 Jews' Selected Intransigent Attitudes, 1980-88

	1980	1985	1988
Hold that Arabs today should not organize politically at all	24.3	27.2	24.8
Hold that the best solution to the Arab minority problem is one of the following			
Arabs will be forced to live outside Israel	*	21.9	20.4
Arabs will live in Israel only if they are resigned to their minority status in a state designed for Jews	*	33.9	25.8
Oppose the use of general strikes by Arabs as a means to improve their situation in Israel	76.2	68.2	55.4
Perceive most Arabs in Israel as primitive	38.2	29.7	*
Favor an increase in surveillance over most Arabs in Israel	42.7	36.9	34.5
Unwilling to have Arab friends	61.5	61.6	60.7
Favor the outlawing of Rakah	51.7	44.8	44.8
Think that Israel should use any opportunity to encourage Israeli Arabs to leave the state	50.3	42.4	39.9
Absolutely unwilling to have an Arab as a superior in a job	45.5	47.4	55.1
Would deny Israeli Arabs the right to vote in Knesset elections	*	24.1	42.8

*Not Asked.

Table 22.6 Jewish Orientation Types by Experienced Impact of the Peace Day Strike, 1988

	Total	Conciliationists	Pragmatists	Hardliners	Exclusionists
Feel that the Peace Day strike (the general strike of Israeli Arabs on December 21, 1987) affected one's attitude toward Israeli Arabs					
Very favorably	3.3	1.8	3.6	1.8	6.9
Somewhat favorably	7.7	12.4	10.1	7.5	1.9
Did not affect	59.3	73.2	59.9	57.3	45.6
Somewhat adversely	17.0	8.4	22.2	14.4	9.1
Very adversely	12.7	4.2	4.3	18.9	27.5

Source: The 1988 survey.

Change in Public Pronouncements and Actions

Systematic material regarding pronouncements and actions of the Jewish public is still scant, and the existing partial evidence does not lend itself so readily to convincing, conclusive interpretation. To illustrate the difficulty in arriving at a plausible explanation, suppose the incidence of anti-Arab public statements, as reported in the press from 1976 to 1991, has risen. At first glance, such a rise can be interpreted as Jewish intransigence; on closer look, it may be the result of a significant, positive increase in Arab-Jewish contacts. The proper meaning also depends on whether the jump in intolerant pronouncements by Jews is limited to a particular segment or takes in a cross-section of the Jewish population. It also makes a real difference whether the response of the press and elites to hostility toward Israeli Arabs is approving or disapproving.

An empirical study of Jewish perspectives on Israeli Arabs by Herzog and Gamson (Herzog, 1990; Herzog and Gamson, 1990) shows the great difficulties in attempting to generalize cross-time trends on the basis of an analysis of themes underlying press articles relating to a small sample of events and dates. These two sociologists analyzed 256 articles from the Hebrew press regarding five critical events in Arab-Jewish relations: the debate over the fate of the Palestinian refugees in 1949, the dispute over a motion to abolish the military government in 1962, the first Land Day strike in 1976, the return of lands to Arab farmers as part of the resolution of the Area 9 question in 1986, and the decision to link tuition fees to army service in 1987. Each event was classified into one of five main interpretive frameworks: hardcore nationalism (which resembles the hardline orientation), liberal nationalism (similar to the pragmatist orientation), Jewish democracy (same as the conciliationist orientation), no problem (no parallel), and equal rights for all (close to the egalitarianist orientation).

The researchers concluded that Jewish public discourse hinges on these five themes, that the civic theme (Equal Rights for All) is marginal in Jewish thinking about Israeli Arabs, and that the trend over the years consists of some strengthening of the hardcore nationalism theme and a further weakening of the already weak civic theme. It is hard to see, given the small number and specificity of the events examined, how these trends can be plausibly deduced from the frequency of the various cognitive schemes over the 1949-87 period. For instance, the hardcore nationalist worldview claims 19% of the articles in 1949, 20% in 1962, 19% in 1976, 48% in 1986, but a low percentage in 1987 (since a different categorization was used in 1987, no comparable figure is provided). Rather than indicating a genuine dramatic rise in hardcore nationalism, the upswing in 1986 in articles colored by this theme may paradoxically be due to the lack of a need to speak up on the part of those agreeing with the government's liberal policy to return some of the lands in Area 9 to their Arab owners. Similarly, the dominant theme in the 74 articles reacting to the government's resolution to impose different tuition fees on students who serve in the army from those who do not was equal rights for all (44.5% of the articles fell into this category). Yet, this strong reaction does not imply, and the researchers wisely refrained from suggesting, that the generally weak, non-Zionist approach has suddenly become dominant in the Israeli Jewish mindset regarding Israeli Arabs. Although this kind of study can trace the development and the subtleties of each orientation toward the Arab minority, its design does not allow the establishment of the relative salience or importance of temporal trends.

Before proceeding with evidence pertaining to what Jews say about and act toward Israeli Arabs, let us first consider the rise in inter-contacts and its meaning for the Jews. The Arab presence in Jewish areas increased steadily and dramatically during the 1970s and 1980s. Most Israeli Arabs continued to be employed in the Jewish sector, in which they also shop and spend some of their leisure time. In view of the perpetual underdevelopment of Israeli Arab villages and towns and the growing Arab purchasing power, many Arabs frequent Jewish commercial centers, cinemas, restaurants, clubs, beaches, and parks. An increasing number of Arab workers and university students also rent rooms and apartments in Jewish metropolitan centers in order to avoid the inconvenience of daily commuting. Of much greater significance is the growing phenomenon of Arabs moving to live permanently in Jewish towns. All the officially classified mixed towns, such as Acre, Haifa, and Ramle, have witnessed a substantial increase in Arab population since the early 1970s; this is due partially to migration from Arab localities. But many Jewish towns have also become mixed since then. They include Natzerat Illit, Nahariya, Rishon Letzion, Beer Sheva, and Eilat (Soffer, 1988: 15). Because of a shortage of housing, poor services, strict social control, and the conservatism of the Arab localities, these Arab families sought a higher quality of life in the Jewish towns while continuing to obtain education and some other vital services from the nearby Arab communities. Jewish discontent was also reinforced by fears of entering "Arab space"; i.e., going into Arab villages and towns and driving on roads bordering Arab areas within the Green Line (Ben-Nahum, 1991). The Jewish feeling of being invaded by Arabs was further intensified by the impact of the partial integration of the West Bank and Gaza Strip into Israel after the 1967 war. By the time the intifada broke out, over one hundred thousand non-citizen Arabs were working in the Jewish sector, an appreciable proportion of them staying there overnight and using Jewish facilities.

The rising penetration of the Israeli Arabs into the Jewish population as workers, members of institutions, users of public facilities, sojourners, and permanent residents has already eradicated Jewish exclusivity in many areas. The Jews feel uneasy about having to share their own "national" space with Arab "outsiders," and clearly resent the loss of exclusivity. In the Jewish neighborhoods and towns where Arabs are present in noticeable proportions, the Jews increasingly also feel the threat of losing dominance. The idea of a Jewish state and the reality of the overwhelming isolation of Arabs in Israel (about 90% of them live in separate localities and use separate institutions) have instilled in the Jews a sense of entitlement to exclusive Jewish space, free of Arab presence; hence, the new phenomenon of Arab penetration makes them feel "invaded." This is a situation that is bound to generate tensions and disputes between Arabs and Jews, but it also indicates an improved phase in Arab-Jewish coexistence, marked by the diminishing isolation of the two communities.

How do Jews actually react to the new reality? We do not really know. In the absence of field studies (except one on Natzerat Illit, to be discussed shortly), we have to turn to the press for information. Press reports are, however, fragmentary and biased toward newsworthy clashes, while clearly tending to ignore amicable contacts. If this assumption is correct, we should also take into account the unknown volume of unreported incidents in interpreting the reported ones.

Press reports regarding life and property losses inflicted on Arabs by Jews no doubt provide the most pertinent, sensitive measure; such incidents usually get reported. The Israeli press in the 1970s and 1980s reported only a small, insignificant number of incidents involving Arab losses of property and life perpetrated by nationalistically motivated Jews. There were virtually no cases of Jewish mobs storming and destroying Arab neighborhoods or seriously injuring or killing Arabs. Violence against Arabs living, working, or using facilities in Jewish towns was also minimal. Jewish vigilantism, which is significant across the Green Line, lacks a parallel in Israel proper. The near absence of Jewish mob violence is remarkable in view of the common Jewish perception of Israeli Arabs as radicalizing and the spread of Jewish encounters with them.

For lack of popular support as well as strict police actions, the several vigilante groups that tried to act against Israeli Arabs soon vanished. One of them was the short-lived *Sikkaryyim* underground, which attacked mostly Jewish left-wing politicians and journalists but also Israeli Arabs. For example, members of this group were reported to have attacked Arabs in the *Hassan Bek* mosque in Jaffa (*Haaretz*, May 5, 1990). Another futile group was *Vatike Hatsanhanim* ("Veteran Paratroopers"), whose aim was to patrol Jewish areas and counterattack Arab suspects (*Yediot Aharonot*, October 10, 1989). The single most important vigilante organization is the Kach Movement, whose members occasionally attack or incite to attack Arabs. The police commonly take countermeasures against Kach provocations and prevent them from deteriorating into mob assaults. There is one infamous case of two Jews, one of whom was then a Kibbutz member, who were convicted of murdering an Arab gas station attendant. The trigger for the murder in December 1984 was press speculation that the unknown murderer of a female Jewish soldier was a nationalistically driven Arab. The convicted murderers, who were caught in 1990, sought pure revenge against the Arab community and chose the attendant at random as an innocent target. The murder shocked the Jewish public, and the Kibbutz tried reconciliation with the victim's family and expelled the convicted member (*Yediot Aharonot*, July 7 and 13, 1990; *Maariv*, July 11 and 17, 1990; *Haaretz*, February 2, 1991). These cases are extremely rare and much less frequent than the number of reverse cases, of Arabs convicted of murdering Jews on nationalistic grounds. In 1989, one Arab was convicted of kidnapping and murdering a soldier (*Haaretz*, November 28, 1989) and another of murdering a Jewish innkeeper in Nahariya (*Haaretz*, June 13, 1989). According to their own testimonies, these Israeli Arabs were nationalistically driven.

In contrast to the scarcity of serious or mob assaults, the number of occasional, individual, light attacks by Jews against Arabs appears to have increased over the years. Most of these incidents involve fights between Arab and Jewish students on university campuses, between Arabs and Jews in swimming areas and national parks, between Jewish and Arab fans at soccer matches, between Arab and Jewish employees in workplaces, as well as clashes in other facilities. The Jews perceive these places as their own turf and feel hurt by the Arab "intruders." For instance, Arab youth dating, courting, or just asking to dance with Jewish girls are often attacked by Jewish youth. All these incidents testify to the increase in the Arab use of what the Jews define as Jewish space and the difficulty they experience in redefining it as a neutral public domain.

One of the more grave incidents, by Israeli standards, was the Ramat Amidar affair. Ramat Amidar is a working-class neighborhood in the privileged town of Ramat-Gan. It is populated by Oriental Jews and included in Project Renewal. Like other poor areas in the metropolitan area of Tel Aviv, Ramat Amidar is a place where more and more Arab university students and workers rent apartments but live there as singles. The local Jewish residents resent the Arab "invaders" and charge them with noise, dirt, overcrowding, sexual harassment, and planting of bombs. These unfounded accusations testify to the Jews' low self-esteem and fear of further status loss resulting from living with outcast Arabs. In late June 1987, scores of Jews stormed an apartment occupied by Arabs and beat them; several days later, the apartment was set on fire. Three of the offending thugs were arrested, convicted, and sentenced. Many of the residents expressed their objections to Arabs living in their midst and made racist statements. A national survey of the Jewish adult population, taken shortly thereafter, revealed a split on the issue among the Jews: 49% were in favor of open occupancy, 44% were against, and 7% were undecided (*Hadashot*, July 3, 1987). Knesset Member Rabbi Kahane was stopped by the police from entering the scene, but a group of leftist Jews staging a demonstration there against Jewish racism faced a hostile reception by the residents. Members of the Interior Committee of the Knesset toured the neighborhood and expressed dismay at the event. The press, the mayor of the town, and many public figures, including the President of the State, strongly censured the attack, invoking the stark memories of pogroms against Jews in the Diaspora. (For accounts, see *Jerusalem Post*, June 26 and 28, 1987; *Yediot Aharonot*, June 26 and 29, 1987; *Haaretz*, editorial, June 28, 1987.)

The Ramat Amidar affair discloses the deep Jewish discontent with the increase of the Arab population in Jewish towns. The mayor of Tel Aviv was quoted as calling for the Judaization of Yaffo (*Yediot Aharonot*, July 12 and 17, 1990). In Acre, where Arabs constitute a quarter of the total population and half of the children, the local Jewish leadership wishes to reduce the Arab population by relocating it, at least partly, to adjacent Arab villages. During the 1989 election campaign for the Acre city government, the failing Likud candidate publicly endorsed a solution of transfer for the Arab problem (*Al-Hamishmar*, December 6, 1988); and in 1991, a Likud deputy-mayor boasted of his endeavors to this effect (Mansur, 1991). In the same campaign, the winning Likud candidate for the mayor of Nahariya voiced vehement opposition to the settlement of Arabs in the town, pledged to take steps to curb the phenomenon, and after assuming office continued to call upon Arabs to leave the town and upon Jews not to rent or sell apartments to Arabs (*Davar*, May 18, 1989; *Haaretz*, May 19, 1989; Chen, 1991). These and other statements fall much short of actual practice because the law unequivocally affirms the Arabs' right to live wherever they choose.

Natzerat Illit is a case that best illustrates the problematic of Arab-Jewish coexistence in Jewish towns and perhaps of what is in store for Israel as a whole for years to come. It is possible to discuss this question in some detail thanks to a study of this town by the anthropologist Rabinowitz (1990). Natzerat Illit was established in 1957, partly on confiscated Arab lands and as part of the project of Judaization of the

Galilee, aiming to break the territorial contiguity and demographic preponderance of the Arabs in the region. In 1987, the population of this exclusive Jewish stronghold numbered 24,500 persons, of whom 3,200 (or 13%) were Arabs. Since the early 1970s, the Arabs of metropolitan Nazareth, which suffers from a shortage of housing, have been buying and renting apartments in Natzerat Illit, where there is a surplus of housing. Yet, the norm among the Jewish townspeople was and still is not to sell apartments to Arabs, and the Labor mayor of the town has publicly echoed Jewish public opinion by speaking against Arab migration to the town. In the early 1980s, *Mana* (an acronym for "Defenders of Natzerat Illit") was formed to fight back by pressuring Jews not to sell to Arabs and by dissuading Arabs not to move in. The organization, influenced by the Kach Movement, issued racist statements and held demonstrations. Despite the protest and pressure, sales to the Arabs have proceeded uninterruptedly because the opposition lacks a legal base and, contrary to Jewish fears, the Arab demand has boosted the real estate market and prices in the town, to the benefit of both sides. Arab-Jewish neighborly relations are good and Jewish stereotypes of Arabs have diminished. The Arab minority in the town consists mostly of middle-class Christians who are as well-off as the predominantly middle-class Ashkenazic majority.

If Arab residence in the town is not economically detrimental to the Jews and if the Arabs are well educated and mannered, why do Jews continue to frown on the Arab settlement in Natzerat Illit? Jews oppose in principle the transformation of the town from an exclusively Jewish to a mixed town. They fear the loss of Jewish dominance following the loss of Jewish exclusivity. They feel that by living in Natzerat Illit, they are pioneers, fulfilling the national goal of Jewish settlement, redeeming the land of Israel, and containing the spread of the Arabs. This is the purpose of their life in the periphery of the country and this is why the city was founded, to begin with, in the Arab heartland. These are the grounds for giving the Jews of Natzerat Illit, like other Jewish towns of the periphery, tax breaks, cheap mortgages, cut-rate housing, lands, and special funds for community development. The Arab migration to the town clearly defeats the mission of Jewish pioneering and settlement, undermines the rationale for extending special privileges to Jews, and makes it harder for the authorities to reserve preferential treatment to Jews.

The more Arabs who move in, the greater are their impact and demands. They insist on their full right as citizens to settle anywhere they like and deny any Jewish claim to an exclusively Jewish town; but during the first two decades of their settlement in Natzerat Illit, they were cautious not to antagonize the Jews. By using the community services of Arab Nazareth, they save the Jews from the double jeopardy of flooding and recasting Jewish services or creating parallel Arab services (schools, churches, mosques, shops, clubs, etc.) in the Jewish town. In 1989, however, for the first time, the Arabs of Natzerat Illit set up a separate election list to the city council, which received the support of 70% of the Arab voters and elected an Arab councillor. The list pressed national along with local issues. Constituting a tenth of the electorate, the Arabs also decided the close race for mayoralty by voting unanimously for the Labor candidate (this was also the case in Acre and Haifa). These political developments mark the reassertion of Arabs as a separate community in Natzerat Illit with new claims and independent power.

Natzerat Illit is a harbinger of Arab-Jewish relations. The Jews there have shown a remarkable contrast between ideological intransigence and behavioral openness. On the one hand, they continue to look with distaste upon Arab migration to the town, see Arab residents as outsiders, and hold to the idea of an exclusively Jewish town; on the other hand, they continue to rent and sell apartments to the Arabs, tolerate and even like them as neighbors, and generally reconcile themselves with the Arab presence. There were no incidents of deadly assaults against Arabs nor significant destruction of Arab property. The police has no choice but to protect the Arabs against Jewish harassment. The Jewish residents cannot stop the Arabs from moving in nor can they tamper with the nationally imposed ideology and policy of Jewish exclusivity. Another lesson that can be drawn from Arab-Jewish relations in Natzerat Illit is that Arab penetration of Jewish areas succeeds when it proceeds gradually. Only at a later stage did the Arabs reassert themselves politically and strive for equal status as residents.

Another case in point is the reaction of the Jewish establishment to widespread manifestations of political extremism and anti-Arab sentiment among Jewish youth during the 1980s. The evidence came from attitudinal surveys of high school students (three of the more comprehensive surveys were sponsored by the Van Leer Jerusalem Foundation and conducted by Zemah of the Dahaf Research Institute; Zemah, 1980, *Haaretz*, October 26, 1987, and London, 1990; another survey was reported in *Haaretz*, September 17, 1990) and from the great demand in high schools for speakers from the radical right. One response to the youth's intolerance was to launch the Education for Democracy program in the high schools and to boost contrived encounters between Arab and Jewish high school students. In view of the charged atmosphere, widespread Jewish fears of Arabs and the significant increase in the number of arranged mixed encounters, one should emphasize the incessant support of the Jewish public for these programs. There were only a few cancellations. Objections were raised by some Rabbis, who were concerned about observance of kashruth by Jewish youth visiting Arab homes and about the danger of assimilation inherent in Arab-Jewish coeducational activities. The Rabbis of Haifa (*Haaretz*, November 8, 1985), Acre (*Hatzoffe*, September 10, 1986), Beit Shean (*Haaretz*, January 13, 1986), and of other towns, and two of the Rabbis who served as Knesset Members on behalf of the Shas Party all voiced strong protests (*Yated Neaman*, June 22, 1988).

The arranged meetings between Arabs and Jews were not confined to high school students, however. They also included meetings and extended discussions between school teachers, principals, writers, intellectuals, academicians, heads of local councils, and other members of the community.

The value of these contrived interactions and exchanges between the two communities is mostly symbolic; that is, the Jews publicly register goodwill and interest in Arab issues and grievances and keep open the lines of communication with fellow Arabs. Although evaluation studies of these programs tend to yield at least partially positive results (e.g., Bar and Asaqla, 1988; Bar, Bar-Gal and Asaqla, 1989), their actual impact is not high, because they are concerned with only a small fraction of the population, are short-lived, and are conducted in non-real life situations.

Another instructive case is the Jewish public reaction to the Kach Movement, whose raison d'etre is activity against Arabs generally and Arabs in Israel particularly. Kach started to operate in the early 1970s, winning in 1984 a seat in the Knesset for its leader, the late Rabbi Kahane. Kach activists made attempts to enter Arab localities, to speak to Arabs, and to distribute leaflets and stage demonstrations there in order to promote the following causes: raising the state's flag, having Arabs sign Israel's Declaration of Independence, threatening them against moving to Jewish areas, convincing them to leave the country, and persuading Jewish women married to Arab men to desert their families and come back to the Jewish fold. Kahane used abusive language in referring to Arabs and introduced bills in the Knesset to ban sexual contact and marriage between Arabs and Jews, to levy a special poll tax on Arab citizens, and to expel Arabs from the country under certain circumstances.

How were these Kach racist activities received by the Jewish majority? There is no doubt that a small minority of Jews endorsed them, yet the rejection of Kach and its anti-Arab pronouncements and actions was by far overwhelming. Kahane and his supporters were not allowed by the police to enter Arab localities. Kahane was stopped from making speeches and holding demonstrations in the Jewish sector either by the police or by Jewish civil rights groups. The latter also organized rallies in solidarity with the Arabs. Numerous statements were made by public figures on both the left and the right denouncing racism and Kach. The Knesset was united in summarily ostracizing Kahane, emptying the floor when he spoke, refusing to table his racist motions, curtailing his right of movement into Arab areas, and passing an amendment to the election law that finally barred his party from participation in the 1988 elections. The treatment of Kahane as an outcast set a precedent in the history of the Knesset. The Kach provocations have unintentionally served the cause of having Jewish elites categorically distancing themselves from racism and reaffirming the Arabs' right to live in Israel and to enjoy equal rights and opportunities. Even the radical right, which entertains the idea of transfer of the Palestinian population, is forced to distinguish itself from the Kach Movement. For instance, Rahavam Ze'evi, the leader of Moledet, has reiterated his position that the transfer policy does not apply to Israeli Arabs (*Knesset Proceedings*, November 8, 1990; Meiri and Bar-Muha, 1991). The Jewish elites' renewed commitment to liberal values, triggered by the need to counteract Kach propaganda, have filtered down to some extent to the Jewish masses.

The liberal trend is also evident in the ambivalence and discord among the Jewish establishment on how to treat the Progressive List for Peace and its leader Mi'ari; this compares with the unanimous rejection of Kach and Kahane. Attempts were made to prevent the participation of both Kach and the PLP in the 1984 and 1988 elections, and the 1985 amendment to the election law was designed to bar both these parties. Yet, the PLP and Mi'ari were not targeted as an outcast, and have become instead a bone of contention between left and right. The right has continued to harass Mi'ari. At the initiative of the right-wing, his parliamentary immunity was revoked in 1987 by the Knesset on charges of participation in a rally in solidarity with the PLO, but this Knesset decision was overturned by the Supreme Court. The Central Elections Committee approved the PLP and disqualified Kach, and the Supreme Court upheld both decisions. In 1990, a Knesset committee, urged by the Likud, recommended the removal of Mi'ari's immunity because of his contacts with PLO officials for the purpose of promoting the Arab refugees' right of return by organizing the operation of the "return ship" to Israel, but the Knesset turned down this recommendation (*Yediot Aharonot*, September 26, 1990; *Haaretz*, October 30 and November 6, 1990; Benziman, 1990). Mi'ari presented his treatment by the Knesset as a test case of the state's treatment of the Arab minority. His position, that his dealings with the PLO should be considered a legitimate political activity and a normal representation of his constituents and that Arab Knesset Members who maintain contacts with the PLO are as entitled to immunity as Jewish Knesset Members who do so, was accepted by the majority of Knesset Members.

Similarly instructive was the Jewish public response to the 1987 government decision to impose a higher university tuition fee on students who do not serve in the army or render a national service ($1,500 instead of the then regular fee of $1,050). The right-wing ministers in the unity government under Shamir's premiership took advantage of the temporary absence from the country of some Labor ministers to pass this decision. Whereas the official rationale was that compensation should be given for money lost by fulfilling military or civil service, the two-scale tuition scheme was publicly perceived, rather, as penalizing Arab students, whom the state does not call for either army or national civil service. The public uproar was unprecedented and unexpected by the government. The new policy was exposed in the press as blatant discrimination and condemned by many Jewish public figures. Most adamant was the Secretary-General of the Labor Party, who said: "This is the worst moral decision ever taken by an Israeli government since the establishment of the state. It places Israel in the same camp with South Africa and Rhodesia. The right-wing has shown its real face: Kahane is a spearhead, not the only one" (*Haaretz*, May 18, 1987). A leading article in the *Haaretz* daily newspaper went so far as to warn against opening "a third front"; i.e., an internal front against the Arab minority in addition to Israel's two external fronts (against the Arab world and against the Palestinians in the occupied territories) (Shtrasler, 1987). The Committee of University Presidents passed a resolution not to execute the government's decision. The National Students Union, controlled by right-wingers at the time, also rejected the distinction between two kinds of students and continued its fight for a universal, low tuition fee. Public pressure built up to abolish the decision, which was rescinded two weeks after its adoption. Many Arabs were deeply moved by the firm Jewish public opinion on the issue.

The fact that during the later years of the 1980s the Kach Movement acted openly as an anti-Arab movement, that attempts were made to stop the PLP, and that the government adopted a resolution against Arab students attests to the substantial ethnocentrism in Israeli society. On the other hand, the Jewish reactions against these phenomena were no doubt even more innovative and impressive. In contrast to the 1950s and 1960s, when pronouncements and actions against Arab citizens could pass unnoticed or even enjoyed public support, they had to face in the late 1980s not only organized Arab protest but also certain Jewish censure and sometimes even an effective opposition.

Policy Change

A policy of domination, rather than consociationalism, toward the Arab minority was determined in 1948, and it has since then remained unchanged in its basic presuppositions, goals, means, and results. A certain policy change toward liberalization did take place over the years, however.

The existing policy toward the Arabs, namely, the combination of equal rights for all with structured Jewish dominance, is derived from Israel's nature as an ethnic democracy. "The main objective is to institutionalize effective domination over Arabs for an unlimited period of time for the purpose both of averting the threat to Israel's national security and Jewish-Zionist character and of harnessing Arab resources on behalf of the Jewish majority" (Smooha, 1982: 75; this article discusses this policy in detail). More specifically, the operative goals have been to keep Arabs law-abiding citizens, to make them accept their status as a permanent minority (prevention of Arab assimilation, promotion of Arab bilingualism and biculturalism, denial of territorial and institutional Arab autonomy, containment of a state-wide Arab leadership, and undermining of a regional Arab majority status), to use them as suppliers of services (provision of labor, lands, and votes to the Jewish sector), and to transform them into Israeli Arabs (a mixture of minorities, cut off from the Palestinian people). These unofficial goals are different from the declared ones of fostering equality and integration while respecting the separate existence of the Arab minority. The means employed to achieve these operative goals are economic dependence (most Arab breadwinners depend on employment in the Jewish economy, and the continued underdevelopment of the Arab localities) and political control (surveillance and restrictions over Arab political activities). It is estimated that this policy has managed to neutralize Arabs as a threat and to exploit their resources, but it has failed to de-Palestinize them. Implementation has also become less strict and less effective over time.

The trend of change in the factors underlying the policy toward the Arabs is mixed. On the one hand, Jewish dependence on Arab resources has diminished. In the post-1967 period, Israeli Arabs ceased to be the only source of cheap, temporary labor because of the extension of full membership and trade-union protection to them by the Histadrut and the availability of low-cost labor from the West Bank, Gaza Strip, and Third World countries. Similarly, the large-scale expropriations of Arab lands before 1967 sharply reduced the need for further confiscations. On the other hand, the Arab vote has become more significant after the changeover of governments in 1977 because of the rise of two Jewish political blocs, which fiercely vie for power. The Jewish perception of the Arabs as a security threat has, however, persisted and to some extent even strengthened since 1976. The highly mobilized and organized Arabs are increasingly suspected of collaboration with their hostile brethren in the occupied territories and the Palestinian diaspora.

To these constraints over possible liberalization of policies toward the Arabs, we must add the persistent, even growing Jewish desire to keep Israel Jewish and Zionist. In fact, the trend of consolidating Israel's Jewish character is quite evident in a number of legislative initiatives taken during the 1980s. These include legal amendments to make the traditional Hebrew law (*din ivrie*) a mandatory source in case of lacunas in the law, to criminalize the public display of signs of identification with the PLO and ban contacts with PLO officials (an amendment to the Prevention of Terrorism Act), and to refuse an election list the right to participate in Knesset elections if it denies Israel to be "the state of the Jewish people" (an amendment to the Election Law). Not less significant are various drafts of a bill of rights deliberated by Knesset or Government committees. All the proposals take for granted the Jewish character of the state and subordinate the fulfillment of human and civil rights to it. For instance, the draft of "The Basic Law: Basic Human Rights," agreed upon by the Government, states that all persons, irrespective of their origin, are equal before the law, but it is legal to practice "relevant" discrimination. The alternative wording suggested for this principle leaves no doubt about what should be regarded as "relevant" (i.e., legal) discrimination: "Any legal provision stemming from the nature of the State of Israel as a Jewish state does not constitute discrimination" (Ministry of Justice, 1989). The 1988 draft of a Constitution for Israel (*Maariv*, January 13, 1988), formulated by a committee of jurists from Tel-Aviv University and supported, among the Jews, by a large popular movement and an appreciable part of the elite, explicitly states in its preamble that Israel is the state of the Jewish people. Although it is not clear if the incontrovertible Jewish character of the state takes precedence over basic human rights, the proposed Constitution formally negates the right to form a party, to take part in a Knesset election, and to table a motion in which Israel's mission as the state of the Jewish people is denied.

The Jewish nature of the state has not been mitigated over the years; however, the trend of change in the separate administrative treatment of the Arabs is evident, in the direction of increasing integration. Arab minority affairs were once managed by the Ministry of Minorities. The separate Ministry was dissolved because it functioned as a guardian of Arab rights, contrary to the nascent policy of allocating low priority to the Arab problem. The military government, the *Shabac* or *Shin Bet* (the internal security service), and the Prime Minister's Advisor on Arab Affairs were in charge of the Arab minority from 1949-1966. In December

1966, the military government was lifted. The separate Arab departments in the various government offices have gradually lost influence, and the regional branches of the Advisor's office were abolished in the 1980s. In 1976, the Druze community was taken off the Advisor's jurisdiction and incorporated into the Jewish mainstream. Since 1984, a Minister has been appointed to take care of minority affairs. Since he is usually without portfolio and budget, this reform signifies a boost in the attention allotted to the concerns of the Arab minority rather than a reinforcement of administrative separation. This trend of decreasing separation is even more striking among the political parties and the Histadrut. By the early 1970s, all the secular Jewish parties admitted Arabs as full members. In 1976, the Histadrut decided to dissolve the separate Arab department and took steps to integrate Arabs into its various units and workers' councils.

These integrative measures are a marked shift from the policy of isolation as a means of control that has been imposed on the Arabs during the 1950s. The idea then was to stifle change by preventing Arabs from allying themselves with liberal Jews (Lustick, 1980). The integrative policy, however, still contains an element of control because it is driven by a firm belief that incorporation into Jewish organizations strengthens Arab dependence on Jews and lessens the hazard inherent in Arab autonomous institutions. The contribution of integration to equality is also not clear under these circumstances. It is worth emphasizing, nonetheless, that since the Arabs suspect any organizational separation initiated by Jews to be discriminatory, they are pleased with the policy shift to encourage Arab integration into the mainstream.

Another historical trend is the loosening of control over the Arab minority. The turning point was certainly the removal of the military government from all of the Arab areas. This fateful decision was the result of mounting political pressure by the opposition, especially by Mapam and Ahdut Haavoda, which formed an alignment with the ruling Mapai Party in 1965. The security forces were divided on whether the time was ripe for lifting military rule: the IDF opposed while the *Shabac* agreed. Experience has shown that the Arabs as a corporate group do not pose a serious security threat (do not form an active fifth column, national resistance movement, or state-wide underground), despite the prevalence of subversive individuals among them. The new policy was based on the solid assumption that the *Shabac*'s deep penetration into the Arab population is effective in deterring, detecting, and punishing subversive elements. A further unfastening of control took place soon after the 1967 war, when the *Shabac* had to relocate its main activities from the Arabs inside Israel to the Arabs in the occupied territories. Another significant step was taken by abolishing the exorbitant authority given to chiefs of the military commands to issue detention orders. "The 1979 Emergency Authorities (Arrests) Law" requires that any administrative detention of a citizen or a permanent resident must be ordered by the Minister of Defense, limited to six months, approved by a civilian judge within 48 hours, and subject to an appeal to the Supreme Court. As a result, the detention of Arab suspects and troublemakers has dropped dramatically since 1979 and is now employed only on rare occasions.

This significant liberalization of control over the Arabs falls short, however, of switching to a policy of trust. That national security has remained the prime concern of the state in its dealing with the Arab minority is best demonstrated in the composition of the *Haavoda Hamerkazit* (Central Committee), the highest state body overseeing Israeli Arabs: it consists of representatives of the army, the *Shabac*, the police, the Prime Minister's Advisor on Arab Affairs, and since 1985, it has been headed by the Minister responsible for Minorities. The Arabs are still distrusted, exempted from military service, and placed under some surveillance. The threat attributed to them continues to be the main justification for retaining the otherwise objectionable 1945 Emergency (Defense) Regulations, which serve as the key internal security legislation. The government does not hesitate to resort to these sweeping internal security powers if necessary. On December 1, 1980, for instance, it banned the convening of the congress of Arab masses, which was supposed to establish an all-Arab representative body. Acting upon secret *Shabac* reports, the government feared that the planned "Parliament of the Arabs in Israel" would set up parallel institutions to the state bodies, coordinate its resistance activities with the PLO and the Arabs in the occupied territories, and call for secession to a Palestinian state if established. On April 12, 1981, the government also outlawed the umbrella organization of nine radical action groups ("The National Coordinating Committee"). During the 1980s, security was invoked to halt planned or ongoing publications in Arabic. For instance, "Al-Raya," the mouthpiece of the Sons of the Village Movement, was ordered to shut down permanently in 1989; "Sout Al-Haq Wal-Huriya," published by the Islamic Movement, was banned for three months in 1990, both these cases on charges of incitement and subversion (*Yediot Aharonot*, March 5, 1989; July 9, 1990). Furthermore, in 1990, the knesset passed the first reading of an amendment to the 1949 Prevention of Terrorism Act that aims to greatly tighten the restrictions and penalties on any body that knowingly or unknowingly, directly or indirectly, receives any financial support from terrorist organizations. If the amendment is finally enacted, the activities of over 200 Israeli Arab non-profit associations that depend on donations from abroad will be seriously threatened (Galnoor, 1990).

The police are increasingly assuming the chief function of control over the Arab community, completely displacing the army, and appreciably reducing the direct involvement of the *Shabac*. The police expanded their role and presence in Arab localities during the 1980s. They are usually more concerned with internal security than with fighting crime in the Arab sector (S. Cohen, 1990). After the outbreak of the intifada, the police commissioner warned against the breakdown of public order in the Arab sector. To deal with the sharp rise in infractions of public order, the *Yasam* (a mobile police force) was formed in 1988 to control disturbances and riots. This unit is in addition to *Malav* (a police department for intelligence and detection), which assists the *Shabac* in interrogations and arrests. The growing centrality of the police in the control of the Arab sector, however, attests to a healthy trend of entrusting a common civilian agency with dealing with the Arabs as civilians.

Another significant trend is a certain reduction over the years in anti-Arab discrimination as a primary component of public policy. In 1952, it was decided that wages and prices must be equal for all population groups (declaring illegal the hitherto practice of paying lower wages to Arab workers and lower prices to Arab farmers); in 1954, the Arabs were accepted as members of the trade unions; in 1959, they were fully allowed into the Histadrut; in 1960, they were granted access to labor exchanges; in 1966, they were liberated from military government; in the early 1970s, they were accepted into Jewish political parties; and in 1980, the citizenship law was amended to make it possible to naturalize thirty thousand Arabs who were until then disenfranchised. Discrimination in budget allocations decreased significantly over the years. A study that compared Arab and Jewish local authorities of equal size showed that the Jewish lead in budgets, which was at a ratio of 13:1 in 1970, had dropped to 3:1 in 1982; and in terms of government grants, the drop was from 23:1 to 5:1 (Al-Haj and Rosenfeld, 1990). The gap in per capita allocation of funds by the Ministry of the Interior continued to narrow during the 1980s, but the slow pace of closure caused considerable protest and numerous shutdowns of the Arab councils. In the summer of 1991, an agreement was achieved between the government and the striking heads of Arab local councils that provided for an increase of 240% in the operations budget of the Arab local governments and for bringing it to a par with that of the Jewish local governments in four years (*Haaretz*, August 27, 1991). The leaders of the Committee of Heads of Arab Local Councils praised the agreement as "a historical decision" (*Al-Ittihad*, August 27, 1991). In the 1970s, only several Arab local councils had approved master plans; by 1991 plans for 90% of the councils were in an advanced stage of approval (*Knesset Proceedings*, July 17, 1991). These zoning plans are supposed to meet the needs of the Arab population up to the year 2010 in terms of lands earmarked for housing, recreation, public facilities, commerce, and industry. The severe problem of 7,000 illegal buildings was drastically reduced by legalizing most of them, following the government's decision in 1989 to adopt the recommendations of the Markowich Commission, and the progress made on master plans. The Minister in charge of Minorities announced a ten-year plan for investing about four billion dollars in infrastructure and in facilities in the Arab sector and in settling the enormous land claims of the Bedouin of the Negev (*Knesset Proceedings*, December 4, 1989).

The policy of land expropriations had changed considerably, as well. In the first years of the state, expropriation (outside the Negev) ran in the hundreds of thousands of dunams; it was down to tens of thousands in the 1960s, then to several thousands in the 1970s, and finally to none in the 1980s. The last wave of formal confiscations took place in 1976; but in practice, most of the expropriated 6,000 dunams were left in the hands of their Arab owners and only in 1990 was an attempt made to take them away. The case of Area 9 set a precedent in land policy. Area 9, in the lower, central Galilee, consisted of 65,000 dunams, of which 12,000 were owned by Arabs and all of which was allocated for use as firing ranges by the army. For many years the access to these lands was restricted and, as a result, constituted a relentless source of dispute between the Arab landowners and the authorities. In August 1986, a committee consisting of Labor ministers decided to abolish Area 9 and to return the lands to their owners (Schiff, 1986). This was a rare case of releasing lands to Arabs. The decision invoked strong criticism from the radical right within and outside the Likud, but otherwise passed quite calmly. The main reason for the impressive policy change from large-scale to virtually no land expropriations was the government's apparent fear of strong Arab resistance, not a lack of lands to take over.

There are also certain indications that the authorities and other Jewish institutions are increasingly aware of the need to consider Arabs as full members of the society and to instill in them a feeling of participation and belonging. A series of steps taken in the 1980s confirms this observation. They include the appointments of an Arab as a consul in Atlanta, Georgia, an Arab to head the branch of Arab education in the Ministry of Education and Culture, three Arabs as members of the Central Committee of the Histadrut, and three Arabs as deputies to the Head of the Center for Local Governments. Other symbolic gestures were the issuing of a stamp in honor of the *Al-Jazar* mosque in Acre, the publication of a telephone book in Arabic, the addition of Arabic subtitles to certain Hebrew TV programs, the awarding every year of several subsistence fellowships to writers in Arabic, frequent public appearances of the President of the State and government ministers in Arab localities and in Arab political and cultural events (e.g., the unprecedented appearance of President Herzog at Rakah's 20th Congress in December 1985, and his message to the 21st Congress in May 1990), and most importantly, the inclusion of an Arab as 1 of 12 persons lighting the torches in the opening state celebration of Independence Day. It is also worth noting that for the first time, a significant number of polls taken during the campaign for the 1988 elections included the Arab population. Since the 1988 elections, the tabulations of results of voting intentions, routinely published in the Hebrew press, include the three predominantly Arab parties as part of the "left" bloc, along with Labor and the small Zionist left parties. In 1989, the Israel Institute of Applied Social Research, under the direction of Elihu Katz, began to include Israeli Arabs as an integral part of its continuing surveys of the Israeli public. Since the early 1980s, Arab speakers are commonly included in panels of conferences or public discussions relating to Israeli Arabs. These signs of goodwill were made without any retraction from the Jewish-Zionist character of the state and without giving up Jewish power, however.

The failing attempt, made on April 12, 1990, to form a narrow, Labor-led coalition government based on the backing of the three predominantly Arab parties exposes the stumbling blocks in allowing the Arabs into Israel's political mainstream. The undertaking fell through when two Knesset Members from the ultra-orthodox Agudat Israel, which had consented to join the coalition, refused to vote for the new government because of its dependence on the Arabs. These Knesset Members and others from the Likud and the radical right declared their principled opposition to the formation of any coalition government dependent on Arabs, who were portrayed as abetting, representing, or taking orders from the PLO. A week before the confidence vote was held in the Knesset, Arafat urged Arab Knesset Members to vote for the Labor coalition. Although publicly repudiated by Arab Knesset Members, the PLO intervention in Israel's internal affairs played into the hands of the right and radical right (*Maariv*, April 8, 1990). The right of Arabs who favor talks between Israel and the PLO to decide whether Labor or Likud heads the government was rejected, while the right of Jews subscribing to the same view was not. Many Jews, especially within the right-wing bloc, believe that a Jew supporting the PLO is naive or mistaken, whereas an Arab supporting the PLO is disloyal and subversive. The Arabs and leftist Jews condemned as "racist" the delegitimation of Arab Knesset Members and the distinction made between them and leftist Jewish Knesset Members (Kafra, 1990). In a message to a rally against racism held in

Nazareth, the President of the State wrote: "It is impossible that parties which solicit the support of the Arab public would disqualify it in the event of a political test. This disqualification stands neither the moral test nor the test of democracy" (*Al-Hamishmar*, April 24, 1990).

The reluctant resort to Arab support by Labor in coalition-making set a historical precedent, however (Shapira, 1990). This was the first time that independent, predominantly Arab parties had ever been candidates for a coalition government. An agreement was signed with them that provided for proceeding with the peace initiative, certain social reforms, and a long list of concessions to the Arab sector aiming to bring it up to par with the Jewish population (the text of the agreement was published in *Haaretz*, June 5, 1990). It is true that the agreement fell short of the demands presented jointly by the three predominantly Arab parties. It also did not provide for the appointment of an Arab as a minister and for the official recognition of the Committee of Heads of Arab Local Councils, and these collective needs were not even pressed as claims by the Arab negotiators. The predominantly Arab parties were not even supposed to be full partners in the coalition government, but to support it as outsiders. Despite all its faults and its delegitimation by part of the Jewish public, the 1990 trial to build a coalition dependent on the Arabs should be considered a significant step forward in the piecemeal, painful process of incorporating the Arab community into the national power structure.

The continuous dispute among the Jews over the best reform of the political system has an Arab dimension. Those in the Likud opposing direct, popular election of the Prime Minister argue that Israeli Arabs will tip the scale by voting for the Labor candidate who accepts the principle of "land for peace." In right-wing eyes, the Arabs do not have the right to decide elections in a Jewish state, especially when most of them presumably vote with an intention to weaken or even undermine the state. Although the Arabs have the right to vote, this right should not be misused; more generally, the prerogative to decide a close race in Israel as the state of the Jewish people should be reserved to Jewish groups. The radical right goes a step further by advocating the denial of the franchise to Arabs who do not serve in the army or who do not render some civil service. Ariel Sharon boasted of the qualitative edge the Likud has over Labor: "Our half [of the electorate] consists of the Jewish majority of the State of Israel. The other [Labor] half was obtained by Jews with the help of Arabs who represent the extremists from among the Arabs in the Land of Israel, who publicly support the PLO, and this is the big difference" (interview in *Yediot Aharonot*, June 15, 1990). On the other hand, Labor and leftist parties, which enjoy Arab electoral support, do not usually question the legitimacy of Arab political rights and do not oppose reforms on these grounds. One method that enjoys the backing of some Knesset Members in both the Likud and Labor camps is that the head of the election list (party) receiving the largest number of valid votes will be the Prime Minister. The Zionist Left parties raised principled objection to this suggestion, accusing its sponsors of scheming to reduce Arabs' participation rate in Knesset elections and to distort their voting options (*Haaretz*, December 19, 1990). Amnon Rubinstein, the leader of Shinui, wrote in this regard: "The suggestion will put the Arabs in Israel into an impossible situation. If they will vote for an Arab list, they will actually vote for the Likud. They will face an immoral dilemma: to give up any independent representation, or to vote for themselves and thereby support a Likud government" (*Yediot Aharonot*, December 23, 1990).

This discussion of trends in policy toward the Arab will conclude with a review of the main findings of a new study, by Benziman and Mansur (forthcoming), of Israeli government policy toward the Arabs in Israel during the entire 1948-90 period. In the third chapter of their book, these two investigative journalists detail the policy, its execution and outcomes. They discern four themes in the policy: population transfer, arbitrary regulation, coexistence, and integration. All of these strategies have been present in the policy since 1948, but in various combinations and doses. Yet, a clear policy change emerges over the years. The initial period is characterized by a transfer of most of the Arab population from the area that became Israel. Government policy was to weather pressures to repatriate the Arab refugees and to encourage emigration of the remaining Arabs. The ensuing period, starting in the early 1950s and ending in 1963, when the hardline Ben-Gurion finally quit office, was marked by arbitrary regulation, or what Lustick calls "a system of control." The Arabs were subordinated through land expropriations, military government, segmentation into clans and religious communities, discrimination, forced underdevelopment, economic dependence, and involuntary isolation from the Jews.

From the mid-1960s to 1976, the dominant motive in policy shifted to coexistence, Arabs and Jews living side by side, with tension and alienation, but also with waning outright compulsion by the state. The military government was abolished, investments in the development of the Arab sector increased, and the Arabs were permitted to mobilize and to air their grievances.

The last period began after the first Land Day strike in 1976. Shocked by the vehement Arab resistance to expropriations of some lands, the government held a discussion of the Arab situation and adopted a new policy of active promotion of integration and equality between Arabs and Jews. All seven Prime Minister's Advisors on Arab Affairs (Toledano,

Sharon, Gur-Arye, Ginat, Gilboa, Tsafrir, and Blai) who served during the 1976-90 period submitted policy proposals to the government, that recommended giving higher priority to the problems of the Arab minority, ways to reduce the discrepancies in life standards between Arabs and Jews, methods to improve Arab integration, measures to lessen Arab disaffection and alienation, means to contain Arab radicalization, and steps to fight Jewish ethnocentrism. In these confidential reports, the Advisors concede government neglect, discrimination, and the partial implementation, and limited effect, of the policies toward the Arabs, and they warn against the danger of impending destabilization of the Arab situation. This post-1976 preoccupation with Arab equality and integration in the Advisors' secret documents contrasts sharply with the officials' mindset in the earlier period, as was candidly conveyed in a public statement by Loubrani, an Advisor on Arab Affairs to Ben-Gurion: "It might have been better if there were no Arab university students. If they had remained hewers of wood, it might have been easier to control them" (*Haaretz*, April 4, 1961; quoted by Shammas, 1983: 37-38).

Conclusion

Although the available evidence is not clearcut, it is more in line with the Jewish accessibility than Jewish intransigence thesis. Survey data for the 1980-88 period show stability and a certain moderation in Jewish attitudes toward Israeli Arabs. The examination of pronouncements and actions, as reported in the press, also reveals that the Jewish public has become less rejecting and more tolerant of Arabs. Policy also changed over time from control toward an emphasis on equality and integration. All these changes took place despite the further legal consolidation of the Jewish character of the state, the Jewish displeasure with the rapid blurring of exclusivity of the various Jewish areas and institutions, and the Jewish perception of the growing Arab militancy as radicalization and rejection of the state.

It is necessary to warn against several misinterpretations of this positive trend, however. First, the change is moderate. Despite improvements over the years, the Arab situation continues to be basically unsatisfactory. Although Jewish attitudes have not stiffened further, neither have they softened substantially, and they are not tolerant and fair at present. The Jews have learned to live with diminishing Jewish exclusivity, but they continue to feel uncomfortable, and even resentful, because of it. Although public policy has shifted from outright domination toward the pursuit of greater integration and equality, it still lacks a real commitment to these objectives. Second, there is no compelling reason to assume that the positive trend will continue, producing in the end higher levels of equality and tolerance for Arabs, and that the trend will not stop or not be reversed. Finally, the Arabs are clearly dissatisfied with the rate and pace of change. They insist on "full equality now," and they feel frustrated by anything less. Like the Jews who misperceive growing Arab militancy as radicalization, the Arabs misperceive piecemeal Jewish moderation as intransigence. Seen from their own perspectives, though both are correct, each side missing the true meaning of change in the other side. Yet, the situation is asymmetric: as the subordinate party to the relation, the Arabs pay a high price for the perpetuation of the status quo and for the painfully slow pace of change among the Jews.

Part Four

CONCLUSIONS

23

Conclusions

This socio-political study of the relations between Arabs and Jews in Israel within its pre-1967 borders seeks to examine the key issues dividing them, to discuss the differences within each side, and to trace trends over the years in the basic orientation of each community toward the other. The analysis is based on four sets of surveys consisting of face-to-face interviews with nationally representative samples of adult men and women from both populations: the 1976 surveys contain 656 Arabs and 148 Jews (these Jews are the only non-representative sample in the entire project, and for this reason they are excluded from the study of trends over time); the 1980 surveys comprise 1,140 Arabs, 1,267 Jews, and 88 Arab and 90 Jewish public figures; the 1985 surveys include 1,203 Arabs, 1,205 Jews, and 137 Arab and 144 Jewish public figures; and the 1988 surveys draw on 1,200 Arabs and 1,209 Jews. The 1976 surveys are reported in *The Orientation and Politicization of the Arab Minority in Israel* (Smooha, 1984), the 1980 surveys in *Arabs and Jews in Israel, Vol. 1* (Smooha, 1989), and the 1985 and 1988 surveys in the present volume.

A detailed examination of the views of Arabs and Jews on 13 central issues relating to their mutual relations shows that a majority on each side disagrees with a majority on the other. This pattern is typical of deeply divided societies. At the same time, there are also certain basic agreements that significantly mitigate the sharp disagreements. In order to gain a real sense of the significance of these discords and accords, let us first look at the majority opinion on each side while ignoring the internal differences.

To indicate only the highlights from the 1985-88 surveys, both communities accept the idea of Arab-Jewish coexistence: the Arabs recognize Israel's right to exist, accept their minority status in Israel but reject its Jewish-Zionist character, whereas the Jews acknowledge the

Arabs' right to live in Israel as a minority with full equal rights but deny them national, collective rights. The Arabs feel that the Jews should reciprocate their acceptance of the legitimate existence of the State of Israel by acknowledging the Palestinians' right to self-determination, allowing the formation of an independent Palestinian state in the West Bank and Gaza Strip alongside Israel, and consenting to negotiate with the PLO. The Jews repudiate these expectations, condemn them as counterproductive for peace, and consider their endorsement by the Arabs to be evidence of Arab disloyalty.

Each group has a different collective national identity. Civic Israeli identity has remained secondary to their separate Palestinian and Jewish national identities. The Arabs see themselves as Palestinians and Israelis, and attempt to forge a new identity that combines both, as do the Jews with their dual Jewish and Israeli identities. This is an impossible mission for the Arabs, however, because of the inherent limits on the development of an Israeli identity by non-Jews in a non-assimilating Jewish state and because of the threats to national security of a strong Palestinian identity. Hence, Jews both fear and negate the Palestinian identity of the Arabs in Israel. The controversy over institutional autonomy for the Arabs falls along similar lines. The Arabs demand non-territorial, institutional autonomy: control over their educational system, a state recognition of Arab national organizations (such as the Committee of Heads of Arab Local Councils), the freedom to form nationalist Arab parties, the right to establish an Arab university, and a proportional share of the national resources. Israel rejects this drive for autonomous institutions because it appears as impinging on its Jewish-Zionist character and engendering secessionist sentiments. It grants Arabs an ethnic (religious, cultural, linguistic) minority status while they pursue a Palestinian national minority status. For the same reasons Jews reject the Arab desire that Arab education should educate Arabs to love Israel as the common homeland of its two peoples (Arabs and Jews) or should instill Palestinian nationalism in them.

Culture and class are other crucial areas of sharp dispute. While the Arabs accept Hebrew as a second language and Israeli Jewish culture as an addition to their core-culture, they resent the Jews' cultural orientation toward the West, wish to see their culture to be an integral part of Israel's national culture, and even would prefer that Israel will become predominantly Arab in culture. The Arabs are also displeased with their position as a working and poor class in Israel's middle class society. Their aspirations for social mobility are high and they urge Israel to bring them as fast as possible on a par with the Jews. The Jews reject these demands and insist on keeping their cultural and class dominance.

Mutual ethnocentrism further divides the two communities. Most Jews distrust most Arabs, and most Arabs distrust most Jews. Both are reserved about meaningful contacts between them, although the Arabs are less reserved than the Jews because they have more to gain from interethnic exchanges. Stereotyping also burdens Arab-Jewish relations, but it is much less virulent than expected. By far the most troublesome component of ethnocentrism is the Jews' expectation of preferential treatment by the state. Many Jews feel that the Jewish state, by its very nature, should extend special privileges and entitlements to Jews, a view that legitimizes the public and individual discrimination against the Arabs. Given the large-scale discrimination against them, the Arabs seek non-discrimination and have not as yet pressed for affirmative action.

The various means of struggle are another key issue. The Arabs embrace democratic procedures as the strategy for advancing their status and condition in Israeli society. They also believe in the efficacy of democracy to affect change and disapprove of the use of extra-legal or violent measures. The Jews assent to these points but object to the Arab endorsement and use of extra-parliamentary politics, especially general strikes and protest abroad. Although these forms of protest are legal, they are considered by the Jews to be illegitimate and an extreme means of struggle.

These disagreements between Arabs and Jews over critical issues show that there is a Jewish consensus from which most Arabs dissent. The thirteen issues at dispute can be reduced to five fundamental controversies. First is the Arab rejection of the ideology of Zionism which makes Israel a Jewish-Zionist state, a special case of the general type of ethnic democracy that combines democracy for all with ethnic dominance. The second cardinal discord stems from the parallel Jewish rejection of Palestinian nationalism which Israeli Arabs accept as the overarching ideology shaping their collective identity, culture, education, and to a certain degree their politics as well. Third, there is a controversy over whether individual rights could and should be fully equal for Arabs and Jews. The Jews expect preferential treatment by the state on the basis of its Jewish nature, their unqualified loyalty, and their fulfillment of all duties (unlike the Arabs who do not discharge military or civic service). Fourth, Jews deny the Arabs' demand for institutional autonomy and for official recognition of the nationalist, Palestinian essence of their institutions. Finally, the Jews oppose Arab participation in the national power structure: they do not allow the Arabs into national coalition politics and into national decision-making bodies.

Arab-Jewish discord is, nonetheless, softened by the factionalism in each community. The Arabs are divided among themselves on the various issues of Arab-Jewish coexistence. They are classified into four types. The accommodationists (7% in the 1988 survey) are persons who accept Israel as a Jewish-Zionist state and work through the Jewish parties to improve their conditions. The reservationists (31%), in tune with the ideology and strategy of the Democratic Arab Party, have reservations about the Jewish nature of the state, organize independently, and actively seek participation in the national power structure through cooperation and even coalition with the Labor and Zionist left parties. Following the lines of the Communist Party and the Progressive List for Peace, the oppositionists (52%) constitute a permanent political opposition that objects to the Jewish-Zionist character of the state and wages an intensive, independent struggle for peace and equality. The followers of the Sons of the Village Movement in Israel and the Rejection Front abroad (10%) reject Israel altogether and wish to replace it with a Palestinian state in the entire area of Palestine. The adherents of the Islamic Movement do not fall into any single type but are scattered into several ones, hovering between the oppositionists and rejectionists.

Similarly, the Jews are split into five orientations toward Israeli Arabs despite the fact that Arab-Jewish coexistence does not figure prominently as an issue in Jewish politics. The egalitarianists, who subscribe to the ideology of the Communist Party and are few in numbers, reject Zionism and Israel's Jewish-Zionist mission and pursue the goal of a secular-democratic state. The conciliationists (11% in the 1988 survey) support the left Zionist view that the Arabs should enjoy full equality while the Jewish character of the state must remain intact. The pragmatists (37%) are followers of the Labor Party's approach that Jewish control can better be maintained by making concessions and compromises to the Arabs. The hardliners (30%) support the strong-arm ideas and policies of the Likud, religious, and radical right parties that the Arabs should adjust themselves to Jewish dominance, otherwise their entitlement to equal rights and opportunities would be restricted. The exclusionists (22%), influenced by the Kach Movement, wish to get rid of the Arabs or to consolidate Jewish rule by forcing them into a formally subordinate status in a non-democratic system.

Arab and Jewish factionalisms soften the plural and polarized nature of Israeli society. The internal disagreements among the Arabs prevent them from forming a unified political bloc or a single election list. The internal discords among the Jews allow Arabs to find Jewish sympathizers, supporters, and allies and to exact certain concessions from the Jews by taking sides in the tough competition for power between the Labor and Likud political camps. These political deals have already been in evidence since the early 1980s. The most outstanding cases in point were the deep Arab involvement in the election of the chairman of the Center for Local Government in 1989 and in the abortive attempt to form a narrow Labor coalition government in 1990. The internal differentiation has also helped to humanize Arabs and Jews in the eyes of the other side. As a result, many Arabs today distinguish among various streams of Zionism and some say that they can live with left Zionism. The Jews are also increasingly distinguishing rejectionist Arabs from others

The examination of trends over time showed a consistent pattern. The attitude change, emerging from the Arab 1976-88 surveys, took two forms. On the one hand, there was a rise in militancy, as manifested in such measures as identities combining Israeli and Palestinian components, approval of a two-state solution, endorsement of general strikes, and disapproval of Israel's Jewish features. On the other hand, there was no rise in measures of rejectionism such as non-Israeli Palestinian identities, support for a state in all of Mandatory Palestine instead of Israel, endorsement of the use of violence, and rejection of Israel's right to exist. These two concurrent trends were also evident in the distribution of the Arab orientation types. From 1976 to 1988 the accommodationists dropped from 13% to 7%, whereas the oppositionists increased from 44% to 52%, both changes reflect a rise in militancy. On the other hand, the proportion of the rejectionists was 13.5% in 1976 and 10% in 1988, demonstrating that rejectionism did not increase during this period.

The trends in leadership, voting, and protest were more or less the same. The main pattern shifted over the years from traditional, hamula, or Jewish-related leaders to modern, politicized, and independent leaders. Leadership styles clearly changed from accommodating to militant, not to rejectionist. There was also a consistent rise in Arab voting for parties or lists not related to the Zionist establishment: 16% in 1955, 23% in 1965, 51% in 1977, and 58% in 1988. Since all these political bodies work within Israel's system, this rise implies an increase in militancy, not in rejectionism. By the same token, Arab protest was modest in both volume and form up to the early 1970s, but has become frequent and intensive since then. Actually the Arabs have been waging a sustained struggle for peace and equality since the mid-1970s, resorting to large demonstrations and general strikes. Arab protest has remained, however, within democratic bounds and corresponded to the standards of extra-parliamentary protest set by Israeli Jews during this period. Most importantly, the Arabs passed the hard test of the intifada. While they expressed their solidarity with the intifada through protests, shipments of relief, and to some extent even illegal activities, they have unequivocally refrained from taking part in the Palestinian uprising. The daily rebellious activities of clashes with the army, fatalities, shutdowns of businesses, popular committees running villages, underground communiques, and so forth are restricted to the occupied territories.

Greater openness marks the parallel trends among the Jews. There was a reduction during the 1980s in such hardline attitudes as disapproval of the Arab use of general strikes and the approval of the view that Israel should encourage Arabs to leave the country. This attitude change is well captured in the increase in the combined proportion of the conciliationists and pragmatists from 41% in 1980 to 48% in 1988, a decrease in the hardliners' strength from 37% to 30%, respectively, and a stability in the part of the exclusionists (22%). An examination of change in the public pronouncements and actions also points to a growing acceptance of Arabs by the Jews. Over the years Jewish localities and institutions have lost their exclusivity because of continuing Arab penetration. Jews have reacted with discontent but without resort to significant violence against Arab persons and property. There was some moderation in the tone of statements against Israeli Arabs, while anti-Arab incitement was counteracted by firm measures (e.g., the strong countermeasures taken against Kach and its late leader). Even a limited liberalization in policies toward the Arabs in Israel has been underway since the mid-1960s. The military government over Arab areas was abolished, Arabs were admitted as full members to the Histadrut and Jewish political parties, the large-scale discrimination in the allocation of resources diminished, and certain symbolic gestures expressing a willingness to incorporate Arabs into the system were made.

These findings on key issues of coexistence, internal factionalisms, and temporal trends better fit the Arab politicization and Jewish accessibility theses than the more common Arab radicalization and Jewish intransigence theses. The Arabs' militancy is amply mainfested in their active opposition to discriminatory policies, fighting for equal rights and opportunities, pursuit of autonomous institutions, and support for Palestinian nationalism. They are law-abiding citizens who tie their fate and future with Israel. If radicalism is defined as a rejection of Israel, minority status, Jews, and Jewish institutions, or as the use of violent or unlawful means against the state, then the Arabs are neither radical nor radicalizing. On the other hand, the Arab radicalization approach fails to make this crucial distinction between militancy and radicalism (or rejectionism). In contrast, the politicization approach emphasizes the Israelization of the Arabs as a counterbalance to their rather normal reassertion of Palestinian identity and affinity. It also stresses the internal political divisions among Israeli Arabs.

In the same vein, these research results confirm the Jewish accessibility perspective. Rather than remaining intransigent or hardening their position further, the Jews and Jewish authorities have opened up to the Arabs, have become more considerate of their needs, and have reduced discrimination against them. The Jews have also become more divided in their orientation toward Israeli Arabs, with supporters of the Labor political camp being more tolerant than the adherents of the Likud camp. The Jewish intransigence approach is unrealistic in underplaying the cumulative, incremental change in the Jewish orientation and in overplaying the large distance that has remained to be traversed in order to bring the Arabs on par with the Jews at both individual and collective levels.

The Arab radicalization and Jewish intransigence theses do not properly account for the basic fact that Israeli Arabs have not turned into a rebellious minority as have the Catholics in Northern Ireland and the Tamils in Sri Lanka, to name just two cases. Furthermore, neither can they explain the moderate degree of rapprochement between Arabs and Jews that took place during the 1970s and 1980s. The theoretical models underlying these theses, especially modernization, control, internal colonialism, dependency, and political economy, do not provide an adequate interpretation of current Arab-Jewish relations and of the long-term trends shaping them.

The alternative Arab politicization and Jewish accessibility theses are not derived from any particular theoretical perspective, except perhaps a general approach stressing national conflicts over resources and values. Two major explanatory factors are suggested, however: one refers to Israeli democracy and another to the Israeli-Palestinian conflict. Both factors are considered to play a negative role in the Arab adjustment to the Jewish state. Since Israeli democracy is neither liberal nor consociational, it does not provide sufficient protection of individual and minority rights. Furthermore, the Palestinian question is a sharp divider between Arabs and Jews. It provides the basis and legitimacy for the state treatment of the Arabs as a threat to national security, for Jews' profound mistrust, and for the exemption of the Arabs from military service that serves as seemingly justifiable grounds for institutional discrimination. As long as the Palestinian issue remains unsettled, the Arabs will continue to find themselves caught in the crossfire between their people and state.

Without denying the adverse implications of these two crucial factors, the alternative approach emphasizes other impacts. There are positive aspects to the nature and dynamics of the Israeli political system – ethnic democracy and democratization. Israel is an ethnic democracy par excellence. It combines extension of social, civic, and political rights to all citizens in conjunction with the dominance and preferential treatment to the Jews. This low-rate democracy, nonetheless, has supplied Arabs with the fundamental tools for conducting an intensive but legal struggle for ameliorating their lot in Israeli society. Yet without the growing overall democratization of the system from the early 1960s onwards, it would be impossible to conceive of favorable change in Arab-Jewish relations. Without democratization, Arabs would not have been liberated from military rule, would not have been able to penetrate Jewish institutions, and could not have carried out the continued fight for peace and equality. By the same token, democratization has enabled the Jews to better differentiate between Israeli Arabs and other Palestinians, to allow Arabs to employ firm democratic procedures for advancing their cause, not to react with backlash and repression to widespread Arab protest, to tolerate Arab entry into exclusive Jewish institutions, and to make limited concessions to Arabs.

Similarly, some of the historical developments in the Israeli-Palestinian conflict are quite positive for the Israeli Arab adaptation to Israel. Most important is the transformation of the Palestinians during the 1948 war from an indigenous to a diaspora people. As a result, a divergence in life conditions and destiny has taken deep root among three segments of the Palestinian people over the years. Israeli Arabs have evolved into a distinct Palestinian group, living in the homeland, and being part of Israel but not part of the Palestinian core (the West Bank and Gaza Strip). The 1967 occupation and even the 1987 intifada did not reverse, stop, or slow down this historical process. Naturalized and non-refugee Palestinians outside the core, especially citizens of Israel, Jordan, and countries in the West are permanently settled and are not likely to move to the State of Palestine if it were established. This is inherent in the very emergence of a diaspora community.

The positive impact of the Palestinian internal divergence on the need felt by Israeli Arabs to reconcile themselves with life as a permanent minority was redoubled by the continuous shift of the Palestinians away from rejectionism since the late 1970s. No doubt, the watershed was the PLO's renunciation of terrorism and its acceptance, in late 1988 of a two-state solution, Israel's right to exist, and UN resolution 242. These and the conspicuous non-participation of Israeli Arabs in the intifada set the Palestinian citizens of Israel apart from the rest of the Palestinian people. Since then, they have increasingly been considered by their brethren as Israeli Palestinians, permanently settled in Israel, who should fight for equal rights within the Jewish state and to work for amicable coexistence with the Jews. The non-Israeli Palestinians do not see the Arab minority problem as an integral component of the wider Palestinian question, would not like to overburden the Palestinian agenda with it, do not want Israeli Arabs to join the intifada, feel that any move that might upset Arab-

Jewish relations could be misused by Israel as a pretext not to disengage from the occupied territories, and wish Israeli Arabs to serve as a lobby for them in Israeli politics. Some of the non-citizen Palestinians even go as far as to suggest that Israeli Arabs have to come to terms with Israel as a Jewish-Zionist state. These developments on the Palestinian scene have legitimized Israel in the eyes of Israeli Arabs and intensified their struggle for peace and equality, rather than alienated them from the state.

Jewish democracy and the Palestinian question will continue to be the chief factors shaping Arab-Jewish relations in Israel for years to come. Despite the ascendance of the radical right during the 1980s, the Israeli political system continues to function as a viable democracy. In the aftermath of the Gulf War, and in spite of Palestinian wrongdoing during the gulf crisis, the continuing intifada, and the extraordinary settlement drive by Israel's nationalist government during 1990-91, the peace process seems in late 1991 to be moving another significant step forward. On the other hand, the mass-immigration of Soviet Jews to Israel is driving a wedge between Arabs and Jews. At least in the short-run and before appreciable and sustained economic growth occurs, the Arabs will be doubly hurt both as Israelis by the depletion of resources (rise in unemployment, cuts in services, shortages in development funds, and inflationary pressures) and as Arabs by their institutionally vulnerable minority status (the expansion of Jewish settlement in Arab areas, preferential treatment of Jews in the allocation of jobs and other resources, and the diminution of the Arabs' demographic and electoral power). The spread of the Islamic Movement will also have some adverse effect. The Movement frowns on Arab secularization, pursues institutional separation and autonomy for the Arabs, and revives lingering Arab doubts about the status of Moslems as a minority in a Jewish state Yet, it is doubtful whether the Islamic Movement will become rejectionist and seek confrontation with the state because its leaders are keenly aware of the constraints imposed by Israel and by the increasingly Israelized Arab population.

These research findings and suggested explanations do not imply that Israeli Arabs have successfully accommodated themselves to the Jewish state and they are content with life as Arabs in Israel, or that Israel need not make any major change in order to improve and stabilize Arab-Jewish coexistence. The central thesis of the study is, rather, that the common views that the Arabs are radical and radicalizing and Jews are intransigent and hardening their orientation toward the Arabs are not substantiated by the available evidence. Put differently, the Arab minority poses to Israel a genuine and difficult problem that can be managed or reduced but is bound to remain insoluble. The Israeli case is a special combination of a common minority problem (cultural disadvantages, ethnic inequality, prejudice, discrimination, and other structural disabilities faced by the minority) with the contradictions built into ethnic democracies where the minority is also handicapped by institutionalized ethnic dominance. In the final analysis, Israel is a state of and for Jews. As such it cannot accord full equality to the Arabs who, in turn, cannot fully identify themselves with the Jewish state.

What can and must be done to manage the Arab minority problem? Various solutions have been offered by different political groups in Israel. One extreme option, with a secular version advocated by the Sons of the Village Movement and a religious version endorsed by some circles in the Islamic Movement, is the formation of a Palestinian state in the entire area of Palestine instead of Israel Another extreme option is the involuntary transfer of the Arab population outside Israel to achieve a purely Jewish state according to Kach's vision. Still, another radical possibility, preferred by some Jewish intellectuals and probably the Communist Party, is to transform Israel into an Israeli state with a new Israeli nationality common to both Arabs and Jews and with free intermixing. Another radical option is a binational state in which the two communities will enjoy equal collective status, Jewish dominance in state and public institutions will be eliminated, resources will be allocated proportionately, and Arabs will be granted autonomy. Although this vision is currently not espoused by any political movement or party in Israel, it actually represents the wishful thinking of many Israeli Arabs. Close to the hearts of many Jewish supporters of the radical right is the idea of turning Israel into a minimally democratic, Jewish state by denying democracy to the Arabs when it conflicts with Jewish interests, establishing a formal system of control over the Arabs, disenfranchising Arabs who do not render a military or civic service, and deporting Arabs who perpetrate sabotage.

All these ideas are not real options because of their substantial digression from the status quo and lack of mass support. The Jewish political mainstream (the Zionist left, Labor, Likud, and most of the religious parties) stand for keeping Israel a democratic Jewish state, characterized by Jewish dominance, Jewish majority, strong ties with Jews abroad, separate identity for Arabs and Jews, extension of preference to Jews in selected areas, and conferral of full individual rights but only limited group rights to the Arabs. On the other hand, the Arab political mainstream (Democratic Front for Peace and Equality, Progressive List for Peace, and Democratic Arab Party) seems to promote the goal of a recognized national minority in a democratic Jewish state. This is an option that falls between the democratic Jewish state option and the binational state option. It provides Arabs with national collective rights such as institutional autonomy, officially recognized leadership and organizations, and receipt of a proportional piece of the national pie. The Jews object because they are reluctant to compromise their dominance and are afraid of Arab secessionism.

Two proposals for significantly reforming Arab-Jewish coexistence are worth mentioning. One is set forth by a team from the Van Leer Jerusalem Foundation (1990). It calls for a new covenant between Arabs and Jews based on the principle of "shared civility," namely, the expansion of the role of citizenship in resource-allocation and culture. In essence, according to this scheme the Arabs should render civil, in lieu of military, service and accept Israel's Jewish-Zionist character in exchange for Jewish respect for their culture, a policy of non-discrimination, and the state's commitment to close the gaps in the level of services between the two sectors. The other policy proposal by Dror (1989) provides for encouraging Arabs to assimilate into Jewish culture and society, creating a status of a non-voting permanent resident for Arabs who wish to be part of the political life of the State of Palestine, and officially recognizing the Arab minority as an autonomous sub-nationality entitled to its own institutions and symbols but also more integrated into the state. Dror suggests the incorporation of Arab elements into the state Jewish symbols (for instance, the addition of a crescent to a corner of Israel's Star of David flag).

These proposals move in the right direction because they expand the consociational arrangements in Israeli democracy, without shifting to a binational state, and allow Arabs more freedom of choice. To manage the Arab minority problem, Israel thus should accept the Arabs' demand for a recognized minority status, recognize their Palestinian nationalism (identity, culture, and education), shift to non-discriminatory policies, institute a bill of individual rights and minority protection, and add some neutral and Arab elements to the state system of symbols in order to enable Arabs to at least partly identify themselves with the state. Such changes will keep Israel a Jewish and a democratic state but with a balance fairer to the Arabs. The new deal will, of course, require a permanent settlement of the Palestinian question through Israel's disengagement from most of the areas in the West Bank and Gaza Strip. The resolution of the wider dispute will allow Arabs to join the Israeli army and thus to remove a main stumbling block that constantly strains their relations with the state and Jews. In the event of peace, Israeli Arabs will step up their struggle for equality and national rights. Concessions made to them will strengthen Israeli democracy without dismantling the Jewish character and Zionist mission of the state.

Part Five

APPENDIXES

A

Methodology of the Surveys

Since each of the volumes on the 1976 and 1980 surveys (Appendix A in Smooha, 1984 and 1989) contains a special, detailed account of the methodology and problems involved in conducting the surveys, especially the Arab ones, a brief review and evaluation of the procedures applied in the 1985 and 1988 surveys will suffice here.

Procedures

Measuring Instrument

A questionnaire, consisting of closed questions, served as the measuring instrument. With one form in Arabic and another in Hebrew, it served Arabs and Jews. Most of the questions were identical, but some were either deleted or adjusted for each respective group. The parallel questionnaire forms were pre-tested on small samples prior to the fieldwork.

The Arabic questionnaire included 189 items in 1985 and 227 in 1988; the Hebrew questionnaire contained 163 and 194 items, respectively, most of which were attitudinal questions on Arab-Jewish relations. About 80 questions in 1985 and in 1988 were the same as in the 1980 survey, and 50 were the same as in the 1976 survey.

The English translation of the questionnaires appears in Appendix B and Appendix C.

Population and Sampling

The population was defined as Arabs and Jews, 18 years old and older, living in Israel within the pre-1967 borders. It excluded non-Arab minorities (Circassians, Bahais, and European Christians), the Palestinian Arab residents of East Jerusalem, Druzes and Jews in the Golan Heights, and Palestinians and Jewish settlers on the West Bank and Gaza Strip.

The sampling framework for the Arab population consisted of all the Arab permanent localities, Bedouin encampments, and mixed Arab-Jewish towns. These clusters were stratified according to region, population size, municipal status, religious composition, level of services, and percentage vote for the Democratic Front for Peace and Equality and the Progressive List for Peace in the 1984 Knesset elections. Of all the stratified Arab localities and mixed towns, 44 were selected in 1985 and 41 in 1988. With minor exceptions, these localities were identical to those in the 1980 sample.

The official list of eligible voters published in May 1985 by the Ministry of the Interior was used to draw a systematic random sample of Arabs from each locality sampled in the 1985 survey. Similarly, the 1988 sample was drawn from an updated, complete population registration list provided by the Ministry of the Interior. The number of respondents in each locality was proportional to its population size.

The Jewish sample, which included 33 localities in both 1985 and 1988, represented a cross-section of 859 towns and villages of various population size, municipal status, region, and voting pattern. In each selected locality, some residential quarters were sampled; and in each chosen quarter, some dwelling units were sampled and the persons living in them were polled by interviewers according to pre-set randomized procedures.

Table A1 lists all the localities included in the 1976, 1980, 1985, and 1988 Arab samples, their social profiles, and the number of interviews actually completed in each. Table A2 does the same with regard to the 1980, 1985, and 1988 Jewish samples.

Fieldwork

Some 1,200 persons were interviewed from each population (1,203 Arabs and 1,204 Jews in 1985; 1,200 Arabs and 1,209 Jews in 1988). The interviews with Arabs were conducted in Arabic by Arab interviewers from mid-May to the end of June 1985 and in March-April 1988; the interviews with Jews were completed in Hebrew by Jewish interviewers during June 1985 and March-April 1988.

Interviewers in the Arab survey were university students hailing from the same locality in which they interviewed (in 44% of the cases in 1985 and 40% in 1988, interviewer and respondent were acquaintances). They were briefed, and their first completed interview was checked. Of the Arab respondents, 82% in 1985 and 75% in 1988 appeared in the original name list and the rest were substitutes (who were, in turn, chosen from a pre-selected random name list). It was necessary to use substitutes for various reasons: change of address, sojourn outside place of residence, misspelled names, sickness, refusal, and so forth.

Table A1 Localities Surveyed in the 1976-88 Arab Samples and Their Statistical Profiles[a]

Locality	Religious Composition	Region	Municipal Status	Population in Thousands	% Vote for DEPE & PLP	Level of Services	1976 Sample[b]	1980 Sample[b]	1985 Sample[b]	1988 Sample[b]
1. Haifa	6	1	1	19.8	51.2	3	37	66	65	73
2. Lod	1	3	1	8.1	31.2	2	27	29	20	19
3. Akko (Acre)	2	1	1	8.3	61.9	2	–	13	19	21
4. Tel-Aviv-Yafo	7	3	1	10.8	43.6	2	–	12	14	14
5. Nazareth	7	1	1	49.4	64.3	3	48	91	96	114
6. Shefaram	7	1	1	19.4	57.1	3	27	42	45	32
7. Tira	1	2	2	12.7	74.8	3	27	28	29	30
8. Baka Al-Gharbia	1	2	2	13.2	41.2	3	29	30	30	29
9. Sakhnin	2	1	2	14.8	77.2	3	28	65	66	66
10. Majd Al-Khrum	1	1	2	7.1	59.2	3	30	32	30	32
11. Daliat Al-Karmel	3	1	2	9.5	10.1	3	20	28	30	30
12. Kfar Yasif	7	1	2	5.8	75.9	3	26	29	30	30
13. Um Al-Fahem	1	2	1	23.1	66.7	3	–	34	31	31
14. Tayba	1	2	2	19.5	64.4	3	–	40	42	42
15. Yirka	3	1	2	7.5	12.1	3	–	14	15	12
16. Kfar Kana[c]	2	1	2	9.7	52.6	3	–	9	21	21
17. Maker	2	1	2	5.7	67.3	1	30	53	28	27
18. Ein Mahel	1	1	2	6.0	51.2	2	28	30	30	29
19. Jat[c]	1	2	2	5.4	44.0	3	28	29	31	30
20. Jisser Al-Zarka	1	3	2	6.0	6.4	1	25	24	25	24
21. Julis	3	1	2	3.5	0.8	2	19	25	26	27
22. Meilya	5	1	2	2.0	53.9	3	25	21	27	27
23. Pkiein	4	1	2	3.3	39.5	3	–	18	19	20
24. Fassuta	5	1	2	2.2	32.9	2	–	16	18	16
25. Faradies	1	3	2	6.2	5.7	2	–	27	30	28
26. Nahaf	1	1	2	5.5	61.0	1	–	26	27	27
27. Marja	1	2	4	0.5	30.0	1	8	27	14	16
28. Naora	1	1	4	1.0	14.5	1	18	23	25	25
29. Sheikh Danun[d]	1	1	3	1.3	60.0	1	16	25	26	28
30. Sajur	3	1	3	2.1	1.2	1	15	24	25	24
31. Eilut	1	1	4	*	*	1	16	15	17	17
32. Buayna	1	1	2	4.0	43.1	1	19	20	20	18
33. Akbara	1	1	4	*	40.3	2	7	10	9	10
34. Mouawiya	1	2	4	1.5	73.0	1	21	20	27	28
35. Bartaa	1	2	4	1.4	11.0	1	–	30	29	21
36. Kabul[e]	1	1	2	5.5	60.0	2	–	–	30	29
37. Busmat-Tivon	1	1	2	4.0	10.7	2	22	29	31	31
38. Hilf	1	1	4	0.6	5.9	1	13	15	17	17
39. Saayda Um Al-Ghnam	1	1	4	0.8	4.5	1	12	10	16	16
40. Huzayil	1	4	4	*	7.6	1	18	20	11	–
41. Aatzam	1	4	4	*	4.0	1	17	19	16	–
42. Abu Rabiaa	1	4	4	*	1.3	1	–	20	12	–
43. Atawna	1	4	4	*	16.7	1	–	19	15	–
44. Rahat[f]	1	4	2	16.8	14.7	2	–	–	19	34
45. Tel Sheva[g]	1	4	2	4.4	3.7	1	–	–	–	35
Total							656	1,140	1,203	1,200

* Not available.

[a] Statistical profiles reflect the situation in 1988.

[b] Interviews with 18-year-olds and older only (excluding 16-17 years old – 66 in 1976 and 45 in 1980).

[c] Because of an intense hamula feud during the fieldwork period, some of the interviews in 1980 were conducted elsewhere.

[d] Ibtin was surveyed instead in 1976 and 1980.

[e] Kabul was added in 1985 to replace half of the quota for Maker.

[f] Rahat was added in 1985 as a settled Bedouin community in the Negev.

[g] Tel Sheva was added in 1988 as a settled Bedouin community in the Negev to replace Huzayil, Aatzam, Abu Rabiaa, and Atawna. These dwindling, scattered Bedouin encampments are settling down in the Bedouin towns of Rahat and Tel Sheva.

Key to Codes in Table

Religious composition: 1. Moslem; 2. mixed, with Moslem majority; 3. Druze; 4. mixed, with Druze majority; 5. Christian; 6. mixed, with Christian majority; 7. mixed, with no majority.

Region: 1. The Galilee; 2. Triangle; 3. Center; 4. Negev.

Municipal status: 1. Municipality; 2. local council; 3. regional council; 4. unincorporated.

Population in thousands: As of end of 1987.

% vote for DFPE and PLP: % of the votes in the 1988 Knesset elections cast for the Democratic Front for Peace and Equality and the Progressive List for Peace.

Level of local services: 1. Low; 2. medium; 3. high.

Whereas the fieldwork in the Arab survey was administered by the research team operating from the University of Haifa, the Jewish survey was contracted to the Dahaf Research Institute, headed by a noted pollster, Dr. Mina Zemah.

Table A2 Localities Surveyed in the 1980-88 Jewish Samples and Their Statistical Profiles

Locality	District	Type	Population in Thousands	% Vote for Right and Religious	1980 Sample	1985 Sample	1988 Sample
1. Tel-Aviv-Yafo	5	1	319.5	51.2	189	147	168
2. Jerusalem	1	1	346.1	66.7	86	85	112
3. Haifa	3	1	223.2	43.4	104	117	82
4. Beer Sheva	6	3	114.6	64.0	39	40	33
5. Ramat Gan	5	2	115.6	51.3	82	81	69
6. Bene Berak	5	2	107.4	86.3	38	20	44
7. Herzliya	5	2	70.2	48.7	34	29	35
8. Holon	5	2	143.6	53.9	101	88	72
9. Petah Tikva	4	2	132.1	60.0	63	64	57
10. Netanya	4	2	114.4	63.8	45	49	–
11. Rishon Letzion	4	2	120.1	54.0	53	72	42
12. Pardes Hana	3	4	16.2	65.2	32	45	20
13. Teveria (Tiberias)	2	2	30.8	79.1	28	25	30
14. Ramle	4	3	43.9	67.3	28	37	25
15. Ashdod	6	3	72.9	71.2	36	23	46
16. Zikhron Yaacov	3	4	5.6	60.4	–	18	–
17. Yavne	4	5	20.1	72.9	23	13	15
18. Rosh Haayin	4	5	11.6	87.4	21	33	11
19. Raanana	4	4	48.0	45.6	16	44	18
20. Afula	2	2	24.2	69.9	27	28	27
21. Beit-Shean	2	5	13.0	82.2	25	28	49
22. Beit-Shemesh	1	5	14.0	75.5	11	11	-
23. Dimona	6	3	25.4	75.2	17	16	27
24. Akko (acre)	2	3	37.2	58.4	30	–	10
25. Kiryat Yam	3	2	31.7	59.9	31	–	–
26. Ofakim	6	5	13.3	78.5	–	–	13
27. Rehovot	4	2	71.9	53.2	–	–	46
28. Ramat Hasharon	4	4	35.4	39.2	–	–	25
29. Kiriat Bialik	3	4	32.4	48.9	–	–	29
30. Ashteol	1	7	0.4	89.8	–	15	–
31. Kfar Bialik	3	6	0.6	28.5	–	13	–
32. Burgata	4	7	0.4	27.6	–	14	–
33. Haniel	4	6	0.3	28.8	–	12	–
34. Yad Rambam	4	9	0.5	92.4	–	8	–
35. Gilgal	4	9	0.6	16.3	–	4	–
36. Maayan Zvi	3	8	0.6	6.2	–	4	–
37. Kfar Massarik	3	8	0.7	1.2	–	8	12
38. Hatzerim	6	8	0.7	4.3	–	7	–
39. Mishmar Hanegev	6	8	0.7	2.9	10	8	–
40. Hahotrim	3	9	0.6	2.2	10	–	–
41. Gaash	4	9	0.6	0.9	10	–	–
42. Kiryat Anavim	1	8	0.4	6.4	10	–	–
43. Tzofit	4	6	0.4	16.7	11	–	–
44. Bareket	4	7	0.5	99.3	11	–	–
45. Beit-Yitzhak	4	6	1.3	20.0	9	–	–
46. Ben Shemen	4	7	0.3	32.2	11	–	–
47. Brosh	6	7	0.3	78.0	10	–	–
48. Geva Karmel	3	7	0.4	34.4	11	–	–
49. Ora	1	7	0.4	65.3	–	–	6
50. Hemed	4	7	0.4	85.9	–	–	15
51. Herev Leaet	4	7	0.4	54.5	–	–	22
52. Peduyim	6	7	0.3	76.0	–	–	17
53. Beit–Hagdi	6	7	0.5	97.4	–	–	5
54. Ramat Yohanan	2	8	0.6	4.4	–	–	15
55. Kfar–Menahem	2	9	0.6	0.2	–	–	8
Not known, other					4	1	4
Total					1,267	1,204	1,209

Key to Codes in Table:

District: 1. Jerusalem; 2. Northern; 3. Haifa; 4. Central; 5. Tel–Aviv; 6. Southern.

Type: 1. Three largest cities; 2. municipality settled by Jews before 1948; 3. municipality settled by Jews since 1948; 4. urban settlement settled by Jews before 1948; 5. urban settlement settled by Jews since 1948; 6. Moshav established before 1948; 7. Moshav established since 1948; 8. Kibbutz established before 1948; 9. Kibbutz established since 1948.

Population in thousands: As of end of 1987.

% vote for right and religious: % of the votes in the 1988 Knesset elections cast for Likud, Tehiya, Tsomet, Moledet, Shas, Agudat Israel, Degel Hatora, and the National Religious Party.

A Leadership Survey

The 1985 study also included interviews, based on the same standard questionnaires used for the general public, with 137 Arab and 144 Jewish leaders. These 281 public figures were selected to represent 4 political currents in each community (each of the 8 currents was represented by about 35 leaders). Political currents are defined according to affiliation with political parties or movements, and leaders were chosen according to roles or positions they assumed. A strenuous effort was made to select a cross-section from each current and to include the most powerful leaders. The method of selection relied on a combination of office holding and reputational rank in the party. Table A3 gives a breakdown of the leaders interviewed by political affiliation and major role.

Table A3 Classification of Leaders by Political Affiliation and Major Role

	Estab. Affil. Arab Lead.	Unaffil-iated Arab Lead.	DFPE & PLP Arab Lead.	Sons of Village Arab Lead.	DFPE & PLP Jewish Lead.	CRM & Mapam Jewish Lead.	Labor Jewish Lead.	Likud Camp Jewish Lead.
Major role								
Cabinet ministers, deputy ministers							4	
Knesset Members	4				3	9	11	13
Top officials	4	2				2	6	5
Heads of local or regional councils	8	17	5			1	9	11
Top officeholders in parties	12		7		10	6	3	
Other officeholders in parties	3		21	31	8	6	1	1
Intellectuals, scholars, journalists	1	12	8		14	10	6	4
Other		1		1	1			
Total	32	32	41	32	36	34	40	34

The Arab leaders are well internally differentiated. Arabs who were affiliated with Jewish parties were classified as "establishment affiliated Arab leaders." They included Knesset members, heads of local councils, and top office holders in the Jewish parties. Less distinguishable are the so-called "unaffiliated Arab leaders," consisting mainly of heads of local councils and members of the intelligentsia, who are at present politically independent, but in most cases used to be identified with the Zionist establishment. The third current contained Arab leaders of the mixed Arab-Jewish election blocs – the Democratic Front for Peace and Equality and the Progressive List for Peace. They are party officials and intellectuals. The last group consisted of activists in the Sons of the Village Movement. They are young men who do not usually hold any other political role and are hardly considered as leaders by the Arab community at large; notwithstanding their marginality, they still represent a distinct political ideology and style. On the other hand, representatives of the fundamentalist Islamic Movement were not included in the Arab leadership sample, because of their scant political involvement at the time of the 1985 study. They emerged as local politicians only in 1988 and as aspirants for national leadership gradually thereafter.

Beyond the differences in political affiliation and roles, these Arab leaders share much in common. As a whole, they are well educated, relatively young (in their forties), ambitious, articulate, uncoopted, and skillful in the craftsmanship of Israeli politics. They also share a basic consensus on peace and equality (with the diminishing exception of the rejectionist activists in the Sons of the Village Movement) and belong to the forum called the Supreme Follow-Up Committee, where they deliberate matters of interest to all Israeli Arabs. Together they constitute a remarkable leadership corps which stands in a sharp contrast to the traditional Arab notables and hamula heads of the previous generation.

The Jewish leaders are markedly discernable. On the left extreme of the political spectrum are the marginal Jewish public figures who are affiliated with the non-Zionist DFPE and PLP. Many of them are political activists or intellectuals. The second group, known as the Zionist left, is composed of leaders of the Citizens' Rights Movement, Mapam, and Shinui. They included many Knesset Members, party officials, and intellectuals. The Labor Party supplied the third category of leaders consisting of cabinet ministers and deputy ministers, Knesset Members, mayors, and intellectuals. In the last current were included leaders affiliated with the Likud Party, Tehiya, and the religious parties. They were composed mostly of Knesset Members and mayors. This was a group of leaders that did not relish cooperation with the survey - some refused to grant an interview and others felt noticeably uneasy with the questions. On the other hand, the sample of Jewish leaders excluded the extreme right, which was vocally represented at the time by the Kach Movement, for the simple reason that Kach lacked a body of leadership beyond Rabbi Kahane and several of his aides.

The Jewish leaders well represented the wide range of opinions within the broad Jewish Zionist consensus on the Arab minority problem. The dissenting non-Zionist left provides a distinctly different view.

A Special Survey

The 1985 survey, like the previous surveys, drew on standard questionnaires with fixed-choice answers. This technique is adequate for polling quickly and cheaply a large sample of people whose responses are comparable and quantifiable. It tends, however, to cause misunderstandings among the respondents and to present the analysts with difficulties of interpretation.

To overcome some of these obstacles, an additional survey of a different kind was taken during 1986. The respondents were asked to clarify or to explain the standard answers they chose to key questions in the questionnaire. Some respondents were also requested to state freely their stand on Arab-Jewish relations in Israel.

About a hundred such semi-structured interviews were conducted. The quota sampling covered four categories of persons: Arab rank and file, Arab leaders, Jewish rank and file, and Jewish leaders. Together they represented various population groups and the major political streams in the Arab and Jewish sectors.

This special survey, especially the interviews with the leaders, who are expectably more articulate and sophisticated than the general public, provided qualitative material that proved helpful in the interpretation of the statistical survey findings.

Evaluation

Representativeness

The samples in the 1985 and 1988 surveys were representative, with a sampling error of 3%. Based on systematic samples drawn from the electorate roster in 1985 and from the population register in 1988, the Arab surveys were more representative than the Jewish samples, which allowed for interviewers' biases in the final selection of respondents.

Representativeness of the Arab samples is demonstrably evident in the close correspondence (measured by less than a 5% deviation) between the sample statistics and the population parameters reported in official records. As shown in Table A4, this holds true for gender, age, religion, and education, and more or less true even for voting in the 1984 Knesset elections. The 1988 Arab sample is, however, biased in favor of the militants as shown in the over-representation of the 18-29 olds and under-representation of persons without schooling and of voters for Jewish parties.

In contrast, the Jewish sample is less representative. Hardly included were, of course, newcomers and others with insufficient knowledge of Hebrew, who constitute about one tenth of the Jewish population. This bias is universal in public polls in Israel. There were gross under-representations of certain demographic categories (e.g., Jews aged 50 years and older, Jews born abroad, and Jews having fewer than 9 years of schooling); but as shown in Table A5, this bias was corrected by weighting the original samples. More serious are the under-representation of voters for the religious parties and the over-representation of voters for Labor and affiliated parties in the 1985 survey. The under-representation of religious Jews causes a liberal-tolerant bias in the figures of the Jewish public in 1985. Zemah, the pollster who was in charge of the fieldwork for the Jewish surveys, claimed that people tend to over-report voting for winning parties, as was the case with the Labor Party, which headed the government when the 1985 survey was taken a year after the 1984 elections. As for the under-representation of religious Jews in 1985, she suggested that it was due to a call by rabbis, following the 1984 elections, not to participate in public opinion polls.

Table A4 Representativeness of the 1985 and 1988 Arab Samples

	The 1985 Survey			The 1988 Survey		
	Sample	Population	Difference	Sample	Population	Difference
Men	54.3	50.0	+4.3	53.8	50.1	+3.7
Age						
18-29	49.2	49.5	-0.3	51.8	45.3	+6.5
30-49	36.1	35.8	+0.3	32.4	36.2	-3.8
50+	14.7	14.7	0.0	15.8	18.5	-2.7
Religion						
Druze	9.6	9.8	-0.2	9.6	9.6	0.0
Christian	14.4	14.4	0.0	14.6	12.8	+1.8
Moslem	76.0	75.8	+0.2	75.8	77.6	-1.8
Years of schooling						
0	15.3	17.0	-1.7	7.8	15.2	-7.4
1-8	42.2	43.8	-1.6	38.3	37.9	+0.4
9-12	32.1	29.1	+3.0	41.7	38.0	+3.7
13+	10.4	10.1	+0.3	12.2	8.9	+3.3
Voting in the 1984 Knesset elections						
DFPE	38.3	33.0	+5.3	36.7	33.0	+3.7
PLP	15.3	18.0	-2.7	19.5	18.0	+1.5
Jewish parties	46.4	49.0	-2.6	43.8	49.0	-5.2

Reliability

The surveys yielded stable, consistent answers. The interviewers rated the degree of comprehension shown by the respondents as adequate: for the Arabs in 1985 – 80% full or reasonable understanding, 18% a certain lack of understanding, and only 2% a lack of understanding (in 1988, the figures were 80%, 16%, and 4%, respectively); for the Jews in 1985 - 78%, 19%, and 3% (and 82%, 16%, and 2% in 1988), respectively. The responses were also consistent from one item to the next. For instance, in the 1985 survey, when respondents were asked at the beginning of the interview which of several Arabic newspapers they read during the past week, 43% of the Arabs reported reading *Al-Ittihad*; when asked again at the end of the interview if they read *Al-Ittihad*, 41% answered positively.

To ensure against falsifications, 18% of all the Arab respondents and 56.5% of all the Jewish respondents in 1985 (and 15% and 28%, respectively, in 1988) were recontacted (the Arabs in person and the Jews by phone) by the fieldwork supervisors. Since these checks covered all interviewers, it is unlikely that the final data included forgeries.

Table A5 Representativeness of the 1985 and 1988 Jewish Samples

	The 1985 Survey			The 1988 Survey		
	Sample	Population	Difference	Sample	Population	Difference
Men	50.8	49.5	+1.3	51.3	49.7	+1.6
Father's place of birth, age and years of schooling						
Israel, 18-34, 0-8	0.1	0.2	-0.1	0.1	0.1	0.0
Israel, 18-34, 9-12	2.7	2.5	+0.2	3.3	3.3	0.0
Israel, 18-34, 13+	1.7	1.4	+0.3	2.0	2.0	0.0
Israel, 35-54, 0-8	0.2	0.2	0.0	0.2	0.2	0.0
Israel, 35-54, 9-12	0.6	0.6	0.0	0.8	0.8	0.0
Israel, 35-54, 13+	0.5	0.5	0.0	0.7	0.7	0.0
Israel, 55+, 0-8	0.2	0.2	0.0	0.3	0.3	0.0
Israel, 55+, 9-12	0.2	0.2	0.0	0.3	0.3	0.0
Israel, 55+, 13+	0.1	0.1	0.0	0.2	0.2	0.0
Asia-Africa, 18-34, 0-8	3.2	3.6	-0.4	1.9	1.9	0.0
Asia-Africa, 18-34, 9-12	16.5	16.4	+0.1	15.3	15.3	0.0
Asia-Africa, 18-34, 13+	4.5	4.3	+0.2	5.1	5.1	0.0
Asia-Africa, 35-54, 0-8	7.2	7.6	-0.4	6.2	6.2	0.0
Asia-Africa, 35-54, 9-12	6.5	6.0	+0.5	8.0	8.0	0.0
Asia-Africa, 35-54, 13+	1.9	1.7	+0.2	2.6	2.6	0.0
Asia-Africa, 55+, 0-8	7.1	7.2	-0.1	7.1	7.1	0.0
Asia-Africa, 55+, 9-12	1.6	1.5	+0.1	2.2	2.2	0.0
Asia-Africa, 55+, 13+	0.5	0.5	0.0	0.6	0.6	0.0
Europe-America, 18-34, 0-8	0.5	0.5	0.0	0.4	0.4	0.0
Europe-America,18-34, 9-12	6.0	6.5	-0.5	5.2	5.2	0.0
Europe-America, 18-34, 13+	6.7	6.9	-0.2	6.2	6.2	0.0
Europe-America, 35-54, 0-8	1.4	1.8	-0.4	1.0	1.0	0.0
Europe-America, 35-54, 9-12	5.5	5.5	0.0	5.6	5.6	0.0
Europe-America, 35-54, 13+	7.4	6.9	+0.5	8.1	8.1	0.0
Europe-America, 55+, 0-8	7.2	7.7	-0.5	6.7	6.7	0.0
Europe-America, 55+, 9-12	6.3	6.3	0.0	6.5	6.5	0.0
Europe-America, 55+, 13+	3.6	3.2	+0.4	3.8	3.8	0.0
Voting in the 1984 Knesset elections						
DFPE, PLP	0.4	0.4	0.0	0.1	0.4	-0.3
CRM, Shinui	6.4	5.0	+1.4	7.0	5.0	+2.0
Labor, Yahad, Ometz	46.6	39.2	+7.4	39.9	39.2	+0.7
Likud	33.1	34.9	-1.8	38.4	34.9	+3.5
Religious parties	5.6	12.1	-6.5	9.1	12.1	-3.0
Tehiya, Kach	6.9	5.8	+1.1	4.6	5.8	-1.2
Other lists	1.0	2.6	-1.6	0.9	2.6	-1.7

Validity

Doubts are often raised whether the respondents, especially the Arabs, gave their "true" opinions. Since Arabs may feel fearful of expressing views hostile to the regime and since most distrust Jews, many might misrepresent their replies.

Despite this possible built-in slant toward accommodation in the Arab data, several considerations assure us that the credibility and correctness of the Arab responses should not be questioned and that they are on a par with the Jewish replies. First, the interviewers' assessments were quite encouraging. Only 11% of the Arab respondents in both 1985 and 1988 were seen by their interviewers as somewhat mistrustful; likewise, only 4.5% in 1985 and 5% in 1988 of the Arab respondents, compared with 5% and 3% of the Jewish respondents, were judged to have provided unsatisfactory or partially invalid information.

Second, in view of the results, it is doubtful that apprehension and self-restraint critically suppressed answers that the other side would consider extremist. To illustrate, in the 1985 surveys, 29% of the Arabs endorsed PLO terrorist actions against the Israeli Army within the Green Line and 36% of the Jews endorsed Jewish terrorist actions against Israeli Arabs who perpetrated nationalist terrorist actions against Israeli Jews.

Third, the surveys distinguished well between groups that are known to differ. Druzes and Galilee Bedouin were predictably less militant than other Arabs. Arabs who were affected by land expropriations or who voted for non-Jewish parties were clearly more radical in orientation than others. Similarly, Jews who reported voting for the Likud, Tehiya, religious, and Kach parties were found to be markedly more anti-Arab and hawkish than other Jews.

Fourth, the virtual constancy of the answers across the 1976-88 surveys on items that are not supposed to vary over time demonstrates the credibility of the material. To illustrate, the proportion of Israeli Arabs today whose families became displaced or internal refugees as a result of the 1948 war was 23.5% according to the 1976 survey, 21% according to the 1980 survey, 20% according to the 1985 survey, and 18% according to the 1988 survey.

Conclusion

It is safe to conclude that the various methodological tests show that the 1985 and 1988 surveys, like the previous ones, produced sound data for both Arabs and Jews.

Apart from the obvious lending of credence to the research findings themselves, this conclusion suggests two broader implications. One implication is that Israelization, which in this context means adoption of Israeli modern standards of thinking and behavior, has already reached an advanced stage among Israeli Arabs. The other implication is that democratization has also progressed to such a degree as to enable Israeli Arabs to express themselves as free citizens. Without the maturation of these two processes since the mid-1970s, survey research could not have succeeded among the Arabs of Israel.

B

The 1985 Questionnaire

Following is an English translation of the questionnaire used for interviewing both Arabs and Jews. Except where indicated, the Arabic-language questionnaire was identical in content and form to the Hebrew-language version. Questions that were presented to Arabs only are marked by an asterisk, and those posed to Jews only are identified by two asterisks. To save space, identical answers to a series of questions are occasionally reproduced in the first question only. The item numbers here are the variable numbers used in the codebook of the computerized records rather than the original numbers in the questionnaire. For this reason there are gaps in the numbers although all items are reproduced as they appear in the original questionnaire.

Interviewer's Introduction to Arab Respondents

The Department of Sociology and Anthropology at the University of Haifa is conducting a survey of Arab-Jewish relations in Israel. For this purpose, 1,200 persons, representing Arabs all over the country, were chosen. You are one of those who were randomly selected for this sample. A similar sample of Jews was also selected for the study. The goal of the research is to ascertain the attitudes of Arabs and Jews toward each other.

All of the information that you provide will be used for scientific objectives only. Your answers will serve to understand better the situation of Arabs in Israel, and hence your cooperation is very important.

The questions that I will present to you do not have right or wrong answers. The purpose is to learn about your stands on a number of topics. I hope that you will take this opportunity to express your opinions freely.

I will read to you the question and the answers related to it, and you are requested to choose the answer that suits you most.

Interviewer's Introduction to Jewish Respondents

I am an interviewer from the Dahaf Research Institute, which is an independent institute for social research. We conduct public opinion polls on various subjects. You were randomly selected as one respondent. Your answers will remain anonymous and be used for scientific objectives only.

The subject matter of the survey this time is Arab-Jewish relations in Israel. The goal of the study is to ascertain the attitudes of Jews toward the Arabs of Israel; i.e., the Arabs who are Israeli citizens and live within the Green Line.

Every question has a number of answers, and you are requested to choose, only after hearing all the possible answers, the one that suits you most.

Text of Questionnaire

1 *Case number.*

6 *To what extent are you interested in problems relating to relations between Jews and Arabs in Israel?*
1 Much — 2 To an appreciable degree
3 To some degree — 4 No

7 *(For Arab respondents:) How often do you have contact with Jews? (For Jewish respondents: "Jews" reads "Arabs.")*
1 Daily — 2 Quite often — 3 Sometimes — 4 Almost never

8 *(For Arab respondents:) Do you have Jewish friends and have you visited their homes over the past two years? (For Jewish respondents: "Jewish" reads "Arab.")*
1 Have no Jewish/Arab friends
2 Have Jewish/Arab friends but have not visited them
3 Have Jewish/Arab friends and have visited their homes over the past two years

9 *(For Arab respondents:) Are you willing to have Jewish friends? (For Jewish respondents: "Jewish" reads "Arab.")*
1 Definitely willing
2 Willing
3 Willing, but prefer Arab/Jewish friends
4 Want to have Arab/Jewish friends only

10 *Are you willing to have your own children or the children of your close family attend a mixed Arab-Jewish classroom?*
1 Definitely willing — 2 Willing
3 Willing, but prefer Arabs/Jews — 4 Want Arabs/Jews only

11** *Are you willing to have an Arab as your own personal doctor?*
1 Definitely willing — 2 Willing
3 Willing, but prefer a Jew — 4 Want a Jew only

12** *Are you willing to work in a place where Arabs and Jews work together?*
1 Definitely willing 2 Willing
3 Willing, but prefer Jews 4 Want Jews only

13** *Are you willing to have an Arab as your superior in a job?*
1 Definitely willing 2 Willing
3 Willing, but prefer a Jew 4 Want a Jew only

14 *Are you willing to live in a mixed neighborhood?*
1 Definitely willing 2 Willing
3 Willing, but prefer Arabs/Jews 4 Want Arabs/Jews only

15 *Are you against or for the possibility that in addition to the separate schools for Arabs and Jews, there will also be new elementary schools where Arabs and Jews who so wish will have their children study in mixed classrooms and in both languages?*
1 Against 2 For

16 *Are you against or for new mixed neighborhoods where Arabs and Jews who so wish will live together?*
1 Against 2 For

17 *Do you think that residential quarters should be separate for Arabs and Jews?*
1 Yes 2 Uncertain 3 No

18 *Do you know how to read and write in Arabic (i.e., can you write a simple letter in Arabic)?*
1 Yes 2 No

19* *Which Arabic newspaper did you read last week?*
1 Did not read any newspaper, but can read Arabic
2 *Al-Ittihad*
3 *Al-Thadamun*
4 An East Jerusalem newspaper
5 *Al-Thadamun* and *Al-Ittihad*
6 *Al-Thadamun* and an East Jerusalem newspaper
7 *Al-Ittihad* and an East Jerusalem newspaper
8 *Al-Ittihad, Al-Thadamun*, and an East Jerusalem newspaper

20* *Which newspapers and broadcasts do you trust most?*
1 Official, non-partisan Israeli newspapers and broadcasts
2 Israeli newspapers of the Jewish left
3 Rakah newspapers
4 Non-Israeli newspapers and broadcasts from the occupied territories, Arab states, or Europe

21 *(For Arab respondents:) Do you know enough Hebrew to conduct a conversation on various matters with an Israeli Jew? (For Jewish respondents: "Hebrew" reads "Arabic," "Jew" reads "Arab.")*
1 Yes 2 No

22 *Do you read and write Hebrew (i.e., can you write a simple letter in Hebrew)?*
1 Yes 2 No

23 *Did you read a Hebrew newspaper last week?*
1 Yes 2 No

24 *What is your opinion of the possibility that modern values and practices will prevail in Israel?*
1 In favor 2 Have reservations 3 Against

25* *Should Arabs in Israel learn modern values and practices from Jews?*
1 Yes 2 Uncertain 3 No

26 *Should Arabs in Israel adopt Jewish values and practices in addition to their own?*
1 In favor 2 Uncertain 3 Against

27 *Should Jews in Israel adopt Arab values and practices in addition to their own?*
1 In favor 2 Uncertain 3 Against

28 *What is your opinion of the possibility that Jews and Arabs should together try to create new common values and practices in addition to their own?*
1 Opposed 2 Tend to oppose 3 Tend to agree 4 Agree

29 *Which type of culture would you wish to have evolve Israel - closer to a Western culture or to an Arab culture?*
1 Distinct Western culture
2 Western culture in which Arab elements are incorporated
3 A mixed culture consisting of Western and Arab elements
4 Arab culture in which Jewish elements are incorporated
5 Distinct Arab culture
6 Opposed to both cultures

30** *Should it be required by law that all street and locality signs be written in both Hebrew and Arabic?*
1 Yes 2 No

31 *Which of the following goals is most desirable for Arab education in Israel today?*
1 To live as a loyal minority member in a Jewish state
2 To love Israel as the common homeland of its two peoples, Arab and Jewish
3 To be a member of the Palestinian people

32 *Which of the following goals is most desirable for Jewish education in Israel today?*
1 To live as a loyal citizen
2 To love Israel as the common homeland of its two peoples, Arab and Jewish
3 To be a member of the Jewish people

33 *(For Arab respondents:) Are you for or against the teaching of Jewish history and culture in Arab schools at a level that would equip any Arab with a good knowledge of Jewish subjects?(For Jewish respondents: "Jewish" reads "Arab" and "Arab" reads "Jewish" or "Jew.")*

1 For 2 Against

34** *Are you for or against the teaching of Arabic in Jewish schools at a level equal to English even if this would require cutting down on other subjects?*

1 For 2 Against

35** *Which language should be the dominant language of the public and state institutions in Israel?*

1 Hebrew 2 Hebrew and Arabic equally 3 Arabic

36 *Should Arab culture be treated as an important part of Israel's national culture?*

1 In favor 2 Have reservations 3 Against

37 *The State of Israel is:*

1 Homeland of Jews only
2 Common homeland of Jews and Arabs
3 Homeland of Arabs only

38** *Should the State of Israel prefer Jews or Arabs?*

1 Prefer Jews to Arabs considerably
2 Prefer Jews to Arabs to some extent
3 Treat both equally
4 Prefer Arabs to Jews to some extent
5 Prefer Arabs to Jews considerably

39** *Should the State of Israel prefer Jews or Arabs in university admissions?*

1 2 3 4 5

40** *Should the state of Israel prefer Jews or Arabs in civil service jobs?*

1 2 3 4 5

41 ** *Should the State of Israel prefer Jews or Arabs in granting social security benefits?*

1 2 3 4 5

42* *Should the State of Israel within the Green Line retain a Jewish majority?*

1 Yes 2 No

43* *Do you accept Israel's right to exist?*

1 Yes 2 Have reservations 3 No

44 *(For Arab respondents:) Should Arabs in Israel resign themselves in principle to a status of a national minority with full civil rights? (for Jewish respondents:) Are you resigned to the Arabs' right to live in Israel as a national minority with full civil rights?*

1 Yes 2 Have reservations 3 No

45 *(For Arab respondents:) Are you resigned to being a minority member in Israel today? (for Jewish respondents:) Are you resigned to the very existence of an Arab minority in Israel today?*

1 Yes 2 Have reservations 3 No

46* *Do you accept Israel's right to exist within the Green Line as a Jewish-Zionist state?*

1 Yes 2 Have reservations 3 No

47 *(For Arab respondents:) It is said that it is all right to use any means necessary to abolish Israel's Jewish-Zionist character. What is you opinion? (To Jewish respondents: "to abolish" reads "to retain.")*

1 Yes 2 Have reservations 3 Against

48** *Do you agree or disagree that a list that both accepts the principles of democracy and Israel's right to exist but opposes its Jewish-Zionist character, should be allowed to run in Knesset elections?*

1 Agree 2 Tend to agree
3 Tend to disagree 4 Disagree

49 *Are you in favor or against the participation in coalition government of existing or new political parties that truly represent the interests of Arabs in Israel?*

1 Definitely in favor 2 In favor
3 Against 4 Definitely Against

50 *After the 1984 Knesset elections the possibility was created of forming a Labor government supported also by the Democratic Front for Peace and Equality (headed by Rakah) and the Progressive List for Peace (headed by Mi'ari and Peled). Are you in principle in favor or against such a government?*

1 Definitely in favor 2 In favor
3 Against 4 Definitely against

51* *The United Nations General Assembly adopted a resolution that Zionism is a racist movement. Do you agree with this resolution?*

1 Agree 2 Have reservations 3 Disagree

52* *What is your opinion of the Law of Return, i.e., the law that accords only to the Jews the right of citizenship upon arrival in Israel?*

1 Retain as is 2 Retain under certain circumstances 3 Repeal

53 *Do you think that Arabs can be equal citizens in Israel as a Jewish-Zionist state and can identify themselves with the state?*

1 Yes 2 Possibly 3 Doubtful 4 No

54** *Should the state impose compulsory or voluntary military service on the Arab citizens?*

1 In favor of compulsory military service
2 In favor of voluntary military service
3 Against

55** *Should the state impose civil service in lieu of military service on the Arabs in Israel?*
1 In favor of compulsory civil service
2 In favor of voluntary civil service
3 Against

56* *If your son (and if you do not have a son, suppose you did) were subject to compulsory military service, would you advise him to serve or to refuse?*
1 Serve 2 Refuse

57* *And if your son were subject to compulsory civil service in lieu of military service, would you advise him to serve or to refuse?*
1 Serve 2 Refuse

58* *And if your son were subject to either compulsory military service or compulsory civil service, what would you advise him to do?*
1 Serve military service 2 Serve civil service 3 Refuse

59 *Should Arabs control and manage their own system of education?*
1 In favor 2 Have reservations 3 Against

60** *Have you heard of the Committee of Heads of Arab Local Councils?*
1 Yes 2 No

61 *Do you consider the Committee of Heads of Arab Local Councils to be truly representative of the interests of Arabs in Israel?*
1 Definitely yes 2 Yes 3 No
4 Definitely no 5 Have not heard of the Committee

62** *What should be the position toward the existing organizing of heads of Arab local councils into a separate committee of their own, in addition to their participation in the Local Government Authority?*
1 Outlaw the Committee 2 Ignore it
3 Negotiate with it without recognizing it 4 Recognize it

The following organizations may be formed by Arabs in Israel and put under their full influence and management. Indicate your opinion of each.

63 *An Arab University.*
1 In favor 2 Have reservations 3 Against

64 *A new Arab radio or television station.*
1 In favor 2 Have reservations 3 Against

65 *An Arab trade union.*
1 In favor 2 Have reservations 3 Against

66 *A new nationalist Arab political party.*
1 In favor 2 Have reservations 3 Against

67 *Which political organization is most desirable for Arabs in Israel under the present circumstances?*

1 To join existing Jewish parties as individuals with equal status
2 To form Arab parties that can reach agreement or cooperate with the existing Jewish parties
3 To belong to non-Zionist parties composed of Arabs and Jews
4 To establish independent nationalist Arab parties
5 No political party organization at all

68 *Do you consider Rakah (Israeli Communist Party) to be truly representative of the interests of Arabs in Israel?*

1 Definitely yes 2 Yes 3 No 4 Definitely no

69 *Do you consider the Progressive List for Peace, headed by Knesset members Mi'ari and Peled, to be truly representative of the interests of Arabs in Israel?*

1 Definitely yes 2 Yes 3 No 4 Definitely no

70* *Do you consider the Committee for Defense of Arab Lands to be truly representative of the interests of Arabs in Israel?*

1 Definitely yes 2 Yes 3 No 4 Definitely no
5 Have not heard of the Committee

71 *In assessing your socioeconomic achievements today, with whom do you compare yourself?*

1 Arabs in Arab countries
2 Arabs in the West Bank and Gaza Strip
3 Inhabitants of the Western World
4 Jews in Israel
5 Palestinian Arabs during Mandatory Palestine

72 *How do you regard the present socioeconomic gap between Jews and Arabs in Israel?*

1 Large 2 Medium 3 Small

73 *How do existing government policies affect the present socioeconomic gap between Jews and Arabs in Israel?*

1 Reduce it 2 Neither reduce nor widen it 3 Widen it

74 *Some say that the Arabs in Israel enjoy equal job opportunities, except in jobs related to national security. What is your opinion?*

1 Agree 2 Have reservations 3 Disagree

75 *Do you think that Arab youth have reasonable chances of fulfilling their occupational aspirations in Israel today?*

1 Yes 2 Possible 3 Doubtful 4 No

76* *To what extent are you satisfied with being an Israeli citizen?*

1 Definitely satisfied 2 Satisfied 3 Not too satisfied
4 Not satisfied 5 Not satisfied at all

77 *Are you satisfied with the cultural and educational services in your place of residence?*
1 Definitely satisfied 2 Satisfied 3 Not too satisfied
4 Not satisfied 5 Not satisfied at all

78 *Is the socioeconomic status of your family better or worse than it was five years ago?*
1 Better 2 Did not change 3 Worse

79 *Do you expect the socioeconomic status of your family in the next five years to be better or worse than it is today?*
1 Better 2 Not to change 3 Worse

80* *Where would you feel more at ease, in Israel or in an Arab country? [See also question 125.]*
1 More in Israel 2 No difference 3 More in an Arab country

81* *Do you feel alien in Israel in your style of life, practices, and values?*
1 To a great degree 2 To a considerable degree
3 To some degree 4 Do not feel alien

82 *(For Arab respondents:) Do you feel that your relations with Jews are on an equal footing?(For Jewish respondents: "Jews" reads "Arabs.")*
1 Always 2 In most cases 3 Often
4 Almost never 5 Have no contact with Jews/Arabs

83 *(For Arab respondents:) When you learn about an action in which an Arab citizen from Israel killed a Jewish citizen on nationalist grounds, how do you feel?(For Jewish respondents: "Arab" reads "Jewish" and "Jewish" reads "Arab.")*
1 Rejoice and justify action
2 Rejoice but do not justify action
3 Sadden but justify action
4 Sadden and do not justify action

Indicate which of the following you consider to be good or bad, and which the Arabs in Israel enjoy or suffer from.

84* *Rise in the standard of living.*
1 Good thing that Arabs enjoy
2 Good thing that Arabs do not enjoy
3 Bad thing that Arabs suffer from
4 Bad thing that Arabs do not suffer from

85* *Social security benefits.*
1 2 3 4

86* *Increase in the standard of education and culture.*
1 2 3 4

87* *The opportunity to develop and modernize.*
1 2 3 4

88* *Change in the status of women.*
1 2 3 4

89* *Democracy.*
1 2 3 4

90* *Greater equality among the Arabs themselves today than formerly.*
1 2 3 4

Let us proceed to questions regarding the Israeli-Arab conflict.

91** *What is your stand on settlements in Judea and Samaria?*
1 In favor 2 Have reservations 3 Against

92** *What is your opinion of the annexation of Judea and Samaria?*
1 In favor of immediate annexation
2 In favor of future annexation 3 Against annexation

93 *What is your stand on the Peace Treaty between Israel and Egypt?*
1 In favor 2 Have reservations 3 Against

94** *Do you consider the Palestinians today to constitute a nation?*
1 Yes 2 No

95** *Do you think that Israel should recognize the Palestinians as a nation?*
1 Yes 2 Only under certain circumstances 3 No

96** *Do you think that the Palestinians have the right to have a state that will include parts of the West Bank and Gaza Strip?*
1 Yes 2 Have reservations 3 No

97 *Are you in favor of establishing a Palestinian state in the West Bank and Gaza Strip alongside Israel?*
1 Yes 2 Only under certain circumstances 3 No

98 *Do you think that Israel should recognize the PLO as the authoritative representative of the Palestinian people?*
1 Yes 2 Only under certain circumstances 3 No

99* *Do you think that the PLO should recognize the State of Israel?*
1 Yes 2 Only under certain circumstances 3 No

(For Arab respondents:) Are you in favor or against each of the following actions carried out today by the PLO against Israeli targets? (For Jewish respondents:) Are you in favor or against each of the following actions?

100 *(For Arab respondents:) Soldiers and military bases in the West Bank, Gaza Strip, and outside Israel. (For Jewish respondents:) Bombing of PLO bases.*
1 In favor 2 Against

101 *(For Arab respondents:) Soldiers and military bases within the Green Line. (For Jewish respondents:) Bombing of refugee camps in retaliation for terrorist attacks.*
1 In favor 2 Against

102 *(For Arab respondents:) Jewish settlers in the West Bank and Gaza Strip. (For Jewish respondents:) Terrorist actions by Jews against Arabs in the territories in retaliation for terrorist attacks.*

1 In favor 2 Against

103 *(For Arab respondents:) Jewish citizens within the Green Line. (For Jewish respondents:) Terrorist actions by Jews against Israeli Arabs in retaliation for terrorist attacks by Israeli Arabs.*

1 In favor 2 Against

104 *Which borders of the State of Israel are you prepared to compromise on in order to reach a peace settlement?*

1 All of Mandatory Palestine where a new state will be established instead of Israel
2 1947 UN partition borders (the Galilee and Triangle not included in Israel)
3 Pre-1967 borders (the Galilee and Triangle included in Israel)
4 Present borders with certain modifications in favor of Israel
5 Present borders with willingness to compromise also in Judea and Samaria
6 Present borders

105 *Should Israel recognize the Palestinian refugees' right of repatriation to Israel within the Green Line?*

1 Yes 2 Only under certain circumstances 3 No

106 *(For Arab respondents:) Should the Palestinians give up the demand for the right of repatriation if this is necessary to reach a peace settlement? (For Jewish respondents:) Should the Jews give up East Jerusalem if this is necessary to reach a peace settlement?*

1 In favor 2 Have reservations 3 Against

107 *Which one of the following political bodies offers the best solution to the Israeli-Arab conflict?*

1 Kach (Kahane's movement)
2 Tehiya, Gush Emunim
3 Likud
4 Labor
5 Citizens' Rights Movement, Peace Now
6 Progressive List for Peace
7 Rakah
8 PLO mainstream (Arafat)
9 Rejection Front

108* *According to the Palestinian National Covenant Jews in Israel today constitute a religious community only, not a people. What is your opinion?*

1 People 2 Religious community only

The following two questions are related to the possibility that the government of Israel would decide to withdraw from most areas of Judea and Samaria for a peace settlement.

109** *If such a decision were taken by a national unity government, including most cabinet ministers of the Likud, how would you react?*
1 Would act against the decision with all means, including violence
2 Would act against the decision with all legal means, including demonstrations and strikes
3 Would act against the decision mostly through persuasion and pressures
4 Would not act at all
5 Would act in favor of the decision

110** *And if the decision on withdrawal were to be taken by a Labor government, how would you react?*
1 Would act against the decision with all means, including violence
2 Would act against the decision with all legal means, including demonstrations and strikes
3 Would act against the decision mostly through persuasion and pressures
4 Would not act at all
5 Would act in favor of the decision

111 *(For Arab respondents:) Do you have relatives in Lebanon? If yes, did anyone of them get hurt in Israel's War in Lebanon? (for Jewish respondents:) Did you, your brother, son, grandson, or father serve in Israel's War in Lebanon? If yes, did anyone of them get hurt in the War?*
1 No 2 Yes, but none got hurt 3 Yes, and someone got hurt

112 *Did Israel's War in Lebanon favorably or adversely affect your attitude toward the State?*
1 Very favorably 2 Somewhat favorably 3 Did not affect
4 Somewhat adversely 5 Very adversely

113 *Did Israel's War in Lebanon strengthen or weaken your belief in Israeli democracy?*
1 Strengthened 2 Did not affect 3 Weakened

114 *Did Israel's War in Lebanon strengthen or weaken your belief in a political (as opposed to a military) solution to the Palestinian question?*
1 Strengthened 2 Did not affect 3 Weakened

115** *One of the goals of Israel's War in Lebanon was to do away with the PLO in Lebanon. Was it justified to go to war for this cause?*
1 Definitely justified 2 Justified 3 Not justified
4 Definitely not justified

116 *Did you participate in protest actions against Israel's War in Lebanon?*
1 Yes 2 No

117 *When thinking of the term "Israeli," whom do you include?*
1 Only Jews 2 Jews and Arabs

118 *Is the term "Israeli" appropriate in describing your identity?*
1 Very appropriate 2. Appropriate 3 Not too appropriate
4 Not appropriate at all

119* *Is the term "Palestinian" appropriate in describing your identity?*
1 Very appropriate 2 Appropriate 3 Not too appropriate
4 Not appropriate at all

120* *Is the term "Israeli Palestinian" appropriate in describing your identity?*
1 Very appropriate 2 Appropriate 3 Not too appropriate
4 Not appropriate at all

121* *How would you define yourself if you had to choose one of the following alternatives?*
1 Arab 2 Palestinian Arab 3 Israeli Arab
4 Israeli 5 Israeli Palestinian
6 Palestinian in Israel or Palestinian Arab in Israel 7 Palestinian

122 *How would you define Arabs in Israel if you had to choose one of the following alternatives?*
1 Arabs 2 Israeli Arabs 3 Israelis
4 Palestinian Arabs 5 Israeli Palestinians
6 Palestinians in Israel or Palestinian Arabs in Israel 7 Palestinians

123 *To whom are Arabs in Israel more similar in style of life and daily behavior?*
1 Arabs in the West Bank and Gaza Strip 2 Jews in Israel

124 *(For Arab respondents:) To whom do you feel closer?*
1 Arabs in the West Bank and Gaza Strip 2 Jews in Israel

(For Jewish respondents:) Are Arabs in Israel more loyal to the State of Israel than are the Arabs in the West Bank and Gaza Strip?
1 Yes 2 No

125* *If you had a choice, where would you feel more at home, in an Arab country or in Israel? [See also question 80.]*
1 In an Arab country 2 In Israel

126* *How many times during the past year did you pay social visits to the West Bank and Gaza Strip?*
1 Never 2 Several times a year 3 Once a month
4 Several times a month 5 Several times a week

127* *How many times during the past year did you pay business visits to the West Bank and Gaza Strip?*
1 Never 2 Several times a year 3 Once a month
4 Several times a month 5 Several times a week

128* *Do you maintain ties with relatives living across the Green Line or in Arab countries?*
1 Yes 2 No, but have relatives there
3 Do not have relatives there

206 *What is your view of Arab self-rule in the Galilee and Triangle?*
1 In favor 2 Have reservations 3 Against

207* *Do you accept the idea that the Galilee and Triangle should remain integral parts of Israel?*
1 Accept 2 Tend to accept 3 Tend to reject 4 Reject

208* *If a Palestinian state were to be established, what should be the future of the Galilee and Triangle?*
1 Integral parts of Israel 2 Parts of a Palestinian state

209 *What is the most appropriate solution to the problem of the Arab minority in Israel?*
1 Arabs will be forced to live outside Israel
2 Arabs will live in Israel only if they are resigned to their minority status in a state designed for Jews
3 Arabs will live in Israel as a national minority with full civil rights
4 Arabs will live in Israel as a national minority recognized by the state and enjoying proper political representation
5 Arabs will live in a Palestinian state to be established in the West Bank, Gaza Strip, the Galilee, and Triangle
6 Arabs will live in a secular-democratic state to be established in all of Palestine instead of Israel

210 *Do you agree or oppose the possibility that Arabs in Israel will organize independently, like Orthodox Jews, in order to advance their vital interests?*
1 Agree 2 Tend to agree 3 Tend to oppose 4 Oppose

211** *Should the closing of the socioeconomic gap between Arabs and Jews be an important and urgent state goal?*
1 Yes, an important and urgent state goal
2 Yes, an important but not urgent state goal
3 Not so important and not so urgent
4 Not important and not urgent

212* *Do you consider the Sons of the Village Movement to be truly representative of the interests of the Arabs in Israel?*
1 Definitely yes 2 Yes 3 No 4 Definitely no

213 *Do you consider the PLO to be truly representative of the interests of the Arabs in Israel?*
1 Definitely yes 2 Yes 3 No 4 Definitely no

214 *To what extent is it possible to improve the Arab situation by acceptable democratic means, such as persuasion and political pressure?*
1 To a great extent 2 To a substantial extent
3 To a certain extent 4 To almost no extent

215* *Are you willing to contribute your time or money for a struggle to change the present situation of Arabs in Israel?*
1 No, not willing
2 No, because it is not necessary
3 No, because of lack of time or money
4 Yes, willing to contribute some
5 Yes, willing to contribute much

Are you in favor, have reservations, or against the use of each of the following means to improve the situation of Arabs in Israel?

216 *Protest actions abroad.*
1 In favor 2 Have reservations 3 Against

217 *General strikes.*
1 In favor 2 Have reservations 3 Against

218 *Boycotts of institutions or plants.*
1 In favor 2 Have reservations 3 Against

219 *Licensed demonstrations.*
1 In favor 2 Have reservations 3 Against

220 *Unlicensed demonstrations.*
1 In favor 2 Have reservations 3 Against

221 *Resistance with force.*
1 In favor 2 Have reservations 3 Against

What is the most appropriate means of struggle that Arabs in Israel should use with regard to each of the following goals?

222* *Equal budgets to Arab and Jewish local councils.*
1 All means, including violence
2 Legal means, including demonstrations and strikes
3 Persuasion and pressures
4 Not a goal for the struggle of Arabs in Israel

223* *Enactment of a special punitive law against discrimination in employment, housing, etc., on religious or national grounds.*
1 2 3 4

224* *Abolition of the special benefits to army veterans and to their families.*
1 2 3 4

225* *Proper compensation for expropriated Arab lands.*
1 2 3 4

226* *Repeal of the Law of Return, i.e., the law granting only to Jews the right to citizenship upon arriving in Israel.*
1 2 3 4

227* *Israel's recognition of the PLO.*
1 2 3 4

228* *The formation of a Palestinian state in the West Bank and Gaza Strip alongside Israel.*
1 2 3 4

229* *Israel's recognition of the Arab refugees' right to repatriation.*
1 2 3 4

230* *Did you participate this year in events commemorating Land Day?*
1 Yes 2 No
3 Was unable to participate (sick, abroad, etc.)

231* *Did you participate during the past two years in a demonstration protesting the treatment of Arabs in Israel?*
1 Never 2 Once or twice 3 Three or more times

232* *Have you endured harassment by the authorities or economic suffering as a result of expressing opinions or taking actions to affect the present conditions of Arabs in Israel?*
1 Not at all
2 Endured political harassment, but not economic suffering
3 Endured economic suffering, but not political harassment
4 Endured political harassment and economic suffering

233* *Do you fear harassment by the authorities or economic suffering if you act strongly to change the situation of Arabs in Israel?*
1 Not at all
2 Fear political harassment, but not economic suffering
3 Fear economic suffering, but not political harassment
4 Fear political harassment and economic suffering

Should each of the following citizen groups be granted or denied the right to vote in national elections?

234** *Arabs in Israel.*
1 Grant 2 Deny

235** *Severe critics of government policy.*
1 Grant 2 Deny

236** *Persons whose loyalty to the state is dubious.*
1 Grant 2 Deny

237** *Zionists who support the formation of a Palestinian state in the West Bank and Gaza Strip alongside Israel.*
1 Grant 2 Deny

238** *Non-Zionists who support the formation of a Palestinian state in the West Bank and Gaza Strip alongside Israel.*
1 Grant 2 Deny

239** *Are security restrictions on Arabs in Israel justified as long as the Israeli-Arab conflict persists?*
1 Yes 2 To some extent 3 No

240** *During a state of unemployment, who should be laid off first - Jewish or Arab citizens?*
1 Jewish citizens should be laid off first
2 Arab citizens should be laid off first
3 Nationality should not be considered

241** *Should Israel seek and use any opportunity to encourage Israeli Arabs to leave the state?*
1 Agree 2 Have reservations 3 Disagree

242** *What is your opinion on outlawing Rakah?*
1 Agree 2 Have reservations 3 Disagree

243** *What is your opinion on outlawing the Progressive List for Peace?*
1 Agree 2 Have reservations 3 Disagree

244** *What is your opinion on outlawing the Kach Movement?*
1 Agree 2 Have reservations 3 Disagree

(For Arab respondents:) Indicate with which of the following statements on Jews in Israel do you agree or disagree. (For Jewish respondents: "Jews" reads "Arabs.")

245 *(For Arab respondents:) Most Jews in Israel do not care about self respect and family honor. (For Jewish respondents:) Most Arabs in Israel will never reach the level of development Jews have reached.*
1 Agree 2 Disagree

246 *(For Arab respondents:) Most Jews in Israel are exploitive. (For Jewish respondents:) Surveillance over most Arabs in Israel should be increased.*
1 Agree 2 Disagree

247 *(For Arab respondents:) It is impossible to trust most Jews in Israel. (For Jewish respondents:) It is impossible to trust most Arabs in Israel.*
1 Agree 2 Disagree

248 *(For Arab respondents:) Most Jews in Israel are racist. (For Jewish respondents:) Most Arabs in Israel are primitive.*
1 Agree 2 Disagree

249 *(For Arab respondents:) Most Jews in Israel do not attribute any value to Arab life. (For Jewish respondents:) Most Arabs in Israel do not attribute any value to Jewish life.*
1 Agree 2 Disagree

250** *Today Israel within the Green Line is a Jewish-Zionist state in which an Arab minority lives. What is your opinion of the Jewish-Zionist character of the state?*
1 It should be strengthened
2 It should remain the same
3 It should be mitigated

251** *What would you prefer if the egalitarian-democratic character of the state stands in contradiction to its Jewish-Zionist character and you must choose between them?*
1 Certain to prefer the egalitarian-democratic character
2 Think to prefer the egalitarian-democratic character, but not certain
3 Think to prefer the Jewish-Zionist character, but not certain
4 Certain to prefer the Jewish-Zionist character

252** *What is your opinion of expropriation of Arab lands within the Green Line for Jewish development?*
1 Agree 2 Have reservations 3 Disagree

253** *What is your opinion of expropriation of Jewish lands for Arab development?*
1 Agree 2 Have reservations 3 Disagree

254** *Does the State of Israel do enough for Arabs in Israel?*
1 Yes, it does too much 2 It does enough 3 No, it does too little

255* *Are you in favor or against expropriation of Arab lands by Arab local councils for the development of Arab localities in Israel?*
1 Definitely in favor 2 In favor 3 Against 4 Definitely against

256 *What should be the policy of the state toward Arabs in Israel?*
1 Continuation of the present policy
2 Increase in surveillance over Arabs
3 Achievement of equality and integration with Jews
4 Allowing Arabs to organize independently and become partners in state institutions
5 Granting Arabs a separate legal status like the autonomy offered to Arabs in the West Bank and Gaza Strip

257 *Some regard Arabs in Israel today as being divided by religion and hamula, some see them as being divided by political opinion, and some do not observe any particular division. What is your view?*
1 They are mostly divided by religion and hamula
2 They are mostly divided by political opinion
3 They are not particularly divided

Indicate the extent to which each of the following statements regarding Arabs in Israel is true or not.

258 *Arabs in Israel hate Jews.*
1 True for almost all of them
2 True for a large proportion of them
3 True for a certain proportion of them
4 True for a small proportion of them
5 True for only individual instances or not true at all

259 *Arabs in Israel are loyal to the State of Israel.*
1 2 3 4 5

260 *Arabs in Israel have reconciled themselves to Israel's existence.*
1 2 3 4 5

261 *Arabs in Israel rejoice at Israel's suffering.*
1 2 3 4 5

262** *Arabs in Israel engage in spying against Israel.*
1 2 3 4 5

Indicate the extent to which each of the following statements regarding Jews in Israel is true or not.

263 *Jews have reconciled themselves to the existence of an Arab minority in Israel.*
1 2 3 4 5

264 *Jews hate Arabs.*
1 2 3 4 5

Indicate whether you are in favor, have reservations, or are against each of the following measures to improve Arab conditions in Israel.

265** *The extension to Arab localities of the same special assistance given to Jewish development towns.*
1 In favor 2 Have reservations 3 Against

266** *The extension to Arab schools of the same special assistance given to disadvantaged Jewish schools.*
1 In favor 2 Have reservations 3 Against

267** *Proper compensation for expropriated Arab lands.*
1 In favor 2 Have reservations 3 Against

268** *Allocation of lands and funds to establish new Arab towns.*
1 In favor 2 Have reservations 3 Against

269** *Enactment of a special punitive law against discrimination in employment, housing, etc., on religious or nationalist grounds.*
1 In favor 2 Have reservations 3 Against

270 *Do you consider Arabs in Israel to be a danger to national security?*
1 To a great degree 2 To a considerable degree
3 To a certain degree 4 No

271** *What is your opinion of a strong-arm policy toward Arabs in Israel?*
1 In favor 2 Have reservations 3 Against

Let's proceed now to general topics.

272 *With regard to the observance of religious tradition, what do you consider yourself?*
1 Very religious
2 Religious
3 Religious to some extent (for Jewish respondents: traditional)
4 Not religious (for Jewish respondents: secular)

273 *(For Arab respondents:) Do you fulfill your duty to pray? (For Jewish respondents:) Do you travel on Sabbath?*
1 No (for Jewish respondents: Yes)
2 Yes (for Jewish respondents: No)

274 *Did you or someone from your immediate family (i.e., brother, sister, father, mother, son, daughter, spouse) become religious during the past five years?*
1 No
2 Yes, myself only
3 Yes, someone from the family, but not myself
4 Yes, both myself and someone from the family

275* *What is your opinion of the traditional practice of loyalty to one's hamula against other hamulas?*
1 Retain as is 2 Modify 3 Abolish

276 *(For Arab respondents:) What should be the average number of children per Arab family in Israel today?(For Jewish respondents: "Arab family" reads "family.")*
1 One or two children 2 Three 3 Four
4 Five 5 Six or more

277* *Do you allow a young single Arab girl to have a boyfriend?*
1 Yes, allow 2 Allow to some extent 3 No

278* *Do you acknowledge a woman's right to choose a husband even against her parents' will?*
1 Acknowledge 2 Have reservations 3 Deny

279* *Since 1948, has there been any expropriation of lands owned by you, your brothers, sisters, parents, or children?*
1 Yes, much 2 Yes, some
3 No, but own land 4 Own no land

280* *Did your family or the family of your father become a refugee family as a result of the 1948 War?*
1 No 2 Yes

281* *Are you of Bedouin origin?*
1 No 2 Yes, a Bedouin from the Negev
3 Yes, a Bedouin from the Galilee

282 *For which list would you vote if elections to the Knesset were held today?*
1 Maarakh (Labor, Yahad-Weizman, Ometz-Horowitz)
2 Likud
3 Mapam
4 Tehiya
5 DFPE (Democratic Front for Peace and Equality)
6 PLP (Progressive List for Peace)
7 CRM (Citizens' Rights Movement)
8 Shinui (Change)
9 Tami (Israel's Tradition Movement)
10 NRP (National Religious Party)
11 Agudat Israel
12 Shas
13 Morasha-Poale Agudat Israel
14 Kach (Kahane)

15 Other lists
16 Have not decided
17 Would not vote

284 *For which list did you vote in the last elections to the Knesset (in July 1984)?*
1 Maarakh 2 Likud 3 DFPE 4 PLP
5 CRM 6 Shinui 7 Yahad 8 Ometz
9 Tami 10 NRP 11 Agudat Israel 12 Shas
13 Morasha-Poale Agudat Israel 14 Tehiya 15 Kach
16 Other lists 17 Did not vote

286* *For which list did you vote in the last local elections (in November 1983)?*
1 A Jewish list
2 A list affiliated to a Jewish party
3 A DFPE or Rakah list
4 A list of or affiliated with the Sons of the Village Movement
5 Other local list
6 Did not vote

287 *Are you a member of any party? Which one?*
1 Not a member 2 Labor 3 Herut
4 Mapam 5 Liberals 6 Rakah
7 PLP 8 Shinui 9 CRM
10 Yahad 11 Tami 12 Agudat Israel
13 NRP 14 Morasha-Poale Agudat Israel
15 Shas 16 Tehiya 17 Kach
18 Other

Now I wish to obtain some information on your background.

289 *Is there a car at the disposal of your family (including a car owned by the workplace which is assigned for use by a family member)?*
1 Yes 2 No

290 *Gender.*
1 Male 2 Female

291 *Age (recorded in two digits).*

293 *Personal status.*
1 Single 2 Married 3 Widowed 4 Divorced

294 *Number of children.*
0 None 1 One child 2 Two children...
13 Thirteen 14 Fourteen or more children

296* *Your spouse (in the last marriage) is from:*
1 Same hamula and same place of residence
2 Same hamula but different place of residence
3 Same place of residence but different hamula
4 Different hamula and different place of residence

297* *How many of your hamula members live in your place of residence?*
1 Fewer than 100 persons 2 100-500
3 501-1,000 4 More than 1,000

298 *Education.*
1 No schooling 2 Incomplete primary
3 Complete primary 4 Incomplete secondary
5 Complete secondary
6 Post secondary, incomplete higher 7 Complete higher

299 *Religion.*
1 Druze 2 Moslem
3 Greek-Catholic 4 Greek-Orthodox
5 Other Christian 6 Jew

300 *What do you do in the main?*
1 Employed (including soldier in professional army)
2 Unemployed (seeking work)
3 Retired
4 Housewife
5 Student
6 Soldier in compulsory service

301 *Are you the head of a family (a husband, a father, or a single, a divorced, or a widowed person living separately)?*
1 Yes 2 No

302 *Work status of head of family.*
1 Employee
2 Employer
3 Self-employed
4 Member of cooperative or Moshav
5 Kibbutz member
6 Unpaid family member
7 Not employed (retired, housewife, student, soldier in compulsory service)

303 *Is the head of family a tenured employee?*
1 Yes 2 No

304 *Who is the employer of the head of family?*
1 Jewish
2 Arab
3 Public institution (State, Histadrut, Local Government, Jewish Agency, University, etc.)
4 Head of family is not employee

305 *Job classification of head of family.*
1 Scientific and academic worker
2 Other professional, technical, and related worker

3 Top administrator and manager
4 Other administrator and manager
5 Top clerical and related worker
6 Other clerical and related worker
7 Big merchant
8 Other sales worker
9 Service worker
10 Farm owner or manager
11 Skilled agricultural worker
12 Unskilled agricultural worker
13 Skilled worker in industry, mining, building, transport, and other skilled worker
14 Other worker in industry mining, building, transport, and other unskilled worker
15 Head of family is unemployed, soldier in compulsory service, living separately

*307*** *Year of immigration.*

1 Born in Israel | 2 Immigrated before 1948
3 1948-1951 | 4 1952-1956
5 1957-1960 | 6 1961-1965
7 1966 or later

*308*** *Father's country of birth.*

1 Born in Israel | 2 Morocco, Tangier
3 Algeria, Tunisia, Libya | 4 Iraq
5 Yemen, Southern Yemen | 6 Syria, Lebanon, Egypt
7 Turkey, Bulgaria, Greece
8 Other countries in Asia and Africa | 9 USSR
10 Poland | 11 Rumania
12 Germany | 13 Anglo-Saxon countries
14 Other countries in Europe and America

*310*** *If you have to define yourself in terms of ethnic origin, which of the following would you choose?*

1 Oriental, Sephardic   2 Ashkenazic   3 Mixed

*311*** *(For Oriental or Sephardic respondents only:) Are you, or anyone of your children, brothers, sisters, or grandchildren married today to an Ashkenazic Jew?*

1 No
2 Yes, only myself
3 Yes, only someone from the family (child, brother, sister, grandchild)
4 Yes, myself and someone from the family

*312*** *(For Ashkenazic respondents only:) Are you, or anyone of your children, brothers, sisters, or grandchildren married today to an Oriental or a Sephardic Jew?*

1   2   3   4

Do you read any of the following newspapers or listen to any of the following radio stations?

414* *Al-Ittihad.*
1 Yes 2 No

415* *Al-Thadamun.*
1 Yes 2 No

416* *Al-Sinara.*
1 Yes 2 No

417* *Al-Kuds.*
1 Yes 2 No

418* *Yediot Aharonot.*
1 Yes 2 No

419* *Maariv.*
1 Yes 2 No

420* *Israeli Arabic radio.*
1 Yes 2 No

421* *The Voice of Peace.*
1 Yes 2 No

We are through. Thanks for your cooperation.

Following is the interviewer's report, to be completed at the end of the interview.

423* *Respondent's sampling listing.*
1 Included in original list
2 Included in replacement list

424 *Duration of interview (recorded in minutes, three digits).*

427* *Do you personally know the respondent?*
1 Yes 2 No

428 *Was another person present during the interview?*
1 No 2 Yes, but did not interrupt
3 Yes and did interrupt

429 *What was the degree of understanding shown by the respondent?*
1 Lack of understanding
2 Certain lack of understanding
3 Reasonable understanding
4 Full understanding

430* *Was there an atmosphere of trust during the interview?*
1 Lack of trust 2 Certain lack of trust
3 Reasonable trust 4 Full trust

431 *What was the overall reliability of the information given by the respondent?*
1 Not reliable
2 Sufficient
3 Good
4 Very good

432** *What was the overall attitude of the respondent toward Arabs in Israel?*
1 Very sympathetic
2 Sympathetic
3 Neutral
4 Mixed, both sympathetic and hostile at the same time
5 Hostile
6 Very hostile

433 *Locality of residence.*

For Arab respondents
1 Haifa
2 Lod
3 Akko (Acre)
4 Tel-Aviv-Yafo
5 Nazareth
6 Shefaram
7 Tira
8 Baka Al-Gharbia
9 Sakhnin
10 Majd Al-Khrum
11 Daliat Al-Karmel
12 Kfar Yasif
13 Um Al-Fahem
14 Tayba
15 Yirka
16 Kfar Kana
17 Maker
18 Ein Mahel
19 Jat
20 Jisser Al-Zarka
21 Julis
22 Meilya
23 Pkiein
24 Fassuta
25 Faradies
26 Nahaf
27 Marja
28 Naora
29 Sheikh Danun
30 Sajur
31 Eilut
32 Buayna
33 Akbara
34 Mouawiya
35 Bartaa
36 Kabul
37 Busmat-Tivon
38 Hilf
39 Saayda Um Al-Ghnam
40 Huzayil
41 Aatzam
42 Abu Rabiaa
43 Atawna
44 Rahat

For Jewish respondents
51 Tel-Aviv-Yafo
52 Jerusalem
53 Haifa
54 Beer Sheva
55 Ramat Gan
56 Bene Berak
57 Herzliya
58 Holon
59 Petah Tikva
60 Netanya
61 Rishon Letzion
62 Pardes Hana
63 Teveria (Tiberias)
64 Ramle
65 Ashdod
66 Zikhron Yaacov
67 Yavne
68 Rosh Haayin

69 Raanana
71 Afula
72 Beit Shean
73 Beit Shemesh
74 Dimona
75 Ashteol
76 Kfar Bialik
77 Burgata
78 Haniel
79 Yad Rambam
80 Gilgal
81 Maayan Zvi
82 Kfar Massarik
83 Hatzerim
84 Mishmar Hanegev

435 *Research group*
1 Arab Public
2 Arab leaders affiliated with the Zionist establishment
3 Unaffiliated Arab leaders
4 Arab leaders affiliated with the DFPE or PLP
5 Arab activists in the Sons of Village Movement
6 Jewish public
7 Jewish leaders affiliated with the DFPE or PLP
8 Jewish leaders affiliated with CRM, Mapam or Shinui
9 Jewish leaders affiliated with Labor
10 Jewish leaders affiliated with Likud, Tehiya, or religious parties

437 *Interviewer's gender.*
1 Male 2 Female

438 *Interviewer's code.*

441 *(For office use:) Verification of the interview.*
1 No 2 Yes

C

The 1988 Questionnaire

Following is an English translation of the questionnaire used for interviewing both Arabs and Jews. Except where indicated, the Arabic-language questionnaire was identical in content and form to the Hebrew-language version. Questions that were presented to Arabs only are marked by an asterisk, and those posed to Jews only are identified by two asterisks. To save space, identical answers to a series of questions are occasionally reproduced in the first question only. The item numbers here are the variable numbers used in the codebook of the computerized records rather than the original numbers in the questionnaire. For this reason there are gaps in the numbers although all items are reproduced as they appear in the original questionnaire.

Interviewer's Introduction to Arab Respondents

The Department of Sociology and Anthropology at the University of Haifa is conducting a survey of Arab-Jewish relations in Israel. For this purpose, 1,200 persons, representing Arabs all over the country, were chosen. You are one of those who were randomly selected for this sample. A similar sample of Jews was also selected for the study. The goal of the research is to ascertain the attitudes of Arabs and Jews toward each other.

All of the information that you provide will be used for scientific objectives and statistical analyses only. Your answers will serve to understand better the situation of Arabs in Israel, and hence your cooperation is very important.

The questions that I will present to you do not have right or wrong answers. The purpose is to learn about your stands on a number of topics. I hope that you will take this opportunity to express your opinions freely.

I will read to you the question and the answers related to it, and you are requested to choose the answer that suits you most.

Interviewer's Introduction to Jewish Respondents

I am an interviewer from the Dahaf Research Institute which is an independent institute for social research. We conduct public opinion surveys and studies on various subjects. You were randomly selected as one of 1,200 respondents. Your answers will remain anonymous and will be used for statistical objectives only.

The study this time is carried out in Israel and several other countries. The goal is to find out what people think about the society and state where they live.

Every question has a number of answers, and you are requested to choose, only after hearing all the possible answers, the one that suits you most.

Text of Questionnaire

1 *Case number.*

For each of the following officeholders indicate whether he has or does not have a very large influence on the society and state in Israel today. Please note, we are asking about a very large influence and not about a certain influence. If there is a certain influence but not a very large influence, indicate that there is no very large influence.

6 *Cabinet ministers.*
1 Have a very large influence 2 Do not have a very large influence

7 *Trade union leaders.*
1 Have a very large influence 2 Do not have a very large influence

8 *Leaders of political parties.*
1 Have a very large influence 2 Do not have a very large influence

9 *Top commanders of the military.*
1 Have a very large influence 2 Do not have a very large influence

10 *Big industrialists.*
1 Have a very large influence 2 Do not have a very large influence

11 *Heads of religion.*
1 Have a very large influence 2 Do not have a very large influence

12 *Top bankers.*
1 Have a very large influence 2 Do not have a very large influence

13 *Editors of the press, radio, and television.*
1 Have a very large influence 2 Do not have a very large influence

14 *Supreme court justices.*
1 Have a very large influence 2 Do not have a very large influence

Think of a country in which you would like to live. We want to ask you a number of questions about the forms of government that you prefer for the country in which you wish to live.

15 *What kind of government would you prefer for such a country?*

1 A government which does all its work well and efficiently, but expects the people to respect and obey it, or

2 A government which tries to help people with problems but does not always do its work well or efficiently

16 *What would you prefer?*

1 A government which is honest, with no bribery or corruption, but without strong and inspiring leaders, or

2 A government with some men who might be a little dishonest but who are strong and inspiring leaders

17 *What would you prefer?*

1 A regime of one political party only, with a single plan for the country's future, or

2 A regime of more than one party, each with its own plan for the country's future

18 *What form of socioeconomic structure would you prefer?*

1 Shops and factories owned by private businessmen who will work hard to make the business grow, or

2 Shops and factories owned by the government elected by the people

19 *What would you prefer?*

1 All people should have the right to own property, or

2 The government should own all property and give it to the people to use

Let us proceed to statements which describe different possible forms of government.

20 *Of the following two forms of government, which one would you prefer?*

1 A government which tries to make all people as equal as possible in wages, housing, and education, even if there is need to impose heavy taxes, or

2 A government which enables people who are clever and hard working to become wealthier than others

21 *What would you prefer?*

1 A government which allows people in provinces and towns to elect councils to make many of their own laws, or

2 A government which makes laws which are the same for all areas of the country

22 *What would you prefer?*

1 A government which controls what newspapers may write to prevent disunity, or

2 A government which allows newspapers to criticize the government and to enjoy freedom of expression

The government can use different means to protect national unity. Which of the following means do you approve of and which do you disapprove of?

23 *Prosecution of political activists who use violence.*
1 Approve 2 Disapprove

24 *Preventive action against opponents of the regime in order to prevent their activity ahead of time.*
1 Approve 2 Disapprove

25 *Collective punishment (punishing whole groups).*
1 Approve 2 Disapprove

26 *Using all military means irrespective of human life.*
1 Approve 2 Disapprove

27 *Seeking political solutions by negotiation.*
1 Approve 2 Disapprove

28 *Think of all areas of your life. What changes, reforms, or improvements would people like you see as being most necessary in the future? (Open question; responses are coded into the following categories).*
1 Personal desires (rise in standard of living, children's wellbeing, education, etc.)
2 Public desires (peace, unity, equality, change of government, etc.) without a mention of Arabs in Israel
3 Public desires with a mention of Arabs in Israel
4 Both personal and public desires without a mention of Arabs in Israel
5 Both personal and public desires with a mention of Arabs in Israel

29 *Which one of the following things is the most important for achieving success in life?*
1 Working hard for personal progress
2 Organizing and standing together as a group
3 Education
4 Experience
5 Connections (knowing the right people)
6 Inheritance
7 Luck
8 Tricks
9 What your parents taught you
10 Religious belief (for Jewish respondents: trustfulness)

31 *Imagine that you win a lot of money in the lottery. On which one of the following would you spend the most?*
1 Investing in a big plant or business
2 Starting a small plant or business
3 Investing in a bank with good interest
4 Enjoying spending money on myself or my family

32 *If you have to choose between the following two kinds of work, which one would your prefer?*
1 A job in a factory or office with a good salary to rely on, or
2 Your own business where you can win a lot or lose a lot

There are a number of foreign governments and organizations which are concerned with Israel's internal affairs. For each one of them indicate if it is mostly helpful, mostly harmful, or have no effect.

33 *The United States.*
1 Mostly helpful 2 Mostly harmful 3 Have no effect

34 *The Soviet Union.*
1 Mostly helpful 2 Mostly harmful 3 Have no effect

35 *The European Community (the Common Market states).*
1 Mostly helpful 2 Mostly harmful 3 Have no effect

36 *Egypt.*
1 Mostly helpful 2 Mostly harmful 3 Have no effect

37 *Jordan.*
1 Mostly helpful 2 Mostly harmful 3 Have no effect

38 *Syria.*
1 Mostly helpful 2 Mostly harmful 3 Have no effect

39 *South Africa.*
1 Mostly helpful 2 Mostly harmful 3 Have no effect

40 *American Jewry.*
1 Mostly helpful 2 Mostly harmful 3 Have no effect

41 *The Vatican.*
1 Mostly helpful 2 Mostly harmful 3 Have no effect

42 *The United Nations.*
1 Mostly helpful 2 Mostly harmful 3 Have no effect

43 *The PLO.*
1 Mostly helpful 2 Mostly harmful 3 Have no effect

There are many countries like Israel in which groups differ from each other "in nationality, religion, language, or culture" (for Jewish respondents: without the words in quotation marks). There are different opinions about the best form of government for these states. Think of Israel and indicate which opinion you accept and which you do not accept for Israel.

44 *Do you accept or do not accept that the country should be divided up, and each nationality, religion, or lingual group will have its own state?*
1 Accept 2 Do not accept

45 *Do you accept or do not accept that the largest group will rule, and the other groups should accept what it will be decided?*
1 Accept 2 Do not accept

46 *And that one group will rule over other groups, and people who refuse to accept this, will have to keep quiet or leave the country?*
1 Accept 2 Do not accept

47 *And that a single party, open to everyone, will rule without opposition?*
1 Accept 2 Do not accept

48 *And that all people will vote for any party they like, and parties will have to form a coalition government that will ensure a share of power for all major groups?*
1 Accept 2 Do not accept

49 *And that all people will vote for any party they like, and the winning party or parties will rule while other parties will be in the opposition?*
1 Accept 2 Do not accept

50 *Which one of the above possibilities do you regard as the best solution for the problem of Israeli Arabs, excluding the Arabs in the territories?*
1 The State of Israel within the Green Line (i.e., without the territories) should be divided up into two states between Jews and Israeli Arabs
2 The Jews will rule, and Israeli Arabs should accept what the Jews will decide
3 The Jews will rule, and Israeli Arabs who refuse to accept this, will have to keep quiet or leave the country
4 A single party, open to Jews and Israeli Arabs, will rule without opposition
5 All people will vote for any party they like, and parties will have to form a coalition government that will ensure share of power for Jews and Israeli Arabs
6 All people will vote for any party they like, and the winning party or parties, will rule while other parties will be in the opposition

51 *And which possibility do you regard as the best solution for the problem of the Arabs in the territories?*
1 Israel should withdraw, so that the Jews and the Arabs in the territories will live in separate states
2 The Jews will rule, and the Arabs in the territories should accept what the Jews will decide
3 The Jews will rule, and Arabs in the territories who refuse to accept this, will have to keep quiet or leave the country
4 A single party, that will be open also to Arabs in the territories, will rule without opposition
5 All people, including the Arabs in the territories, will vote for any party they like, and parties will have to form a coalition government that will ensure a share of power for Jews and for Arabs in Israel and the territories
6 All people, including the Arabs in the territories, will vote for any party they like, and the winning party or parties will rule while other parties will be in opposition

Is each of the following things important or not important to you?

52 *Is being an Israeli citizen important or not important to you?*
1 Important 2 Not important

53 *Being a Moslem/a Christian/a Druze/a member of the Jewish faith?*
1 Important 2 Not important

54 *Being a member of the Arab nation/Jewish people?*
1 Important 2 Not important

55 *Being a person with a certain occupation, education, and lifestyle?*
1 Important 2 Not important

56 *Being a person living in the homeland?*
1 Important 2 Not important

57 *Being religious or non-religious/religious, traditional, or secular?*
1 Important 2 Not important

58 *Being a member of the Arab minority/Jewish majority in Israel?*
1 Important 2 Not important

59 *Being a member of the Palestinian people/being a sephardic (an Oriental) or an Ashkenazic?*
1 Important 2 Not important

60* *Being a member of a certain hamula?*
1 Important 2 Not important

61 *Now you are asked to go again over the above list of affiliations and identities and to pick from it the one which is the most important to you.*
1 Being an Israeli citizen
2 Being a Moslem/a Christian/a Druze/a member of the Jewish faith
3 Being a member of the Arab nation/Jewish people
4 Being a person with a certain occupation, education, and lifestyle
5 Being a person living in the homeland
6 Being religious or non-religious/religious, traditional, or secular
7 Being a member of the Arab minority/Jewish majority in Israel
8 Being a member of the Palestinian people/being a sephardic (an Oriental) or an Ashkenazic
9* Being a member of a certain hamula

62 *What is your second most important identity?*
1 2 3 4 5 6 7 8 9

63 *And what is your third most important identity?*
1 2 3 4 5 6 7 8 9

Here are a number of things which people say about social affairs in Israel. Could you tell me whether you agree or disagree with each statement.

64 *Whether one likes it or not, when groups with different nationality, religion, language, or culture live in one country, one group will control another.*
1 Agree 2 Disagree

65 *Even very different groups living in one country can easily accept each other as they are, and respect each other's mutual rights.*
1 Agree 2 Disagree

66 *In the State of Israel the most important differences are between rich and poor in each nationality group, even more than the differences between Jews and Israeli Arabs.*
1 Agree 2 Disagree

67 *Obviously there are differences between Jews and Israeli Arabs, but they should be kept out of politics.*
1 Agree 2 Disagree

68 *Groups with different nationality, religion, language, or culture make a country socially richer and more interesting.*
1 Agree 2 Disagree

69 *The gap in power between Jews and Israeli Arabs is such that no important change in power relations is possible for the long run.*
1 Agree 2 Disagree

70 *Open conflict between Jews and Israeli Arabs will cause everyone to lose in the long run.*
1 Agree 2 Disagree

71 *Israeli Arab youth have a reasonably good chance of reaching their goals in life.*
1 Agree 2 Disagree

Here are more things which people say about social affairs in Israel, and I wish to ask you with which one you agree and with which one you disagree.

72 *One must be very cautious with people, you cannot trust the people who live and work around you.*
1 Agree 2 Disagree

73 *I am afraid that our children might never enjoy as high a standard of living as we used to have.*
1 Agree 2 Disagree

74 *Poor people have only themselves to blame for their situation.*
1 Agree 2 Disagree

75 *Whatever my personal efforts are in Israel, I will not get the education and job I am entitled to.*
1 Agree 2 Disagree

76 *I am envious of what the wealthy people have and feel I should have the same.*
1 Agree 2 Disagree

77 *One should be sure that something really works before taking a chance on it.*
1 Agree 2 Disagree

78 *If you try to change things, you usually make them worse.*
1 Agree 2 Disagree

79 *I feel uncertainty and fear about my future.*
1 Agree 2 Disagree

80 *There is very little a person like me can do to improve the life of people in Israel.*
1 Agree 2 Disagree

81 *Even ordinary people can make progress, if they help each other.*
1 Agree 2 Disagree

82 *I prefer to work hard and take risks in order to earn a lot of money than to have a secure job without high salary.*
1 Agree 2 Disagree

People trust certain persons and not others. Indicate which of the following kinds of persons you trust and which you do not trust.

83 *Friends.*
1 Trust 2 Do not trust

84 *Family members.*
1 Trust 2 Do not trust

85 *Neighbors.*
1 Trust 2 Do not trust

86 *People of my religion/ethnic group.*
1 Trust 2 Do not trust

87 *Arabs. (For Jewish respondents: "Jews.")*
1 Trust 2 Do not trust

88 *All citizens of the state.*
1 Trust 2 Do not trust

89 *People with the same work and life conditions as mine.*
1 Trust 2 Do not trust

90 *People from my locality.*
1 Trust 2 Do not trust

91 *With which description of the social inequalities in the country do you agree more?*
1 Most of the wealth is held by a small minority at the expense of the majority who are poor people
2 A majority of people are in the middle class, with a small minority who are rich or poor

92 *In the past five years, has inequality between rich and poor in the country increased, decreased or remained the same?*

1 Increased 2 Decreased 3 Remained the same

93 *Between which of the following groups are there the most important differences in Israel today?*

1 Between poor and rich
2 Between religious and non-religious Jews
3 Between Sephardic and Ashkenazic Jews
4 Between Israeli Arabs and Jews

94 *Think of the conflicts which have recently developed between the two groups that you indicated. What do you feel?*

1 I fear that quiet and cooperation between these two groups have become impossible
2 In spite of everything, quiet and cooperation between these two groups can still be achieved

95 *Do you have Jewish friends and have you visited their homes over the past two years? (For Jewish respondents: "Jewish" reads "Arab.")*

1 Have no Jewish/Arab friends
2 Have Jewish/Arab friends but have not visited them
3 Have Jewish/Arab friends and have visited their homes over the past two years

96 *Are you willing to have Jewish friends? (For Jewish respondents: "Jewish" reads "Arab.")*

1 Definitely willing 2 Willing
3 Willing, but prefer Arab/Jewish friends
4 Willing to have Arab/Jewish friends only

97** *Are you willing to have an Arab as your superior in a job?*

1 Definitely willing 2 Willing
3 Willing, but prefer a Jew 4 Willing to have a Jew only

98 *Are you willing to have your daughter (if you do not have a daughter, suppose you do) marry a Jew? (For Jewish respondents: "a Jew" reads "an Arab.")*

1 Definitely willing 2 Willing
3 Willing, but prefer an Arab/a Jew
4 Willing to have an Arab/a Jew only

99 *Which type of culture would you wish to have evolve in Israel -closer to a Western culture or closer to an Arab culture?*

1 Distinct Western culture
2 Western culture in which Arab elements are incorporated
3 A mixed culture consisting of Western and Arab elements
4 Arab culture in which Jewish elements are incorporated
5 Distinct Arab culture
6 Opposed to both cultures

100 *Which of the following goals is most desirable to Arab education in Israel today?*
1 To live as a loyal minority member in a Jewish state
2 To love Israel as the common homeland of its two peoples, Arab and Jewish
3 To be a member of the Palestinian people

101 *Which of the following goals is most desirable for Jewish education in Israel today?*
1 To live as a loyal citizen
2 To love Israel as the common homeland of its two peoples, Arab and Jewish
3 To be a member of the Jewish people

102** *Which language should be the dominant language of the public and state institutions in Israel?*
1 Hebrew 2 Hebrew and Arabic equally 3 Arabic

103 *The State of Israel is:*
1 Homeland of Jews only
2 Common homeland of Jews and Arabs
3 Homeland of Arabs only

104** *Should the State of Israel prefer Jews or Arabs?*
1 Prefer Jews to Arabs considerably
2 Prefer Jews to Arabs to some extent
3 Treat both equally
4 Prefer Arabs to Jews to some extent
5 Prefer Arabs to Jews considerably

105** *Who should be admitted to the universities?*
1 The brightest persons, regardless if Jews or Israeli Arabs
2 Mostly Israeli Arabs
3 Mostly Jews
4 Jews and Israeli Arabs according to their proportion in the population

106** *And who should get civil service jobs?*
1 The brightest persons, regardless if Jews or Israeli Arabs
2 Mostly Israeli Arabs
3 Mostly Jews
4 Jews and Israeli Arabs according to their proportion in the population

107* *Should the State of Israel within the Green Line retain a Jewish majority?*
1 Yes 2 No

108* *Do you accept Israel's right to exist?*
1 Yes 2 Have reservations 3 No

109 *(For Arab respondents:) Should Arabs in Israel resign themselves in principle to a status of a national minority with full civil rights? (For Jewish respondents:) Are you resigned to the Arabs' right to live in Israel as a national minority with full civil rights?*

1 Yes 2 Have reservations 3 No

110 *(For Arab respondents:) Are you resigned to being a minority member in Israel today? (For Jewish respondents:) Are you resigned to the very existence of an Arab minority in Israel today?*

1 Yes 2 Have reservations 3 No

111* *Do you accept Israel's right to exist within the Green Line as a Jewish-Zionist state?*

1 Yes 2 Have reservations 3 No

112** *Do you agree or disagree that a list that both accepts the principles of democracy and Israel's right to exist but opposes its Jewish-Zionist character, should be allowed to run in the Knesset elections?*

1 Agree 2 Tend to Agree 3 Tend to disagree
4 Disagree

113 *According to your own understanding and definition of what Zionism is, are you:*

1 Zionist 2 Non-Zionist 3 Anti-Zionist

114* *The United Nations General Assembly adopted a resolution that Zionism is a racist movement. Do you agree with this resolution?*

1 Agree 2 Have reservations 3 Disagree

115 *Do you think that Arabs can be equal citizens in Israel as a Jewish-Zionist state and can identify themselves with the state?*

1 Yes 2 Possibly 3 Doubtful
4 No

116* *If your son were subject to either compulsory military service or compulsory civil service, what would you advise him to do?*

1 Serve military service 2 Serve civil service 3 Refuse

What kind of leader do Israeli Arabs need now?

117* *A leader who is concerned with the practical day-to-day needs of Israeli Arabs.*

1 Very important 2 Not very important

118* *A leader who is able to bargain and achieve reasonable compromises.*

1 Very important 2 Not very important

119* *A leader who is feared by Jews.*

1 Very important 2 Not very important

Think of leaders of Israeli Arabs who live in the country or abroad.

120* *Who do you prefer most? (Open question; responses are coded according to the following categories).*
1 Arab leaders of the Israeli Communist Party
2 Arab leaders of the Progressive List for Peace
3 Non-partisan Israeli Arab leaders
4 Arab leaders affiliated with Israeli Jewish parties
5 Arab activists in the Sons of the Village Movement
6 Arab leaders on the West Bank and Gaza Strip
7 Arab leaders of the PLO mainstream
8 Arab leaders of the PLO Rejection Front
9 Other Arab leaders
10 Jewish leaders
11 Other leaders

122* *And who else do you prefer most?*
1 2 3 4 5 6 7 8 9 10 11

124* *From the following list, who do you prefer most? (Note: respondents were given names only, without the identifying information in parentheses).*
1 Tawfiq Tubi (Knesset Member, leader of the Israeli Communist Party, Christian)
2 Mouhamad Wattad (Knesset Member, Mapam Party, Moslem)
3 Ibrahim Nimr Hussein (independent, Chairman of the Committee of Heads of Arab Local Councils, Moslem)
4 Kamel Daher (one of the top leaders of the Progressive List for Peace, Moslem)
5 Amal Nasr A-Din (Knesset Member, Herut Party, Druze)
6 Yasir Arafat (leader of the PLO mainstream)
7 Abu Musa (leader of the PLO Rejection Front)
8 Abdul Wahab Darawshe (Knesset Member, Moslem, ceded from the Labor Party to form the Democratic Arab Party)
9 Sheikh Abdallah Darwish (a top leader of the Islamic Movement)
10 Mouhamad Mi'ari (Knesset Member, the leader of the Progressive List for Peace, Moslem)
11 Tawfiq Zayad (Knesset Member, Israeli Communist Party, mayor of Nazareth, Moslem)
12 Zaydan Atshi (Knesset Member, Shinui Party, Druze)

126* *Who else in the list do you prefer?*
1 2 3 4 5 6 7 8 9 10 11 12

128* *Can Arab leaders whom you prefer be efficient in promoting the interests of Israeli Arabs?*
1 Yes 2 No

206* *Would you support Arab leaders whom you prefer even if they act in a way you do not understand?*
1 Yes 2 No

207* *Do you consider the Committee of Heads of Arab Local Councils to be truly representative of the interests of the Arabs in Israel?*
1 Definitely yes 2 Yes 3 No
4 Definitely no 5 Have not heard of the Committee

208 *Which political organization is most desirable for Arabs in Israel under the present circumstances?*
1 To join existing Jewish parties as individuals with equal status
2 To form Arab parties that can reach agreement or cooperate with the existing Jewish parties
3 To belong to non-Zionist parties composed of Arabs and Jews
4 To establish independent national Arab parties
5 No political party organization at all

209* *When you think about your progress in life, in your work and home, with whom do you compare yourself most often?*
1 Ashkenazic Jews 2 Israeli Arabs 3 Oriental Jews
4 Residents of Western countries
5 People like you ten years ago
6 Rich people

210 *Do you think that Arab youth have reasonable chances of fulfilling their occupational aspirations in Israel today?*
1 Yes 2 Possible 3 Doubtful 4 No

211* *To what extent are you satisfied with being an Israeli citizen?*
1 Definitely satisfied 2 Satisfied 3 Not too satisfied
4 Not satisfied 5 Not satisfied at all

212 *Is the socioeconomic status of your family better or worse today than it was five years ago?*
1 Better 2 Did not change 3 Worse

213 *When you learn about an action in which an Arab citizen from Israel killed a Jewish citizen on nationalist grounds, how do you feel? (For Jewish respondents: "an Arab" reads "a Jewish" and "a Jewish" reads "an Arab.")*
1 Rejoice and justify action 2 Rejoice but do not justify action
3 Sadden but justify action 4 Sadden and do not justify action

214 *What is your stand on the Peace Treaty between Israel and Egypt?*
1 In favor 2 Have reservations 3 Against

215** *Do you think that the Palestinians have the right to have a state that will include parts of the West Bank and Gaza Strip?*
1 Yes 2 Have reservations 3 No

216 *Are you in favor of establishing a Palestinian state in the West Bank and Gaza Strip alongside Israel?*
1 Yes 2 Only under certain circumstances 3 No

217* *Are you willing to move to a Palestinian state if one was established alongside Israel?*
1 Yes 2 Only under certain circumstances 3 No

218 *Do you think that Israel should recognize the PLO as the authoritative representative of the Palestinian people?*

1 Yes 2 Only under certain circumstances 3 No

219 *(For Arab respondents:) Do you think that the PLO should recognize the State of Israel?*

1 Yes 2 Only under certain circumstances 3 No

(For Jewish respondents:) If the PLO will undergo a basic change, and it will announce its recognition of the State of Israel and its willingness to stop terrorist actions completely, should Israel then be ready or not ready to conduct peace negotiations also with the PLO?

1 Definitely should 2 Should 3 Should not
4 Definitely should not

220 *Should the solution to the Palestinian question include also the settlement of the land dispute between Israeli Arabs and the state?*

1 Yes 2 Only under certain circumstances 3 No

221 *Should negotiations to settle the Palestinian question include also a solution to other problems of Israeli Arabs?*

1 Yes 2 Only under certain circumstances 3 No

222* *Should the solution to the Palestinian question include also compensations to Jews from Arab countries for the property they left there?*

1 Yes 2 Only under certain circumstances 3 No

223 *Which borders of the State of Israel are you prepared to compromise on in order to reach a peace settlement?*

1 All of Mandatory Palestine, in which new state will be established instead of Israel
2 1947 UN partition borders (the Galilee and Triangle not included in Israel)
3 Pre-1967 borders, i.e., without the West Bank, Gaza Strip, East Jerusalem, and the Golan Heights (the Galilee and Triangle included in Israel)
4 Pre-1967 borders with certain modifications in favor of Israel
5 Present borders with willingness to compromise also in Judea and Samaria
6 Only present borders

224 *Should Israel recognize the Arab refugees' right of repatriation to Israel within the Green Line?*

1 Yes 2 Only under certain circumstances 3 No

225 *(For Arab respondents:) Should the Palestinians give up the demand for the right of repatriation if this is necessary to reach a peace settlement? (For Jewish respondents:) Should the Jews give up East Jerusalem if this is necessary to reach a peace settlement?*

1 In favor 2 Have reservations 3 Against

226 *When thinking of the term "Israeli," whom do you include in it -only Jews or both Jews and Arabs?*

1 Only Jews 2 Jews and Arabs

227 *Is the term "Israeli" appropriate in describing your identity?*

1 Very appropriate 2 Appropriate 3 Not too appropriate
4 Not appropriate at all

228* *How would you define yourself if you had to choose one of the following alternatives?*

1 Arab 2 Palestinian Arab 3 Israeli Arab
4 Israeli 5 Israeli Palestinian
6 Palestinian in Israel or Palestinian Arab in Israel 7 Palestinian

229 *How would you define Arabs in Israel if you had to choose one of the following alternatives?*

1 Arabs 2 Israeli Arabs 3 Israelis
4 Palestinian Arabs 5 Israeli Palestinians
6 Palestinian in Israel or Palestinian Arab in Israel 7 Palestinian

230* *To whom do you feel closer -to Arabs in the West Bank and Gaza Strip or to Jews in Israel?*

1 Arabs in the West Bank and Gaza Strip 2 Jews in Israel

231 *(For Arab respondents:) If you had a choice, where would you feel more at home, in an Arab country or in Israel?*

1 In an Arab country 2 In Israel

(For Jewish respondents:) Are Arabs in Israel more loyal to the State of Israel than are the Arabs in the West Bank and Gaza Strip?

1 Yes 2 No

232* *Do you accept the idea that the Galilee and Triangle should remain integral parts of Israel?*

1 Accept 2 Tend to accept 3 Tend to reject
4 Reject

233 *What is the most appropriate solution to the problem of the Arab minority in Israel?*

1 Arabs will be forced to live outside Israel
2 Arabs will live in Israel only if they are resigned to their minority status in a state designed for Jews
3 Arabs will live in Israel as a national minority with full civil rights
4 Arabs will live in Israel as a national minority recognized by the state and enjoying proper political representation
5 Arabs will live in a Palestinian state to be established in the West Bank, Gaza Strip, the Galilee, and Triangle
6 Arabs will live in a secular-democratic state to be established in all of Palestine instead of Israel

234** *Should the closing of the socioeconomic gap between Arabs and Jews be an important and urgent state goal?*
1 Yes, an important and urgent state goal
2 Yes, an important but not urgent state goal
3 Not so important and not so urgent goal
4 Not important and not urgent goal

235 *To what extent is it possible to improve the Arab situation by acceptable democratic means, such as persuasion and political pressure?*
1 To a great extent 2 To a substantial extent
3 To a certain extent 4 To almost no extent

Following are a number of methods Arabs in Israel can use to advance their interests. For each of them, indicate if you are in favor,. have reservations, or against.

236 *Protest actions abroad.*
1 In favor 2 Have reservations 3 Against

237 *General strikes.*
1 In favor 2 Have reservations 3 Against

238 *Unlicensed demonstrations.*
1 In favor 2 Have reservations 3 Against

239* *Resistance with force.*
1 In favor 2 Have reservations 3 Against

What is the most appropriate means of struggle that Arabs in Israel should use with regard to each of the following goals?

240* *Equal budgets for Arab and Jewish local councils.*
1 All means, including violence
2 Legal means, including demonstrations and strikes
3 Persuasion and pressures
4 Not a target

241* *Israel's recognition of the PLO.*
1 All means, including violence
2 Legal means, including demonstrations and strikes
3 Persuasion and pressures
4 Not a target

Which of the following means of struggle, that Israeli Arabs use to improve their situation in the country, is good and which is not good?

242* *Demonstrations.*
1 Good 2 Not good

243* *General strikes.*
1 Good 2 Not good

244* *Shutdowns of schools.*
1 Good 2 Not good

245* *Shutdowns of local councils.*
1 Good 2 Not good

246* *Voting for the Democratic Front for Peace and Equality and for the Progressive List for Peace.*
1 Good 2 Not good

247* *Voting for the Jewish parties.*
1 Good 2 Not good

248* *Did you participate in the Peace Day strike which was held on December 21, 1987?*
1 Yes 2 No
3 Sick, was abroad, housewife, retired, unemployed

249 *(For Arab respondents:) Did the events in the territories that began on December 9, 1987 affect or did not affect your attitude toward the State? (For Jewish respondents:) Did the Peace Day strike, i.e., the general strike of Israeli Arabs on December 21, 1987, affect or did not affect your attitude toward Israeli Arabs?*
1 Very favorably 2 Somewhat favorably 3 Did not affect
4 Somewhat adversely 5 Very adversely

250** *Should Israeli Arabs be granted or denied a right to vote in Knesset elections?*
1 Be granted 2 Be denied

251** *And should non-Zionist persons who support the formation of a PLO-headed Palestinian state in the West Bank and Gaza Strip alongside Israel be granted or denied the right to vote in Knesset elections?*
1 Be granted 2 Be denied

252** *Should Israel seek and use any opportunity to encourage Israeli Arabs to leave the country in order to reduce their number in the population?*
1 Agree 2 Have reservations 3 Disagree

253** *What is your opinion of outlawing of Rakah?*
1 Agree 2 Have reservations 3 Disagree

254 *Do you agree or disagree that it is impossible to trust most Jews in Israel? (For Jewish respondents: "Jews" reads Arabs.")*
1 Agree 2 Disagree

255** *What would you prefer if the egalitarian-democratic character of the state stands in contradiction to its Jewish-Zionist character and you must choose between them?*
1 Certain to prefer the egalitarian-democratic character
2 Think to prefer the Jewish-Zionist character, but not certain
3 Think to prefer the Jewish-Zionist character, but not certain
4 Certain to prefer the Jewish-Zionist character

256** *Does the State of Israel do enough or not enough for the Arabs in Israel?*
1 Yes, it does too much 2 It does enough
3 No, it does too little

257 *What should be the policy of the state today toward Arabs in Israel?*
1 Continuation of the present policy
2 Increase in surveillance over Arabs
3 Achievement of equality and integration with Jews
4 Allowing Arabs to organize independently and become partners in state institutions
5 Granting Arabs a separate legal status like the autonomy offered to the Arabs in the West Bank and Gaza Strip

258 *What proportion of Arabs in Israel have reconciled themselves to Israel's existence?*
1 All or almost all of them 2 A large proportion of them
3 A certain proportion of them 4 A small proportion of them
5 Only individual instances or none

259 *What proportion of Jews have reconciled themselves to the existence of an Arab minority in Israel?*
1 All or almost all of them 2 A large proportion of them
3 A certain proportion of them 4 A small proportion of them
5 Only individual instances or none

260** *Do you consider Arabs in Israel to be a danger to national security?*
1 To a great degree 2 To a considerable degree
3 To a certain degree 4 No

261** *What is your opinion of a strong-arm policy toward Arabs in Israel?*
1 In favor 2 Have reservations 3 Against

Do you agree or disagree with each of the following statements regarding Israeli Arabs?

262* *Unity among Israeli Arabs is more important even than loyalty to the state.*
1 Agree 2 Disagree

263* *The political struggle of Israeli Arabs is proceeding well and must continue.*
1 Agree 2 Disagree

264* *The strength of the Jews opposing Israeli Arabs makes it very doubtful whether Israeli Arabs will achieve the goals of their struggle.*
1 Agree 2 Disagree

265* *The political goals of Israeli Arabs are so important that any sacrifice is worthwhile, no matter how painful.*
1 Agree 2 Disagree

266* *Violence and killing can never be justified, no matter how important the Israeli Arab struggle.*
1 Agree 2 Disagree

267* *Some regard Arabs in Israel today as being divided by religion and hamula, some see them as being divided by political opinion, and some do not observe any particular division. What is your view?*
1 They are mostly divided by religion and hamula
2 They are mostly divided by political opinion
3 They are not particularly divided

268* *Does Islamic fundamentalism in Israel affect or does not affect the relations between the Arab religious communities in Israel?*
1 Favorably 2 Does not affect 3 Adversely

269* *Does Israel's War in Lebanon affect or does not affect the relations between the Arab religious communities in Israel?*
1 Favorably 2 Does not affect 3 Adversely

270* *To what degree is there competition for civil service jobs between the Arab religious communities in Israel?*
1 To a great degree 2 To a considerable degree
3 To a certain degree 4 Almost none

Let us proceed now to general topics.

271 *To what degree are you satisfied or dissatisfied with your life as an Arab in Israel? (For Jewish respondents: "an Arab" reads "a Jew.")*
1 Very satisfied with my life as an Arab/a Jew in Israel
2 Satisfied
3 Neither satisfied nor dissatisfied -in the middle
4 Dissatisfied
5 Very dissatisfied with my life as an Arab/a Jew in Israel

272 *With regard to the observance of religious tradition, what do you consider yourself?*
1 Very religious 2 Religious
3 Religious to some extent (for Jewish respondents: traditional)
4 Not religious (for Jewish respondents: secular)

273 *How often do you pray?*
1 Regularly 2 Often 3 Sometimes
4 Hardly ever 5 Never

274** *Do you travel on Sabbath?*
1 Yes 2 No

With which of the following religious beliefs do you agree and with which do you disagree?

275 *I believe in a life after death, where good people will be rewarded and bad people will be punished.*
1 Agree 2 Disagree

276 *I am convinced that my own religion is the only true one.*
1 Agree 2 Disagree

277 *I try hard to live my daily life according to the teachings of my religion.*
1 Agree 2 Disagree

278 *I can be happy and enjoy life without believing in a God.*
1 Agree 2 Disagree

279 *I believe that there are hidden forces of good and evil which may help or harm me.*
1 Agree 2 Disagree

280 *I believe in some form of existence after death.*
1 Agree 2 Disagree

281 *I regularly attend a Mosque/a church/a Hilweh/a synagogue.*
1 Agree 2 Disagree

282 *I feel very close to people of my own religion, whatever their nationality, education, wealth, or political views are.*
1 Agree 2 Disagree

283 *No matter what people's religious beliefs are, the only important thing is that everybody leads a moral life and is a good human being.*
1 Agree 2 Disagree

284 *What should be the average number of children per Arab family in Israel today? (For Jewish respondents: "Arab family" reads "family.")*
1 One or two children 2 Three 3 Four 4 Five
5 Six or more

285* *Do you allow a young single Arab girl to have a boyfriend?*
1 Yes, allow 2 Allow to some extent 3 No

286* *Since 1948, has there been any expropriation of lands owned by you, your brothers, sisters, parents, or children?*
1 Yes, much 2 Yes, some 3 No, but own land
4 Own no land

287* *Did your family or the family of your father become a refugee family as a result of the 1948 War?*
1 No 2 Yes

288 *For which list would you vote if elections to the Knesset were held today?*
1 Maarakh (Labor) 2 Likud 3 Mapam 4 Tehiya
5 DFPE (Democratic Front for Peace and Equality, Rakah)
6 PLP (Progressive List for Peace)
7 CRM (Citizens' Rights Movement
8 Center (Shinui) Party
9 Tsomet
10 NRP (National Religious Party)
11 Agudat Israel
12 Shas
13 Poale Agudat Israel

14 Kach
15 Other lists
16 Have not decided
17 Would not vote

290 *What is your second choice?*
1 2 3 4 5 6 7 8 9 10 11 12 13 14 15
16 17

292* *If a new, independent Arab party, that strives to participate in the coalition government in order to advance the interests of Israeli Arabs, were to be established, are you willing to vote for it?*
1 Definitely willing 2 Willing 3 Not willing
4 Definitely not willing

293* *If Knesset Member Darawshe were to establish an independent list, headed by him, and the other parties would remain the same, for which list would you vote then?*
1 Maarakh (Labor) 2 Likud 3 Mapam 4 Tehiya
5 DFPE (Rakah) 6 PLP
7 List headed by Darawshe 8 CRM
9 Center (Shinui) Party 10 Tsomet
11 NRP 12 Agudat Israel 13 Shas
14 Poale Agudat Israel 15 Kach 16 Other lists
17 Have not decided 18 Would not vote

295 *Which kind of government would you prefer to be formed after the next elections to the Knesset?*
1 Labor government 2 Likud government
3 National unity government

296 *Maarakh (Labor) says it would not form a coalition government with the DFPE (Rakah) or Progressive List for Peace. The Likud says that it would not form a coalition government with Kach (Kahane). (For Jewish respondents: "it would form"). To what degree will this affect your voting in the next elections to the Knesset?*
1 Certain to affect 2 Think to affect
3 Think not to affect 4 Certain not to affect

297* *Does your decision for which list to vote in the next elections to the Knesset stem more from considerations of struggle for peace or more from considerations of struggle for equality?*
1 Much more from considerations of struggle for peace
2 More from considerations of struggle for peace
3 More from considerations of struggle for equality
4 Much more from considerations of struggle for equality

298 *For which list did you vote in the last elections to the Knesset (in July 1984)?*
1 Maarakh (Labor) 2 Likud 3 DFPE 4 PLP
5 CRM 6 Shinui 7 Yahad 8 Ometz
9 Tami 10 NRP 11 Agudat Israel

12 Shas 13 Morasha-Poale Agudat Israel
14 Tehiya 15 Kach
16 Other lists 17 Did not vote

300 *Are you a member of any party? Which one?*
1 Not a member 2 Labor 3 Herut
4 Mapam 5 Liberals 6 Rakah
7 PLP 8 Center Party (Shinui)
9 CRM 10 Yahad (Weizman)
11 Tami 12 Agudat Israel
13 NRP (including Morasha) 14 Poale Agudat Israel
15 Shas 16 Tehiya 17 Tsomet
18 Kach 19 Other

302 *Are you a member of the Histadrut (General Federation of Labor)?*
1 Yes 2 No

303 *Gender.*
1 Male 2 Female

304 *Age (two digits).*

306 *Personal status.*
1 Single 2 Married 3 Widowed 4 Divorced

307 *Number of children in the family (two digits).*

309 *What was the last class in school you completed?*
1 No schooling 2 Incomplete primary
3 Complete primary 4 Incomplete secondary
5 Complete secondary 6 Post-secondary, incomplete higher
7 Complete higher

310 *What was the last class in school your father completed?*
1 2 3 4 5 6 7

311 *Religion.*
1 Druze 2 Moslem 3 Greek-Catholic
4 Greek-Orthodox 5 Latin
6 Maronite 7 Protestant 8 Jew

312 *Can you read and write in Arabic, i.e., can you write a simple letter in Arabic?*
1 Yes 2 No

313* *Did you read an Arabic newspaper last week?*
1 Yes 2 No

314 *(For Arab respondents:) Do you know enough Hebrew to conduct a conversation on various matters with an Israeli Jew? (For Jewish respondents:) Do you know enough Arabic to conduct a conversation on various matters with an Israeli Arab?*
1 Yes 2 No

315 *Can you read and write in Hebrew, i.e., can you write a simple letter in Hebrew?*
1 Yes 2 No

316 *Did you read a Hebrew newspaper last week?*
1 Yes 2 No

317 *What do you do in the main?*
1 Employed (including soldier in professional army)
2 Unemployed (seeking a job)
3 Retired (ask the following three questions with regard last full-time job before retirement)
4 Housewife (skip next two questions)
5 Student (skip next two questions)
6 Soldier in compulsory service (skip next two questions)

318 *What kind of work do you do? (Open question; a two-digit classification with the tens digit indicating economic branch and each category also including related occupations not elsewhere classified).*
0 Academic workers in life services: biologists, biochemists, agronomists
1 Academic workers in physical sciences: chemists, physicists
2 Architects and engineers
3 Physicians, dentists, and practical dentists
4 Pharmacists and veterinarians
5 Jurists: Dayanim (judges in religious courts), judges, lawyers
6 Academic workers in social sciences: statisticians, mathematicians, economists, psychologists, sociologists
7 Academic workers in humanities and translators
8 Lecturers and professors in universities
9 Instructors in post-secondary non-academic colleges and teachers in high schools
10 Teachers, principals, and inspectors in intermediate divisions (junior high schools), primary schools, and kindergartens
11 Accountants
12 Workers in religious services: Rabbis, Kashruth inspectors, lawyers in religious courts, Sheikhs, clergymen
13 Writers, journalists, actors, composers, musicians, sculptors, painters, practical artists (fashion designers, commercial artists, etc.), producers, stage managers, photographers
14 Social workers, probation officers, youth guides
15 Nurses and related para-medical workers: nurses, opticians, physiotherapists, technicians in medicine
16 Technicians in life, chemical, and physical sciences
17 Engineering technicians
18 System analysts and computer programers
19 Other professionals and technicians: ship officers, airplane pilots, extension workers
20 Elected members of government: the President, members of parliament, cabinet ministers, deputy ministers, heads of local governments

21 Managers and administrators in central and local governments: department heads in civil service, secretaries of local governments, hospital administrators, prison workers, police officers, fire department officers
22 Managers in professional agencies and institutions in life, physical, and engineering sciences (but not directors-general)
23 Managers in professional agencies and institutions in humanities, social sciences, and law
24 Non-public managers of production or commercial units, banks, insurance companies, hotels, universities
30 Clerical supervisors and inspectors
31 Bookkeepers, cashiers, bank tellers, post office clerks
32 Typists, secretaries, keyboard operators
33 Stockroom attendants and stock control clerks
34 Telephone, telegraph, and radio operators
35 Transport and communications supervisors: railway station workers, postmasters, post office supervisors
36 Bus or train conductors, mail carriers, post office workers, messengers
37 General clerical office workers
38 Clerks not elsewhere classified: receptionists, library clerks, technical clerks
40 Proprietors working in wholesale trade
41 Proprietors working in retail trade: store owners, gas station owners
42 Technical salesmen, traveling salesmen, manufacturing agents, buyers, managers in department stores or supermarkets
43 Insurance agents, real estate agents, stockbrokers, travel agents, advertising agents, auctioneers, custom agents, assessors
44 Salespersons, gas station attendants, models
45 Peddlers, newsvendors, and other distributors of goods
50 Proprietors working in catering and lodging services (restaurants, coffeehouses, kiosks, hotels, motels)
51 Cooks
52 Waiters and bartenders
53 Managers of catering and lodging services and hotel chambermaids
54 Housekeepers: housemaids, cookmaids, nursemaids
55 Launderers and dry cleaners
56 Hairdressers, barbers, cosmeticians
57 Protective service workers: policemen, detectives, firefighters, guards
58 Guides, stewards, teacher's aides, dental assistants
59 Other service workers: undertakers, doorkeepers, janitors, street sweepers, dishwashers, kitchen helpers
60 Farm owners working in their farms
61 Farm managers and foremen
62 Skilled workers in agriculture
63 Fishermen
64 Farm machinery operators: tractor drivers
65 Operators and foremen in farm product processing plants

66 Unskilled workers in agriculture: foresters, pickers, farmhands
70 Raw metal processing workers: foremen, metal castors, rolling-mill workers, metal workers, and coaters
71 Blacksmiths, tinsmiths, welders, toolmakers, locksmiths, and other finished metal workers
72 Fitters, assemblers, and machine and vehicle repairmen
73 Pipefitters and plumbers
74 Electrical fitters and electrical equipment, radio, and electronics makers: fitters and assemblers of electronics, electricians of vehicles, telephone installers and repairmen, building electricians
75 Assemblers and fitters of watches, jewelry, and precision instruments
76 Diamond cutters and finishers
77 Workers in food processing, tobacco, and beverages: bakers, food cookers, dairy product makers, butchers, millers, drink makers
78 Wood product makers and carpenters
79 Textile workers: fiber preparers, spinners, weavers, knitters, dyers
80 Tailors, dressmakers, and sewers
81 Shoemakers and leather goods makers
82 Printing trade workers
83 Skilled workers in other shops and industries: skilled workers in chemical processing, dental technicians, ceramic workers, glass workers, musical instrument makers and repairmen, computer operators, quality control workers
84 Miners, quarry workers, well drillers
85 Building construction workers
86 Operators of digging, earth moving, road building and hoisting machines
87 Ship and train personnel: sailors, train drivers
88 Drivers of buses, trucks, and taxis
89 Painters and whitewashers of buildings, automobiles, furniture
90 Porters and longshoremen
91 Unskilled workers in clerical and mineral processing: treaters of chemicals, paper makers, refiners
92 Unskilled workers in plastic and rubber production
93 Unskilled workers in food production, tobacco, and beverages
94 Engine and pump operators and oilers
95 Packers and labellers
96 Unskilled workers in mineral processing
97 Other unskilled workers in industry
9 Other unskilled workers in construction
99 Other unskilled workers

320 *What is your work status?*

1 Employee | 2 Employer
3 Self-employed | 4 Member of cooperative or Moshav
5 Kibbutz member | 6 Unpaid family member
7 Not employed (housewife, student, soldier in compulsory service)

321 *How many people live in this household? (i.e., persons who live together permanently and prepare their meals in common) (two digits).*

323 *Who is the main breadwinner in this household?*
1 Yourself 2 Your spouse 3 Your father
4 Your mother 5 Another relative
6 None (pension, welfare, etc.) 7 Other

324 *What kind of work does the breadwinner do? (Open question; same classification as in question 318).*

326 *What was the work with the highest rank which your father held? (Open question; same classification as in question 318).*

328 *To what socioeconomic level do you belong?*
1 Upper class 2 Upper-middle class 3 Middle class
4 Lower-middle class 5 Lower class

406** *What is your country of birth?*
1 Born in Israel 2 Morocco, Tangier
3 Algeria, Tunisia, Libya 4 Iraq
5 Yemen, Southern Yemen 6 Syria, Lebanon, Egypt
7 Turkey, Bulgaria, Greece
8 Other countries in Asia and Africa
9 USSR 10 Poland
11 Rumania 12 Germany
13 Anglo-Saxon countries
14 Other countries in Europe and America

408** *What is your father's country of birth?*
1 2 3 4 5 6 7 8 9 10 11 12 13 14

410** *If you have to define yourself in terms of ethnic origin, which of the following possibilities would you choose?*
1 Oriental or Sephardic 2 Ashkenazic 3 Mixed

We are through. Thanks for your cooperation.

Following is the interviewer's report, to be completed at the end of the interview.

411* *Respondent's sampling listing.*
1 Included in original list 2 Included in replacement list

412 *Duration of interview.*
1 Less than an hour
2 An hour to less than an hour and a half
3 An hour and a half to less than two hours
4 Two hours to less than two and a half hours
5 Two and a half hours and longer

413* *Do you personally know the respondent?*
1 Yes 2 No

414 *Was another person present during the interview?*
1 No 2 Yes, but did not interrupt
3 Yes and did interrupt

415 *What was the degree of understanding shown by the respondent?*
1 Lack of understanding 2 Certain lack of understanding
3 Reasonable understanding 4 Full understanding

416* *Was there an atmosphere of trust during the interview?*
1 Lack of trust 2 Certain lack of trust
3 Reasonable trust 4 Full trust

417 *What was the overall reliability of the information given by the respondent?*
1 Not reliable 2 Sufficient 3 Good
4 Very good

418 *Locality of residence.*

For Arab respondents:
1 Haifa 2 Lod 3 Akko (Acre)
4 Tel-Aviv-Yafo 5 Nazareth 6 Shefaram
7 Tira 8 Baka Al-Garbia
9 Sakhnin 10 Majd Al-Khrum
11 Daliat Al-Karmel 12 Kfar Yasif 13 Um Al-Fahem
14 Tayba 15 Yirka 16 Kfar Kana
17 Maker 18 Ein Mahel 19 Jat
20 Jisser Al-Zarka 21 Julis 22 Meilya
23 Pkiein 24 Fassuta 25 Faradies
26 Nahaf 27 Marja 28 Naora
29 Sheikh Danun 30 Sajur 31 Eilut
32 Buayna 33 Akbara 34 Mouawiya
35 Bartaa 36 Kabul 37 Busmat-Tivon
38 Hilf 39 Saayda Um Al-Ghnam
40 Rahat 41 Tel-Sheva

For Jewish respondents
51 Tel-Aviv-Yafo 52 Jerusalem 53 Haifa
54 Beer Sheva 55 Ramat-Gan 56 Bene Berak
57 Herzliya 58 Holon 59 Petah Tikva
60 Rosh Haayin 61 Rishon Letzion 62 Pardes Hana
63 Teveria (Tiberias) 64 Ramle 65 Ashdod
66 Akko (Acre) 67 Yavne 68 Raanana
69 Kiryat Bialik 70 Afula 71 Beit-Shean
73 Dimona 74 Ora 78 Hemed
79 Herev Leaet 80 Peduyim 81 Beit-Hagdi
82 Rehovot 84 Ramat Hasharon 85 Ofakim
86 Ramat Yohanan 87 Kfar Masarik 88 Kfar Menahem

420 *Research group.*
1 Jewish sample 2 Arab Sample

421 *Verification of the interview.*
1 No 2 Yes

423 *Date of completion of interview.*

References

Al-Haj, Majid. 1991. *Education and Social Change among the Arabs in Israel.* Tel Aviv: International Center for Peace in the Middle East.

______. Forthcoming. "The Impact of the Intifada on the Orientation of the Arabs in Israel: The Case of a Double Periphery." In *Framing the Intifada: Media and People,* edited by Akiba Cohen and Gadi Wolsfeld. Norwood, NJ: Ablex Publishing Corporation.

Al-Haj, Majid and Avner Yaniv. 1983. "Uniformity or Diversity: A Reappraisal of the Voting Behavior of the Arab Minority in Israel." Pp. 139-64 in *The Elections in Israel 1981,* edited by Asher Arian. Tel Aviv: Ramot Publishing, Tel Aviv University.

Al-Haj, Majid and Elihu Katz. 1989. "Peace: Arab and Jewish Attitudes." *Jerusalem Post,* August 4.

Al-Haj, Majid and Henry Rosenfeld. 1990. *Arab Local Government in Israel.* Boulder, CO: Westview Press.

Algazi, Yosef. 1990. "The Arabs in Israel Request Autonomy." *Haaretz,* July 27. (Hebrew).

Bar, Haviva and Jaber Asaqla. 1988. *Encounters between Jewish and Arab Youth in Givaat Haviva: Evaluation of Attitudes Before and After.* Jerusalem: The Israel Institute of Applied Social Research. (Hebrew).

Bar, Haviva, David Bar-Gal, and Jaber Asaqla. 1989. *The School for Peace at Neve Shalom/Wahat Al-Salam, 1985-1988, Encounters between Jewish and Palestinian-Arab Youth.* Jerusalem: The Israel Institute of Applied Social Research.

Be'er, Yizhar. 1990. "Faisal Husseini: The Making of a Leader." *New Outlook* 33, 1-2 (March): 24-27.

Ben-Nahum, Arnon. 1991. "Geography of Fear." *Haaretz,* August 7. (Hebrew).

Benziman, Uzi. 1990. "No Stopping on the Downgrade." *Haaretz,* November 8. (Hebrew).

Benziman, Uzi and Attallah Mansur. Forthcoming. *The Government Policy toward the Arabs in Israel, 1948-1990, Processes of Decision Making and Implementation*. Jerusalem: Keter. (Hebrew).

Chen, Yael. 1991. "This Is Not Because I'm Racist." *Haaretz*, May 6. (Hebrew).

Cohen, Oren. 1990. "They Want Autonomy, Too." *Hadashot*, June 8. (Hebrew).

Cohen, Raanan. 1985. *Processes of Political Organization and Voting Patterns of Arabs in Israel (In Four Election Campaigns to the Knesset, 1973-1984)*. Two Parts. M.A. Thesis. Tel Aviv: Department of the Middle East, Tel Aviv University. (Hebrew).

______. 1989. *The Political Developments of the Arab Minority in Israel as Reflected by Parliamentary Voting Patterns, 1948-1984*. Doctoral Dissertation. Tel Aviv: Tel Aviv University. (Hebrew).

______. 1990. *Complexity of Loyalties: Society and Politics: The Arab Sector in Israel*. Tel Aviv: Am Oved. (Hebrew).

Cohen, Stanely. 1990. *Crime, Justice and Social Control among the Arabs in Israel*. Tel Aviv: International Center for Peace in the Middle East.

Committee on Civil Service. 1989. *Report of the Public-Professional Committee on an Overall Examination of the Public Service and Bodies Supported by the State's Budget*. Two Volumes. Jerusalem: The Government's Printer. (Hebrew).

Connor, Walker. 1984. *The National Question in Marxist-Leninist Theory and Strategy*. Princeton, NJ: Princeton University Press.

Dar, Yoel. 1979. "The Soil that Grows Up Violators of National Security." *Davar*, May 30. (Hebrew).

Diskin, Avraham. 1989. "Statistical Aspects of Voting in the Arab Sector." Pp. 22-34 in *The Arab Vote in Israel's Parliamentary Elections, 1988*, edited by Jacob M. Landau. Jerusalem: The Jerusalem Institute for Israel Studies. (Hebrew).

Dotan, Shmuel. 1991. *Reds: The Communist Party in Eretz Israel*. Kfar Sabba: Sevna Hasoffer. (Hebrew).

Dror, Yeheskel. 1989. *A Grand Strategy for Israel*. Jerusalem: Academon. (Hebrew).

Eizenbach, Zvi. 1989. "Recent Changes in Fertility among Israeli Moslems." *Hamizrah Hehadash* 32, 125-128: 80-96. (Hebrew).

Falah, Ghazi. 1990. "Arabs versus Jews in Galilee: Competition for Regional Resources." *GeoJournal* 21, 4 (August): 325-36.

Friedman, Thomas. 1987. "An Islamic Revival is Quickly Gaining Ground in an Unlikely Place: Israel." *The New York Times*, April 30.

Gal, John. 1989. *The Arab Vote in the 1988 Elections*. Givaat Haviva: Institute for Arab Studies.

Galnoor, Itzhak. 1990. "'Preventing Terror': Just an Excuse." *Israeli Democracy* (Winter): 10-11.

Ghanem, Asa'd and Sarah Ozacky-Lazar. 1990. "The Green Line, 'Red Lines,' and the Intifada." *Sekirot* 3. Givaat Haviva: Institute for Arab Studies. (Hebrew).

Ginat, Joseph. 1986. "The Arab Vote: Protest or Palestinization?" Pp. 151-67 in *The Elections in Israel 1984*, edited by Asher Arian and Michal Shamir. Tel Aviv: Ramot Publishing, Tel Aviv University.

Gur-Arye, Benyamin. 1982. "The Follow-Up Committee Will Bring About Radicalization." *Leket* 22 (November): 21-25. (Hebrew).

Gvirtz, Yael. 1990. "Opening the Stitches." *Davar*, February 2. (Hebrew).

Ha'etzni, Nadav. 1990. "On Small Fire (in the Meantime)." *Ha'ir*, June 26. (Hebrew).

Haidar, Aziz. 1990. *The Arab Population in the Israeli Economy*. Tel Aviv: International Center for Peace in the Middle East.

______. 1991. *Social Welfare Services for Israel's Arab Population*. Boulder, CO: Westview Press.

Haidar, Aziz and Elia Zureik. 1987. "The Palestinians Seen through the Israeli Cultural Paradigm." *Journal of Palestine Studies* 16, 3 (Spring): 68-86.

Hamaissi, Rasem. 1990. *Planning and Housing among the Arabs in Israel*. Tel Aviv: International Center for Peace in the Middle East.

Herzog, Hanna. 1990. "The Right to Be Included: Israeli Jewish-Arab Relations." *Discussion Paper* 3-90. Tel Aviv: Pinhas Sapir Center for Development, Tel Aviv University.

Herzog, Hanna and William Gamson. 1990. *Culture and Cognition in America and Israel*. Report. Jerusalem: US-Israel Binational Science Foundation.

Hofman, John and Nadim Rouhana. 1976. "Young Arabs in Israel: Some Aspects of a Conflicted Social Identity." *Journal of Social Psychology* 99: 75-86.

Horowitz, Dan and Moshe Lissak. 1989. *Trouble in Utopia: The Overburdened Polity in Israel*. Albany, NY: State University of New York Press.

Horowitz, Donald L. 1985. *Ethnic Groups in Conflict*. Berkeley: University of California Press.

Israeli Communist Party. 1959. *Report of the 13th Congress*. Tel Aviv: Israeli Communist Party. (Hebrew).

______. 1986. *The 20th Congress*. Tel Aviv: Central Committee, Israeli Communist Party. (Hebrew).

JCSS Study Group. 1989. *The West Bank and Gaza: Israel's Options for Peace*. Tel Aviv: The Jaffee Center for Strategic Studies, Tel Aviv University.

Kafra, Michal. 1990. "Second Rate Knesset Members." *Maariv*, May 4. (Hebrew).

Katz, Elihu and Majid Al-Haj. 1989. "Options: Dovish, Hawkish and Local Arab." *Jerusalem Post*, August 25.

Klausner, Samuel Z. 1991. "Diaspora in Comparative Perspective." Pp. 194-221 in *Eretz Israel, Israel, and the Jewish Diaspora*, edited by Menachem Mor. Lanham, MD: University Press of America.

Klein, Menahem. 1989. "The PLO's Two-Year Lesson." *Haaretz*, December 8. (Hebrew).

Kretzmer, David. 1990. *The Legal Status of the Arabs in Israel*. Boulder, CO: Westview Press.

Kuper, Leo. 1990. "The Genocidal State: Overview." Pp. 19-51 in *State Violence and Ethnicity*, edited by Pierre van den Berghe. Niwot, CO: University Press of Colorado.

Landau, Jacob M. (ed.). 1989. *The Arab Vote in Israel's Parliamentary Elections, 1988*. Jerusalem: The Jerusalem Institute for Israel Studies. (Hebrew).

Landras, Israel. 1990. "Autonomy? And What Next?" *Davar*, July 13. (Hebrew).

Lehman-Wilzig, Sam. 1990. *Stiff-Necked People, Bottle-Necked System: The Evolution and Roots of Israeli Public Protest, 1949-1986*. Bloomington, Indiana: IN: University Press.

______. 1991. "Copying the Master: Patterns of Israeli-Arab Protest, 1950-1990." Paper Read at the Conference on The Arab Minority in Israel: Dilemmas of Political Orientation and Social Change. Tel Aviv: The Dayan Center, Tel Aviv University.

Lerner, Natan. 1984. "Affirmative Action in Israel." Pp. 110-53 in *International Perspectives on Affirmative Action*. Conference Report. New York: The Rockefeller Foundation.

London, Yaron. 1990. "Half of the Youth Favor Transfer." *Yediot Aharonot*, May 29. (Hebrew).

Lustick, Ian. 1980. *Arabs in the Jewish State: Israel's Control of a National Minority*. Austin, TX: University of Texas Press.

______. 1990. "The Changing Political Role of Israeli Arabs." Pp. 115-31 in *The Elections in Israel 1988*, edited by Asher Arian and Michal Shamir. Boulder, CO: Westview Press.

Mansur, Attallah. 1987. "How the Next Strike Will Be," "Lessons from the General Strike." *Haaretz*, June 21 and 28. (Hebrew).

______. 1991. "Lip Service in Arabic." *Haaretz*, March 20. (Hebrew).

Mar'i, Sami K. 1978. *Arab Education in Israel*. Syracuse, NY: Syracuse University Press.

Mayer, Thomas. 1989. "The 'Moslem Youth' in Israel." *Hamizrah Hehadash* 32, 125-128: 10-20. (Hebrew).

Meiri, Shmuel and Yossi Bar-Muha. 1991. "The Walls of Acre Were Not Toppled by the Transferer." *Kolbo*, August 9. (Hebrew).

Ministry of Defense. 1984. *Protocol of a Meeting with the Representatives of the Progressive List for Peace.* Tel Aviv: Office of the Ministry of Defense. (Hebrew).

Ministry of Justice. 1989. "Basic Law: Basic Human Rights." A Draft Approved by the Ministerial Committee on Legislation and Law Enforcement. Jerusalem: Ministry of Justice. (Hebrew).

Ozacky-Lazar, Sarah and Asa'd Ghanem. 1990. "Autonomy for Arabs in Israel – An Initial Discussion." *Sekirot* 5. Givaat Haviva: Institute for Arab Studies. (Hebrew).

Paz, Reuven. 1990. "The Islamic Movement in Israel and the Municipal Elections of 1989." *Jerusalem Quarterly* 53 (Winter): 3-26.

Peres, Yochanan and Nira Yuval-Davis. 1969. "Some Observations on the National Identity of the Israeli Arab." *Human Relations* 22, 3 (July): 219-33.

Rabinowitz, Dan. 1990. *Relations between Arabs and Jews in the Mixed Town of Natzerat Illit, Northern Israel.* Doctoral Dissertation. Cambridge: Department of Social Anthropology, University of Cambridge.

Regev, Avner. 1989. *The Arabs in Israel: Political Issues.* Jerusalem: The Jerusalem Institute for Israel Studies. (Hebrew).

Reiss, Nira. 1991. *The Health Care of the Arabs in Israel.* Boulder, CO: Westview Press.

Reiter, Yitzhak. 1989. "The Democratic Arab Party and Its Position on the Orientation of the Arabs in Israel." Pp. 63-84 in *The Arab Vote in Israel's Parliamentary Elections, 1988*, edited by Jacob M. Landau. Jerusalem: The Jerusalem Institute for Israel Studies. (Hebrew).

Rekhess, Elie. 1986. *Between Communism and Arab Nationalism: Rakah and the Arab Minority in Israel (1965-1973).* Doctoral Dissertation. Tel Aviv: Tel Aviv University. (Hebrew).

______. 1989. "Israeli Arabs and the Arabs of the West Bank and Gaza: Political Affinity and National Solidarity." *Asian and African Studies* 23, 2-3 (November): 119-54.

Rouhana, Nadim. 1984. *The Arabs in Israel: Psychological and Social Dimensions of Collective Identity.* Doctoral Dissertation. Detroit, MN: Wayne State University

______. 1986. "Collective Identity and Arab Voting Patterns." Pp. 121-49 in *The Elections in Israel 1984*, edited by Asher Arian and Michal Shamir. Tel Aviv: Ramot Publishing, Tel Aviv University.

______. 1989. "The Political Transformation of the Palestinians in Israel: From Acquiescence to Challenge." *Journal of Palestine Studies* 18, 3: 38-59.

______. 1991. "Palestinization among the Arabs in Israel: The Accentuated Identity." Paper Read at the Conference on The Arab Minority in Israel: Dilemmas of Political Orientation and Social Change. Tel Aviv: The Dayan Center, Tel Aviv University.

Ryan, Stephen.1990. "Ethnic Conflict and the United Nations." *Ethnic and Racial Studies* 13, 1 (January): 25-49.

Schiff, Ze'ev. 1986. "Area 9 – The End." *Haaretz*, August 31. (Hebrew).

Schiff, Ze'ev and Ehud Ya'ari. 1989. *Intifada: The Palestinian Uprising – Israel's Third Front*. New York: Simon and Schuster.

Segev, Tom. 1990. "The Last Taboo." *Haaretz*, June 8. (Hebrew).

Shamir, Michal. Forthcoming. "Political Intolerance among Masses and Elites in Israel: A Reevaluation of Elitist Theory of Democracy." *Journal of Politics* (November, 1991).

Shammas, Anton. 1983. "Diary." Pp. 29-48 in *Every Sixth Israeli*, edited by Alouph Hareven. Jerusalem: The Van Leer Jerusalem Foundation.

Shapira, Boaz. 1990. "Peres' Only Achievement." *Haaretz*, April 27. (Hebrew).

Shtrasler, Nehamya. 1987. "An Independent State in the Galilee." *Haaretz*, May 19. (Hebrew).

Smooha, Sammy. 1974. "On behalf of a Palestinian Entity." *New Politics* 11, 2 (Spring): 44-51.

______. 1982. "Existing and Alternative Policy towards Arabs in Israel." *Ethnic and Racial Studies* 5, 1 (January): 71-98.

______. 1984. *The Orientation and Politicization of the Arab Minority in Israel*. Haifa: The Jewish-Arab Center, University of Haifa.

______. 1989. *Arabs and Jews in Israel. Vol. 1. Conflicting and Shared Attitudes in a Divided Society*. Boulder, CO: Westview Press.

______. 1990. "Minority Status in an Ethnic Democracy: The Status of the Arab Minority in Israel." *Ethnic And Racial Studies* 13, 3 (July): 389-413.

Soffer, Arnon. 1988. *The Demographic and Geographic Situation in Eretz Israel: Is It the End of the Zionist Vision?* Haifa: Author's Printing. (Hebrew).

_______. 1990. Review of Smooha's Arabs and Jews in Israel, Vol. 1. *Contemporary Sociology* 19, 6 (November): 817-19.

Springborg, Robert. 1990. Review of Smooha's Arabs and Jews in Israel, Vol. 1. *Annals* 508 (March): 196-97.

Sullivan, John L., Michal Shamir, Nigel Roberts, and Patrick Walsh. 1984. "Political Intolerance and the Structure of Mass Attitudes: A Study of the United States, Israel and New Zealand." *Comparative Political studies* 17, 3 (October): 319-44.

Tal, Yerah. 1985. "The Trial of the Assassins of Dani Katz: The End." *Haaretz*, October 16. (Hebrew).

Van Leer Jerusalem Foundation. 1990. *A Civil Covenant between the Arab and Jewish Citizens of Israel*. A Revised Draft (September). Jerusalem: The Van Leer Jerusalem Institute.

Weitzer, Ronald. 1990. *Transforming Settler States: Communal Conflict and Internal Security in Northern Ireland and Zimbabwe*. Berkeley: University of California Press.

Yiftachel, Oren. 1990. *Public Policy and Political Stability in a Biethnic Democracy: The Influence of Israel's Land Use Planning on Arab-Jewish Relations in the Galilee*. Doctoral Dissertation. Perth: University of Western Australia; Haifa: The Technion.

Yuchtman-Ya'ar, Ephraim and Yochanan Peres. 1991. "Public Opinion and Democracy after Three Years of Intifada." *Israeli Democracy* (Spring): 21-25.

Zemah, Mina. 1980. *The Attitudes of the Jewish Majority toward the Arab Minority in Israel*. Interim Report. (Mimeographed). Jerusalem: The Van Leer Jerusalem Foundation. (Hebrew).

Zureik, Elia T. 1979. *The Palestinians in Israel: A Study in Internal Colonialism*. London: Routledge and Kegan Paul.

______. 1987. Review of Smooha's The Orientation and Politicization of the Arab Minority in Israel. *International Journal of Middle East Studies* 19, 2 (May): 225-27.

______. 1991. "The Impact of the Intifada on the Palestinians in Israel." Working Paper Read at the University of Haifa.

Index